Windows System Center 2022

Foundation of Windows unified IT management platform

Dujon Walsham

www.bpbonline.com

First Edition 2025

Copyright © BPB Publications, India

ISBN: 978-93-65897-678

All Rights Reserved. No part of this publication may be reproduced, distributed or transmitted in any form or by any means or stored in a database or retrieval system, without the prior written permission of the publisher with the exception to the program listings which may be entered, stored and executed in a computer system, but they can not be reproduced by the means of publication, photocopy, recording, or by any electronic and mechanical means.

LIMITS OF LIABILITY AND DISCLAIMER OF WARRANTY

The information contained in this book is true to correct and the best of author's and publisher's knowledge. The author has made every effort to ensure the accuracy of these publications, but publisher cannot be held responsible for any loss or damage arising from any information in this book.

All trademarks referred to in the book are acknowledged as properties of their respective owners but BPB Publications cannot guarantee the accuracy of this information.

To View Complete
BPB Publications Catalogue
Scan the QR Code:

www.bpbonline.com

Dedicated to

My Mother

About the Author

Dujon Walsham is currently a director owner of two IT technology companies, namely Walsham Solutions and the co-founder of SecQube. His expertise evolves around the System Center technology stack, Modern Management and Cyber Security.

He is a newly joined member of the Microsoft MVP Alumni after being a 3x Microsoft MVP within the Enterprise Mobility sector.

In addition to being the author of this book, he has written another book named "Self Motivation: Anyone can do IT if I did IT" which focuses on the journey of starting within the IT industry from 18 years old up until the launch of his first company, Walsham Solutions.

He has, over the years, managed to achieve over 20+ Microsoft certifications and is a regular technical community contributor consisting of various articles and blogs that follow a subject series structure. He has also made various appearances on webinars, notably SCOMATHON, SCOMATHIN Coffee Break sessions, the Microsoft Endpoint Summit led by the Modern Endpoint Management group on Linkedin and other Microsoft MVP-related webinar events, as well as regular speaker sessions with IT training provider JustIT, where his career started. From being the first 18-year-old to partake in the adults-only course in 2006 to help encourage other young people to get active within the IT industry.

Aside from the technical aspects, he is also active in the community and gives back in various ways, such as being the sponsor for the Dulwich Hamlet Juniors Under 11 football team for which he was once a player, as well as working alongside his former primary school church of St Pauls Church of England Primary school.

About the Reviewer

Steve Miles works in a senior technology role for the cloud practice of a multi-billion turnover European IT distributor.

He is a Microsoft Most Valuable Professional (MVP), Microsoft Certified Trainer (MCT), and an Alibaba Cloud MVP. He has 25+ years of technology experience in hosted datacenter services, hybrid, and multi-cloud platforms, and a previous military career in engineering, signals, and communications.

Steve is the author of many books on Microsoft technologies with a focus on Azure, AI and data as well as security.

Steve is a petrolhead and can also be found tinkering with cars when he is not writing.

Acknowledgement

I would like to thank everyone here at BPB Publications for their great support throughout the creation of this book and the overall process of getting us from the beginning to the end of this journey.

I would also like to thank the technical reviewers of this book for their detailed feedback, who did a great job in helping shape the book; these things help to bring out the best in any technical author as well as the overall publication of this book.

I also appreciate all the readers who will find this book of interest as it is a subject area I am very passionate about. I thank everyone mentioned here once again.

Preface

This book is integral to developing a complete understanding of the power that System Center brings, especially within the new 2022 versions. We find that specialists or Subject Matter Experts might be experts in one or two products; quite rarely will you see individuals profficient in more than two, so we want to take everyone whether beginning or expert level on the full journey. This book serves to be a solid foundation for understanding System Center, to which the reader can build and expand on a certain product or more.

This book is targeted towards just technical readers, engineers, and architects but also for stakeholders and other business centered roles so that each individual can understand what each product represents and the benefits that it can provide for your environment. It is important for each product to be represented not only by its technical attrubutes, but also by what it can contribute to BAU practices as well as scalability for the future.

The book comprises 16 chapters covering each individual product within the System Center family. The first two chapters help establish the foundation of what System Center is and what it can do and introduce the readers to the advancements and new features introduced into their 2022 versions.

Additionally, Chapter 3 focuses on Microsoft Configuration Manager. Though it is a product that is not part of the System Center suite anymore, it is still a product that integrates well with the family product set. This chapter kicks off the journey with the book dedicating two chapters to each product with one representing the design aspect and the other representing the implementation aspect.

In order to keep up to date with the latest developments and cloud adoptions, we also explore how the System Center family plays a part, in not only the integration with having a hybrid environment between on-premise and Azure but also how the hybrid milestone can also transition into full modern management in Chapter 15.

Lastly, we look to detail the best practices and real-world scenarios so that we can understand the balance between what we should do and what is actually being applied more commonly within organizations.

Chapter 1: Introduction to Microsoft System Center– This chapter starts off by explaining the purpose of what the suite of System Center products can bring as a whole and then goes into what each product does individually.

Chapter 2: Latest Updates and Features– This chapter analyses all the latest updates available to each product in System Center and the new features that have been introduced into each product.

Chapter 3: OS and Application Deployment Optimization of Configuration Manager– Kicking off with the first product to dive into is Microsoft Configuration Manager through exploring its design scenarios, how to centralize management of all your endpoints and servers' various roles, and the part in which it plays with its collaboration with Intune.

Chapter 4: Deployment and Administration of Microsoft Configuration Manager– This chapter details on how to implement Configuration Manager and how to administer the product with various common tasks to configure the product to where it needs to be to apply any best practices applicable and to examine the real world scenarios.

Chapter 5: Monitoring Infrastructure with System Center Operations Manager– This chapter dives into Operations Manager to provide the reader with how the product can monitor your infrastructure and how best to design the solution to fit your requirements.

Chapter 6: Deployment and Administration of System Center Operations Manager– This chapter explores the implementation of Operations Manager using everything that we have left from the previous chapter to understand how to design the solution. We will then explore how we can administer the product with how to manage the monitoring solutions for our environment and how we can enhance our monitoring going forward, concluding with the best practice and real-world scenarios.

Chapter 7: Service Reporting and Analytics with System Center Service Manager– This chapter then goes on to the next product with Service Manager, where we look into how it can help with the ITSM (IT Service Management) framework and its integrations with the other products with System Center we also look how to design a solution where all information is consolidated and how we can prepare a Configuration Management Database.

Chapter 8: Deployment and Administration of System Center Service Manager– This chapter then follows on from the previous chapter by exploring how to implement and configure Service Manager. Here, we will get into detail on how exactly we configure integrations configurations, and populate the Service Manager, whether native or bespoke configurations, to help build the product to fit your environment.

Chapter 9: Building Scalable and Resilient Orchestration Environments– This chapter focuses on System Center Orchestrator, where we learn how to design a product that is able to automate processes and workflows whether they are one-time, continuous, or reoccurring (BAU – Business As Usual) tasks to be carried out. We will outline the design of its integrations with other products within the System Center family and other core Microsoft products.

Chapter 10: Deployment and Administration of System Center Orchestrator– This chapter follows on from the previous chapter by exploring how to fully implement Orchestrator and install and configure the integrations we require. It also goes into the development of the automated processes so that they can correctly and precisely perform.

Chapter 11: Virtualization with System Center Virtual Machine Manager– This chapter will be around Virtual Machine Manager and how we can design a solution that is able to centralize all of our hypervisor environments. We will analyze all the core roles that can be added once the solution has been installed, as well as outline all of the different templates that it can use.

Chapter 12: Deployment and Administration of System Center VMM – This chapter will, in step-by-step detail, show how we can install Virtual Machine Manager and how we can administer the product by adding our hypervisor environments and servers into the Virtual Machine Manager fabric. We will also cover in more technical detail how to create and configure various templates which will help to centralize, administer, and maintain our virtual environment.

Chapter 13: Creating and Managing Backups with System Center DPM – This chapter covers Data Protection Manager, where we will explore how this solution fits for all of our backup and disaster recovery scenarios.

Chapter 14: Deployment and Administration with System Center DPM – This chapter incorporates everything we have learned within the previous chapter and puts this into practice by showing how we can transition a design into a full implementation. Here, we will explore how we are able to manage our environment with a Data Protection Manager to allow for backups to take place and how we can plan for a recovery in a DR (Disaster Recovery) scenario.

Chapter 15: Standardizing Managing and Governance for Hybrid Settings– This chapter examines how System Center plays a part in not only the centralized management of our on-premise environment but also on how this can be extended to a hybrid environment where everything can be managed jointly through on-premise and cloud-based technologies. We will touch on how each individual product can integrate as well as prepare for the transition into full cloud management and hybrid scenarios.

Chapter 16: Conclusion and Future Trends– This chapter wraps up everything we have learned within the book to provide a conclusion on where we see the products in System Center individually as well as altogether. We look at the future trends and explore all of the active technical communities to further our understanding and expertise of System Center.

Coloured Images

Please follow the link to download the
Coloured Images of the book:

https://rebrand.ly/3e5c4c

We have code bundles from our rich catalogue of books and videos available at **https://github.com/bpbpublications**. Check them out!

Errata

We take immense pride in our work at BPB Publications and follow best practices to ensure the accuracy of our content to provide with an indulging reading experience to our subscribers. Our readers are our mirrors, and we use their inputs to reflect and improve upon human errors, if any, that may have occurred during the publishing processes involved. To let us maintain the quality and help us reach out to any readers who might be having difficulties due to any unforeseen errors, please write to us at :

errata@bpbonline.com

Your support, suggestions and feedbacks are highly appreciated by the BPB Publications' Family.

Did you know that BPB offers eBook versions of every book published, with PDF and ePub files available? You can upgrade to the eBook version at www.bpbonline.com and as a print book customer, you are entitled to a discount on the eBook copy. Get in touch with us at :

business@bpbonline.com for more details.

At **www.bpbonline.com**, you can also read a collection of free technical articles, sign up for a range of free newsletters, and receive exclusive discounts and offers on BPB books and eBooks.

Piracy

If you come across any illegal copies of our works in any form on the internet, we would be grateful if you would provide us with the location address or website name. Please contact us at **business@bpbonline.com** with a link to the material.

If you are interested in becoming an author

If there is a topic that you have expertise in, and you are interested in either writing or contributing to a book, please visit **www.bpbonline.com**. We have worked with thousands of developers and tech professionals, just like you, to help them share their insights with the global tech community. You can make a general application, apply for a specific hot topic that we are recruiting an author for, or submit your own idea.

Reviews

Please leave a review. Once you have read and used this book, why not leave a review on the site that you purchased it from? Potential readers can then see and use your unbiased opinion to make purchase decisions. We at BPB can understand what you think about our products, and our authors can see your feedback on their book. Thank you!

For more information about BPB, please visit **www.bpbonline.com**.

Join our book's Discord space

Join the book's Discord Workspace for Latest updates, Offers, Tech happenings around the world, New Release and Sessions with the Authors:

https://discord.bpbonline.com

Table of Contents

1. **Introduction to Microsoft System Center** 1
   Introduction 1
   Structure 1
   Objectives 1
   Overview of Microsoft System Center 2
      Products within Microsoft System Center 2
      Microsoft System Center Configuration Manager 3
   Benefits and importance of System Center products 3
      Microsoft System Center Operations Manager 3
      Microsoft System Center Virtual Machine Manager 6
      Microsoft System Center Orchestrator 7
      Microsoft System Center Service Manager 8
      Microsoft System Center Data Protection Manager 10
      Microsoft Configuration Manager 11
   Conclusion 13
   Points to remember 14
   Multiple choice questions 14
      Answers 15
   Key terms 16

2. **Latest Updates and Features** 17
   Introduction 17
   Structure 17
   Objectives 18
   Latest updates for System Center 18
      Update release cycle for System Center 18
      Microsoft System Center Operations Manager 20
      Microsoft System Center Virtual Machine Manager 20
      Microsoft System Center Orchestrator 20
      Microsoft System Center Service Manager 21
      Microsoft System Center Data Protection Manager 21
      Microsoft Configuration Manager 21

- Latest features for System Center 22
  - *Microsoft System Center Operations Manager* 22
  - *Microsoft System Center Virtual Machine Manager* 23
  - *Microsoft System Center Orchestrator* 24
  - *Microsoft System Center Service Manager* 25
  - *Microsoft System Center Data Protection Manager* 25
  - *Microsoft Configuration Manager* 25
- Best practice for upgrading System Center 26
  - *Upgrade order* 26
  - *Pre-production environmental testing* 27
  - *Disaster recovery* 27
  - *Supported requirements level* 28
  - *In-place versus side by side* 28
- Conclusion 29
- Points to remember 29
- Multiple choice questions 30
  - *Answers* 31
- Key terms 31

3. OS and Application Deployment Optimization of Configuration Manager 33
- Introduction 33
- Structure 33
- Objectives 34
- Configuration Manager topology structure 34
  - *Configuration Manager Server roles* 34
    - Management point 35
    - Cloud Management Gateway Connection Point 36
  - *Consolidated topology* 36
  - *Multi-server role topology* 37
  - *Site servers topology* 37
  - *Central administration sites* 38
    - Primary site 38
    - Secondary site 39
- Recommended requirements for scalability 39
  - *Hardware requirements* 39
    - Site systems 40

   Core Configuration Manager roles 40
   Disk space 41
   Clients 42
  Structured Query Language Server requirements 42
  Operating System requirements 43
   Supported OS versions for servers 43
   Supported OS versions for clients 44
   Windows 10 Support 44
   Windows 11 Support 44
   Role limitations 45
 Future planning for modern management 46
  Modern management using Intune 46
   Co-management 47
   Hybrid Entra ID in co-management 48
  From Microsoft Configuration Manager to Intune 49
   Operating System device management prerequisites 49
   Application migration 49
   Windows update process migration 50
 What role will the Configuration Manager play 52
  Application deployment and Operating System deployment 53
 Configuration Manager lab requirements 53
  Central administration site environment 53
  Standalone primary site environment 55
 Conclusion 56
 Points to remember 56
 Multiple choice questions 57
  Answers 58
 Key terms 58

4. Deployment and Administration of Microsoft Configuration Manager 59
 Introduction 59
 Structure 60
 Objectives 60
 Primary stand-alone Configuration Manager deployment 60
  Windows server prerequisites 60
  Active Directory schema extensions 63

- Windows Assessment and Deployment Kit 64
- Structured Query Language Server permissions 66
- Firewall requirements 66
- Pre-installation prerequisites 67
- Primary site installation 68

Multiple child sites Configuration Manager deployment 71
- Central administration site installation 71
- Add primary site server to central administration site 73
- Add secondary site server to the primary site 74

Site system status validation of Configuration Manager 75
Component status validation of Configuration Manager 77
Administration of Configuration Manager 79
- Adding additional roles 79
- Database replication 80
  - Replication schedule 81
  - Monitoring of replication 81
- Discovering devices 81
  - Discovery methods 81
  - Client installation account 82
  - Boundary and boundary group set up 83
  - Deploying agents to devices 84
- Cloud attach device management 85
- Upgrade process 86
- Important logs for upgrade process 88

Best practices 88
- Administration 88
  - Upgrading Microsoft Configuration Manager 88
  - Usage of the central administration site 89
- Monitoring 89
  - Create custom queries 89
  - Add reporting services point 89
- Software library 89
  - Non-complicated applications 89
  - Maintenance Windows 90
- Assets and Compliance 90

   Collection creation strategies 90
   Configuration baselines over software metering 91
  Real-world scenario 91
   Administration 91
   Monitoring 91
   Software library 92
   Assets and Compliance 92
  Conclusion 93
  Points to remember 93
  Multiple choice questions 94
   Answers 95
  Key terms 95

5. Monitoring Infrastructure with System Center Operations Manager 97
  Introduction 97
  Structure 97
  Objectives 98
  Operations Manager topology structure 98
   Operations Manager roles 98
   Single management topology 100
   Multi management topology 100
   Untrusted domain and Demilitarized Zone topology 100
  Planning for monitoring 100
   Hardware requirements 101
   Operating System requirements 101
   Structured Query Language Server requirements 102
   Operations Manager limitations 102
   Management packs 103
    Microsoft management packs 103
    Third-party management packs 104
    Community-based management packs 105
    Management pack authoring: Operations Manager console 106
    Management pack authoring and Visual Studio VSAE 106
   Run-As accounts 108
   Override strategy 109
   Microsoft 365 and Microsoft Azure monitoring 110

Data retention	*110*
Multihoming	111
Justification for multihoming	*111*
Disaster recovery versus multihoming configuration	*112*
Azure Monitor	112
System Center Operations Manager Managed Instance planning	*113*
Log Analytics planning	*114*
Integration with Operations Manager	*114*
Operations Manager lab requirements	115
Single management server lab	*115*
Multi-management server lab	*116*
Demilitarized Zone server lab	*116*
Multihoming server lab	*117*
Conclusion	117
Points to remember	118
Multiple choice questions	118
Answers	*119*
Key terms	120

6. Deployment and Administration of System Center Operations Manager ... 121

Introduction	121
Structure	122
Objectives	122
Operations Manager single management server deployment	122
Windows Server Operating System installation media	*123*
Installing server roles and features	*123*
Reporting server: Windows Server prerequisites	*124*
Structured Query Language server reporting services	*124*
Service account requirements	*125*
Firewall requirements	*125*
Installing single management server	*126*
Installing management server	*127*
Installing Operations Console	*128*
Installing web console	*129*
Installing reporting server	*130*
Installing Audit Collection Services Collector	*130*

- Operations Manager multi-management server deployment 131
  - Adding additional management servers 131
    - Installing Gateway Server 133
- Management resource pool health validation of deployment 134
  - Operations Manager services validation 134
    - Resource pool validation within the Operations Console 135
- Administration of Operations Manager 138
  - Installing management packs 138
    - Troubleshooting 139
  - Creating management packs 139
    - Creating a new management pack 139
  - Creating resource pools 141
  - Creating a Run As account 141
    - Creating UNIX/Linux accounts 142
  - Creating Run As profiles 142
  - Adding new agents 143
  - Adding a Windows Agent through Automatic discovery 144
  - Adding a Windows Agent through Advanced discovery 144
  - Adding a Windows Agent through manual installation 145
  - Adding a UNIX or Linux Agent through automatic discovery 147
  - Azure Log Analytics setup 148
  - Upgrading Operations Manager 149
    - Monitoring alerts 151
- Best practices 152
  - Creating closed alerts view 152
  - Tuning management packs 153
  - Default management pack 153
  - Testing management packs 154
- Real-world scenario 154
  - Console versus Visual Studio in Management packs 154
- Conclusion 154
- Points to remember 155
- Multiple choice questions 155
  - Answers 156
- Key terms 156

7. Service Reporting and Analytics with System Center Service Manager 157

- Introduction 157
- Structure 157
- Objectives 158
- Service Manager topology structure 158
  - *Service Manager roles* 158
  - *Single management server topology* 159
    - Scenario one 159
    - Scenario two 159
    - Scenario three 160
  - *Multi-management server topology* 160
  - *Hardware requirements* 160
  - *Operating System requirements* 161
  - *Structured Query Language Server requirements* 162
- Product connector planning 162
  - *Data warehouse connector* 163
  - *Active Directory connector* 164
  - *Configuration Manager connector* 164
  - *System Center Operations Manager CI connector* 164
  - *System Center Operations Manager alert connector* 165
  - *System Center Virtual Machine Manager connector* 165
  - *System Center Orchestrator connector* 165
  - *Exchange connector* 166
  - *Connectors via System Center Orchestrator* 166
  - *Planning for connector usage* 166
    - Connectors to use 167
    - Scheduling connector sync 167
    - Deciding on System Center Operations Manager connectors 167
- Information Technology Service Management planning 168
  - *Activity management* 169
  - *Change management* 169
  - *Incident management* 169
  - *Problem management* 169
  - *Release management* 169
  - *Fulfilling service request* 170

  Developing templates..*170*
  Development of workflows..*171*
 Configuration Management Database design...171
  Up-to-date information..*171*
  Views for custom Configuration Item classes...*172*
 Disaster recovery...173
  Additional management servers..*173*
  Secure storage backup..*173*
 Service Manager lab requirements...174
  Single management server...*174*
  Single management server and data warehouse...*174*
  Multi management server and data warehouse..*175*
 Conclusion..176
 Points to remember...176
 Multiple choice questions...177
  Answers...*178*
 Key terms..178

8. Deployment and Administration of System Center Service Manager 179
 Introduction..179
 Structure..180
 Objectives..180
 Service Manager installation...180
  Management Server..*180*
  Data warehouse server...*180*
  Self-Service Portal...*181*
   Self-Service Portal Internet Information Services installation................*181*
  Service Manager console..*182*
  Windows Server OS installation media..*182*
   Installation of server roles and features...*183*
  Service Manager prerequisites...*183*
   Installing Microsoft SQL Server Analysis Management Objects...........*184*
   Installing Microsoft OLE DB Driver for SQL..*184*
  Service account requirements..*185*
  Firewall requirements..*185*
  Management server installation..*186*

Management Server encryption key backup	188
Additional Management Server installation	188
Data warehouse reporting prerequisites	189
Data warehouse server installation	191
Connector configuration	193
Setting up the data warehouse connector	193
Setting up the Active Directory connector	195
Setting up the Configuration Manager connector	196
Setting up the Operations Manager Alert connector	196
Setting up the Operations Manager CI connector	198
Setting up the Orchestrator connector	198
Setting up the Virtual Machine Manager connector	199
Self-Service configuration	199
Administration of the Service Manager	200
Management packs	200
Adding management packs	201
Creating new management packs	201
Creating new templates	201
Creating workflows	202
Publishing to Self-Service Portal	202
New request offering	203
New service offering	204
Creating custom views for Configuration Management database	205
Creating folder	206
Creating view	206
Upgrading the Service Manager	206
Best practices	207
Real-world scenarios	207
Conclusion	208
Points to remember	208
Multiple choice questions	209
Answers	210
Key terms	210

9. Building Scalable and Resilient Orchestration Environments 211

Introduction 211

- Structure ... 211
- Objectives ... 212
- Orchestrator topology structure ... 212
  - Orchestrator roles ... 212
  - Single Runbook server topology ... 213
  - Multi-Runbook server topology ... 213
  - Hardware requirements ... 214
  - Operating System requirements ... 214
  - Structured Query Language Server requirements ... 214
- Product integration planning ... 215
  - Integration packs ... 215
  - Native integration packs ... 216
  - Microsoft-based integration packs ... 217
    - Planning for Active Directory integration ... 218
    - Planning for Configuration Manager integration ... 219
    - Planning for Operations Manager integration ... 220
  - Planning for Service Manager integration ... 221
  - Planning for Virtual Machine Manager integration ... 221
  - Planning for Data Protection Manager integration ... 223
    - Third-party integration packs ... 224
- Service Management Automation ... 224
  - Web service ... 225
  - Runbook Worker ... 225
  - PowerShell module ... 225
  - Choosing Orchestrator, Service Management Automation or both ... 225
- Service Manager connectors ... 226
  - Custom connectors ... 226
  - Syncing Orchestrator Runbooks to the Service Manager ... 227
- Disaster recovery ... 227
  - More Runbook servers ... 227
  - Data Store Configuration ... 227
  - Orchestrator Data Protection Manager integration ... 227
- Orchestrator lab requirements ... 228
  - Consolidated topology ... 228
  - Scalable topology ... 229

	Conclusion 230
	Points to remember 230
	Multiple choice questions 231
	Answers 231
	Key terms 232
10.	**Deployment and Administration of System Center Orchestrator** 233
	Introduction 233
	Structure 234
	Objectives 234
	Single runbook server installation 234
	Installing splash screen 234
	.NET Framework 3.5 Installation Media 235
	Orchestrator account requirements 236
	Firewall requirements 237
	Orchestrator installation 237
	Multi-runbook server installation 239
	Installing additional runbook 239
	Administrating Orchestrator 241
	Deploying manager tasks 241
	Register integration packs 241
	Deploy integration packs 242
	Deploy Runbook Designer servers via deployment manager 243
	Deploy runbook servers via deployment manager 243
	Configuration of integration packs 244
	Active Directory Integration Pack Configuration 245
	System Center 2022 Operations Manager 246
	Creating runbooks 247
	New runbook 247
	Edit runbook 247
	Creating runbook workflows 248
	Global settings 253
	Testing runbooks 254
	Update Orchestrator (Update Rollups) 255
	Best practices 256
	Multiple integration pack connections 256

Effective error handling	256
Consoles for integration packs	258
PowerShell handling	258
Real-world scenarios	258
Upgrading to Orchestrator 2022	258
Clearing authorization cache	259
Runbook limits	259
Distributed Component Object Model permission issues	259
Conclusion	259
Points to remember	260
Multiple choice questions	260
Answers	261
Key terms	261

11. Virtualization with System Center Virtual Machine Manager 263

Introduction	263
Structure	263
Objectives	264
Virtual Machine Manager topology structure	264
Virtual Machine Manager roles	264
Virtual Machine Manager post-installation roles	264
Single management server topology	265
Virtual environment management planning	265
Hardware requirements	266
Operating System requirements	266
Structured Query Language requirements	267
Virtual Machine Manager limitations	267
Hypervisor platform management decisions	268
Infrastructure role planning	268
Library servers	268
PXE servers	270
Update servers	271
Storage planning	271
Network planning	272
Logical networks	272
Virtual environment template design	273

	Physical host profile design *274*
	Operating System of host server *274*
	Hardware configuration *274*
	Operating System configuration *274*
	Virtual machine profile design *275*
	Templates design *277*
	Disaster recovery 278
	Virtual Machine Manager lab requirements 279
	Single management server *279*
	High availability or mixed hypervisor environment configuration *279*
	Conclusion 280
	Points to remember 281
	Multiple choice questions 281
	Answers *282*
	Key terms 282
12.	**Deployment and Administration of System Center VMM** **283**
	Introduction 283
	Structure 284
	Objectives 284
	Virtual Machine Manager single management server deployment 284
	Management server *284*
	Windows Assessment Deployment Kit *284*
	Structured Query Language Server Command Line Utilities *285*
	Virtual Machine Manager console *286*
	Virtual Machine Manager service accounts *286*
	Firewall requirements *286*
	Virtual Machine Manager installation *287*
	Virtual Machine Manager multi-manager server deployment 289
	Adding additional management servers *289*
	Administration of the Virtual Machine Manager 290
	Adding infrastructure servers *290*
	Library server *291*
	Pre-boot Execution Environment server *292*
	Update server *292*
	Adding Storage *292*

Adding networking	293
Logical Networks	293
Logical Switches	293
Adding hosts	294
Host groups	294
Hyper-V hosts: Domain network	294
Untrusted domain Hyper-V Hosts	296
Perimeter network Hyper-V Hosts	296
VMware ESXi Hosts	298
Profiles creation	299
Hardware profiles	299
Guest Operating System profiles	300
Creating Virtual Machines	301
Create Virtual Machines with Virtual Machine templates	302
Importing resources to the library server	303
Bare metal deployment hosts	304
Physical computer profile	304
Adding host for provisioning	305
Managing hosts and Virtual Machines	305
Upgrading the Virtual Machine Manager	306
Best practices	307
PRO tips for System Center Operations Manager integration	307
Monitoring Virtual Machine Manager	307
Real-world scenarios	307
Managing vCenter servers	308
Conclusion	308
Points to remember	308
Multiple choice questions	309
Answers	310
Key terms	310
13. Creating and Managing Backups with System Center DPM	**311**
Introduction	311
Structure	311
Objectives	312
Data Protection Manager topology structure	312

    Data Protection Manager roles *312*
    Single management server topology *312*
    Hardware requirements *313*
    Operating System requirements *313*
    Structured Query Language requirements *313*
  Product integration planning 314
    Product recognition *314*
    Managing VMware *315*
    System Center Orchestrator *316*
    System Center Operations Manager *316*
  Backup scheduling design 316
    Protection group structuring *317*
    Data retention planning scheduling *317*
  Disaster recovery 318
  Data Protection Manager lab requirements 319
    Data Protection Manager 2022 lab setup table *320*
  Conclusion 320
  Points to remember 321
  Multiple choice questions 321
    Answers *322*
  Key terms 322

14. Deployment and Administration of System Center DPM **323**
  Introduction 323
  Structure 324
  Objectives 324
  Data Protection Manager deployment 324
    Management server *324*
        Structured Query Language Server management tools 324
    Structured Query Language Server *325*
        Reporting services 325
        Data Protection Manager 2022 support files 325
        Data Protection Manager service accounts 326
    Firewall requirements *327*
        Data Protection Manager installation 327
  Technology backup configuration 329

   Manage VMware credentials..*329*
  Administration of Data Protection Manager 331
   Add storage *331*
   Add servers *332*
    Windows servers | Not behind firewall *333*
    Windows Servers –Behind firewall | Trusted domain *333*
    Windows Servers | Behind firewall | Non-trusted domain *334*
    VMware servers *335*
   Create protection group *336*
   Manage protection group..*337*
    Adding new group members *337*
    Perform consistency check...*338*
    Recover from protection group backup *338*
    Alert monitoring *340*
    Report administration *340*
    Upgrade Data Protection Manager...*341*
  Best practices 343
   Disk pool structure *343*
  Real-world scenarios 343
   Tape backup *343*
   Product placement against other third-party products *344*
  Conclusion 344
  Points to remember 344
  Multiple choice questions 344
   Answers *345*
  Key terms 346

15. Standardizing Management and Governance for Hybrid Settings 347
  Introduction 347
  Structure..347
  Objectives..348
  Managing hybrid environments using Microsoft System Center 348
   Microsoft Configuration Manager *348*
  Governance policies and compliance across hybrid infrastructure 353
   Intune..*353*
    Compliance policies *354*

Hybrid Autopilot profiles	*356*
Group policy to Intune migration	*358*
Integrating Cloud platforms for centralized management	358
System Center Operations Manager	*359*
System Center Virtual Machine Manager	*359*
System Center Data Protection Manager	*360*
Conclusion	360
Points to remember	361
Multiple choice questions	361
Answers	*362*
Key terms	362

16. Conclusion and Future Trends 363

Introduction	363
Structure	363
Objectives	364
Recap of key concepts and learnings	364
Microsoft Configuration Manager	*364*
System Center Operations Manager	*364*
System Center Service Manager	*365*
System Center Orchestrator	*366*
System Center Virtual Machine Manager	*366*
System Center Data Protection Manager	*367*
Future trends in data center management using System Center	367
System Center 2025	*367*
Configuration Manager updates	*368*
Entra ID and modern management	*369*
Future of the System Center	*370*
Notable links to follow	*370*
Conclusion	371
References	371

Index **373-380**

CHAPTER 1
Introduction to Microsoft System Center

Introduction

In this chapter, we will go into an overview of the whole System Center suite. Given its long history through most of the products in the suite and some coming into the suite later in the years and taking into account that we will be discussing System Center 2022 as the current latest version, this will be a great way of combining the history from then all the way up to now. Explaining the benefits and importance of the System Center products will be key in this chapter and to set the overall tone before proceeding further in this book.

Structure

This chapter will cover the following topics:
- Overview of Microsoft System Center
- Benefits and importance of System Center products

Objectives

The objectives will be to have a greater understanding of the roles that each product plays within System Center as well as its overall purpose. We will also learn the specifics of the roles and the benefits which come along with each product individually as well as altogether.

Overview of Microsoft System Center

To talk of exactly what Microsoft System Center will be perhaps the most exciting part which will set off the tone and foundation for the reader. A topic such as this has been given various interpretations as to exactly what its role is, and here we hope to consolidate a lot of those same thoughts as well as to provide a new light to its purpose to shine the light on its latest and greatest form.

Overall Microsoft System Center is essentially a suite of products which is used to manage your environment by form of centralization, bringing everything together to provide a **Single-Pane-Of-Glass (SPOG)** investigation of your environment.

The purpose of Microsoft System Center can hold as much excitement as the person who provides their **Subject Matter Expert (SME)** opinion to summarize. To show an example we will say that Microsoft System Center can potentially do anything and everything you want it to for your IT environment. The key is really in how you utilize it as well as understanding what you would require the suite for.

Aimed at simplifying data center management, Microsoft System Center really poses every solution for the reader to be able to take on the journey of developing the right solution, and with various depth of levels of what the suite can bring complement each product and should bring excitement to the person who wants to divulge further into the products.

The centralization performed by the suite mainly operates on an agent managed based solution. Meaning that an agent is normally pushed onto the servers or client devices which are required to be managed by a particular product, which then feeds information back to a primary management point which can capture that information. The only product which does not share this kind of operation would be Orchestrator, which we will touch on later in this chapter.

Products within Microsoft System Center

These are the current products that exist within the suite:
- **Microsoft System Center Operations Manager (SCOM)**
- **Microsoft System Center Virtual Machine Manager (SCVMM)**
- **Microsoft System Center Orchestrator (SCO)**
- **Microsoft System Center Service Manager (SCSM)**
- **Microsoft System Center Data Protection Manager (SCPDM)**

> **Note:** You may notice that Microsoft System Center Configuration Manager is missing from the product list, Due to rebranding the Configuration Manager product is no longer part of the actual suite, but this book will cover Configuration Manager as well as the explanations of it is rebranding and purpose.

Each product plays an individual but integral role within the family of System Center with each being a powerful centralized solution. In the next topic we will explore the role that each product plays.

Microsoft System Center Configuration Manager

What happened to Microsoft System Center Configuration Manager? To provide some background to this, Configuration Manager was originally a Microsoft System Center product from 2007. However, with the focus and drive into modern management, configuration has gone into various different rebrandings over the years and now stands out as a separate solution, but it still however remains an integral piece of the System Center suite regardless.

It is perhaps the most popular product of the suite, with the other being Microsoft System Center Operations Manager. Both share a similar history of developments, that is, being introduced into the suite from Configuration Manager, starting from its original name of **Systems Management Server (SMS)** and the operations manager being **Microsoft Operations Manager (MOM)**.

Returning to Configuration Manager, its official name is now Microsoft Configuration Manager, which belongs to the overall solution of Microsoft Endpoint Manager or is simply known as endpoint management, which represents a centralized solution for both on-premises and cloud-based device management.

The reader can expect this book to also dive greatly into this product with its roots being in the System Center suite.

Benefits and importance of System Center products

Now that we understand the suite, we can now start to explore the roles in which each product plays, its capabilities and how they are fully utilized within your data center management.

Microsoft System Center Operations Manager

This specific product takes care of one of the core principals of managing your data center environment, that is, monitoring. Microsoft System Center Operations Manager is the official centralized monitoring solution for the System Center suite.

This product is a beast of a solution and is a true and key example of being able to do anything and everything with it. The purpose of this product is to to pull all your environment into a centralized look and to assess the health state of your environment which is observed as a whole and broken down into several segments to build an overall picture.

This is achieved through an agent-based rollout to the devices which you want to monitor. Although, primarily aimed at servers you also hold the capability of extending this to your client devices as well.

The way in which the operations manager functions to monitor the health state of your environment is by utilizing a logical container called management packs. Each management pack consists of a set of monitors and rules. Generally, they contain the following types of objects to make up the overall management pack which are:

- Classes
- Discoveries
- Monitors
- Rules
- Tasks
- Views

To provide more context to each of them let us go through each one so we can understand how these play a role.

Classes are the logical IDs which represent a discovered instance. For example, let us take, *Windows computers*; this is defined as an actual class which represents Windows computers as written in the name. Classes then contain properties which then stand out as the attributes for a class.

Another example of this looking at Windows computers you would have a property which is called **principal name** which is the name of the Windows computer. If you were to develop a custom class for a management pack, and you named it something like **Test App Computers** you may have common property names to represent each discovered instance such as:

- Name
- Version

These attributes then make up the class which we are looking to define. Another part of the properties within a class is the definition of a **key property** which is used to identify an instance within a class as being unique. Hence, if we know that the name of a computer will be unique on each device, we could define that as the key property for which operations manager will be able to recognize and set apart from the rest.

> *Tip:* **In the realms of best practice the most efficient way to define a key property would be to utilize a Graphic User Interface Identity (GUID) which is highly unlikely for another instance or device to share.**

Looking at the next layer would then be the **Discoveries** side, which is used to find the instances of the class that we define. Hence, if we want to find computers that have the test application as well as the properties of name and version, we would create a discovery that would run a process or a script that can then identify if a specific computer meets the criteria for the targeted class that the discovery is running for. Once it has been discovered, the properties that we outlined earlier will also be populated from the discovered information.

Monitors are what it is all about now when it comes to showcasing the power of the operations manager. Here is where we define a criterion very similar to a discovery, but in this case, this is where we would assess the health state of a managed instance. Providing another example let us say we want to check the running state of a windows service, the monitor would check on a specified interval if whether that service was running on that computer. Typically monitors have a healthy status and error status, but you can also have a middle ground where you can report on a status which can be labelled as a warning.

> *Tip:* It is always best to know when to define a monitor health status as an error or warning. Best practice would advise that an error health status prompts for an urgent response, whilst a warning status would be more to let you know that something is starting to become serious unless it is not investigated or addressed. Improper health statuses can set a domino effect of false positives or negatives

Rules are very similar to monitors, however the fundamental difference between them is that they do not have to have a necessary bearing on the health status. In other words, monitors normally have an auto-resolution function for where it detects if something is healthy or unhealthy and will switch between them. Rules on the other hand can report one status which may not have to define two states or any auto-resolution. Rules can also be used as a process which could be like a scheduled task that bear no health status recognition, or even to perform collection of metrics such as performance counters that you would get in something like **performance monitor** (**perfmon**).

Tasks are handy options which are presented within an operations manager console that can be ran either on an agent managed computer or on the actual server itself. This provides a great way for an administrator to find out more information or to perform certain actions conveniently without having to go directly to an agent managed computer or run anything outside of operations manager.

Then finally to complete the management pack is the visual which showcases your discovered instances which are done through **views**. They can come in a variety of types but overall, they visually display the health status and information for everything which has been discovered and monitored.

These management packs can either be created by the administrator of operations manager or there are several official vendor-based management packs which natively come from Microsoft, as well as other third-party vendors also.

Everything then ties together to showcase the strength of how operations manager is a true powerhouse for a monitoring solution.

Microsoft System Center Virtual Machine Manager

Another powerful product, in fact, is one of the slightly overlooked out of the System Center suite but addresses another important principle of centralized management, and in this case, it involves the centralization of your virtual environment.

Virtual Machine Manager helps organizations to show your entire virtualization environment within your data center with a focus on being able to fully manage, optimize and provide scalability for your environment.

Your management capabilities can provide a lot and not limited to the following:
- Creation of new virtual server hosts
- Creation of new virtual machines
- Templates for server hosts and machines
- Centralized repository for your software

In real-world cases, a lot of environments will utilize either a Hyper-V environment or a VMware environment, and as expected, most may use a product such as VCenter for their VMware environment, whilst Virtual Machine Manager has a focus on the management of Hyper-V environements. You can also can manage your VMware environment and can prove to be an even more powerful tool if you are to operate in a hybrid scenario where you may use both hypervisor platforms.

To expand on the scalability side this is quite important especially when you take into consideration the growth of a business, and this is where Virtual Machine Manager can assist.

The template bullet point opens a great convenience so that when we must build a new server on demand, a virtual machine template would have a profile already pre-configured. Now profiles essentially have a configuration already preset for a VM to fit in terms of minimum and recommended requirements.

Another side to the great part of being able to support a hybrid type of setup, we must consider the actual placement of new servers when it comes to the correct hosts on where to place a new virtual machine which would be rated by the resources available on the desired host. These options provide great flexibility all around, and even though a product such as this may not get utilized as much, it is one to be recognized and should be encouraged to expand upon.

Microsoft System Center Orchestrator

Perhaps it is the best name within the System Center suite because the name Orchestrator simply says it all!

The Orchestrator's purpose is literally to bring **everything** together. Everything meaning every single Microsoft System Center product within the suite.

This product has the ability to integrate all products, including fundamental Windows services such as Active Directory, to be all connected to build powerful and complex automated workflows that help not only the administrative effort on small tasks but also enrich very detailed and complicated processes and workflows which are either carried out manually or semi-automatically.

Its perhaps the smallest tool in a sense as well because of the solution being driven by a small console. However, just like its other relatives within the suite they rely on the server roles which play specific key roles to be able to have workflows carefully load balanced across to provide an efficient flow of processes.

The processes which we speak of are defined in orchestrator as runbooks. Runbooks you could say are quite similar to how operations manager management pack's function. Runbooks contain a series of actions that come from a System Center product, Active Directory, or various other foundational services within Windows to provide an instructed set of actions to complete to perfect a workflow process being successful.

In the traditional way in which operations manager uses management packs to represent specific Microsoft products or third-party products to monitor, orchestrator utilizes a similar mechanism which are called **integration packs**. Each integration pack allows the administrator to configure the connection setup to the desired product in which the integration pack represents.

Here is an example of how Orchestrator would work:

Let us say we have an integration pack that represents none other than Microsoft System Center Operations Manager. This pack then contains a series of different actions that can be added into a runbook like the following example:

- Create alert
- Get alert

However, what if we also have the Active Directory integration pack as well, we then have another set of actions specific to Active Directory with some examples being:

- Create user
- Get user

Now, with this type of setup, we will want to define an automated process that would help us with the onboarding of a new user, such as being alerted when a new account was created. With the setup we have, we could construct a runbook that would contain a step that performs get user, and then another that runs the step **create alert**. With this workflow, we could go into the get user action and define an additional filter, such as being created today or in 24 hours; if it finds an account, we can then create an alert in SCOM, which would state a new account has been created in Active Directory.

Now if you take that example and then imagine all the integration packs and the number of workflows and processes which your data center has that could be essentially transformed into an automated workflow, that is orchestrator.

As we go further into this chapter keeping mind what has been discussed previously, when you understand all of the benefits and importance of each product once you refer back to here you can understand the type of power System Center really has when you take in consideration the vital role in which orchestrator can play.

Microsoft System Center Service Manager

The next product that we will discuss is the one that now considers another principle, another solution that can bring everything together in a similar fashion as the Orchestrator. However, in this case, this product brings everything together in more of an **IT Service Management (ITSM)** and **Configuration Management Database (CMDB)** way which helps us build a framework across your whole environment to where it can be administered by a centralized helpdesk team to help deliver IT services across the spectrum.

One of the common features this product has with operations manager is its use of management packs. These logical containers are the same as well being able to orchestrate them using similar Microsoft products such as Visual Studios and other specific product tools. However, instead of using them for monitoring capabilities they are more to extend the recognition of other classes of information. This may help the connectors you create which we will go into further.

We bring to you Microsoft System Center Service Manager, a solution which again brings together all your System Center products altogether to have an automated service management solution which would allow you to provide IT services with all the collated inventory from your data center environment.

Now, to paint the picture of how the service manager works, let us first look into the aspects of the ITSM modules that we may recognize, such as:

- Change management
- Incident management
- Service request management
- Problem incident management

With these types of services, you would need to have the correct information on the **Configuration Instance's** (**CI**) to refer one of the requests with such as information of a particular service, application or even a computer.

Now let us really paint the picture. So with the CMDB, which is populated from the connections with other System Center products, let us say again, operations manager. We could pull in all the discovered monitored computers within SCOM. Once this is stored within the CMDB in service manager, when someone in the IT service team or an end user were to raise let us say an incident, then they could select their computer which was discovered within the CMDB. It would then provide the IT service team the information they need to understand the issue and how the setup is on that user as well as machine.

The best part of service manager is that what we have described is one part of the product. The other side to this powerhouse is its relationship with System Center orchestrator. Orchestrator is officially labelled as the **custom connector** for service manager.

To provide context to this, connectors are what service manager uses to connect to different System Center products or technologies such as Active Directory and even exchange. The same way orchestrator uses integration packs to setup connections to other System Center products also.

The following connectors can be configured within Service Manager:

- **Configuration manager**: Integration with Microsoft Configuration Manager for asset inventory
- **Operations manager (CI connector)**: Integration with operations manager for asset inventory
- **Operations manager (alert connector)**: Integration with operations manager for monitoring inventory
- **Active Directory**: Integration for Active Directory inventory
- **Orchestrator**: Integration to synchronize runbooks created within orchestrator
- **Exchange**: Integration to synchronize emails from mailboxes
- **Data warehouse**: Connection to a server which allows for historical data to be stored for service manager

Hence, what does this mean for Orchestrator and service manager? Do we remember the Orchestrator Runbooks we spoke of in the previous section? The Orchestrator Runbooks that we spoke of in the earlier section, can be brought into the service manager fold and these can be linked to the same IT service requests in which we mentioned above. This means not only can you have a full scale ITSM solution, but potentially have automated workflows which would then also be able to work on a requests behalf to provide a potential solution or at least a discovery scenario for troubleshooting.

Another benefit in which the product provides is also a self-service portal which will allow users to be able to request for specific services which will be applicable to themselves the user or to their device.

Let us look at another example:

Let us say we would want to request a license for an application we have installed on our device which is currently running as a trial version. A user could go into the portal and select this specific service and be provided with a form to enter some basic details about the request. Now let us wrap in everything we spoke about earlier about what this product can do with having some bullet points which may represent some fields which we may have in our self-service request form with a fully populated CMDB:

- **Select an application**: We can select the application which is on our device
- **Select user affected**: The logged in user will be detected from the initial sign-in, of course we can select another user if making a request on someone's behalf
- **Select affected device**: If you are the affected user then your primary device will also be pre-selected or can be chosen.

Once the user has submitted the request, the IT service team then has all the information required to proceed, with the service request.

Overall, the possibilities are endless when it comes to using a product such as service manager, and its other product counterparts only make the product even more powerful thus complimenting each other.

Microsoft System Center Data Protection Manager

Perhaps the most underrated of them all however, is responsible for a crucial principle for our data center environment, which is around backup solutions, which aids us in our disaster recovery planning.

With the benefits and descriptions provided within all the other sections of System Center products, you should be able to envisage on how a product like this can also be just as powerful as the rest. When you take into consideration that it is the most underrated or underutilized of them all, you will understand why this may even prove to be a must have within your environment.

Data Protection Manager, as self-explanatory as it is; it is the backup and recovery solution product of the family.

Now, let us see why this product is important and why we should use it when there are several other backup solutions? Why would we not be able to just use SQL backups?

The main reason is that it is a System Center product, which would mean this would be optimized on how to backup System Center products the best way, in this case, its capability of being able to focus on Virtual Machine Manager level backups provides a great point of integration to look after the disaster recovery of your hypervisor estate. Not only that, but the product is also optimized for the scheduling of all these backups as well.

When taking into consideration a tool that will perform all your backups and that it is able to work specifically how you want it to, one of the big things a customer would want. It is its plug-in and integration capabilities. If a customer is already a System Center household, it would make sense for them to take advantage of a backup solution that is already part of the same family. This would also help keep things together when it comes to backing up the rest of the other products too.

Though backing up the SQL database and snapshots of a database will also provide great help, with a product , such as Data Protection Manager, you will be able to ensure that there is a product which has its best interests also.

A product such as this can have **application aware** backup strategies for the core Microsoft products such as exchange and SQL server, but in the book later we can also display on how we can expand on the application aware level backup strategies too.

Microsoft Configuration Manager

Once again, though no longer part of the System Center family, it is perhaps the most popular product of them all whether inside or outside the suite.

This is not a case of what they would call *saving the best for the last*, but mainly because of the history that this product has and the evolution it has taken, it is indeed a product that must be talked about.

Configuration manager is the product that you want when it comes to tverall device management, when we talk about the following areas:

- Deployment of operating systems
- Patch management compliance
- Asset inventory
- Software library deployment

The preceding list alone probably captures a small percentage of what Configuration Manager is capable of.

As of most recent years, this product has gone through a numerous number of changes to the actual name with its departure from the System Center suite mainly in name, but this has not been reflected within the integrations with all the other System Center products which we can see as follows:

- System Center Orchestrator (integration packs)
- System Center Service Manager (connectors)
- System Center Operations Manager (management pack + further integration)

So let us explain the benefits of Configuration Manager and the role that it plays alongside the System Center suite. Configuration manager takes care of the OS compliance, and this includes from a complete lifecycle of building a bare metal machine, managing the device, and having its device managed within its software library and various compliance policies.

Due to the size of the product, it can be used for perhaps 15% of the overall product without having to really touch any other areas. Hence, let us explore some ways in which Configuration Manager is utilized.

We can go through all the elements and give some more context to each so we can lay out the areas in which this product can be used for.

Operating System Deployment (OSD) represents being able to build bare metal machines to a complete user-ready state. However, this area also represents the upgrading of operating systems also through a process called **task sequences**. These can represent both building a machine as well as upgrading a current machine as well. This area can collate operating system images, and contains the ability to apply the latest windows updates to the operating system images.

Software library optimization, we look at the focus of the deployment of applications and packages. Everything from deployment scheduling as well as the correct form of detection of existing applications discovered on the managed devices within Configuration Manager, and this then leads into another in which Configuration Manager can be responsible for.

Asset and compliance, typically the name of a tab within the console itself, but this represents the **user interface (UI)** centralization of all managed devices within Configuration Manager by logical containers called **collections**. These can also be created to represent users also. These containers help the foundation in terms of deploying any of the applications or task sequences by aiming them specifically at a group of devices or users which have a primary device in which they are assigned to. However, in addition to this kind of role, there is also the asset intelligence aspect whereby, in the way of reports, you can pull up information about hardware and software inventory.

Then the next area of roles in which the Configuration Manager is also known for looking after is patch compliance. When we speak of patch compliance, we talk about the windows updates compliance of being able to perform the following types of actions:

- Synchronization of windows updates
- Summarization of updates required on devices
- Automation of windows update and synchronization

The importance that Configuration Manager plays in terms of patch compliance is the integration that it has with the native feature of the **Windows Server Update Services (WSUS)** role. The benefits of an integration such as this is the workflow combined where Configuration Manager can control the overall management of the updates compliance which then gets extended onto areas such as:

- Patch compliance reporting
- Device update summarization
- Updating of Operating System images with windows updates

The other side, which is also worth providing more context into, is, of course, what separates the Configuration Manager product away from the suite in general, and that would be the optimized focus into the cloud with its integration with Azure and Endpoint Manager, also known as **Intune**.

Now, all the products in System Center do indeed have an integration or a cloud ready version, but in the case of Configuration Manager there is a push going towards modern management. Modern management represents the model of Configuration Manager eventually no longer being performed in an on-premises base but all within the cloud using the Endpoint Manager portal.

As there is of course hesitance for most organizations to move across into this realm due to being unsure of the readiness of their environment or perhaps overall doubt of whether they want to proceed in this away, Configuration Manager has a mode which can be configured which is called co-management.

Co-management is a hybrid solution that allows organizations to be able to utilize both on-premises management with Configuration Manager but also be able to utilize the capabilities of endpoint management. Typically, this can be controlled by editing the workload affinity between both technologies. This is normally a good way to ease the transition into modern management with a view to assessing the readiness and ensuring an organization can move into modern management.

Overall, Configuration Manager does have a staple in foundational products to exist within your data center environment, and though it may no longer be considered a System Center product, its roots are indeed still there and play an integral part in showcasing the suite overall.

Conclusion

To summarize, it is always best to understand exactly what a technology such as System Center provides, as well as breaking down each individual product so that the reader understands that each product has the capability of being a powerhouse on its own depending on what type of solution you are looking for.

There could have been information around the history of the product from its very first version all the way up to now like other sources of information around System Center, but here we want to provide actual excitement to the reader who is then influenced to want to be the practitioner.

A couple of products in this suite do fall under the radar and so the conclusion wants to help shed lighter on the actual capabilities of these products so that we can rekindle back more interest and how they can help solve a lot of potential issues or bottlenecks that may exist within your data center environment which you may or may not be aware of.

Knowing the benefits of what each product provides is critical. When it comes to assessing your requirements, you should always look to make the solution fit the business requirements rather than let the business requirement fit the solution.

Also, the inclusion of Configuration Manager is still important for this chapter, whether it remains a part of the overall suite. It is roots will always be in the System Center field historically as well as technically.

In the next chapter, we will cover all the latest versions which are available for each System Center product as well as all of the new features which come along. Combined this will illustrate a greater understanding of how the updates are released as well as the new features tied to each one.

Points to remember

- Microsoft System Center is a centralized data center management solution.
- Five core products make up System Center being operations manager, service manager, Virtual Machine Manager, Orchestrator, and Data Protection Manager.
- Microsoft Configuration Manager is no longer part of the System Center suite.
- Operations Manager is the monitoring product solution.
- Service Manager is the ITSM product solution.
- Orchestrator is the workflow and automation product solution.
- Virtual Machine Manager is the hypervisor management product solution.
- Data Protection Manager is the backup product solution.
- Except for Orchestrator, all System Center products, including Microsoft Configuration Manager, are agent based managed products.
- Orchestrator is the official custom connector solution for Service Manager.

Multiple choice questions

1. What are the products that make up the Microsoft System Center Solution?
    a. Operations Manager, Configuration Manager, Virtual Management Manager, Data Protection Manager, Orchestrator, Service Manager
    b. Operations Manager, Virtual Machine Manager, Data Protection Manager, Orchestrator, Configuration Manager
    c. Operations Manager, Virtual Machine Manager, Data Protection Manager, Orchestrator, Service Manager

d. Service Manager, Active Directory, Configuration Manager, Service Manager, Endpoint Manager

2. **How would you summarize the role that System Center plays?**
    a. System Center is a centralized data center management solution
    b. System Center is an automation suite
    c. System Center integrates with Active Directory to create users
    d. System Center is a single product solution for centralized management

3. **What is the full name of the abbreviation SCVMM?**
    a. System Center Virtual Machine Manager
    b. System Center Virtual Management Manager
    c. System Center Various Management Manager
    d. Solution Centralization Virtual Machine Manager

4. **Which products integrate to build custom connections?**
    a. Configuration Manager and Operations Manager
    b. Orchestrator and Service Manager
    c. Orchestrator and Operations Manager
    d. Data Protection Manager and Virtual Machine Manager

5. **What is the reason why Configuration Manager is no longer a System Center product?**
    a. Configuration Manager is still part of System Center
    b. Configuration Manager has been retired
    c. Product is a cloud solution only
    d. Rebranding and focus to Modern Management

Answers

1. c
2. a
3. a
4. b
5. d

Key terms

- **Agent managed device:** A device which is managed by an installed agent which reports back to a management point.
- **Single Pane of Glass (SPOG):** A centralized viewing which allows for multiple or all components to be viewed through a **Graphical User Interface (GUI)**
- **Hybrid:** A cross between two or more platforms in which control can be balanced between those platforms.
- **Logical containers:** An object which is contained within a product which is another micromanaged from of management within the product.

Join our book's Discord space

Join the book's Discord Workspace for Latest updates, Offers, Tech happenings around the world, New Release and Sessions with the Authors:

https://discord.bpbonline.com

CHAPTER 2
Latest Updates and Features

Introduction

Keeping yourself updated is very important in the world of IT, but perhaps even more important is keeping the System Center suite fully updated for what it represents, being the centralized management for our whole estate, which also plays a part in keeping our managed estate updated.

What also comes with the latest versions and updates are of course, bug fixes, different tweaks, etc. However, the more exciting part is the distinguishing new features that not only provide a benefit to all our updated managed environment but also to our System Center products, which we will look into in detail within this chapter.

Structure

This chapter will cover the following topics:
- Latest updates for System Center
- Latest features for System Center
- Best practice for upgrading System Center

Objectives

The objectives learned will be to be aware of the latest updates and versions available to System Center in general as well as per each product where we will cover how the latest versions are released and find out more about those updates in terms of what new features come along. Also learned will be the overall best practice to adapt in the real scenario when it comes to the upgrading of any System Center products within your organization.

Latest updates for System Center

A key element in ensuring the efficient operation of products and their support is the application of the latest updates. This is crucial to ensure that we are fully updated and can take advantage of the latest features, bug fixes, and compatibility with the most recent operating systems and products.

However, there are many components to understand how updates are applied and retrieved for each product so we will explore this further.

Update release cycle for System Center

Before we go into the latest updates available for each product, we should understand exactly how System Center's structure is around actual updates.

Again, reiterating about Microsoft Configuration Manager is not part of the suite, even when it was part of the suite its update structure was different compared to the rest which we will cover later this chapter.

Hence, focusing on the actual suite itself the update structure on the high level goes by the year or its release, hence the name of the latest release being System Center 2022 and following the tradition of the previous versions being 2019, 2016 and 2012 respectively.

Then, moving lower down the hierarchy of updates, the primary updates are distributed in the form of update rollups, normally known by its abbreviation of UR.

Update rollups normally come in a form of a `.msp` file which contains a collation of several fixes as well as updates to the designated product. Most of the update rollups are normally targeted to specific server roles for the product in which they must be applied and in a specific order to ensure that the product is upgraded correctly.

The times of releases when it comes to update rollups for System Center can vary. Sometimes, there can be a group release where **Update Rollup 1 (UR1)**, for example, might have an applicable update for every product or might leave out one or two. This would be, of course, dependent on the bugs that have been reported on each product and if there is scope to add more features.

In some cases, there can be small hotfixes that can be made available to a specific product if there is an urgent bug fix that may need to be rectified.

Update rollups and hotfixes are normally available to download from the Microsoft Update Catalog site or by the KB article which references them. You do also have the ability to synchronize the updates with **Windows Server Update Services (WSUS)** but there are a lot of moving parts in terms of upgrading in this way which will also be covered later in this chapter.

Now, for Configuration Manager, the update cycle is slightly different as they go through a release process in which new build versions are released every quarter and follow a number pattern of which would follow as 03, 07, and 11. For example, if we take an older version of Configuration Manager, you will see the following versions:

- 2103
- 2107
- 2111

Each of which are released in the next quarter. The process where new updates are applicable are synchronized through its management console as opposed to having an update rollup structure like the other System Center products. This is something which has remained like this since its earlier rebranding of being known as **Current Branch**.

Though this process exists, you do also have the capability of being able to install a base version of Configuration Manager at a specific build version so that once your Configuration Manager is up and running then, you will be able to apply the latest version to your environment.

It is worth noting that Configuration Manager also does have hotfixes, but they come specifically to the version you are running. This means that if you were on a version such as 2203, then the hotfixes for this version will only be available to you once you have upgraded the version.

Configuration Manager has what we call minor and major upgrades. Minor, meaning that the build number version would change, and the fixes and updates would be applied. However, in a major upgrade, not only would the Configuration Manager server environment be affected, but it will also allow for a new version of the Configuration Manager agent and the console.

Now that we have established the structure of how the updates cycle works in System Center and Configuration Manager we can now proceed to the individual products to see what the latest updates are for each.

Note that the top entry represents the current version of System Center 2022, except for Microsoft Configuration Manager.

Microsoft System Center Operations Manager

At the time of writing this book, the following latest versions are reported (see *Table 2.1*):

Role	Build Version	Release Date	Description	KB Article
All server components	10.22.10118.0	March 2022	Current Version	N/A
All server components	10.22.10565.0	December 2022	Update Rollup 1	KB502245
Agent	10.22.10110.0	December 2022	Update Rollup 1	KB5020318
SCX Agent	1.7.0-0	December 2022	Update Rollup 1	KB5020318

Table 2.1: Microsoft System Center Operations Manager update rollup table

The next table shows the hotfixes applicable for Operations Manager:

Role	Build Version	Release Date	Description	KB Article
All server components	10.22.10575.0	July 2023	Update Rollup 1 – GB Compliance	KB5029601

Table 2.2: Microsoft System Center Operations Manager hotfix table

Microsoft System Center Virtual Machine Manager

At the time of writing this book, the following latest versions are reported (see *Table 2.3*):

Role	Build Version	Release Date	Description	KB Article
All server components	10.22.1287.0	March 2022	Current Version	N/A
All server components	10.22.1508.0	November 2022	Update Rollup 1	KB5019272

Table 2.3: Microsoft System Center Virtual Machine Manager update rollup table

Microsoft System Center Orchestrator

At the time of writing this book, the following latest versions are reported (see *Table 2.4*):

Role	Build Version	Release Date	Description	KB Article
All server components	10.22.2.0	April 2022	Current Version	N/A
All server components	10.22.6.1	January 2023	Update Rollup 1	KB5021420

Table 2.4: Microsoft System Center Orchestrator update rollup table

The next table shows the hotfixes applicable for Orchestrator:

Role	Build Version	Release Date	Description	KB Article
All server components	10.22.8.9	July 2023	Hotfix	KB5029810

Table 2.5: Microsoft System Center Orchestrator update rollup table

Microsoft System Center Service Manager

At the time of writing this book, the following latest versions are reported (see *Table 2.6*):

Role	Build Version	Release date	Description	KB Article
All server components	10.22.1068.0	March 2022	Current Version	N/A
All server components	10.22.1219.0	June 2023	Hotfix	KB5021792

Table 2.6: Microsoft System Center Service Manager hotfix table

Microsoft System Center Data Protection Manager

At the time of writing this book, the following latest versions are reported (see *Table 2.7*):

Role	Build Version	Release Date	Description	KB Article
All server components	10.22.123.0	May 2022	Current Version	N/A
All server components	10.22.148.0	November 2022	Update Rollup 1	KB5019645

Table 2.7: Microsoft System Center Data Protection Manager update rollup table

Microsoft Configuration Manager

At the time of writing this book, the following latest versions are reported (see *Figure 2.8*):

Role	Build Version	Release Date	Description	KB Article
All server components	5.00.9106	April 2023	Build 2303	N/A

Table 2.8: Microsoft System Configuration Manager update table

Latest features for System Center

With the latest version of System Center comes a multitude of new features. In this topic we will show the latest features for each product which will go from the base version of the latest release and going through the latest updates and the features these bring.

> Note: A full list of the latest features can be found here: https://learn.microsoft.com/en-us/system-center/scom/whats-new-in-om?view=sc-om-2022

Microsoft System Center Operations Manager

A full list of the latest features can be found here *What's new in Operations Manager | Microsoft Learn-* **https://learn.microsoft.com/en-us/system-center/scom/whats-new-in-om?view=sc-om-2022**:

Following is the list of new updates that the Operations Manager brings. As the list of features can be extensive, we will include the more popular or highlighted features which will relate to the reader more:

- **Enhanced Role Based Access Control (RBAC):** RBAC is a multi-layered permission control specified by role names. For example, Administrator, power user, read-only, etc. This already exists within Operations Manager, but its latest feature is the addition of a read-only role as well as the ability to assign more granular permissions and delegated control, which refers to a similar Active Directory feature where you can delegate specific permissions to another user/group on a container level basis.
- **NTLM Features for Reporting Services:** This is an additional feature which allows you to add an **New Technology Lan Manager** (**NTLM**) to be configured during installation of the Reporting Services role to allow higher authentication.
- **Alert closure enrichments:** In previous versions closing an open alert whilst a managed object in Operations Manager was unhealthy was not possible. This has now been changed.
- **SHA2 certificate support:** This relates specifically to more Linux based agents which in previous versions encrypted to SHA1. The latest version now encrypts to SHA2.
- **Obtain alert data via REST API by group:** This might be a tad beyond scope as this feature relates to obtaining alert data from the Operations Manager in the

form of REST API, which is geared towards foreign integration or other Microsoft application integrations from using a `groupID` attribute.

- **Obtain FQDN source for alerts:** Here is a feature which allows the administrator to trace the source of an alert, **Fully Qualified Domain Name (FQDN)** in this case relates to the management pack it came from.
- **Sort option for overrides:** Overrides are changes which you can make to components within a management pack such as monitors, rules, and discoveries. More a GUI type of enhancement where if you set overrides for Operations Manager, you can view the list and sort them in columns.
- **Enhanced install experience:** Optimized experience for installs of Operations Manager if you have used custom methods or custom install paths for previous versions or current versions pre update rollup or hotfix.
- **Dependency of local system account removed:** The local system account normally used as a default for the default action account which is used to perform regular SCOM duties such as agent installs etc, this is no longer mandatory.
- **Change tracking enhancements:** Any changes made within SCOM are now kept within a folder to view them when needed.
- **Azure migrate integration:** This is an integration feature that allows you to migrate on-premise devices managed within your SCOM environment to Azure via the console.

With the release of UR1, here are the latest features which represent this:

- **Structured Query Language (SQL) 2022 server support**: This allows for SQL Server 2022 to be used for installing Operations Manager onto.
- **SCOM Managed instance integration support**: This allows for integration between SCOM and the SCOM MI (Managed Instance) to allow for the cloud version of Operations Manager.

Microsoft System Center Virtual Machine Manager

> Note: A full list of the latest features can be found here What's new in System Center Virtual Machine Manager | Microsoft Learn- https://learn.microsoft.com/en-us/system-center/vmm/whats-new-in-vmm?view=sc-vmm-2022

Following is a list of new updates which Virtual Machine Manager brings. As the list of features can be extensive, we will include the more popular or highlighted features which will relate to the reader more:

- **Windows Server 2022 host and guest support**: Windows Server 2022 is an officially supported OS for hypervisor hosts and virtual machines.

- **Windows 11 support**: Windows 11 is an officially supported OS for virtual machines.

With the release of UR1, here are the latest features which represent this:
- **VMware vSphere and ESXi support for 7.0 to 8.0**: Now supporting the management of VMware ESXi hosts and vSphere servers for version 7.0 and 8.0.
- **SQL Server 2022 support**: This allows for SQL Server 2022 to be used for installing Virtual Machine Manager onto.
- **Smart card sign-in support**: Support for signing into the SCVMM console with smart cards.
- **64 virtual networks support**: SCVMM can now support up to 64 virtual networks.

Microsoft System Center Orchestrator

> Note: A full list of the latest features can be found here What's new in System Center Orchestrator | Microsoft Learn- https://learn.microsoft.com/en-us/system-center/orchestrator/whats-new-in-orch?view=sc-orch-2022

Following is the list of new updates that Orchestrator brings. As the list of features can be extensive, we will include the more popular or highlighted features which will relate to the reader more:
- **System Center 2022 integration pack release:** With new releases of Orchestrator will come the latest version of the integration packs for each System Center product and core Microsoft technologies.
- **New web console and web API**: The web console is similar to the runbook designer application but in a web-based form. In previous releases the web console and API were using XML, this has now been changed over to using JSON to optimize the user experience of the web console.
- **Orchestrator now 64-bit**: Orchestrator is now recognized as a 64-bit application whereas previous versions have all been 32-bit based.

With the release of UR1, here are the latest features which represent this:
- **SQL Server 2022 support**: This allows for SQL Server 2022 to be used for installing Virtual Machine Manager onto.
- **.NET Core 6 support**: Orchestrator now has a dependency on .NET Core 6.

Microsoft System Center Service Manager

> Note: There are actually no new features Service Manager within the System Center 2022 suite. There is still a hotfix which fixes multiple bugs which can be found here Hotfix for System Center 2022 Service Manager - June 2023 (KB5021792) - Microsoft Support

Microsoft System Center Data Protection Manager

> Note: To see a full list of the latest features for Data Protection Manager this can be found here: What's new in System Center DPM | Microsoft Learn.

Following is the list of new updates which Data Protection Manager brings. As the list of features can be extensive, we will include the more popular or highlighted features which will relate to the reader more:

- **Windows Server 2022 support:** You can now install SCDPM on Windows Server 2022 as well as the backup of Windows Server 2022 workloads
- **VMware vSphere 7.0 support**: Support for backing up virtual machines on VMware vSphere 7.0 servers

With the release of UR1, here are the latest features which represent this:

- **SQL Server 2022 support**: This allows for SQL Server 2022 to be used for installing Virtual Machine Manager onto.
- **End of support for vSphere 6.0**: Backing up any virtual machines based on a vSphere 6.0 server is no longer supported going forward.

Microsoft Configuration Manager

> Note: A full list of the latest features can be found here: What's new in version 2303 - Configuration Manager | Microsoft Learn.

Following is the list of new updates that Configuration Manager brings. As the list of features can be extensive, we will include the more popular or highlighted features which will relate to the reader more:

- **Cloud attached new features**: Cloud attach is an integration between Configuration Manager and Endpoint Manager to sync devices into the Endpoint Manager portal. More features have been added here such as opting for endpoint security reports and more advancements to syncing devices using cloud attach.
- **Authorization failure audit messages**: It is now possible to see audit logs of authorization failure issues.

- **SQL Server 2022 support**: You can now install Microsoft Configuration Manager on SQL Server 2022 for all different site server levels.
- **Maintenance window schedules offset**: It is now possible to create schedules for maintenance windows where you can begin schedules with an offset of days.
- **Deprecated features**: Features no longer supported evolve around Microsoft Store for business as this has been retired.

Best practice for upgrading System Center

The idea of this topic is to really cover the real-world scenarios and best practices approach across various areas when it comes to the upgrading of System Center in general.

Upgrade order

Rather than go through each product, there is an overall way of approaching the upgrade paths for the whole suite. The first part of this is around the actual order of the products. Please see the following list, which illustrates the order in which they should be upgraded in:

- Microsoft System Center Orchestrator
- Microsoft System Center Service Manager
- Microsoft System Center Data Protection Manager
- Microsoft System Center Operations Manager
- Microsoft Configuration Manager
- Microsoft System Center Virtual Machine Manager

Now, the preceding order is more fitting for environments who are either using every single product or at least where products are integrated together where an upgrade can cause considerable impact.

Taking the Orchestrator for example, this contains an integration pack for every product in the list underneath itself, and where multiple runbooks are using activities which relate to each product by its management pack. If you were to upgrade a product underneath you could potentially break the workflow if Orchestrator cannot to talk to the technology. Which is why it goes first on the list.

Service Manager now connects to Orchestrator as a connector to get the runbooks into the fold, as well as its connectors to other products which can have a dependency on which version is running where, hoping all of them are on the same version.

From Data Protection Manager all the way through to Virtual Machine Manager, whilst they can be integrated with each other they do not hold any top-level bearing where upgrading one of them can potentially stop **Business As Usual** (**BAU**) service from continuing.

Pre-production environmental testing

A sandpit is extremely handy in these cases, where you do not have to touch a production environment and then you are planning and testing can be performed in an environment which is not related to the production environment, thus maintaining BAU and having a recognized process behind you. This is handy for when you were to go into change management to raise a change to perform the upgrade of any product within System Center.

In most cases, environments have three sectors for this, which are:

- Development
- Pre-production
- Production

Some can get the terms of development and pre-production environments mixed up but there is a fundamental difference within them and its normally in the titles that they hold.

Both environments are defined as testing platforms, but the fundamental difference is that development environments are more for experimental use, where higher resistance of stress testing can be tolerated without affecting production environments.

Pre-production, on the other hand, is an environment that is ideally an exact replica of production. Hence, if you were to carry out big changes then testing this out in an environment which is a close replica of production will give the user a much clearer idea of what would happen when testing is successful, but also give an even clearer picture if things were to go horribly wrong. This is where you would rather perform upgrade tasks or any tasks that can cause considerable changes to the environment.

Disaster recovery

Though we have a product such as Data Protection Manager, we would still need to account for disaster recovery for the same product as well, so a backup solution for a so to speak.

However, you will most certainly need to ensure that you have sufficient backups of your environment, testing as mentioned previously as well as a detailed backout plan which will allow you to revert to its original state to carry out BAU work.

There are many ways in which disaster recovery is introduced such as:

- **Environmental level**: This can involve backups of the server estate. If this is a virtual environment, then virtual machine backups and snapshots play a big role where it can be recovered to its last known state.
- **SQL server level**: System Center products all use a SQL Server database. Therefore, backing up of the databases is crucial if wanting to reinstall the product back and have it returned to its last known working configuration state.

- **Real world scenario:** Environmental level backups are a good way of having backups. However, most System Center products have multiple server roles, and if you want to have a full restoration then recovering multiple servers can become troublesome. This is of course dependent on the product you are applying this to.

Supported requirements level

Another area to take into serious consideration is the current hardware and software requirements that are applicable to System Center 2022.

If you are using System Center 2019 or levels below, then your highest level of OS could most likely be Windows Server 2019. Taking this into account you will also have to think about your SQL requirements which may run up to SQL Server 2016.

Before going ahead with any upgrade, you need to ensure that your environment meets the recommended requirements before proceeding. Depending on the practices of your environment, you maybe in a good position to upgrade. However, if you follow practices in which regular updating may not be possible, then you may have a situation where these prerequisites can become a huge administrative effort, and these would need to be addressed before you can proceed with the upgrade of any product.

Real world scenario: For in-place upgrades, there can be a lot of additional updates on the Operating System level which can make the process of doing an in-place upgrade much more difficult depending on how far apart the requirements are from the minimum and recommended levels, which is where a side-by-side migrate can mitigate a lot of issues and can be the more popular choice.

The next section relates to this as well.

In-place versus side by side

In relation to the previous area, which was detailed, if you did happen to have an environment that is not running on specifications to support an upgrade, then another option is the consideration of performing a side-by-side upgrade.

A side-by-side upgrade essentially means that you would perform a clean installation of a product with a view of replicating the previous environment configuration, whether that be on the same version or lower. Once this has been satisfied then you would then have the ability to then retire the previous environment after a successful build has been carried out.

When discussing the recommended requirement levels, it may perhaps be assumed that it is primarily referring to an in-place upgrade. Whilst there can be more bearing around that scenario, a side-by-side upgrade also has the same requirement and though it may keep BAU intact there is still a lot of planning and analysis which would need to be carried out.

Benefits of a side-by-side migration may mean nothing is affected on the BAU side, but on the other hand if you investigate the security structure of your environment there could be some permissions, policies or other forms of hardening which could be very specific to the servers which are running the System Center products. If this cannot be replicated within the new environment then there could be a much bigger issue. This is one scenario of many, but no task of this magnitude should be performed without very careful testing.

Conclusion

To summarise this chapter, this will be looked at as a pivotal referencing point for understanding the latest versions and updates of System Center.

At the time of writing this chapter these would be the latest avaialble. However, you must also remain up to date with the latest releases that will go beyond this book by accessing the links which are related to each of the sections detailing the latest features as well to ensure that you remain fully updated as well as fully supported.

You will also have noticed that a lot of the latest features which come from each product may bear some similarities, which is primarily due to the recommended specifications sharing the same prerequisites, especially when it comes to operating system and SQL server levels.

These are something which you must bear in mind as when you do approach the decision of when and where to upgrade you will need to consider a multitude of scenarios which will impact your environment.

Beforehand, it is great if you maintain your documentation for your environment, and even better if you have diagrams which display a high level as well as a low-level design which will help guide you to the correct decision.

This chapter will work in conjunction very well with your existing documentation to understand how to proceed with any present and future upgrades.

In the next chapter, we will look at Microsoft Configuration Manager and the role it plays within a datacentre environment. We will be looking at how we can design Configuration Manager to help centralize an environment.

Points to remember

- Updates can come in form of update rollups and hotfixes.
- Configuration Manager differs from regular update rollups and hotfixes by synchronization of the latest updates via its console.
- Update rollups and hotfixes use a `.msp` file extension.
- Configuration Manager updates come through on a quarterly basis.

- Products such as Service Manager do not have any updates to the latest version being 2022.
- Most products can share the same new features due to the evolution of the operating system releases; update rollups can introduce the support for new versions or the product can have this natively.
- Upgrade order should be followed if you are utilizing all System Center products or if any of the products are integrated with each other.
- Understand the importance of disaster recovery for when planning to perform any upgrades.
- Know the differences between an in-place upgrade and side-by-side upgrade and balance out whether your environment meets the requirement for either one, but also analyze which is the most appropriate one.

Multiple choice questions

1. What is the name of the update which is used to upgrade the current version of a System Center product?
    a. Update hotfix
    b. Hotfix
    c. Update Rollup
    d. Patch

2. Which System Center product has no new features in its latest release?
    a. Service Manager
    b. Orchestratror
    c. Configuration Manager
    d. Data Protection Manager

3. Name the most common feature within new versions of System Center products (choose all that apply).
    a. VMware ESXi support
    b. Windows Server 2022 support
    c. SQL Server 2022 support
    d. All of the above

4. Which product is recommended as the first System Center technology to upgrade first?

   a. Operations Manager

   b. Virtual Machine Manager

   c. Data Protection Manager

   d. Orchestrator

5. What are the core areas to take into consideration when understanding best practices for a System Center upgrade?

   a. Disaster Recovery

   b. In Place Upgrade or Side by Side Upgrade

   c. Pre production testing

   d. All the above

6. How does Configuration Manager obtain its updates?

   a. Synchronization through the console

   b. Windows Updates

   c. Microsoft Update Catalog

   d. All the above

Answers

1. c
2. a
3. b, c
4. d
5. d
6. a

Key terms

- **BAU**: Business as usual which refers to the general working day in which normal activities which happen in order to maintain current service.

- **Update rollup**: An update which upgrades the selected product or technology in order to add new features and fix bugs detected.

- **Hotfix**: An update similar to an update rollup but normally doesn't have the control to perform a major upgrade within the build version of the targeted technology.

- **Disaster recovery**: A strategy which looks over the maintenance of any issues which may arise that might cause the environment to experience downtime which can potentially interrupt BAU.

- **In-place upgrade**: An upgrade path which a product is upgraded to the latest version on its original servers and structure which has the older version of a technology still installed.

- **Side-by-side upgrade**: An upgrade path which another environment is stood up to take the place of the current environment with a view to migrate to the newer environment.

Join our book's Discord space

Join the book's Discord Workspace for Latest updates, Offers, Tech happenings around the world, New Release and Sessions with the Authors:

https://discord.bpbonline.com

CHAPTER 3
OS and Application Deployment Optimization of Configuration Manager

Introduction

In this chapter, we will investigate the planning and design for Microsoft Configuration Manager. This area will be applicable for most versions of this technology as the same key areas have to be taken in consideration especially when looking into how the solution will be used. Scalability is also a key area in which we will want to analyse when planning a new design, however we will also discover the upgrade paths which would need to be taken in order to be applicable. In Microsoft Configuration Managers case, it will be the **Current Branch** (**CB**) versions and its prerequisites we would need to consider which we will dive into.

Moreover, included will be a minimum and recommended requirement level to where the reader can develop a lab environment which they can use to follow through with the next chapter so you can gauge a practical as well as a theoretical understanding.

Structure

This chapter will cover the following topics:
- Configuration Manger topology structure
- Recommended requirements for scalability
- Future planning for modern management

- What role will the Configuration Manager play
- Configuration Manager lab requirements

Objectives

This chapter aims to make the reader understand all the different topologies that Configuration Manager has, and due to the complexity of this product, there are very vast options each comes with its pros and cons depending on the solution that the reader is trying to achieve.

Another objective is for the reader to understand the future of the solution using this product from considering the overall scalability of the structure they choose to implement, and to outline its best practices. There will also be comprehensive preparation for the specifications of lab requirements which will help the reader on a practical basis on how to build Configuration Manager using the information learned within this chapter.

Configuration Manager topology structure

Microsoft Configuration Manager has multiple topologies to take into consideration, and out of all of the products to speak about in this book this has the largest number of roles, which also makes the amount of topologies to consider much more complicated.

Here we will cover each type of topology, first going by the higher level which evolves around the number of servers which would be used.

Configuration Manager Server roles

Before we start exploring all the different topologies, it is important that you understand every single individual role which can be configured in Configuration Manager. This way when you progress deeper into the chapter you will understand the importance where some roles are mandatory or optional within the preset configurations provided to you.

It is all important to know that any server which holds a role in Configuration Manager is then considered a **site system server**.

> Note: There are a couple of roles that may still exist in Configuration Manager depending on the version you have which are now deprecated which would be the Asset Intelligence Role and Application Catalog roles.
>
> Here are all of the Configuration Manager server roles listed below with a breakdown of what each role does.

Management point

A management point server represents a central point in which all agent managed devices report into. Information reported to the management point can consist of both hardware and software inventory, overall health status, and a key role for downloading and reading the latest policies.

By default, its communication works in a one-way pull connection, where agents contact the management point at regular intervals to obtain the latest information and report to it. Let us now look at the following:

- **Distribution point:** The distribution point is responsible for the content stored within Configuration Manager, which can be downloaded by an agent depending on the deployments which have been allocated to either the object or the object-based collection.
- **site database server:** This role represents the server that holds the **Structured Query Language (SQL)** database for the Configuration Manager server.
- **SMS provider:** This role traditionally is on the first Configuration Manager server you install which holds the link between the server and the ConfigMgr database, WMI classes and data configuration.
- **Software update point:** Normally shortened as the SUP role, this is responsible for the windows update patching feature within Configuration Manager.
- **Service connection point:** This role is responsible for going out to the internet and pulling down the latest updates and hotfixes available for Configuration Manager. Moreover, it is responsible for the downloading and installing of the updates.
- **Data warehouse point:** A role which had been newly introduced into Configuration Manager from when rebranded as CB. This role handles a data warehouse functionality where it can extend the data retention period for various tables and views within the Configuration Manager database, which in turn allows the administrator to keep historical data for further auditing review purposes.
- **Reporting services point:** This role has a dependency on an existing SQL **Server Reporting Service point (SSRS)** to configure this correctly and is used to be able to run native Configuration Manager reports as well as providing an option to create custom reports for Power BI.

> **Note:** In order to create custom reports for Configuration Manager whether normal SSRS reports or Power BI, these will require additional programs such as Microsoft SQL Report Builder. Or for Power BI you can use Power BI Desktop or the Power BI report builder report.

Cloud Management Gateway Connection Point

This role is required when you are planning to utilize the **Cloud Management Gateway (CMG),** which is for internet-based device management. The connection point is responsible for reporting and connecting to the CMG. Let us now look at the following roles:

- **Endpoint protection point**: This role is used for managing your device's windows defender agent which will enable you to create antivirus and malware policies, while allowing you to deploy the latest signatures and updates to the defender agents.
- **Enrollment proxy point**: This role allows the Configuration Manager point to be able to enroll Mac and mobile devices. This is due to be deprecated soon due to Endpoint Manager being able to do this.
- **Fallback status point**: This role is used when agent push installations fail, and the failure messages can be reported back to the fallback status point.
- **State migration point:** When a new device is going through a Task Sequence process involving a new operating system in which user state data is to be migrated from an old device to a new device.

Consolidated topology

A consolidated setup in Microsoft Configuration Manager is perhaps the simplest and easiest topology to have. This scenario means that all roles are held just on one server. A typical consolidated setup by default normally would typically include the following roles:

- Management point server
- Distribution point server
- site database server
- SMS provider

There is an option which you can perform within the setup itself called the express install. It will provide you with a pre-configured setup which will speed up the overall process, which we will cover in the next chapter.

The particular high-level topology described is based on a scenario of a quick setup for a Microsoft Configuration Manager environment which may not be utilized as proof of concept, lab environment setup or even a solution which may not prove to be business critical.

The scenarios outlined focus on this type of high-level topology quite well. There is nothing stopping this type of configuration to still have a business-critical service, however there can be several drawbacks to this type of scenario if Microsoft Configuration Manager is intended to be a business critical service.

Take, for example, the fact that it is a consolidated setup, which then creates a single point of failure. Whereas if this server goes down, then Microsoft Configuration Manager would simply collapse. Having said this, from a disaster recovery perspective, it could nullify the scenario as recovering one server that has all the roles could help bring it to a last known state much quicker than a multi-role scenario, which we will talk about later.

Another drawback is then the resource strain. The SQL Server and databases all being on the same server can cause performance issues if you do not have the correct or sufficient specifications to be able to accommodate this setup.

Multi-server role topology

A multi-server role topology is where you will have more than one windows server (or some cases client OS device) to hold different Configuration Manager roles.

This topology is normally the preferred method due to the avoidance of a single point of failure. To paint out the scenario even further, the consolidated setup would contain the following roles all on one server:

- Management point server
- Distribution point server
- site database server
- SMS provider

In this case, though the first Configuration Manager server would still hold the management point and distribution point role. These roles can then be installed on different individual windows servers where they can be the primary management point or distribution point for the assigned sites.

In theory both high level topologies are the same as nothing would stop an administrator from wanting to scale a consolidated setup to a multi-server role topology as the process is really based on adding additional site system servers to have server roles on them.

However, one of the more convenient features in this topology is that you would have a separate server which would hold the site database server which also allows for further mitigation from the single point of failure.

Site servers topology

The lower level of the topologies is then the actual site servers, which is where the managed devices are assigned to site servers are identified by three attributes, the **Fully Qualified Domain Name (FQDN)**, the site server description and as well as its site code.

A site code is a three-character ID that identifies the site in which a managed device is assigned to.

Central administration sites

The **Central Administration Site (CAS)** is the parent site which would hold the information of all the child sites from underneath its hierarchy.

> Note: Though a central administration site still can be used within Configuration Manager, it is considered a deprecated server role with the main site server recommended to be a primary site is encouraged to move away from this setup as soon as possible to adopt a primary site topology.

From a CAS site, you can then have child sites such as:
- Primary site
- Secondary site

We will cover the sites mentioned previously in much more detail in the next sections.

The topology of a CAS works very similar to how an Active Directory parent domain works, where the parent or also called the **root** is used for a logical parent container to house the rest of the child domains, or in Configuration Managers case the child sites.

During the later times of Configuration Manager and through its rebranding, the CAS site has been deprecated with the best practice and recommended approach is to start with a primary standalone site. You will still be able to have child sites underneath the primary site which are referred to as secondary site servers.

With the child sites, each site will then have a database and file replication schedule which works to keep all the site fully updated and asynchronous.

In addition, the following roles are applicable to be installed on the CAS server:
- Data warehouse service point
- Reporting services point
- Service connection point
- Software update point
- Endpoint protection point
- Asset intelligence point

Primary site

The primary site is the new standard for first time installation of Configuration Manager. From the installation of the site, you will get the following site system roles by default:
- Management point server
- Distribution point server
- SMS provider

There is also an optimized option which the user can select which will pre-select most of the configuration which will skip several windows around the configuration of the communication protocol for the roles mentioned which can either be HTTP or HTTPS.

> **Note:** HTTP protocol is a deprecated option in Configuration Manager. However, you do have the option to use Enhanced HTTP which does use a form of self-signing certificates which is the next best option other than going to full HTTPS.

A primary site has Secondary sites which can be assigned as child sites. They would then report to the primary site as its parent and participate in regular database and file replications between the sites to ensure they are fully update through the asynchronous connection they share.

Secondary site

A secondary site is a small logical site which is looked at as an extension to the primary site. The database is normally embedded within the primary site database, as well as the connection to site via the Configuration Manager is not applicable.

By default, agents that are assigned to the secondary site may use the server roles which are appointed to this site, but they will still show the site code identifier as the primary site.

Recommended requirements for scalability

Now that we have established the understanding of all of the different roles which Configuration Manager has and all of the high level and low-level topologies, the next area to take into consideration are the recommended requirements. This is to explore the various limitations we have in these areas.

This will help understand not only our current position, but to also see a future picture of how the overall Configuration Manager solution will look when considering how scalable our environment is.

> **Note:** To see the most updated requirement information for Microsoft Configuration Manager this can be seen here. https://learn.microsoft.com/en-us/mem/configmgr/core/

Hardware requirements

The first level of requirements we will need to firstly, look into the hardware requirements, which will cover all of the resource specifications we would require. This will also help plan our scalability.

Here, we will outline the official Microsoft hardware requirements and provide additional information and perspective on the scalability.

Site systems

In *Table 3.1*, we outline the hardware requirements specific to each site type:

Site type	High level topology	CPU (Cores)	Memory	Memory allocation for SQL (%)
Primary	Consolidated	16	96	80
Primary	Multi-server role	16	72	90
Primary	Remote SQL	8	16	N/A
CAS	Consolidated	20	128	80
CAS	Multi-server role	16	96	90
CAS	Remote SQL	8	16	90
Secondary site	N/A	8	16	N/A

Table 3.1: Site systems requirements table

To provide a more summarized context for the high-level topology column please refer to the following definitions for a recap:

- **Consolidated**: All server roles installed on a single Windows Server
- **Multi-server role**: ConfigMgr roles are split across several Windows Servers
- **Remote SQL**: The SQL Server and database is held on a separate Windows Server

The requirements outlined previously represent the recommended levels of which your hardware would need to be at to be able to run Configuration Manager at a sufficient level. It must also be considered, whether you are using physical servers or a virtual server environment.

The primary site server specifications outlined in the preceding table also is applicable to a scenario in which the primary site is a child of the CAS site.

Core Configuration Manager roles

The following table represents the recommended specifications of individual roles which you can install, these are reflective of the same roles mentioned earlier in this chapter:

Role	CPU (Cores)	Memory	Disk Space (GB)
Management Point	4	8	50GB
Distribution Point	2	8	OS Default

Role	CPU (Cores)	Memory	Disk Space (GB)
Software Update	8	16	OS Default
*All other site system roles	4	8	50

Table 3.2: Core Configuration Manager roles table

This table is mainly fitting for the multi-server role topology where you would have a separate Windows Server for each role. You may also choose to have more than one role on a Windows Server in a multi-server role topology as well.

In cases like these, to achieve the best scalability you could use the higher recommended specification between the roles to select.

Disk space

The following table outlines the disk space required from minimum levels and detailing the scalability on the number of clients you are planning to manage with Configuration Manager:

Usage	Minimum Space	25,000 Clients	50,000 Clients	100,000 Clients	150,000 Clients	700,000 Clients (CAS Setup)
Configuration Manager Usage	25GB	50GB	100GB	200GB	300GB	200GB
Site Database	75GB for every 25,000 clients	75GB	150GB	300GB	500GB	2TB
Site Database Logs	25GB for every 25,000 clients	25GB	50GB	100GB	150GB	100GB
TempDB Logs	As needed	As needed	As needed	As needed	As needed	As needed

Table 3.3: Disk space hardware requirement table

The table details outline the disk requirement scale plans to show how much you would need to increase the minimum space requirements, depending on the number of clients you will be managing within Configuration Manager. Setting up a CAS is also used to vastly increase the number of clients you can manage if you are a very large organization.

Clients

The clients have quite a vast requirement breakdown, this section will cover mainly what the managed device hardware specification will need to be so that they are managed at optimum level (refer to the following table):

Resource	Minimum level
Processor	Default OS Requirement
Memory	Default OS Requirement
Disk Space	500mb

Table 3.4: Clients hardware requirement table

Generally, the default OS specifications will be enough to run the actual Configuration Manager client. Where the disk space is concerned, this is at the minimal level. Its recommended level here would be 5GB which is to account for the client cache that each agent has. The client cache reserves a default portion of the hard disk space at 10%, which is where the 500mb minimum requirement comes into play.

Structured Query Language Server requirements

Following is a table that outlines the supported versions of SQL Server that can be used to host Microsoft Configuration Manager:

SQL version	SQL Cumulative Update (Minimum)	Configuration Manager Version (Minimum)	CAS	Primary site	Secondary site
SQL Server 2022 – Standard/Enterprise		2303	Yes	Yes	Yes
SQL Server 2019 – Standard/Enterprise	CU5		Yes	Yes	Yes
SQL Server 2017 – Standard/Enterprise	CU2		Yes	Yes	Yes
SQL Server 2016 – Standard/Enterprise	Recommended maximum CU Level		Yes	Yes	Yes
SQL Server 2014 – Standard/Enterprise	Recommended maximum CU Level		Yes	Yes	Yes

SQL version	SQL Cumulative Update (Minimum)	Configuration Manager Version (Minimum)	CAS	Primary site	Secondary site
SQL Server 2012 – Standard/Enterprise	Recommended maximum CU Level		Yes	Yes	Yes
SQL Server 2017 Express	CU2		No	No	Yes
SQL Server 2016 Express	Recommended maximum CU Level		No	No	Yes
SQL Server 2014 Express	Recommended maximum CU Level		No	No	Yes
SQL Server 2012 Express	Recommended maximum CU Level		No	No	Yes

Table 3.5: SQL Server requirements table

It is recommended to use the latest SQL Server version if you are running the latest version of Configuration Manager.

Operating System requirements

Here are the tables which outline the **Operating System (OS)** requirements. The tables will go into detail which are the supported levels in terms of servers holding site system server roles, as well as devices which will contain the Configuration Manager agent.

Supported OS versions for servers

The following table details the OS versions supported for the Configuration Manager site system roles focusing specifically on Windows Server OSs:

Operating System	Configuration Manager Version (Minimum)	All Server Role Support
Windows Server 2022	2107	Yes
Windows Server 2019		Yes
Windows Server 2016		Yes
Windows Server 2012 R2		Yes
*Windows Server 2012 (x64)		Yes

Table 3.6: Site system OS requirements table

Supported OS versions for clients

The following table shows the supported OS versions for devices which are managed by Configuration Manager via an installed agent:

Operating System	Configuration Manager Version (Minimum)
Windows Server 2022	
Windows Server 2019	
Windows Server 2016	
Windows Server 2012 R2	
*Windows Server 2012 (x64)	
Windows 11	2107
Windows 10 (20H2 Minimum)	

Table 3.7: Client-managed OS requirements table

Note: Windows Server 2012 is supported but is at the lowest of the table and should have view to upgrade ASAP. This applies to only the x64 architecture version only. The 32-bit (x86) architecture version of Windows Server 2012 is not supported.

Windows 10 Support

There are various versions of Windows 10 build versions which may be available within your environment. By bare minimum your Windows 10 devices should be at least at the level of 20H2 to be fully supported (refer to the following table):

Operating System	Configuration Manager Version (Minimum)
22H2	2207
21H2	2111
LTSC 2021	2111
21H1	2111
20H2	2111

Table 3.8: Windows 10 Support table

Windows 11 Support

Currently, all build versions of Windows 11 are supported, though best practice would recommend that you try to maintain your Windows 11 devices at the most updated levels (refer to the following table):

Operating System	Configuration Manager Version (Minimum)
22H2	2207
21H2	2111

Table 3.9: Windows 11 Support table

Role limitations

Another critical area for consideration when it comes to the overall future scalability of Microsoft Configuration Manager, is to consider all the limitations which you may potentially run into, depending on the design that you choose.

The following outline these limitations, which will help to guide the scalability:

- **Central administration site:** Here are the maximum limitations for the Central administration site:
    - A maximum of 25 primary sites can be added to a central administration site
    - A maximum of 700,000 clients can be added to a central administration site
    - A maximum of 25,000 clients on the MacOS operating system can be added to a central administration site
    - A maximum of 100,000 mobile devices can be added to a central administration site
    - A maximum total 825,000 clients can be added to a central administration site
- **Primary site:** Here are the maximum limitations for the primary site server:
    - A maximum of 25 child secondary sites can be added to a primary site
    - A maximum of 13 management points can be added to a primary site
    - A maximum of 250 distribution points can be added to a primary site
    - A maximum total 825,000 clients can be added to a primary site
- **Secondary site:** Here are the maximum limitations for the secondary site server:
    - A single management point is the maximum for the secondary site
    - A maximum of 15,000 windows clients can be added to a secondary site
    - A maximum of 250 distribution points scan be added to a secondary site
- **Management point:** Here are the maximum limits of connections which a management point can handle:
    - A maximum of 25,000 client connections can be supported by a management point

- o A maximum of 1,000 mobile connections can be supported by a management point
- o A maximum of 10,000 MacOS client connections can be supported by a management point
- **Distribution point:** Here are the maximum limits of connections which a distribution point can handle:
  - o A distribution point can communicate with a single management point
  - o A maximum of 15,000 windows client connections can be supported by a distribution point
  - o A maximum of 250 distribution points can be assigned to a single site
- **Fallback status point:** Here are the maximum limits of connections which a fallback status point can handle:
  - o A maximum of 100,000 client connections can be supported by a fallback status point
- **Software update point:** Here are the maximum limits of connections which a software update point can handle:
  - o A maximum of 25,000 client connections can be supported by a software update point on a consolidated setup.
  - o A maximum of 150,000 client connections can be supported by a software update point on a multi-server role setup.

Future planning for modern management

With the future of Microsoft Configuration Manager, the push for modern management is now becoming more crucial for the transition of introducing cloud management for our endpoint devices.

With the introduction of endpoint manager which can evolve around both technologies being Microsoft Configuration Manager and Intune, there are again many scenarios to consider when planning for this potential move.

In this topic we will touch on the role in which Intune plays and layout all the areas to take into consideration when looking into the future planning of modern management.

Modern management using Intune

Microsoft Intune is the endpoint manager portal which exists within Azure and is used to the endpoint management solution which is responsible for the overall modern management solution. Its capabilities are similar to Configuration Manager but more optimized for cloud purposes.

In Configuration Manager, devices are managed from using an installed agent, in Intune devices are enrolled using the **Mobile Device Management (MDM)** policy, which can be achieved through various ways such as:

- Windows Autopilot
- Group Policy
- Co-management via Configuration Manager
- Manual enrollment through Company Portal

Due to various constraints and prerequisites for environments to reach the readiness required to use Intune, there have been various methods of being able to move to Intune to ease the transition, with one of those being an integration method called Co-Management.

> **Note: Devices require sufficient licensing before they can enroll to Intune and accept the conditions of the Intune MDM policy. To see more in regard to the license requirements please refer to here https://learn.microsoft.com/en-us/mem/intune/fundamentals/licenses .**

Co-management

Co-management is a solution which involves an integration between both Microsoft Configuration Manager and Intune, which formally creates the Microsoft Endpoint Manager solution

The benefit of this solution is a checkpoint to be able to assess an organizations readiness for transitioning Soley into Intune, by being able to maintain the use of Configuration Manager as well.

With this solution comes Co-management Workload affinity which controls the certain roles which Configuration Manager would be responsible for, and for what Intune would be responsible for. There is also an option in which you can pilot a certain workload feature where Intune does not have to look after the workload for every device, but for certain segregated devices which we will cover later in this chapter.

The affinity option also applies to co-management in general, where you can choose to select all your devices managed in Configuration Manager to be enrolled into co-management, of course it will only select the applicable devices that are eligible to have co-management.

Following workloads which can be co-managed between both Configuration Manager and Intune:

- **Compliance policies**: Compliance workloads are a set of rules which define whether a device meets the criteria to have access to resources on the network.
- **Device configuration:** The device configuration workload works as a group configuration for both the **endpoint protection** and **resource access policies** workloads. Adjusting this affinity will apply to both.

- **Endpoint protection:** This workload controls where the endpoint protection/Windows Defender policies will come from. If selecting Intune, then you will retrieve the policies from both Configuration Manager and Intune.
- **Resource access policies:** These policies are around the method of resource access which can be applicable for Wi-Fi, VPN, e-mail and certificate based access.
- **Client apps:** This can be a very important workload, as this controls where you will receive your application and package distribution from. If you decide to select Configuration Manager, then you will ONLY get applications from Configuration Manager. If you choose Intune, then you will be able to receive application distributions from both Configuration Manager and Intune.
- **Office click-to-run apps:** This workload controls where the Office 365 applications will be deployed from.
- **Windows update policies:** This workload controls where the windows update policies will come from whether it be Configuration Manager via its **Automatic Deployment Rules** (**ADRs**) or the Intune windows update rings.

Co-management also contains other features such as Cloud attach, which allows you to upload all the Configuration Manager device records into Intune, where they will be listed as ConfigMgr devices. When any of the devices uploaded here become "co-managed", you will see the "Managed By" column change.

Hybrid Entra ID in co-management

Hybrid Entra ID is when a device is registered to the Entra ID and is joined to the on-premises Active Directory.

If wanting to perform a co-management scenario with Configuration Manager and Intune, devices are required to have a Hybrid Entra ID record registered first before the co-management enablement can take place on the managed device.

This topic is a very interesting one alongside co-management, due to the various moving parts in the infrastructure when it comes to having a hybrid environment. Though it will allow an organization to be eased into Modern Management via a hybrid environment, the architecture can get quite complicated and involve a lot of dependencies to support it and can get even more complicated when introducing Windows Autopilot into the mix to extend the hybrid environment.

Prerequisites for co-management that already have a dependency on a Hybrid Entra ID environment are as follows:
- **Entra ID Connect**: Entra ID Connect is a tool which is used to perform the synchronization of AD objects from your on-premises domain to the Entra ID domain
- **Intune MDM policy configuration**: The MDM policy contains the policy in which devices integrate with to agree to be managed by the Intune portal. There is of

course a license requirement before devices can use Intune to enroll to. The policy can be defined by a scope of selected users via a group, or all users can be given the permission to enroll devices to Intune.

- **Entra ID device setting configuration:** This is a setting which is found within your Entra ID which allows the administrator to configure the settings of which users are allowed to join their devices to Entra ID. This can be defined by a scope of selected users via a group, or all users can be given the permission to join devices to the Entra ID domain.
- **Configuration manager co-management policy configuration**

From Microsoft Configuration Manager to Intune

When doing the real planning for the migration of Configuration Manager to Intune, whether that be straight from Configuration Manager to Intune or with co-management in place, there are several areas to consider and plan for when it comes to the future preparation of migrating to the cloud.

Operating System device management prerequisites

The first which is perhaps the biggest stumbling block for a lot of organizations is the operating system requirement for windows devices.

There are a few things in which you need to know regarding which devices are eligible to be fully supported when it comes to Intune management:

- Home editions are not supported
- Windows 10 1909 minimum gets the best out of intune

When you look at a lot of environments, in a real-world case scenario there can be the potential of legacy devices which may range from Windows 10 devices below 1909 and even lower. This can be the prompt for a lot of organizations to go to co-management first, to be able to support that estate until its feasible to move across.

> Note: The recommended level being 1909, mainly because Windows Autopilot if wanting to use the pre-provisioning mode (legacy name known as White Glove) you would need 1909 as a minimum to be able to perform this. Though 1909 is out of support it is a level which should be seen as a minimum standard with the recommended standard being Windows 10 22H2 or supported bare minimum of 20H2.

Application migration

Another area is the application estate which you have in your Configuration Manager estate. These would need to be moved over to your Intune tenancy to be able to continue the same level of support provided within Configuration Manager.

Types of applications that can be created within Intune are:
- **Line of Business (LOB) application**: This means any application which uses an `.msi` format.
- **Win32 application**: This is the equivalent to creating an application in Configuration Manager where utilizing detection methods, requirements, and installation commands.

> Note: Win32 applications are looked at as the best way to go due to issues of blending both LOB and Win32 applications together when using Windows Autopilot.

Windows update process migration

Moving further into the future planning of the transition into modern management is the windows update process. Configuration Manager uses the software update point roles and the **Automatic Deployment Rules (ADR)**, in Intune this process is looked after using profiles called update rings.

Update rings work very similar to ADR rules, and they have the following update rings available:
- Feature update rings
- Device driver rings
- Quality update rings

A new feature is also available within Intune which is known as Autopatch, which is an automated process that will configure all of the devices to be able to obtain the latest updates automatically for the following products:
- Windows OS
- Microsoft 365 applications
- Microsoft Edge
- Microsoft Teams

> Note: Windows Autopatch also contains its own license requirements. To know more about the Autopatch license requirements please refer to here https://learn.microsoft.com/en-us/windows/deployment/windows-autopatch/prepare/windows-autopatch-prerequisites

For future planning, the administrator would need to look through the current processes defined within Configuration Manager and then assess how they will be able to duplicate the same vulnerability patching workflow defined in Configuration Manager to Intune

Windows Autopilot

Windows Autopilot is a workflow which enables a device to be built, but also to be automatically onboarded into your Intune tenancy. This is achieved from using an autopilot profile which is assigned to a device in Intune by using either its Intune record, or the device can be imported manually into Intune within the autopilot portal.

Devices can be imported manually by a `.csv` file which is generated from using an installed PowerShell module, or an autopilot profile can be assigned to devices within Intune where you have an option to convert all assigned devices to autopilot devices which saves the time of importing devices manually.

> Note: To see more into the process of how to generate a .csv file to import devices to Intune please refer to here https://learn.microsoft.com/en-us/autopilot/add-devices

Autopilot is very similar to how Configuration Manager would use a task sequence, but in this particular case, autopilot does not reinstall an operating system a push an operating system to the device but rather registers the device to your Intune tenancy so that once the operating system is installed or setup from a **Out of Box Experience (OOBE)** state, the device is then recognized as having an autopilot profile assigned in which the end user or administrator is prompted to enter the credentials for their device to be onboarded.

Here, you would configure the areas that a user would typically see within the OOBE estate, such as region, keyboard configuration, whether the primary user account would be a normal user or have administrative rights on the machine, where you can define the name of the device. Here, you can use variables to preconfigure the name i.e. you could have something like "**Windows-%Serial%**" which would in turn create a device name like Windows-12345.

There are two methods of autopilot which exist which are:
- **User driven autopilot:** A user will be able to sign in and see the progress of the autopilot process run through.
- **Pre-provisioning autopilot:** Legacy known as Whiteglove which is used to complete the autopilot process and then to be turned off. Once the device is then handed to the primary user they would then be able to log in straight away without having to see the autopilot process like the previous method.

In conjunction to an autopilot profile another profile is used called an **Enrollment Status Page (ESP)** which is used to design the pages in which the user will see whilst the autopilot process is taking place. An ESP can also control which applications can be installed onto the device during the autopilot process. This part is constructed where a device is deemed as not being considered **built** unless certain applications defined within the ESP have installed first.

In addition to two methods of autopilot there are also two options in terms of how the device is onboarded with one being an Entra ID enrollment, and a Hybrid Entra ID enrollment which we had touched on earlier within the chapter.

Entra ID enrollment simply means once the autopilot has completed, the device will then be joined to the Entra ID domain only, which is the true essence of modern management going forward. However, when it comes to co-management and supporting a hybrid environment of utilizing both an Entra ID and on-premises AD, the Hybrid Entra ID version will allow a device to join both domains. This is achieved from two further components within the process:

- **Intune AD Connector:** The Intune AD Connector is a tool in Intune which is used to create a computer object within your on-premises AD by using the device record registered within autopilot. So that when you do build a device using a Hybrid Entra ID autopilot profile, it will then be joined to both domains.
- **Domain join profile:** A domain join profile is a configuration profile defined in Intune which is used to be assigned to devices in Intune so that when using a Hybrid Entra ID autopilot profile, it has the right details to your on-premise AD such as the domain name, its computer name and also the organizational unit it will be placed into.

Note: One drawback in the computer name configuration in the domain join profile is the inability to use variables, like the normal autopilot profile configuration. It is used more as a prefix rather than a whole name definition. The prefix is only up to 15 characters, whilst the rest of the name is then randomized.

What role will the Configuration Manager play

With Configuration Manager being a huge suite on its own, the planning of Configuration Manager architecture it would need to be understood the type of role or roles it will play, and this will define the usage as well as the overall business criticality Configuration Manager will play within your environment.

Here are some examples of some defined roles:

- **Vulnerability patching**: You can use Microsoft Configuration Manager as a solution to only look after patching through the WSUS/software update point role, given the flexibility it provides and its ability to go through the Configuration Manager workflow.
- **Legacy device management**: Similar to as noted in the co-management solution mentioned earlier, legacy device management maybe required if you have devices which are not modern management ready, but again also used in conjunction to support the vulnerability patching as well.

- **Asset intelligence**: This is not to be confused with the deprecated role of the asset intelligence sync role, but more within its functionality of obtaining regular inventory for both hardware and software and its reporting functionality.

This can be used as a great source of obtaining asset intelligence information, as well as being an asset to integrations with products like Microsoft System Center Service Manager to help populate its CMDB.

Application deployment and Operating System deployment

The most used scenario of all being the application deployment lifecycle, where you can rollout software to all of your managed devices, as well as having the ability to be able to build bare metal devices to a fully functioning machine using a base OS or custom OS images created from previous captures.

> Note: Configuration Manager also has additional features which can ease the OS deployment workflows into Intune by taking care of the onboarding through the task sequence process, as well as options to run reports that can generate the hardware hashes so that devices can be imported into autopilot.

Configuration Manager lab requirements

With everything taken into consideration from all the previous topics, we will look into the appropriate lab requirements to which the user can use in order to be able to fully understand all of the capabilities in which Configuration Manager as while stepping through the rest of this book.

> Note: The following requirement tables are applicable for a true to size environment where an organization can support these specifications. The reader does not have to create a lab to match the exact processor and memory requirements if these are not possible. For the purpose of the information in the book to carry out practical testing a 4 core and 4-8GB memory will be fine.

Central administration site environment

Though the future of the central administration site is being deprecated and advised to collapse/remove from your existing environment. If you are wanting to fully understand how Configuration Manager works for existing environments as well as a more enriched understanding over its environment, then building a lab with a CAS structure is a great way to go when following not only this book but additional reading material, studying and future planning ahead.

The ideal requirements recommended if using a consolidated or multi-server role environment are given in the following table.

- **Consolidated:** This lab requirement focuses on a structure in which all of the Configuration Manager roles exist on one server, therefore will have its own specifics on the resource requirements seen in the following table:

Component	Requirement
Processor	16 Cores
Memory (GB)	96
Memory Allocated to SQL (%)	90%
Disk Space	At least 100GB
Operating System Version	Windows Server 2022
SQL Server Version	SQL Server 2022
Client Operating Systems	Windows 11 Windows 10 (22H2) Windows Server 2022 Windows Server 2019

Table 3.10: CAS consolidated requirement table

- **Multi-server environment:** This lab requirement focuses on a structure in which the Configuration Manager server roles are split up onto individual servers, where in these cases may not be as intensive on the resource demands:

Component	Requirement
Processor	16 Cores
Memory (GB)	72
Memory Allocated to SQL (%)	80%
Disk Space	At least 100GB
Operating System Version	Windows Server 2022
SQL Server Version	SQL Server 2022
Client Operating Systems	Windows 11 Windows 10 (22H2) Windows Server 2022 Windows Server 2019

Table 3.11: CAS mult- server environment

Standalone primary site environment

The recommended and most common (and simpler) architecture for Configuration Manager would be of course having a standalone primary site server. Overall, it saves the time of planning to remove a child site from being parented by a CAS server.

The ideal requirements recommended if using a consolidated or multi-server role environment are given in the following table.

Consolidated: This lab requirement focuses on a structure in which all of the Configuration Manager roles exist on one server, therefore, will have its specifics on the resource requirements seen in the following table:

Component	Requirement
Processor	20 Cores
Memory (GB)	128
Memory Allocated to SQL (%).	90%
Disk Space	At least 100GB
Operating System Version	Windows Server 2022
SQL Server Version	SQL Server 2022
Client Operating Systems	Windows 11 Windows 10 (22H2) Windows Server 2022 Windows Server 2019

Table 3.12: Standalone primary site consolidated requirement table

Multi-server environment: This lab requirement focuses on a structure in which the Configuration Manager server roles are split up onto individual servers, where in these cases may not be as intensive on the resource demands:

Component	Requirement
Processor	16 Cores
Memory (GB)	96
Memory Allocated to SQL (%)	90%
Disk Space	At least 100GB
Operating System Version	Windows Server 2022
SQL Server Version	SQL Server 2022
Client Operating Systems	Windows 11 Windows 10 (22H2) Windows Server 2022 Windows Server 2019

Table 3.13: Standalone primary site multi server role requirement table

Conclusion

It is important for the reader to understand every topology from high level to low level so they can visualize how their overall architecture will be. Moreover, it is equally important to understand every role which exists within Configuration Manager so that the reader can understand how they will want their Configuration Manager solution to function and the various roles it will play to decide its criticality within the BAU side.

When building your Configuration Manager solution, another area to take into account is the scalability to support the growth that your environment will require when more devices and users are onboarded, which then requires further changes to your infrastructure requirements and resources.

It is also important for the reader to understand how modern management works and its relationship with Configuration Manager, so they are not only aware, but prepared for when it is time to make the transition.

Lastly, the lab requirements outlined will help the reader as well as the environment which needs to grow their knowledge and have a suitable sandpit to develop a POC before they can establish the solution which they require within their infrastructure.

In the next chapter, we will put everything we have learned on this chapter to apply it to the implementation and configuration of Microsoft Configuration Manager, where we will explore how to install and configure the technology.

Points to remember

- Any servers introduced to Configuration Manager with a functioning role is known as a site system server
- High-level topologies detail how many servers are used within a design; low level topologies are for the type of site server used to manage devices
- The two high-level topologies are consolidated and multi-server role
- The three low-level topologies are central administration site, primary site and secondary site
- Plans for scalability must be factored into each growth for further accommodation of more client devices to be managed
- Intune is the modern management solution moving forward when wanting to manage devices within the cloud
- Co-management is the solution that involves the integration between both Configuration Manager and Intune
- Various defined roles or planned designs determine the usage, role and criticality in which Configuration Manager will play

Multiple choice questions

1. **Which one is a site server used in Configuration Manager?**
   a. Central administration site server
   b. Primary site server
   c. Secondary site server
   d. All of the above

2. **What is the name of the solution which integrates both Configuration Manager and Intune?**
   a. CAS
   b. Co-management
   c. Modern management
   d. Endpoint manager

3. **How would you be able to support up to 750,000 clients in a Configuration Manager setup?**
   a. Using a primary site server only
   b. Using a central administration site server
   c. Multiple child sites
   d. 128GB of memory

4. **What is definition of a Hybrid Entra ID Setup?**
   a. Devices being joined to Entra ID and on-premises AD
   b. Devices being able to join the Entra ID domain
   c. Devices being able to enroll to Intune
   d. All of the above

5. **Which role is required if wanting to obtain historical data for Configuration Manager?**
   a. Distribution point
   b. Software update point
   c. Management point
   d. Data warehouse point

6. **What is the maximum number of primary sites you can have?**
   a. 25
   b. 250

c. 2500

d. 25,000

Answers

1. d
2. b
3. b
4. a
5. d
6. a

Key terms

- **CAS**: Central administration site server is a parent server for child sites
- **Hybrid Entra ID**: A setup which allows for devices to be part of both Entra ID and on-premise AD
- **Modern management**: A solution which involves devices being soley managed by Intune
- **Sandpit**: Definition of a lab environment which can be used to test or provide a proof of concept with
- **MDM**: Mobile device management which is a policy which allows for devices to be enrolled into Intune

Join our book's Discord space

Join the book's Discord Workspace for Latest updates, Offers, Tech happenings around the world, New Release and Sessions with the Authors:

https://discord.bpbonline.com

Chapter 4
Deployment and Administration of Microsoft Configuration Manager

Introduction

This chapter will concentrate on the development and deployment of Microsoft Configuration Manager. The importance of this chapter is to illustrate the setup of Microsoft Configuration Manager and the overall deployment so we can ensure the design plan that we specified in the previous chapter allows us to have a healthy setup. There will also be some troubleshooting points to help the reader understand the common and, in some cases, uncommon issues that can arise during the development and deployment process.

It will also provide an in-depth look into the overall administration of Microsoft Configuration Manager as well as outline its best practices. The administration side is what will allow an engineer to perform their **Business as Usual (BAU)** tasks, but also within the administrative side, another area that would enrich the BAU tasks and overall **user interface (UI)**, is where the best practices come in. Best practices are normally looked at as a professional and recommended level to what you should do and not do, but we can also understand that a real-world scenario can conflict with this, so we will look to outline the differences between both.

Structure

This chapter will cover the following topics:
- Primary stand-alone Configuration Manager deployment
- Multiple child sites Configuration Manager deployment
- Site system status validation of Configuration Manager
- Component status validation of Configuration Manager
- Administration of Configuration Manager
- Best practices
- Real-world scenarios

Objectives

This chapter will introduce the readers to a full coverage on how to install Configuration Manager, covering all of the main topologies and traditional roles which come native with certain topologies, as well as additional roles which can be used to further scale your deployments. We will also be looking at how we are not only able to administer Configuration Manager but also how to maintain and keep the product fully updated.

Primary stand-alone Configuration Manager deployment

After the previous chapters, which outlined hardware and software requirements, topologies, and various roles and limitations, we are now ready to proceed with the deployment of our Configuration Manager solution.

In this particular topic, we will focus on the implementation of a primary stand-alone server, which is, by best practice, the recommended topology to go with where the **Central Administration Site** (**CAS**) is due to be a deprecated model.

Windows server prerequisites

These prerequisites are all based on the checks that the Configuration Manager will perform before allowing you to proceed with the installation.

Here, we will outline all the checks involved and define their criticality to allowing or stopping the installation:
- **Server roles:** The first parts of the prerequisites are based on various roles like server roles. The following roles would need to be installed:
    - Web Server (IIS)

- o Windows Server Update Services
- **Server features**: The following features would need to be installed:
  - o .NET Framework 3.5 features
  - o .NET Framework 4.8 features
  - o **Background Intelligent Transfer Service (BITS)**
  - o **Remote Differential Compression (RDC)**
- **Windows server OS installation media**: Before you follow the instructions, there are some other tasks you need to complete first. This is because one of the server features is .NET Framework 3.5, which can only be installed when you have the installation media of the Windows Server OS. You either have this mounted to the computer or copied locally to the system drive, where you can point to the directory.
- **Windows Server Update Services (WSUS) database**: This is primarily for informational purposes, but when following the instructions for installing the WSUS role within the Server Manager, you will be prompted with options to use a **Windows Internal Database (WID)** or a **Structured Query Language (SQL)** Server.

  As a best practice, it is better to utilise the SQL Server in order to be able to take full advantage of SQL backup strategies as well as better database maintenance and performance benefits.
- **Installation of the server roles and features**: To install the server roles, perform the following steps:

Note: The instructions which outline installing the WSUS is applicable if you are installing this role on the same server as the primary Site Server

1. Click the start menu.
2. Go to the **Server Manager** console.
3. In the top right-hand corner select manage: Add roles and features.
4. Before you begin, Click **Next**.
5. **Select installation type:** Ensure the role-based or feature-based installation is selected. Then click **Next**.
6. **Select destination server:** Ensure that the select a server from the server pool has your server selected then click **Next**.
7. **Select server roles:** Select the following roles:
   a. Web Server (IIS)
   b. Windows Server Update Services

8. Click the **Add Features** button within the dialogs when they pop, then click **Next**.
9. Select the following features:
   a. .NET Framework 3.5 Features: .NET Framework 3.5 (includes .NET 2.0 and 3.0)
   b. .NET Framework 4.8 Features: .NET Framework 4.8, ASP.NET 4.8
   c. .NET Framework 4.8 Features: ASP.NET 4.8
   d. .NET Framework 4.8 Features: WCF Services: HTTP Activation
   e. .NET Framework 4.8 Features: WCF Services: TCP Port Sharing
   f. **BITS**
   g. **BITS**: IIS Server Extension
   h. Remote Differential Compression
10. **Web Server Role (IIS):** Click **Next**.
11. Select the following role services:
    a. Web Server: Common HTTP Features: Default Document
    b. Web Server: Common HTTP Features: Directory Browsing
    c. Web Server: Common HTTP Features: HTTP Errors
    d. Web Server: Common HTTP Features: Static Content
    e. Web Server: Common HTTP Features: WebDAV Publishing
    f. Web Server: Web Server Health and Diagnostics: HTTP Logging
    g. Web Server: Web Server Health and Diagnostics: Logging Tools
    h. Web Server: Web Server Health and Diagnostics: Request Monitor
    i. Web Server: Web Server Health and Diagnostics: Tracing
    j. Web Server: Performance: Static Content Compression
    k. Web Server: Performance: Dynamic Content Compression
    l. Web Server: Security: Request Filtering
    m. Web Server: Security: Windows Authentication
    n. Web Server: Application Development: .NET Extensibility 4.8
    o. Web Server: Application Development: ASP.NET 4.8
    p. Web Server: Application Development: ISAPI Extensions
    q. Web Server: Application Development: ISAPI Filters
    r. Web Server: Management Tools: IIS Management Console
    s. Web Server: Management Tools: IIS 6 Management Compatibility

t. Web Server: Management Tools: IIS 6 Management Compatibility: IIS 6 Metabase Compatibility

u. Web Server: Management Tools: IIS 6 Management Compatibility: IIS 6 WMI Compatibility

Then click **Next**.

12. **Windows Server Update Services**: Click **Next**.
13. **Select role services:** Unselect the **WID Connectivity** and select **SQL Server Connectivity**. Then click **Next**.
14. **Content location selection**: Enter a location in the Store updates in the following location (choose a valid local path on *server.server.com* or a remote path) text box. Then click **Next**.
15. **Database instance selection: DB Instance** - Enter the name of the database instance. If it is a default instance you should be able to just enter the server name of the SQL Server. Click the **check connection** button to verify connectivity and then click **Next**.
16. **Confirm installation selections:** Click on the **Specify an alternate source path link at the bottom of the window**.
17. **Specify alternate source path**: Enter the path of the installation media to point to the following folder, that is, **D:\Sources\SxS**. Then click **OK**.
18. **Confirm installation selections:** Click **Install**.

Once completed, you will need to now perform the post-deployment configuration for your WSUS role to be able to be fully activated.

To do so, perform the following steps:

1. Click the start menu.
2. Go to the **Server Manager** console.
3. Click on the flag icon, which should have a warning exclamation mark next to it.
4. Select the launch post-installation tasks for the WSUS and wait for it to complete.

Once this is completed, everything will be installed.

Active Directory schema extensions

For the Configuration Manager to fully publish objects in the Active Directory, the schema must be extended within your Active Directory.

The file required can be found in your Configuration Manager installation media. To extend the schema, perform the following steps:

1. Open the Configuration Manager installation media.

2. Copy the **SMSSETUP\BIN\x64\extadsch** file over to your domain controller.
3. Log onto your domain controller.
4. Open Command Prompt using administrative privileges.
5. Enter the location of the file into the command prompt and then hit *Enter* to run **C:\MEM_Configmgr_2203\ SMSSETUP\BIN\x64\extadsch**.

You should now start to see some log lines get created with then a confirmation of the schema now being extended.

> **Note:** At the time of writing this book, 2203 was the base version of Configuration Manager when downloading the installation media. When Configuration Manager is installed you will have the option to upgrade to the latest version afterwards.

After this part is completed, we will then need to create the containers within the **Active Directory Service Interfaces** (**ADSI**) to allow for objects to be created for the Configuration Manager site server.

To do this, perform the following steps:

1. Log onto the domain controller or a server that contains the ADSI Edit tool.
2. Click on the start menu and select **Windows Administrative Tools**: ADSI Edit.
3. Right-click the **ADSI Edit** in the left-hand pane and select **Connect To**.
4. Accept the defaults and click **OK**.
5. Browse to the Default Naming Context: Top Level Folder: CN=System
6. Right-click the **CN=System** folder and select **New** object.
7. Create Object: Select a class: Select container.
8. Enter the name **System Management** in the value box and then click **Next**.
9. Once created, right-click the **CN=System Management** folder and select **Properties**.
10. Select the **Security** tab and click the **Add** button.
11. Select the **Object Types** button and select the **Computers** object type. Then click **OK**.
12. Enter the name of the server you will use as the primary server then click **Check Names** to verify the computer object, then click **OK**.
13. Click **Apply**, then click **OK**.

Windows Assessment and Deployment Kit

The Windows ADK is a software prerequisite that is required for Microsoft Configuration Manager to be able to operate the **operating system deployment** (**OSD**) and manage the deployments of new bare metal machines.

There are two parts of the Windows ADK, which are as follows:
- Windows ADK Kit
- Windows ADK Windows PE Kit

In the past both would be in the same package, but now these have now been split up as separate packages.

The Windows ADK kit contains all of the tools required to be able to manage OSD components, but the Windows PE represents a different part which is where Configuration Manager uses images referred to as boot images.

Boot images are used to load computers into the WinPE from a **Pre-Execution Environment** (**PXE**) boot process. During the WinPE screen, they are presented with a screen that will show a dialog for password entry, allowing them to see the list of task sequences available to them in which they can build the computer.

The WinPE part of the ADK kit works by having boot images use the WinPE components, which are then loaded into the boot image, allowing it to work correctly during this process.

The versions used are very important when it comes to Configuration Manager. Using the incorrect versions of either both kits or the kits not being at the correct level for Configuration Manager can cause much bigger issues down the line, as well as failing the Configuration Manager prerequisites.

The following table shows the compatibility for each version:

Windows ADK version	Configuration Manager version (Minimum)
Windows 11 (10.1.22621.1)	2203
Windows 11 (10.1.22000)	2111
Windows Server 2022 (10.1.20348)	2111
Windows 10 2004 (10.1.19041)	2111

Table 4.1: Configuration Manager and Windows ADK compatibility table

> **Note:** The updated requirement information for support around the supported versions of ADK kits and Configuration Manager can be seen here:
>
> Support for the Windows ADK - Configuration Manager | Microsoft Learn

Download and install Windows ADK through the following steps:
- **How to download**: The latest downloads of the Windows ADK kits can be found here. **Download and install the Windows ADK | Microsoft Learn**
- **How to install**: Once downloaded, to install you will need to perform the following:

- **Windows ADK kit installation:** The steps to download Windows ADK kit are as follows:
    1. Click on the **ADK setup** set up file.
    2. **Specify location:** Select the installation path, then click **Next**.
    3. **Windows kits privacy:** Select whether you allow Microsoft to collect insights for the windows kits then click **Next**.
    4. **License agreement**: Accept the license agreement, then click **Next**.
    5. **Select the features you want to install**: Click **Install**.
- **Windows ADK PE kit installation:** The steps to download Windows ADK PE kit are as follows:
    1. Click on **ADK win** PE setup file.
    2. **Specify Location:** Select the installation path, then click **Next**.
    3. **Windows kits privacy**: Select whether you allow Microsoft to collect insights for the windows kits then click **Next**.
    4. **License agreement**: Accept the license agreement, then click **Next**.
    5. **Select the features you want to install:** Click **Install**.

Structured Query Language Server permissions

From the initial SQL Server setup, you need to ensure that the computer account of the server on which you will install the primary site server has local administrator privileges on the SQL Server itself, as well as the SQL Server instance.

This is also covered within the *Pre-installation prerequisites section* with the table outlined in *Table 4.2*.

Firewall requirements

Core roles installed into the primary site server are as follows:
- Management point
- Distribution point

You will need to take into account the firewall requirements for these from a site server perspective as well as for the clients and SQL Server connections. The following table helps outline these specific firewall requirements:

Firewall direction	Port used	Protocol type	Transmission Control Protocol (TCP) or User Datagram Protocol (UDP)
Client to management point	80	HTTP	TCP
Client to management point	443	HTTPS	TCP
Client to management point	10123	Client notification	TCP
Client to distribution point	80	HTTP	TCP
Client to distribution point	443	HTTPS	TCP
Client to distribution point	8005	Express updates	TCP
Site Server to Distribution Point	445	**Server Message Block (SMB)**	TCP
Site server to distribution point	135	**Remote Procedure Call (RPC)** Endpoint mapper	135
Site server to distribution point	Dynamic	RPC	Dynamic
Site server to SQL Server	1433	SQL default port	TCP

Table 4.2: Configuration Manager firewall ports table

It is worth noting that each port displayed in the table represents the default port of each protocol mentioned. Assuming that you will want to use the default ports, these can also be changed if there are possible conflicts against technologies that may already be utilizing these ports on the same servers for whatever reason.

The full list of each firewall requirement for each site system server can be viewed here: **Ports used for connections - Configuration Manager | Microsoft Learn**

Pre-installation prerequisites

When stepping through the Configuration Manager installation, you will see a prerequisite checker window, which will run a series of checks to ensure that the criteria are met in order to proceed with the installation.

Figure 4.1 outlines some prerequisites that you may come across which are specific to the latest version of Configuration Manager:

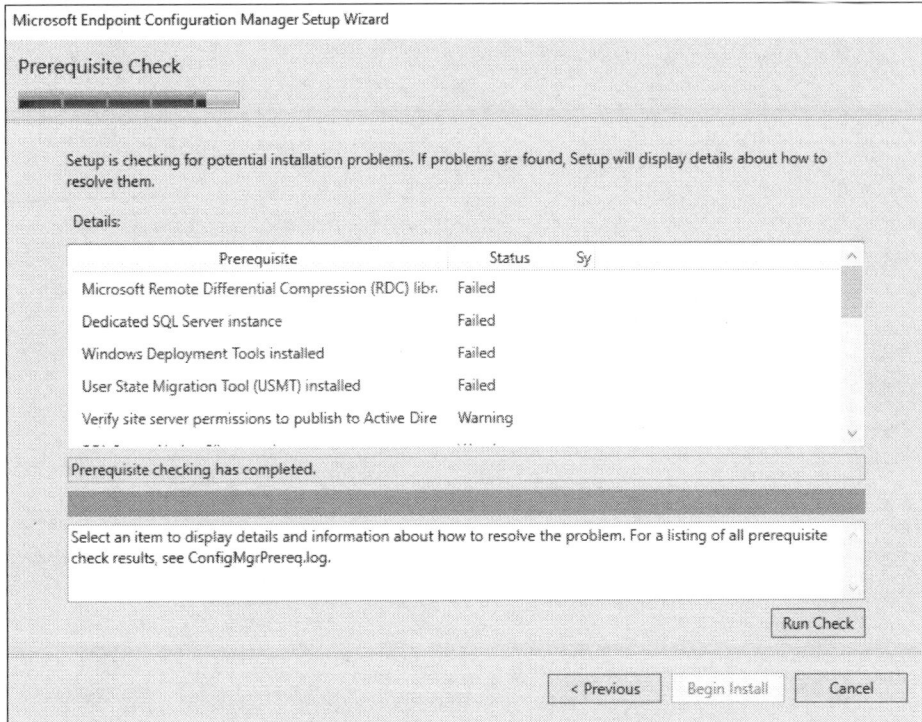

Figure 4.1: Pre-installation prerequisite checker

To see an extensive list of all the prerequisites for Configuration Manager, you can use the following link: **https://learn.microsoft.com/en-us/mem/configmgr/core/servers/deploy/install/list-of-prerequisite-checks**

Primary site installation

Once everything above has been verified and checked, we will proceed with the deployment of Configuration Manager.

To begin this, perform the following steps:

1. Open the installation media and run the `splash.hta` file.
2. When the Microsoft Endpoint Configuration Manager splashes window launches, click the **Install** button.
3. **Microsoft Endpoint Configuration Manager Setup Wizard:** Before you begin: Click **Next**.
4. **Getting Started:** Available setup options: Select the first option, then click **Next**.

> Note: The tick box below represents an express installation setup which would preconfigure all of the next screens we will see through this topic. This would be applicable if you were using a consolidated setup where the SQL instance is on the same server as seen in *Figure 4.2*:

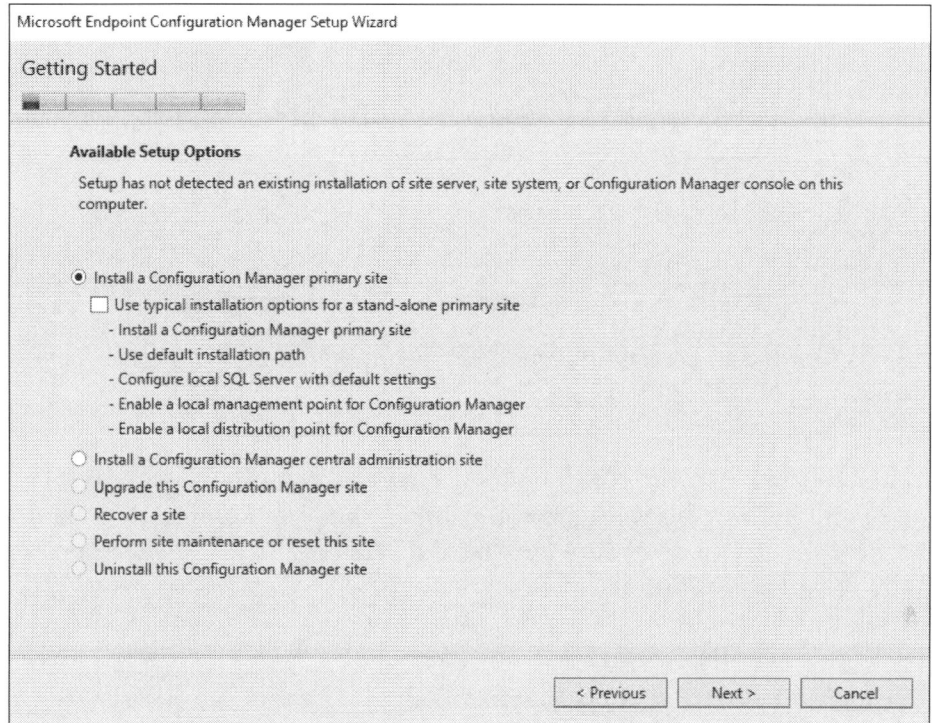

Figure 4.2: *Available setup options window*

5. **Product key:** Enter the product key for your Configuration Manager product and select the correct date for your Software Assurance expiration date. Then click **Next**.

> Note: A Software Assurance agreement is something that allows you to obtain regular updates and the latest version of your System Centre products as well as Configuration Manager.

6. **Product license terms**: Select **I accept these License Terms and Privat Statement for each license term**, then click **Next**.
7. **Prerequisite downloads**: This page is used to download all the prerequisite files needed for the Configuration Manager installation to continue. If you do not have these downloaded, you will need to use the first option, which is to download the required files, so you will require an internet connection for this point. Create a folder locally or point to an appropriate network location where these will be

downloaded using the **Browse** button. Click **Next** to begin the download. If you already have these files downloaded, then you can select the **use previously downloaded files** option and do the same as previously done, then click **Next**:

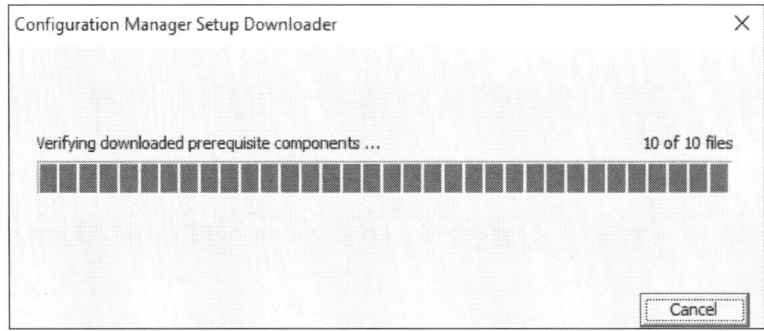

Figure 4.3: Configuration Manager setup downloader dialog

8. **Server language selection:** Select the appropriate languages applicable to your environment, then click **Next**.

9. **Client language selection:** Select the appropriate languages applicable to your environment, then click **Next**.

10. **Site and installation settings:** Enter a three-character identification for your site code, then enter a name for your site. For example, as we are creating a primary site we could use *PRI* and the site name as *Test Organization Primary Site*. Select whether you want to install the Configuration Manager console and define the location where then click **Next**.

11. **Primary site installation:** Select the install the primary site as a stand-alone site, then click **Next**. Accept the notification pop up reminding you of your selection then click **Next**.

12. **Database information**: Enter the details of your SQL Server and instance name. Ensure you have taken into account the firewall requirements for this point. The database name will always follow the default naming convention of CM (site code). For example, if your site code is *PRI* then your database name would be CM_PRI. Click **Next**.

13. **Database information**: Check if the default paths defined for your SQL database file and log file are correct, then click **Next**.

14. **SMS provider settings**: Specify the server that will hold the SMS provider server or you can accept the default of the primary site server holding this role then click **Next**.

15. **Client computer communication settings**: Select your communication settings depending on your PKI setup. If you want to use HTTPS only, select all site system roles that accept only HTTPS communications from clients. If you do not have this in place, then you can select configure the communication method on each site

system role where you are given the option to select clients will use HTTPS when they have a valid PKI certificate and HTTPS-enabled site roles are available, then click **Next**.

16. **Site system roles**: Select the client connection communication methods for the Management and distribution point roles. If you are using HTTP, then select HTTP. If you have your PKI infrastructure in place, then select **HTTPs**. Then click **Next**.

17. **Diagnostic and usage data**: Click **Next**.

18. **Service connection point setup**: If you plan for this server to be responsible for obtaining the latest updates, click **Next**. Ensure that you have an internet connection if using this role. Alternatively, you can select another server to have this role. If you are not planning on installing this role for now, click **Skip** this for now.

19. **Settings summary**: Look through the summary of your Configuration Manager and then click **Next**.

20. **Prerequisite check**: Wait for the prerequisite checks to complete. If a warning is shown, look through to understand what has been flagged and address it appropriately if it will negatively affect your setup. Any showing up as failed will need to be sorted before you can continue. Once everything has been passed you can proceed to click **Begin Install**.

Multiple child sites Configuration Manager deployment

This section will cover the process of adding child sites to your Configuration Manager. We will explore this in multiple areas.

If we go with this particular model, the CAS can be a top-level parent for all child sites. Though this method is to be deprecated and recommended against in best practice, for the purpose of the book, we will outline to the reader the process and the significance of its use.

Central administration site installation

To begin, perform the following steps:

1. Open the installation media and then run the `splash.hta` file.
2. When the Microsoft Endpoint Configuration Manager splash window launches, click the **Install** button.
3. **Microsoft Endpoint Configuration Manager Setup Wizard:** Before You Begin: Click **Next**.

4. **Getting started:** Available Setup Options: Select the Install configuration manager CAS option. Then click **Next**.
5. **Product key:** Enter the product key for your Configuration Manager product and also select the correct date for your Software Assurance expiration date. Then click **Next**.

Note: A Software Assurance agreement is something which allows you to obtain regular updates and the latest version of your system centre products as well as Configuration Manager.

6. **Product license terms**: Select the **I accept these License Terms and Privat Statement for each license term**, then click **Next**.
7. **Prerequisite downloads**: This page is used to download all of the prerequisite files needed for the Configuration Manager installation to continue. If you do not have these downloaded, then you will need to use the first option, which is, **Download required files so you will require an internet connection for this point.** Create a folder locally or point to an appropriate network location where these will be downloaded using the Browse button, then click **Next** to begin the download. If you have these files downloaded, you can select the **Use previously downloaded** files option and do the same as previously done, then click **Next**.
8. **Server language selection:** Select the appropriate languages applicable to your environment, then click **Next**.
9. **Client language selection:** Select the appropriate languages applicable to your environment, then click **Next**.
10. **Site and installation settings:** Enter a three-character identification for your site code, then enter a name for your site. For example, as we create a primary site, we could use CAS and the site name as *Test Organization Central Administration Site*. Select whether you want to install the Configuration Manager console and define the location, then click **Next**.
11. **CAS installation:** Specify whether this will be the first site in a new hierarchy or if this site will expand an existing stand-alone primary site into a hierarchy. Select the **Install as the first site in a new hierarchy**, then click **Next**.
12. **Database information**: Check if the default paths defined for your SQL database file and log file are correct, then click **Next**.
13. **Database information**: Check if the default paths defined for your SQL database file and log file are correct, then click **Next**.
14. **SMS provider settings**: Specify the server which will hold the SMS provider server or you can accept the default of the primary site server holding this role, then click **Next**.
15. **Diagnostic and usage data**: Click **Next**.

16. **Service connection point setup**: If you are planning on this server to be responsible for obtaining the latest updates, you can click **Next**, but ensure that you have an internet connection. Alternatively, you can select another server to have this role. If you are not planning on installing this role for now then you can click **Skip this for now**.

17. **Settings summary**: Look through the summary of your Configuration Manager and then click **Next**.

18. **Prerequisite check**: Wait for the prerequisite checks to complete. If any warning is shown, understand what has been flagged and address it appropriately if they will negatively affect your setup. If any shows up as failed will need to be sorted before you can continue. Once everything has been passed you can proceed to click **Begin Install**.

Add primary site server to central administration site

Once you have established a CAS, you can then start to add child sites to your hierarchy, in this case, primary site servers.

To add a child site to your CAS, perform the following steps:

1. Perform the steps 1- 8 from the previous Central Administration Server section above.

2. **Primary site installation:** Select the **Install the primary site as a stand-alone site**, then click **Next**. Accept the notification pop-up reminding you of your selection, then click **Next**.

3. **Database information**: Enter the details of your SQL Server and instance name. Ensure you have taken into account the firewall requirements for this point. The database name will always follow the default naming convention of CM (site code). For example, if your site code is PRI, then your database name would be CM_PRI. Click **Next**.

4. **Database information**: Check the default paths defined for your SQL database file and log file are correct then click **Next**.

5. **SMS provider settings**: Specify the server which will hold the SMS provider server or you can accept the default of the primary site server holding this role, then click **Next**.

6. **Client computer communication settings**: Select your communication settings depending on your PKI setup. If you want to use HTTPS only, then select **All site system roles accept only HTTPS communications from clients**. If you do not have this in place currently, then you can select **Configure the communication method on each site system role** where you are given the option to select **Clients**

will use HTTPS when they have a valid PKI certificate and HTTPS-enabled site roles are available** then click **Next**.

7. **Site system roles**: Select the client connection communication methods for the Management Point and Distribution point roles. If using HTTP currently then select **HTTP** or if you have your PKI infrastructure in place then select **HTTPs**. Then click **Next**.

8. **Diagnostic and usage data**: Click **Next**.

9. **Service connection point setup**: If you are planning on this server to be responsible for obtaining the latest updates you can click **Next** but ensure that you have an internet connection if using this role. Alternatively, you can select another server to have this role. If you are not planning on installing this role for now then you can click **Skip this for now**.

10. **Settings summary**: Look through the summary of your Configuration Manager and then click **Next**.

11. **Prerequisite check**: Wait for the prerequisite checks to complete. If any show as warning, look through to understand what has been flagged and address appropriately if they will negatively affect your setup. Any which show up as Failed will need to be sorted before you can continue. Once everything has been passed you can proceed to click **Begin Install**.

Add secondary site server to the primary site

If you are required to add additional child sites to a primary site server, you can add secondary sites which will attach the primary site server as the parent.

To add secondary sites, perform the following steps:

1. Open the Microsoft Configuration Manager Console.

2. **Go to the administration**: Site configuration: Sites

3. Right-click the primary site listed in the console and select **create secondary site**.

4. **Before you Begin:** Welcome to the Create Secondary Site Wizard: Click **Next**.

5. **General:** Specify settings for a new secondary site. Enter the site code for your secondary site and select the server which will hold this role. Enter a site name for the secondary site then click **Next**.

6. **Installation source files:** Specify the location of the Configuration Manager installation source files. Keep the default of copy installation source files over the network from the parent site server then click **Next**.

7. **SQL Server settings:** Specify the SQL Server settings to be used for this secondary site installation. Select whether you want to use a SQL Server Express edition for

your secondary site database or if you want to use an existing SQL Server to host the database. Then click **Next**.

8. **Distribution point**: Specify distribution point settings. If the server you have selected does not have all the IIS components, then select the **Install and Configure IIS** if required by Configuration Manager then click **Next**.
9. **Communication**: Select the communication protocol in which devices will use to connect to the distribution point. Click **Next**.
10. **Drive settings**: **Specify drive settings for this distribution point**: Select the appropriate drives in which distribution point data will be stored. Then click **Next**.
11. **Content validation**: Specify the content validation settings. Content validation is a check performed on a regular interval to ensure all packages are integrity checked to verify they are using the correct package files and information. If you wish to enable this tick the **Validate content on a schedule** box then click **Next**.
12. **Boundary groups**: Specify the boundary groups to associate with this site system. Boundary groups are parent group for objects called boundaries which associate a managed device to a site system via a network discovery method such as IP ranges, Active Directory Site or IP subnet. Select the appropriate ones and then click **Next**.
13. **Summary**: Confirm the settings. Review the information you have configured and then click **Next**.

After this has been done the secondary site will be ready to go.

Site system status validation of Configuration Manager

Once Microsoft Configuration Manager has been fully deployed, and upgraded or if any maintenance is done, a way for us to validate its health status is by going through the site system status validation.

This view shows the health status of each site system that holds a Configuration Manager role and is normally reported via status messages. Status messages are codes and notifications that go between the **software development kit** (**SDK**) and the database to be able to communicate the issues being identified on that particular server.

To access this view, perform the following steps:

1. Open the Microsoft Configuration Manager console.
2. Go to **Monitoring**: **System Status**: **Site Status**

Here, you will see a list of all of the site servers and their health status, as seen in *Figure 4.4*:

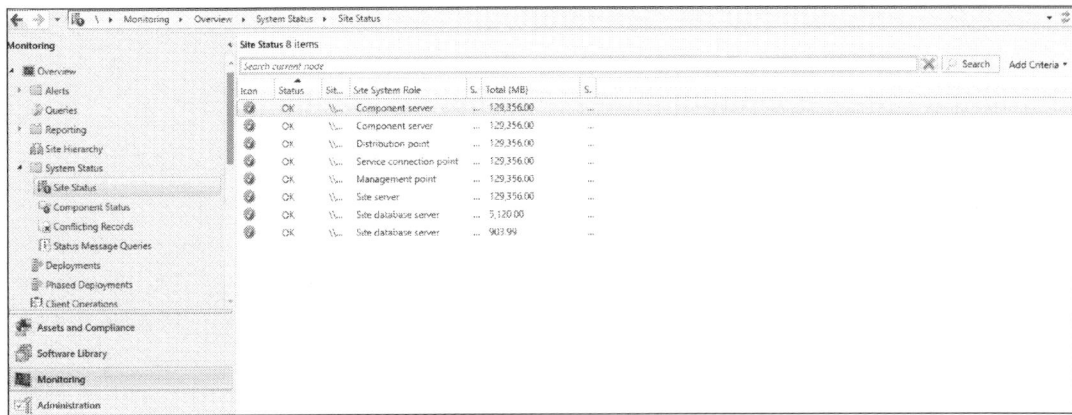

Figure 4.4: Site status view

The health statuses for the site servers come in the following three levels of severities:
- OK (Information if not an issue)
- Warning
- Error

To further examine issues or information on the status, you can right-click and select **Show Messages**: **All**.

You will be presented with a dialog that will ask you to specify the date range of the status messages. Then click **OK** to see the messages as shown in *Figure 4.5* and *Figure 4.6*:

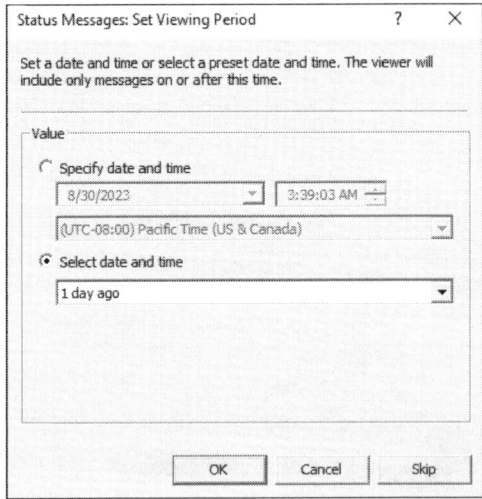

Figure 4.5: Status message viewing period dialog

Message visible after clicking **OK**:

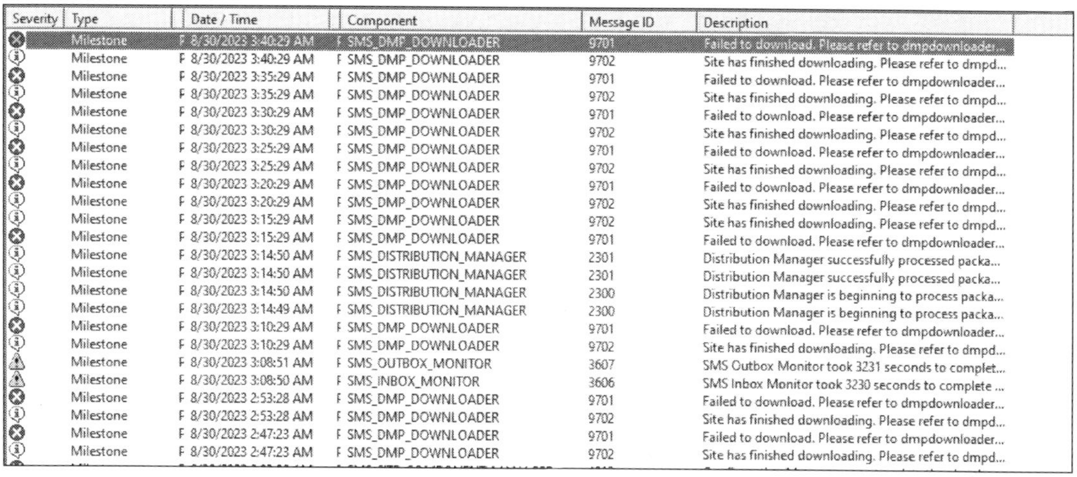

Severity	Type	Date / Time	Component	Message ID	Description
	Milestone	F 8/30/2023 3:40:29 AM	F SMS_DMP_DOWNLOADER	9701	Failed to download. Please refer to dmpdownloader...
	Milestone	F 8/30/2023 3:40:29 AM	F SMS_DMP_DOWNLOADER	9702	Site has finished downloading. Please refer to dmpd...
	Milestone	F 8/30/2023 3:35:29 AM	F SMS_DMP_DOWNLOADER	9701	Failed to download. Please refer to dmpdownloader...
	Milestone	F 8/30/2023 3:35:29 AM	F SMS_DMP_DOWNLOADER	9702	Site has finished downloading. Please refer to dmpd...
	Milestone	F 8/30/2023 3:30:29 AM	F SMS_DMP_DOWNLOADER	9701	Failed to download. Please refer to dmpdownloader...
	Milestone	F 8/30/2023 3:30:29 AM	F SMS_DMP_DOWNLOADER	9702	Site has finished downloading. Please refer to dmpd...
	Milestone	F 8/30/2023 3:25:29 AM	F SMS_DMP_DOWNLOADER	9701	Failed to download. Please refer to dmpdownloader...
	Milestone	F 8/30/2023 3:25:29 AM	F SMS_DMP_DOWNLOADER	9702	Site has finished downloading. Please refer to dmpd...
	Milestone	F 8/30/2023 3:20:29 AM	F SMS_DMP_DOWNLOADER	9701	Failed to download. Please refer to dmpdownloader...
	Milestone	F 8/30/2023 3:20:29 AM	F SMS_DMP_DOWNLOADER	9702	Site has finished downloading. Please refer to dmpd...
	Milestone	F 8/30/2023 3:15:29 AM	F SMS_DMP_DOWNLOADER	9702	Site has finished downloading. Please refer to dmpd...
	Milestone	F 8/30/2023 3:15:29 AM	F SMS_DMP_DOWNLOADER	9701	Failed to download. Please refer to dmpdownloader...
	Milestone	F 8/30/2023 3:14:50 AM	F SMS_DISTRIBUTION_MANAGER	2301	Distribution Manager successfully processed packa...
	Milestone	F 8/30/2023 3:14:50 AM	F SMS_DISTRIBUTION_MANAGER	2301	Distribution Manager successfully processed packa...
	Milestone	F 8/30/2023 3:14:50 AM	F SMS_DISTRIBUTION_MANAGER	2300	Distribution Manager is beginning to process packa...
	Milestone	F 8/30/2023 3:14:49 AM	F SMS_DISTRIBUTION_MANAGER	2300	Distribution Manager is beginning to process packa...
	Milestone	F 8/30/2023 3:10:29 AM	F SMS_DMP_DOWNLOADER	9701	Failed to download. Please refer to dmpdownloader...
	Milestone	F 8/30/2023 3:10:29 AM	F SMS_DMP_DOWNLOADER	9702	Site has finished downloading. Please refer to dmpd...
	Milestone	F 8/30/2023 3:08:51 AM	F SMS_OUTBOX_MONITOR	3607	SMS Outbox Monitor took 3231 seconds to complet...
	Milestone	F 8/30/2023 3:08:50 AM	F SMS_INBOX_MONITOR	3606	SMS Inbox Monitor took 3230 seconds to complete ...
	Milestone	F 8/30/2023 2:53:28 AM	F SMS_DMP_DOWNLOADER	9701	Failed to download. Please refer to dmpdownloader...
	Milestone	F 8/30/2023 2:53:28 AM	F SMS_DMP_DOWNLOADER	9702	Site has finished downloading. Please refer to dmpd...
	Milestone	F 8/30/2023 2:47:23 AM	F SMS_DMP_DOWNLOADER	9701	Failed to download. Please refer to dmpdownloader...
	Milestone	F 8/30/2023 2:47:23 AM	F SMS_DMP_DOWNLOADER	9702	Site has finished downloading. Please refer to dmpd...

***Figure 4.6**: Status message viewer*

The status viewer in *Figure 4.6* provides a breakdown of the health status of each component that exists on the site server. The message ID column represents the code which refers to the description of the issue outlined.

Similar to the capabilities of the standard Windows event viewer, you have the ability to further filter messages in Window to see more specific messages depending on the criteria in which you have selected.

Component status validation of Configuration Manager

Similar to the topic above, the component status is of a similar view to the site status viewer, however, in this case its focus is on all the specific components on each site server rather than solely the site server itself.

To see this view, perform the following steps:

1. Open the Microsoft Configuration Manager console.
2. Go to Monitoring: System status: Component status.

You can then see the view, as shown in *Figure 4.7*:

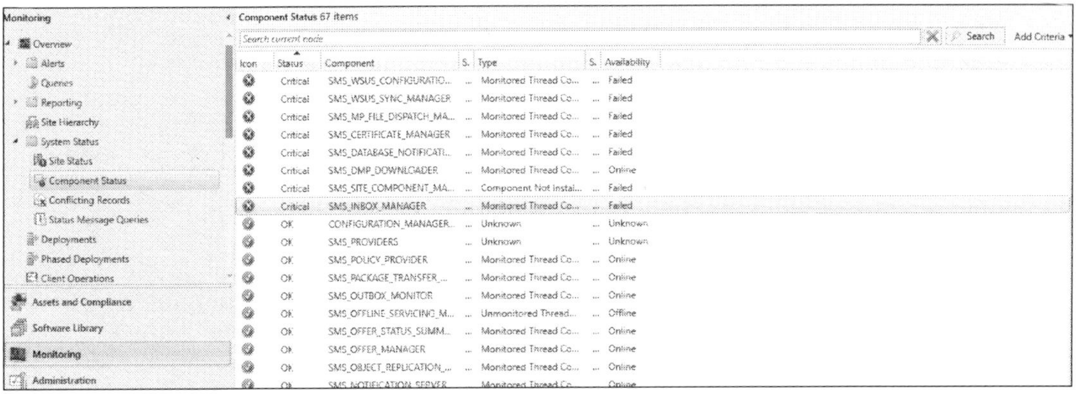

Figure 4.7: Component status view

Though you can use the next tool shown next, it can mostly be launched from this view due to the detail displayed regarding the status of each component in reference to the column, which details whether a component is online, offline, or even unknown.

If you right-click any component and select **Start**: **Configuration Manager Service Manager**.

This will then launch an internal tool for Configuration Manager, which will show a list of all components, and component services, and display them as running or stopped, as seen in *Figure 4.8*:

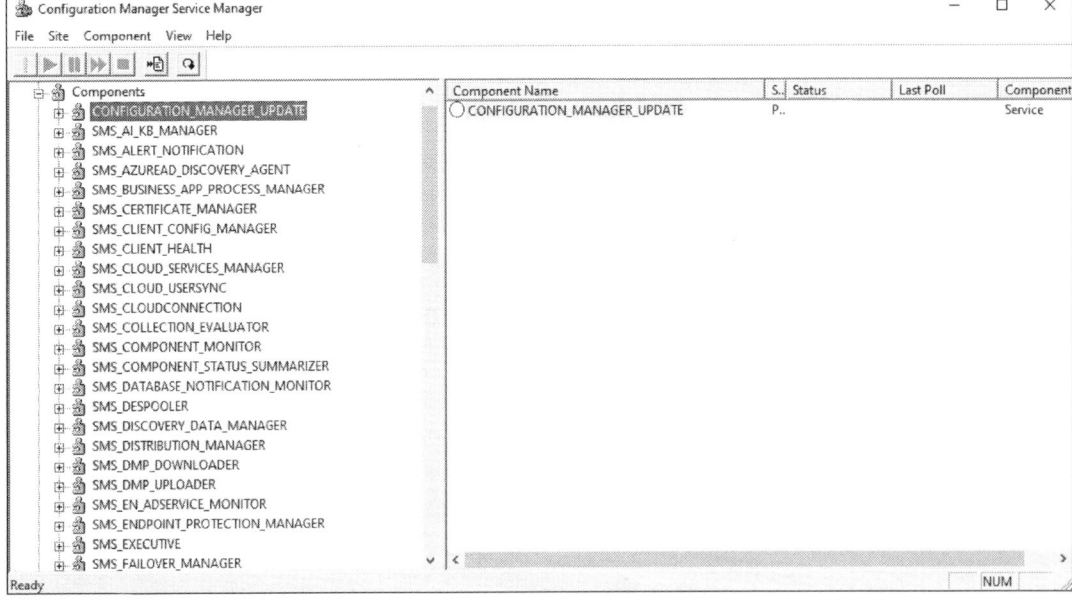

Figure 4.8: Configuration Manager Service manager

Components relating to different site system roles within Configuration Manager are listed here in which services can be queried to find out their running status, as well as being started or stopped, as seen in *Figure 4.9*:

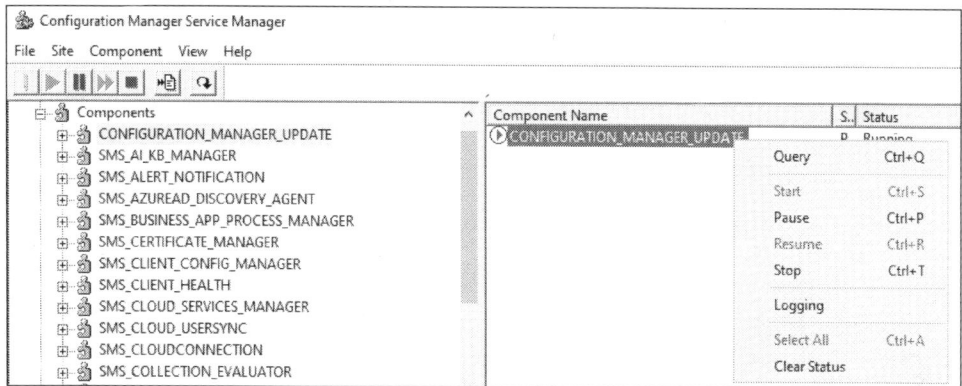

Figure 4.9: Queried component status in Configuration Manager service manager

Administration of Configuration Manager

After your Configuration Manager has been set up, we are ready to start administration tasks that you would normally go through in the ongoing management of your environment.

There are several areas for administration when it comes to this product, but in this book we will focus on the main features that require little to no additional configuration. We will apply *Chapter 3, Streamlining OS and Optimising Application Deployment with Microsoft Configuration Manager*, common areas, as well as features that are introduced into the latest versions that help enrich common administrative tasks.

Adding additional roles

In the previous chapter, we explained the definitions for all the roles that can be installed within the Configuration Manager.

Though there are different options when adding new roles, most of the overall wizards and processes are the same, so we will go through the process of adding an additional role to either an existing Windows server or a new Windows server. Perform the following steps:

1. Open the Microsoft Configuration Manager console.
2. Go to **Administration**: **Site Configuration**: **Server and site systems roles**.
3. Right-click and select **Create Site System Server**. If you want to add a site system server role to an existing server, you can right-click on one of the servers listed in this view and then select **Add Site System roles**.

4. **General:** Select a server to use as a site system. Verify the server used to add roles to or select the correct Windows server to which you will be adding roles to. Select an appropriate site system installation account, then click **Next**.

5. **Proxy:** Specify internet proxy server. Configure appropriately if you have a proxy that the servers need to go through. If not, then click **Next**.

6. **System role selection**: Specify roles for this server. Select the required role/s and proceed to their configuration:

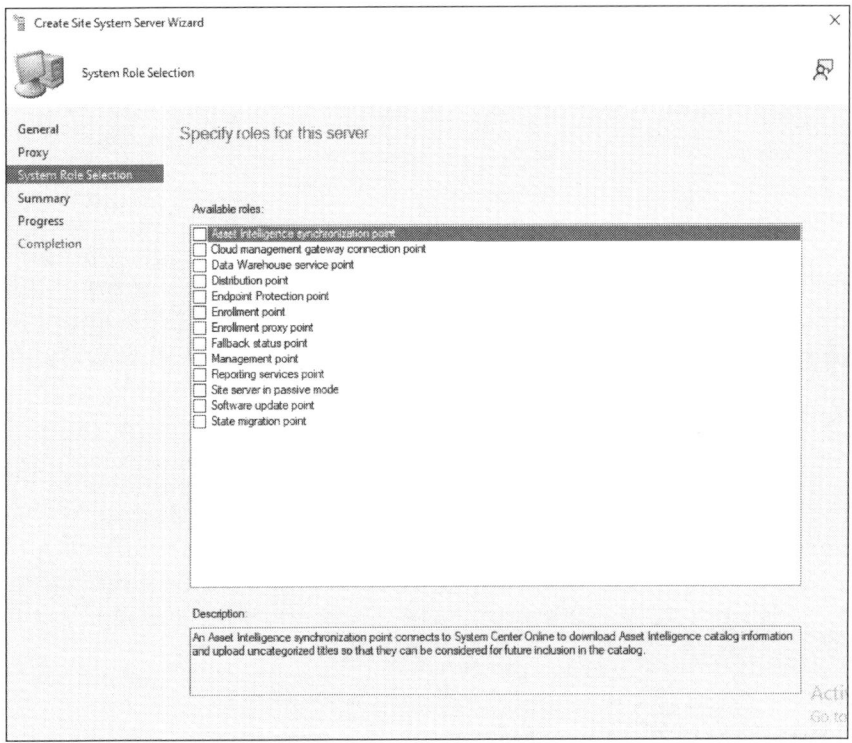

Figure 4.10: Site system roles list

7. **Summary:** The wizard will create a new site system server with the following settings. Check through your configuration, then click **Next**.

> **Note: When adding roles to either the CAS server or primary site server, there will be roles which are only available to specific ones if you are utilizing an environment with a CAS setup.**

Database replication

This comes into play when you have multiple sites. The database replication is when the parent site and child sites perform an asynchronous replication between each other to ensure that all sites are fully updated with the latest information.

Though this is autonomous, you may want to configure some administrative tasks depending on the setup of your Configuration Manager in the future.

Replication schedule

The schedule for replications is normally configured to tailor to appropriate times when the sites should replicate. By default, it will be anytime but to change the same, perform the following steps:

1. Open the Microsoft Configuration Manager Console.
2. Go to **Administration**: **Overview**: **Hierarchy and Configuration**: **Database replication**
3. Right-click either of the links and select link properties

Here, you can configure the scheduling and additional alerts whenever replication fails.

Monitoring of replication

The instructions on how to monitor the replication between the sites managed within **Microsoft Endpoint Configuration Manager (MECM)** are:

1. Open the Microsoft Configuration Manager Console
2. Go to **Monitoring**: **Overview**: **Database replication**

Here, you can see further details on replication details and use additional tools such as the replication link analyzer, to troubleshoot further.

Discovering devices

Another important administrative task is discovering devices so that your Configuration Manager environment can manage them.

There are several moving parts to this process overall. We will lay them out in an appropriate order so the reader can understand how each component plays a part in the discovery of devices.

Discovery methods

Firstly, we need to look at the discovery methods in Configuration Manager, which are responsible for finding objects within the Active Directory. As we discover devices, we will mainly look at the Active Directory system discovery, which can be found in the Administration: Hierarchy Configuration: Discovery methods area of the console. The Active Directory system discovery properties is shown in the following figure:

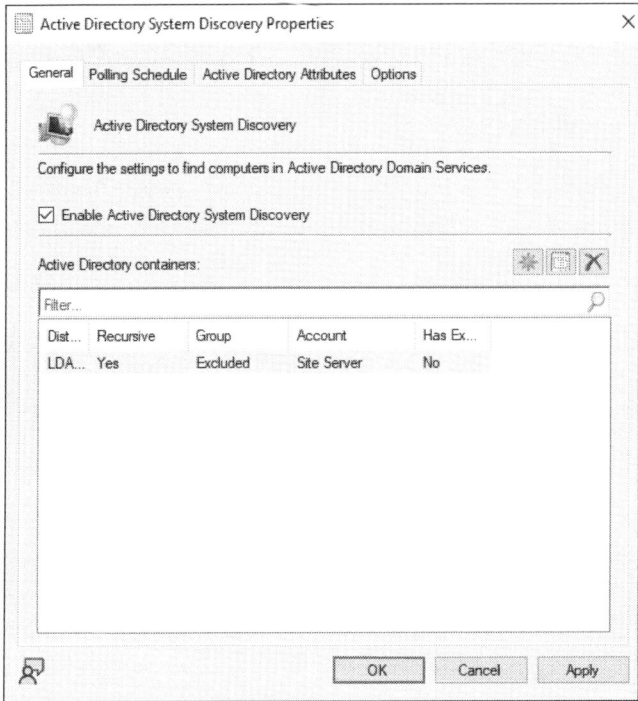

Figure 4.11: Active Directory system discover properties

Here, you can configure which Active Directory containers to target, the polling schedules, and additional attributes to synchronize for your objects. Once configured, you can right-click the discovery and perform a Run Full Discovery Now action, which will start polling Active Directory for system objects.

Client installation account

To install the actual client on the device, we need an account that has appropriate privileges to connect to the device via the network and copy the installation files onto that device. Which is controlled here. To configure the client installation account, perform the following:

1. Open the Microsoft Configuration Manager Console.
2. Go to **Administration**: **Site Configuration**: **Sites**
3. **General:** Right-click the site you want, then select **Client Installation Settings**: **Client push installation**:

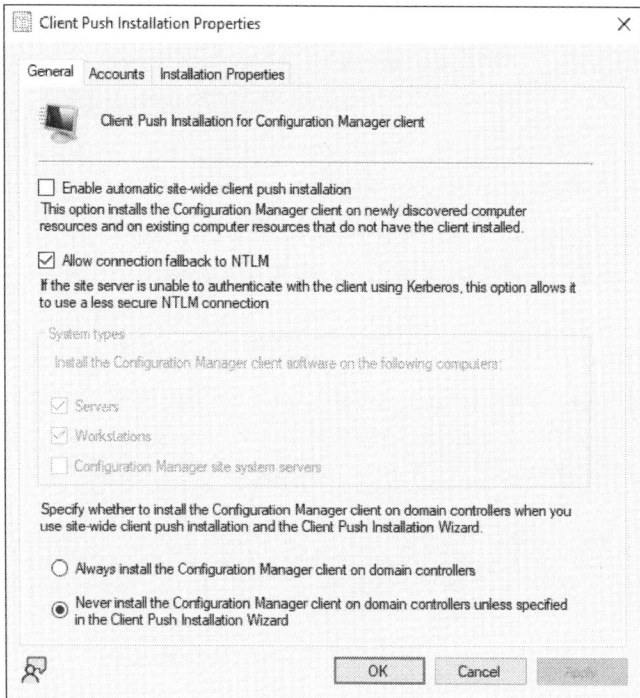

Figure 4.12: Client push installation properties dialog

4. **Accounts:** Select the account which will be used to install the agent.

5. **Installation properties:** Enter any additional properties to customize the installation of your Configuration Manager client. For a full list of additional properties, click here: **https://learn.microsoft.com/en-us/mem/configmgr/core/clients/deploy/about-client-installation-properties**

Boundary and boundary group set up

To ensure that devices get assigned to the correct sites and the site system servers attached to them, we need to formulate the creation of boundaries. To do so, perform the following steps:

1. Open the Microsoft Configuration Manager console.
2. Go to **Administration**: **Hierarchy settings**: **Boundaries**.
3. Right-click and select **Create Boundary**.

Here, you can create the boundary settings and select the type of boundary you want to create, whether that is based on an **Active Directory (AD)** site, IP range, or IP subnet. Enter a description which will help identify what the boundary is for then click **OK**.

Once this has been completed, you will need to create a boundary group which can contain one or more boundaries. This will be assigned to the appropriate site for devices to be managed by.

To setup the boundary groups, perform the following:

1. Open the Microsoft Configuration Manager console.
2. Go to **Administration**: **Hierarchy settings**: **Boundary groups**
3. Right-click and select **Create Boundary Group**
4. **General:** Enter a name for your boundary group which will help to correspond to what the group is for, and add correct boundaries to it.
5. **References**: Configure the site assignment which indicates where devices will be assigned to. If you want to add specific management and distribution points, state migration or software update points to this boundary, then you can do so. Click **OK** when ready.

Deploying agents to devices

Now, we are ready to start deploying agents to devices. This action can be done in the following ways:

- Through individual device.
- By collection.
- By hierarchy settings (will be covered later in this chapter).

For the purpose of this book, we will show you how to do this via device/collection. The steps are as follows:

1. Open the Microsoft Configuration Manager Console
2. Go to **Assets and Compliance: Overview**: **Devices**
3. Right-click a device and select **Install Agent**.
4. **Before you begin:** Installation Configuration Manager client wizard**:** Click **Next**.
5. **Installation options:** Specify client push options. Select the bottom option Install client software from a specified site, then toggle the exact site you want the device to be managed by. The other options for domain controllers are ONLY if installing a client on a **Domain Controller** (**DC,**) and the second option is more if a device already has a client installed. Click **Next**.
6. **Summary:** Confirm the settings. Click **Next** to begin the installation.

To check the progress of the client deployments you can check the `ccm.log` file located in the `Program Files\Microsoft Configuration Manager\logs\ccm.log`. This log will show the attempts to copy the client files to a device and if it was successful.

Cloud attach device management

The current branch and latest versions of Configuration Manager have introduced in the Cloud, attach feature which allows for devices managed within Configuration Manager to be uploaded into Intune, and the ability to enable co-management. We understand the process of configuring the Cloud attach feature and provide some details around co-management side.

To configure, perform the following:

1. Open the Microsoft Configuration Manager Console.
2. Go to **Administration**: **Overview**: **Cloud services**: **Cloud attach**
3. Right-click and select **Configure Cloud Attach**.
4. **Cloud attach:** Cloud attach settings. Click the **Sign In** button so you can sign into your Azure tenancy. The account you sign into will need appropriate rights to manage Azure. Click **Next** to proceed.
5. **Summary:** Confirm the settings. Review the configuration, then click **Next** to create the cloud attach feature.

This will enable devices to be uploaded into the Endpoint Manager admin center and enable endpoint analytics, as seen in *Figure 4.13* and *Figure 4.14*:

Figure 4.13: Intune Windows devices showing ConfigMgr devices

Once all applicable devices have been detected within your Configuration Manager environment, they will show in your Intune portal as managed by ConfigMgr. The device records will be able to show Configuration Manager-specific information for that device.

In addition, devices will be uploaded into the Intune endpoint analytics feature, which replaces the deprecated desktop analytics. This feature is introduced as an integrated add-on to Configuration Manager and can draw up baseline statistics on device performance, compliance, and readiness for work-anywhere scenarios.

Figure 4.14 shows the endpoint analytics scores which breakdown the baseline of all devices managed within your Intune portal:

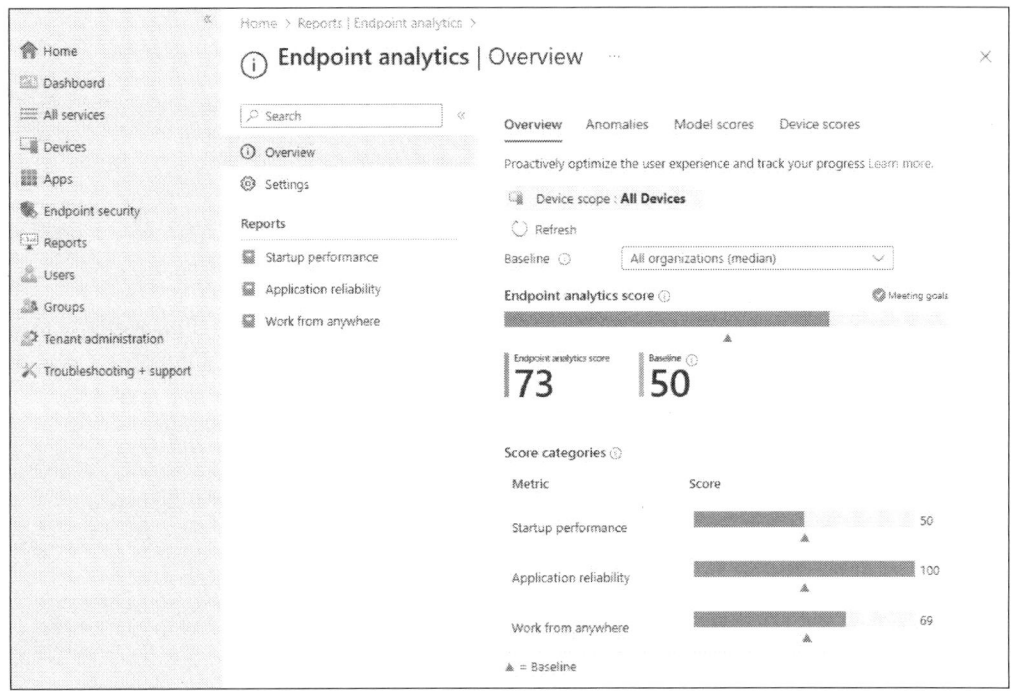

Figure 4.14: Endpoint analytics overview

> **Note:** Cloud attach also configures Co-Management to be enabled, but there are still various parts to its full configuration. To see more of this, click here:
>
> https://learn.microsoft.com/en-us/mem/configmgr/comanage/how-to-enable

Upgrade process

The process of upgrading Configuration Manager is different from entering the current branch phase. The following instructions will help you install the latest updates and hotfixes for Configuration Manager:

1. **Synchronization of latest updates**: To synchronize the latest updates, perform the following steps:

    a. Open the Microsoft Configuration Manager Console.

b. Go to **Administration**: **Overview**: **Updates and serving**.

c. Select the **Check for Updates** button. You will see a notification message stating that the updates will be synchronized. Check after a few minutes to see when they arrive.

2. **Download and install update**: Once the update has been synchronized with Configuration Manager, we can then look to download and install the update. To do so, perform the following steps:

   a. Go to **Administration**: **Overview**: **Updates and serving**.

   b. Select the update you want, right-click, and select **Download**.

   c. Check after a few minutes and the state will have changed from **Available for Download** to **Ready to Install**.

   d. Right-click and select **Install Update Pack**, as shown in *Figure 4.15*, where you can see a list of the updates synchronized and available:

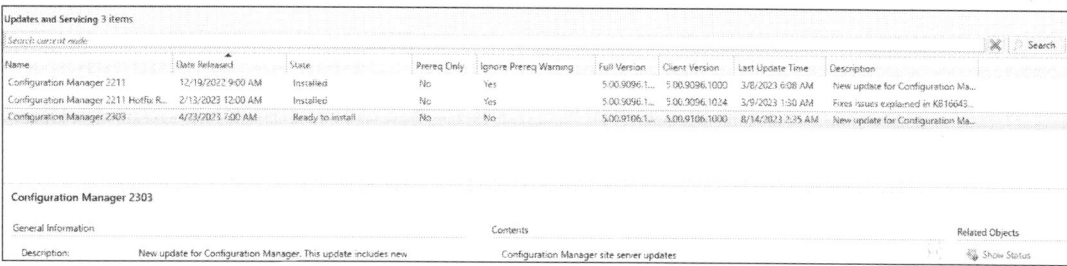

Figure 4.15: Features and updates view

   e. **General:** Configuration Manager: Click **Next**.

   f. **Features:** Features included in the update pack. Select features you want to add to your Configuration Manager then click **Next**.

   g. **Client update options:** Client update settings. Select your preferred way to test your client update package, then click **Next**.

   h. **License Terms:** Review and accept the terms for this update pack. Select **I accept these License Terms and Privacy Statement**, then click **Next**.

   i. **Cloud attach:** Cloud attach settings. If you are using Cloud, attach, keep this enabled and sign into your Azure tenant. If not, you can untick **Enable Cloud**, attach, and click **Next**.

   j. **Summary:** Confirm the settings. Click **Next** to begin the process.

At this point, the prerequisites check will commence, and you can find the progress of this through **Monitoring**: **Updates and Servicing Status part of the console**.

Once the prerequisites check is done, it will show in the console as **Prerequisites Check Completed**.

Important logs for upgrade process

The service connection point role is responsible for the upgrade process outlined. If this role is configured on the same server as the site server, then you will expect to see all of the log files in the same location as the Configuration Manager logs file.

If this role is held on another server, the logs outlined will be on that server, which you would need to browse to.

Here are the following logs which will help see the progress of an update in a verbose look:
- **CMUpdate.log**: Shows the progress of the upgrade.
- **Hman.log**: This contains the verbose information for the update progress.
- **DMPDownloader.log**: Contains the details for when the update is downloading.
- **DMPUploader.log**: Contains the details for database changes.

To view all the logs which are derived from the Service connection point role, you can find these here **https://learn.microsoft.com/en-us/mem/configmgr/core/plan-design/hierarchy/log-files**

Best practices

Best practices are recommended ways of operating, which have been proven and tested by various administrators and experts.

They are not designed to be set in stone as often different scenarios come into play. These can dictate how you design, administer, and implement Configuration Manager, which is a great transition into the real-world scenario topic that will go into later.

The best practices have been outlined and broken down by the pages within the console.

Administration

Here, we will outline best practices which can be applied for all areas within the **Administration** tab of the MECM console.

Upgrading Microsoft Configuration Manager

To ensure that you do not run out of support for your Microsoft Configuration Manager environment and are ahead of the game, make sure that you are running the latest version and that your environment is requirement-specific ready.

This means that if you are running an older version or if a new version has significant changes that will require you to upgrade your resources, OS, or hardware, then it is best to plan ahead accordingly.

Usage of the central administration site

Though this topology is not officially deprecated, it is recommended that you do not use it due to some unnecessary complications involved in managing your environment. There may be many cases where a CAS site is not actually needed, especially if you are not planning to manage more than 500,000 clients.

Since version 2002 as a feature was introduced, it gives you the option to remove the CAS from your topology.

Monitoring

Here, we will outline best practices which can be applied for all areas within the **Monitoring** tab of the MECM console.

Create custom queries

Queries, which can be seen in the Monitoring: Overview: Queries part of the console, are searches that are run against the **Windows Management Instrument (WMI)** SDK using a language called **Windows Management Instrument Query Language (WQL)**, helps retrieve desired information on demand, which can be based on things such as vast areas around device inventory.

It is good to have some of these created so that you are able to run these incase of any reporting, auditing, or general queries. These can also be used as membership rules for collections created in Configuration Manager also.

Add reporting services point

This role is handy to have, as it has hundreds of native reports which help to pull out any data from the Configuration Manager database around anything across administration, monitoring, software library and assets, and compliance-specific information. This works well in conjunction with the custom queries above when wanting to understand more information.

Software library

Here we will outline best practices which can be applied for all areas within the **Software Library** tab of the MECM console.

Non-complicated applications

When it comes to the creation of applications, the fastest and least complicated method normally resides with `.msi` extension applications as they bypass various windows concerning the deployment types.

In scenarios where you do not have applications that are already .MSI, some organizations use various tools to perform **Medium-Scale Integration (MSI)** packaging to transform executables and other file extensions into a recorded transaction that captures all system changes to an MSI file. Some may even contain MST files and additional cab files which can be added into the installation/uninstallation commands.

Maintenance Windows

Maintenance Windows is essential for when you have various deployments that could be set up to run during various times of the day, especially taking into account BAU activities that could be interrupted with reboots and different types of delays.

Ensure that you have appropriate maintenance Windows created for the correct times for any deployments to commence, and make note of where you have created them. Too many Windows can create confusion and mess if you are trying to troubleshoot why devices are not receiving any advertisements.

Assets and Compliance

Here we will outline best practices which can be applied for all areas within the Assets and Compliance tab of the MECM console.

Collection creation strategies

Whether these be user collections or device collections, it is best to have the right strategy for creating collections, in other words, ensure they are meaningful.

Collections should have an overall purpose for its criteria of why objects belong to them, for example:

- **Active Directory membership based**: Based on AD group memberships or Organizational units.
- **Deployment specific**: Based on the deployment you will be creating it for. New memberships can be added to the deployment.
- **Inventory specific**: Based on what software is installed, not installed, or if it is on a specific version.
- **Operating system specific**: Collections created by the Operating System level devices are on.
- **Testing collections**: Any form of test should contain devices that are not critical to any usage so that correct testing can be performed.

Having these types of collections defined will help the overall flow of your Microsoft Configuration Manager environment and are perfectly laid out to know exactly where devices are and their specific reasons.

Configuration baselines over software metering

Configuration baselines are objects that measure the compliance level for specific criteria on a device. Software metering is a native function within Configuration Manager that collects metrics on how software is used and how often it is used. As handy as software metering is, it is extremely resource intensive and is often recommended not to use this method. If you want to collect anything specific, it is better to use the configuration baselines as these are a lot easier and dish out resource usage more on the client device, thus allowing the data to be reported back to Configuration Manager 2222.

Real-world scenario

Real-world scenarios outline the reality of working with Configuration Manager. They essentially explain in detail the pros and cons of using certain methodologies and provide a future heads up of what to be aware of currently as well as futuristically.

Administration

Here, we will outline real-world scenarios that are applicable to the areas found within the **Administration** tab of the MECM console:

- **Upgrading Microsoft Configuration Manager**: It is important to stay fully updated. However, we also have to take into account the business constraints of a major upgrade especially if there is a drive to stay at the absolute latest versions.

  It is better to be at the version level just before the latest version. This allows the environment and business enough time to assess the steadiness of the latest release. Especially when hotfixes, rollups, and some bugs can actually be reported, which could result in the environment experiencing some downtime or hindrance to BAU operations.

Monitoring

Here we will outline real-world scenarios which are applicable to the areas found within the Monitoring tab of the MECM console:

- **Importance of SQL and PowerShell queries**: This applies to all System Centre and Microsoft Configuration Manager technologies. When it comes to the overall control and understanding of the product, it is beneficial for the administrator to be efficient in using SQL queries and PowerShell.

  The database has various views that allow you to see lots of information. vSMS_r_ system is a view that will show data on all the managed devices in Configuration Manager. As for PowerShell, there is the native PowerShell module, which can be launched from the console, as well as the SDK, which can be called using a **Get-**

`WMIObject` or `Get-CIMObject` command. The more efficient you are with these methods of queries, the better you can get out of Configuration Manager.

Software library

Here we will outline real-world scenarios which are applicable to the areas found within the **Software Library** tab of the MECM console:

- **PowerShell methodology of application/package creation:** In continuation of the application best practice, sometimes it is not possible to escape using just the `.MSI` applications, but there are various ways to consolidate multiple installation commands, files, and other configurations that are part of more complicated packaging.

  This is where it is better to use a specialized tool such as *PSAppDeploy*, where you can utilize a mechanism that can install, uninstall, and repair applications all from a Powershell workflow, allowing you to configure the entire experience end to end. It is imperative to test the installation or uninstallation on a test device before packaging, as well as testing the deployment through Configuration Manager so you can get two different results from outside and inside Configuration Manager.

Assets and Compliance

Here we will outline real-world scenarios which are applicable to the areas found within the Assets and Compliance tab of the MECM console:

- **Unknown computer/required task sequence deployment**: This is used as the norm in a lot of environments, but it also bears the highest risk of things going wrong. Unknown computer support essentially allows for any device connected to the network to possess the capability of PXE booting to rebuild the machine.

  Of course, with the right structuring and processes in place, this does not have to be an issue, but a slip in deploying a task sequence as required could spell total disaster. It is even worse if the task sequence has been chosen to be applicable to all managed devices as well as PXE.

  Best practice would perhaps suggest that devices be pre-staged, where they are imported into Configuration Manager so they are recognized beforehand, as opposed to making them available for any machine on the network, but in real-world scenarios, this is not the case.

The same applies to deploying required task sequences and why it is important to not push anything to top-level collections, such as:

- All systems
- All desktop and server clients
- All users

Or any collection that includes business critical servers or anything that is not controlled membership based.

Conclusion

The Configuration Manager can be configured with various topologies. Therefore, it is important to outline all possible methods for setting up and installing different types of site servers.

In addition, when it comes to the overall administration of Configuration Manager various materials cover every administrative task in great detail throughout various versions. We evidently want to highlight some of those core actions and focus on administrative tasks that have been newly introduced into the later versions of the current branch as well.

When managing Configuration Manager, it is important to consider the best practices and real-world scenarios. They both provide a balance of recommendations to be aware of, where the real-world scenarios can differ from best practices and outline how Configuration Manager can be commonly used.

In the next chapter, we will focus on the first product of the System Centre suite which will be the Operations Manager where we will look to cover the design approach and whole structure of how Operations Manager is used to monitor your environment.

Points to remember

- Windows ADK prerequisite comes in two parts which have to be configured correctly to utilize the management of the latest Windows versions utilizing Operating System deployment.
- CAS will use primary sites such as child sites and primary stand-alone sites and take secondary sites as child sites.
- Site System statuses focus on health per each server that holds a site system server role.
- Component statuses focus on the health of each role and outline the server to which the component belongs.
- Cloud attach allows for Configuration Manager devices to be uploaded to Intune for additional management.
- Downloading the latest updates requires an active internet connection.
- Review the best practices and real-world scenarios to understand how to run your Configuration Manager efficiently.

Multiple choice questions

1. What is the name of the site server which can be added to primary site servers as a child site?

    a. Secondary site server

    b. Primary site server

    c. Central Administration Site server

    d. All of the above

2. What is the name of the process the Configuration Manager upgrade goes through before it proceeds with the actual upgrade?

    a. . Pingb

    b. Readiness checker

    c. Content replication

    d. Prerequisites checker

3. How do we extend the schema for Active Directory so that we have permissions to publish to Active Directory?

    a. Run extadsch then create container in ADSI.

    b. Create container in ADSI, then run extadsch.

    c. Install Microsoft Configuration Manager, then create container in ADSI.

    d. Open Active Directory Users and Computers, then create container.

4. What is the name of the prerequisite required to be able to use Operating System deployment functionalities in Configuration Manager?

    a. RDS

    b. OOBE

    c. Windows PE

    d. Windows ADK

5. How do the devices know where to be assigned to a specific site in Configuration Manager?

    a. Site code

    b. Discovery Methods

    c. Boundaries

    d. Distribution Point

6. In a real-world scenario, what is the best advice for upgrading Configuration Manager?

   a. Upgrade to the latest available version.

   b. Upgrade when the servers crash.

   c. Wait until your support date is expired.

   d. Upgrade to the version just before the latest version.

Answers

1. a
2. d
3. a
4. d
5. c
6. d

Key terms

- **Distribution content**: This represents the content within Configuration Manager that has been added to a distribution point where software library content is stored and can be distributed to managed devices.
- **WQL**: Known as the Windows Management Instrument Query Language recognized in Configuration Manager as the language used to query the WMI SDK.
- **EULA**: End User License Agreement, which is to be assigned before moving on to use any software.
- **Cloud attach**: Cloud attach is the functionality that allows for Configuration manager devices to be uploaded to Endpoint Manager.
- **Microsoft Endpoint Manager**: Another term for the Intune portal.

Join our book's Discord space

Join the book's Discord Workspace for Latest updates, Offers, Tech happenings around the world, New Release and Sessions with the Authors:

https://discord.bpbonline.com

CHAPTER 5
Monitoring Infrastructure with System Center Operations Manager

Introduction

In this chapter, we will look into the planning and design for the **System Center Operations Manager (SCOM)**. This area will be applicable for most versions of this technology as the same key areas have to be taken into consideration especially when looking into how the solution will be used. Scalability is also a key area we will want to analyze when planning a new design, but we will also discover the upgrade paths that would need to be taken in order to be applicable for System Center 2022. For the Operations Manager, we will look into all scenarios we may encounter, whether it is a straightforward single-domain design or if it includes a workgroup or **Demilitarized Zone (DMZ)** focus.

There is also included a minimum and recommended requirement level at which the reader can develop a lab environment, which they can use to follow through with the next chapter, so you can gauge a practical as well as a theoretical understanding.

Structure

This chapter will cover the following topics:

- Operations Manager topology structure

- Planning for monitoring
- Multihoming
- Azure Monitor
- Operations Manager lab requirements

Objectives

The objective of this chapter is to provide the reader with an understanding of all the roles available within the Operations Manager and provide their description and the part each of them will play. This will help the reader or administrator understand what components are required to carry out the perfect design for their monitoring solution.

In conjunction, the reader will also understand the impact and changes between legacy versions and the latest features in which 2022 carries along for the Operations Manager. Typical areas around requirements and specifications will change to adapt to the latest Operating System releases and provide a structure that will allow the readers or administrator to construct a lab worthy of further testing with a view for possible production development going forward.

Operations Manager topology structure

SCOM has a few topology structures that cover common areas such as internal monitoring within your domain, external monitoring from DMZ zones, and Cloud-based monitoring.

We will discuss the different types of structures that the Operations Manager has. First, we will cover all the roles that the Operations Manager has, providing more context for how these apply to the outlined topologies given within the topic.

Operations Manager roles

To understand the structure of the Operations Manager, we must first look into all the roles which can be used and the roles they play within the Operations Manager:

- **Management server**: A management server is the focal point for any agent-managed device in SCOM. It is important to note that the first management server will always contain a core function called **Root ManagementSserver** (**RMS**). It works by being the main functionality controller regarding the addition of different server roles, however, this is the name it was referred to in older versions of SCOM.

  With the latest version of SCOM, the RMS function is embedded and referred to as an RMS emulator, which can be moved to different SCOM management servers when required.

From the initial build of a management server, it will create the following logical objects:

- **Resource pool**: A resource pool is a logical container that groups management servers together to provide a load-balanced functionality. By default, there is an all-server resource pool that contains all management servers. Additional ones can be created where required.
- **Management group**: A management group is somewhat similar to how Configuration Manager uses a site code where it is an identification to link a managed agent to the correct management server or servers that are part of the management group to provide the correct monitoring solution.

- **Reporting server**: The reporting server is a role that enables the SCOM environment the ability to run reports against the management servers to pull off monitoring inventory from managed devices.

  On initial installation of any reporting server role, it will follow native reports from the default management packs that come along with SCOM. Different management packs installed in Operations Manager may contain their own types of native reporting which we will explore further in this chapter.

- **Gateway server**: Gateway servers essentially sit within areas where your domain or network might not necessarily have access or authentication, whether that be Active Directory or Kerberos-based.

  The gateway servers then relate to a management server which reports its health status and acknowledges it as another management server where agents can be assigned.

Note: Essentially, management servers can manage devices within a DMZ without the need of a gateway Server, but we will explore further why this is not recommended.

- **Web console server**: The web console server is a web version of the Operations Manager console that is accessible via the IIS website on the preferred server where it will be installed. The web console is not 100% reflective of the Operations Manager **Graphical User Interface** (**GUI**) console but of a web-based alternative.

  The older version of the web console used to have a dependency on Silverlight but as it has retired, the latest SCOM version are based on full HTML5.

- **Audit Collection Services (ACS)**: The ACS role forwards security audit events that come from the Windows event log for the Operations Manager to process and collect. This, in turn, can be viewed within the SCOM console so that it can be viewed within the monitoring workflow.

  The role is primarily installed on the management server, and has a dependency on another component for this feature, the ACS forwarded, where the ACS server collects the security audit events from.

Single management topology

A single management server is the simplest structure. Within a single environment in SCOM, there is a logical group container referred as a management group. This management group contains the connection information for an agent to be monitored by that specific SCOM infrastructure.

A single management topology is always going to be considered as the initial setup or foundation of any structure in which you may look to expand on when considering the scalability for your monitoring solution. Once this has been deployed, additional management servers can be added anytime, which would then involve into a multi-management topology scenario.

> Note: More than one management group can be connected to a management server, however, additional management groups require an additional management server and operational database to manage the group from the console.

Multi management topology

Multiple management servers help to provide a load-balanced support for your monitoring solution. These can be grouped within a logical container called a resource pool.

An advantage of having multiple management servers is that the load-balance of SCOM managed agents can be assigned to different management servers which is important depending on the design of your architecture.

Untrusted domain and Demilitarized Zone topology

This structure is more complicated due to its dependency on a **Public Key Infrastructure (PKI)** infrastructure required to properly introduce certificate-based authentication.

Multiple management servers are recommended if you are considering this, as these will be the focal points for different server roles called gateway servers.

> Note: For gateway servers you need a management point which will be its parent. There is no minimum requirement of needing more than one management server, but really to avoid having a single point of failure.

Planning for monitoring

Planning for monitoring is a tasking exercise, as you will need to consider not just the native features of Operations Manager also the additional third-party and custom requirements as well.

The following topic will look to work through all the areas that make up the planning for monitoring design so that the reader will understand the categories involved to ensure that you design and implement the correct monitoring solution.

Hardware requirements

We have broken down different types of topologies that can be implemented by the Operations Manager, explaining all the server roles involved in making them.

The best way to understand decision-making is to outline the minimum and recommended requirements that will allow you to understand the better fitting solution.

Table 5.1 outlines the hardware minimum requirements that all of the Operations Manager roles require:

Operations Manager role	CPU (Cores)	CPU (GHz)	Memory (GB)	Disk space (GB)
Management server	4	2.66	8	10
Gateway server (Windows)	4	2.66	8	10
Gateway server (Network Device)	8	2.66	32	10
Gateway server (Unix Devices)	4	2.66	4	10
Web console server	4	2.66	8	10
Reporting server	4	2.66	8	10

Table 5.1: Operations Manager hardware requirements

Operating System requirements

Table 5.2 represents the Operating System levels that should be used for Operations Manager 2022.

The last columns indicate whether the roles specified can be run on a desktop experience GUI Windows Server Operating System or if they can be run on the Windows Server Core versions which have no GUI:

Operations Manager role	Windows Server version	Windows Server edition	Windows Server GUI	Windows Server Core
Management Server	2019/2022	Standard/Datacenter	Yes	Yes
Gateway Server	2019/2022	Standard/Datacenter	Yes	Yes
Web Console	2019/2022	Standard/Datacenter	Yes	No
ACS	2019/2022	Standard/Datacenter	Yes	No

Operations Manager role	Windows Server version	Windows Server edition	Windows Server GUI	Windows Server Core
Reporting Server	2019/2022	Standard/Datacenter	Yes	No

Table 5.2: Operations Manager Operating System requirements

Structured Query Language Server requirements

Table 5.3 shows the **Structured Query Language (SQL)** server versions that are applicable for the Operations Manager to hold both the Operations Manager and Datawarehouse Databases:

SQL Version	SQL cumulative update (Minimum)
SQL Server 2022: Standard/Enterprise	
SQL Server 2019: Standard/Enterprise	CU8
SQL Server 2017: Standard/Enterprise	Latest

Table 5.3: Operations Manager SQL Server requirements table

> Note: As of writing this book the latest cumulative update for SQL Server 2017 is CU31, which can be found here: Download Microsoft® SQL Server® 2017 Latest C   https://www.microsoft.com/en-US/download/details.aspx?id=56128umulative Update from Official Microsoft Download Center

Operations Manager limitations

Table 5.4 summarizes the view of the maximum levels in which the Operations Manager can manage in terms of monitored objects.

To see the full list, you can visit the following link: **https://learn.microsoft.com/en-us/system-center/scom/system-requirements?view=sc-om-2022#capacity-limits-for-operations-manager.**

The following table provides a list of Operations Manager limitations:

Limitation item	Value
Maximum agents managed by Management server (Windows)	3000
Maximum agents managed by gateway server (Windows)	2000
Maximum agents managed by Management server (Windows)	1000
Maximum agents managed by gateway server (Windows)	200

Limitation item	Value
Network Devices between two resource pools	2000
Network Devices by one resource pool with three or more management servers	1000

Table 5.4: Operations Manager limitations table

Management packs

The management pack side of monitoring planning is slightly more complicated as we need to understand our options from the beginning.

First, let us look at the default management packs that come along with Operations Manager 2022. These are primarily around platforms like Windows and UNIX/Linux and all default management packs that make for the Operations Manager monitoring. You can view the full list on the following link: **https://learn.microsoft.com/en-us/system-center/scom/manage-mp-installed-during-seutp?view=sc-om-2022**

After this point, we then need to capture the following information:

- Operating System monitoring
- Applications to monitor
- Critical business services
- Company URL health state
- SQL database monitoring

These are some common and core examples of points to consider accommodating management pack strategy.

There are a few methods in how this can be achieved.

Microsoft management packs

There are official management packs made available from Microsoft that will be applicable to most core Windows products such as:

- Windows Server Operating System
- Microsoft SQL Server
- System Center products (Service Manager, Orchestrator, Virtual Machine Manager, Data Protection Manager).

These management packs already contain a comprehensive number of monitors and rules, which will accommodate all the core components so that they can be fully monitored. It is as simple as importing them into the Operations Manager console, which we will cover further in the next chapter.

Another example of how the official Microsoft management packs are fully ready to use is looking into the SQL Management pack. The latest version would be able to break down the categorized components in the following ways:

- SQL Server version
- SQL Server database
- SQL Server database engine
- SQL Server instance
- SQL Server always on

The preceding categories would be defined as **classes** carrying their own attributes to identify the discovered inventoried data. They, in turn, would also contain various monitors and rules applied to each class to define the health status.

> **Note:** By default, the Operations Manager 2022 has a management pack for recognizing Windows servers and Windows clients but requires an additional management pack be able to fully monitor the Operating Systems:

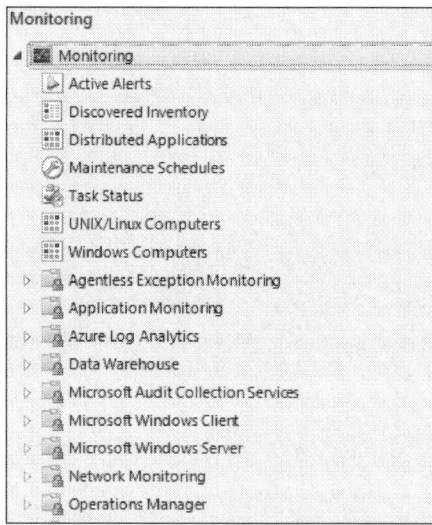

Figure 5.1: Operations Manager management pack in monitoring tab view

Third-party management packs

Third-party management packs are officially built management packs but specifically from third-party vendors that developed them other than Microsoft.

These management packs are aimed specifically at technologies or hardware components that are not Microsoft-specific and can be aimed at technologies such as *VMWare*, *HP*, and *Dell*, to name a few. These management packs can either be made available directly with the vendor or by an organization that makes third-party management packs.

Another fundamental difference between these and the *Microsoft* packs is the additional costs that require the purchase of a license to use the product. These can be based on various license models, such as on a perpetual basis, per year or even based on the hardware resources of the servers which you are using.

Community-based management packs

Community-based management packs are developed by various members of the IT community. These types of management packs are inspired by community demands for which management packs might not exist in the form of Microsoft official releases or are not available from third-party vendors.

It is not uncommon for these management packs to come unsealed, which means that the management pack can be edited freely with either native OS applications, such as Notepad, or using additional tools to edit XML files.

In some cases, community management packs and management packs from Microsoft/Third-parties are generally sealed, which means that the management packs cannot be edited as they are sealed with an encryption key to keep the **Extensible Markup Language (XML)** configuration locked, as shown in the following figure:

Name	Version	Sealed
Data Warehouse Internal Library	10.22.10118.0	Yes
Data Warehouse Library	10.22.10118.0	Yes
Default Management Pack	10.22.10118.0	
Distributed Application Designer Library	7.0.8447.6	Yes
Health Internal Library	7.0.8447.6	Yes
Health Library	7.0.8447.6	Yes
Image Library (System Center)	10.22.10118.0	Yes
Image Library (System)	7.5.8501.1	Yes
Image Library (UNIX/Linux)	10.22.1019.0	Yes
Image Library (Windows)	7.5.8501.1	Yes
Instance Group Library	7.5.8501.1	Yes
Microsoft Audit Collection Services	10.22.10118.0	Yes
Microsoft Change Tracking Report Library	10.22.10118.0	Yes
Microsoft Data Warehouse Reports	10.22.10118.0	Yes
Microsoft Generic Report Library	10.22.10118.0	Yes
Microsoft Service Level Report Library	10.22.10118.0	Yes
Microsoft System Center Advisor	10.22.10118.0	Yes
Microsoft System Center Advisor Internal	10.22.10118.0	Yes
Microsoft System Center Advisor Resources (ENU)	10.22.10118.0	Yes
Microsoft System Center Application Monitoring 360 SLA	1.0.0.0	
Microsoft System Center Application Monitoring 360 Template Library	10.22.10118.0	Yes
Microsoft System Center Operations Manager Library	10.22.10118.0	Yes
Microsoft System Center Visualization Network Library	10.22.10118.0	Yes
Microsoft SystemCenter OperationsManager Summary Dashboard	10.22.10118.0	Yes

Figure 5.2: Installed management pack list in Operations Manager console

Management pack authoring: Operations Manager console

The next alternative where the monitoring that you require does not exist in any form of an existing management pack is the authoring of a management pack by the administrator.

The most convenient way is to develop one from the Operations Manager console where you can have an authoring tab in the console allowing you to create some common components within a management pack such as:

- Monitors
- Rules
- Attributes (Classes)
- Discoveries
- Tasks

There are also additional components you can create that are slightly more specific. They are labeled as Management pack templates where you can create object-specific monitoring such as **Transmission Control Protocol (TCP)** Ports, Services, UNIX/Linux log files, SQL databases, and web application monitoring.

Management pack authoring is quite handy when you have bespoke monitoring that is only specific to your environment and does not exist in an existing management pack.

However, you will need to consider the drawbacks of developing a management pack in this way, as there might be a need to create something slightly more complex where some options are not available to you. This is where the next section will be handy for more advanced administrators of Operations Manager.

Management pack authoring and Visual Studio VSAE

In addition to Management pack authoring, a more complex way is utilizing Visual Studios to create management packs. An additional add-on tool called **Visual Studio Authoring Extensions (VSAE)** is required to develop management packs with Visual Studio.

This add-on allows Visual Studio to create management packs for both Operations Manager and Service Manager. The VSAE add-on is version specific and should be the same as the Visual Studio version which you are running.

At the time of writing this book, Visual Studio 2022 was the latest version. Therefore, you would need to install the VSAE 2022 add-on, which would provide you with the ability to create Operations Manager and Service Manager management packs to the 2022 versions of the respective products.

Authoring management packs here is primarily done in XML format and this is where the complexity comes in. You would need to understand not just the XML language but also the components you are looking to create. You are, of course, given component examples that show the administrator how the format looks so you can follow and edit accordingly.

Figure 5.3 is an example of a management pack fragment for creating a new class in Visual Studio:

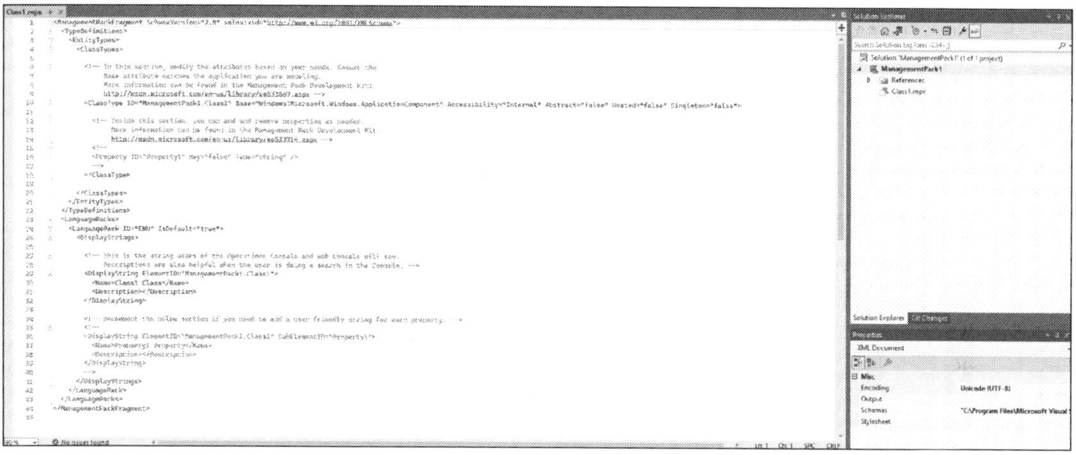

Figure 5.3: Visual Studio class component for management pack

When looking to construct discoveries within Visual Studio, they will be in the form of a template, which we can see in *Figure 5.4*, which shows a grouping of discoveries within one file:

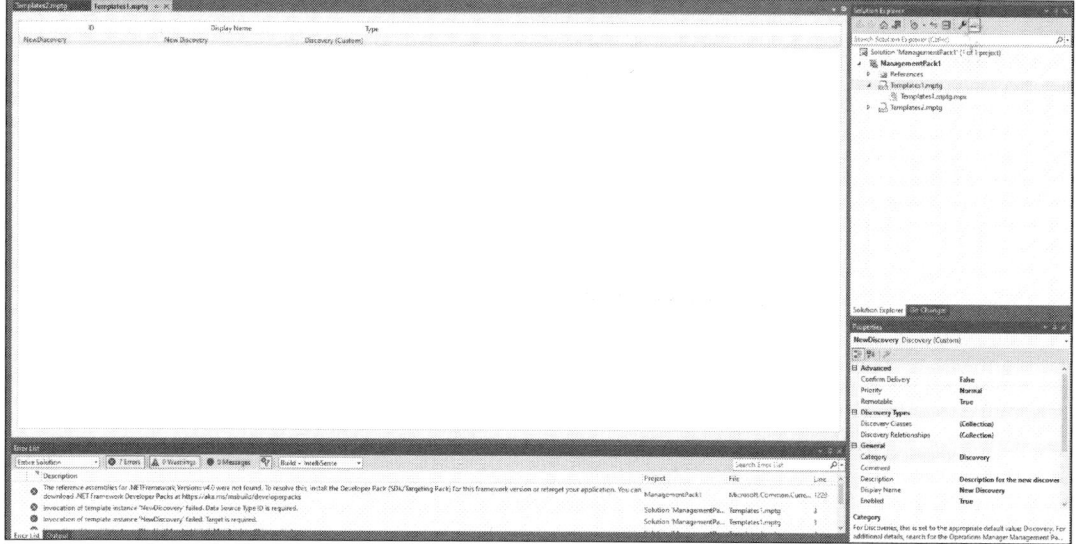

Figure 5.4: Visual Studio discovery component for the management pack

The same format is also used for monitor components which can be seen within *Figure 5.5* displaying a similar format:

Figure 5.5: Visual Studio discovery component for the management pack

> **Note:** There are third-party products which can perform management pack authoring that removes the complexity of developing management packs in Visual Studio. However, it is recommended to understand how it looks and reads in XML first to have a foundational understanding of how management packs are constructed.

Run-As accounts

Run-As accounts play an interesting role when it comes to the right permissions to use to appropriately operate Operations Manager and its aid in discovering and monitoring objects correctly with the management packs.

To break this down further, there are two parts to this, which are as follows:

- Run-As profile
- Run-As account

The Run-As profiles are profiles that hold the Run-As accounts. Run-As profiles are normally attached to components within management packs, which require a profile that would, in turn, hold a Run-As account or accounts that have the correct permissions to discover the objects.

For example, let us take the SQL Management pack. Typically, they have at least two Run-As profiles, one for discovery and one for monitoring. This means that one profile is dedicated to utilizing Run-As accounts that have enough permissions to discover SQL

Server components, while the monitoring Run-As profile utilizes Run-As accounts that have enough permissions to monitor SQL Server components. It could be that one account does both, but this depends on the structure you have.

The Run-As account, on the other hand, is the credentials that make up the account that will be used in a Run-As profile. The credentials can be as following:

- Windows
- UNIX/Linux
- Simple password
- **Simple Mail Transport Protocol (SMTP)**

These are various types of credentials that can be used to create your Run-As account, and then these credentials can be distributed to specific servers which will utilize them or can be distributed to all.

The main Run-As account is known as the action account which is used to perform all default actions for Operations Manager. By default, it can be the system account, but depending on how you install Operations Manager, you can define whether this be a local-based or domain-based account.

Override strategy

Overrides are more of an action that involves changing the configuration of components within management packs where you can decide if they should be enabled, disabled or run in a different way.

In the case of planning for monitoring you should have an understanding about all technologies and software your environment is responsible for and see if the default configurations of the management pack monitors and rules fit in well with your environment.

For example, let us say your Windows Servers are known for having disk drives with a small amount of space and this is perhaps a regular occurrence which is driven by whichever roles they play within your environment. If you were to import the Windows Server Operating System management pack, to define your own monitor or rule what would report on low space, you have to take into account the warning thresholds and critical thresholds.

Warning threshold may typically set a default of 10% free space of the drive remaining while critical may typically be set at a default of 5% free space remaining. This would create a ton of alerts (also known as an alert storm) and could cause chaos for monitoring administrators. If you are using an integration with a ticketing system this could also cause a domino effect of ticket storms.

So, within your monitoring plans, you need to understand the impact of the default monitoring configurations and, where appropriate, develop the strategy of making the correct overrides to work alongside your monitoring solution supporting your architecture as a whole.

Microsoft 365 and Microsoft Azure monitoring

Most organizations may utilize the Cloud services within Azure and have an existing tenancy. One native feature within Operations Manager 2022 is possessing the ability to link your Microsoft 365 subscription or your Microsoft Azure tenancy to Operations Manager you are able to include the Cloud resources into your monitoring solution.

You will, of course, need existing subscriptions to configure the monitoring integration.

Data retention

Data retention is more specific towards the data warehouse functionalities of the Operations Manager, and is perhaps the most overlooked area of monitoring planning.

To provide an overview, data retention is how long current and historical data is kept. This is an important piece to account for.

First, let us look into the operational database of Operations Manager that looks after everyday activities. There is a retention configuration that must be considered here. So let us take a look at the following objects that are accounted for:

- Resolved alerts
- Event data
- Performance data
- Task history
- Monitoring job data
- State change events data
- Performance signature
- Maintenance mode history
- Availability history

The preceding list represents all types of records that the Operations Manager database has where the settings for grooming activities need to be changed. Not all types of records may be required to be kept for long periods of time, so assessing which types are more important will help the data retention planning going forward by adjusting the number of days you want to hold onto

The other side of data retention is data warehouse activities, which have a much bigger historical data storage procedure. The grooming configuration is perhaps more complex than the Operations Manager database where retention configurations can go into several months up to several years and are typically configured by utilizing SQL queries to adjust the time frames for which data is kept.

To see a full list of the data retention categories for the data warehouse, refer to the following link: **https://learn.microsoft.com/en-us/system-center/scom/manage-omdwdb-grooming-settings?view=sc-om-2022**

> Note: In older versions of Operations Manager, a tool was available which can be used to configure the grooming settings for the data warehouse called the DWDataRP tool which would perform the SQL actions to change the retention periods.

Multihoming

Multi homing is a process where you have more than one Operations Manager environment, and both environments essentially monitor each other.

This type of structure can be beneficial when you want to split-up monitoring roles between both environments. In some cases, it is also used as a form of disaster recovery.

There are many scenarios we can explore here, but for the purposes of monitoring planning we need to understand more about what we want to know and understand before proceeding down this route.

Justification for multihoming

When it comes to planning the monitoring, we first need to understand if we actually require multihoming.

There are normally two scenarios in which multihoming can be useful which we touched in in the overview. They are as follows:

- Security
- Disaster recovery

The security side of it could be more than segregating multiple environments where the monitoring requirements are different. For example, if you want to split the responsibility of a type of monitoring then you may want to consider scenarios which splits out the management groups for specific monitoring purposes, such as:

- **Management Group 1**: Monitoring for Active Directory
- **Management Group 2:** Monitoring for SQL Servers
- **Management Group 3:** Monitoring for Azure

This structure would then split out the monitoring responsibilities, therefore avoiding a single point of failure if anything were to happen with any of the management servers in the resource pools that belong to the management groups.

Another side to security is splitting out the types of environments, which may follow a process. These environments are:

- Development environment
- Pre-production environment

In this type of structure, you can have management packs that can be tested on specific machines depending on the management group to which the agent is connected.

On the disaster recovery side of the spectrum, use the same type of structure for both management groups to replicate configurations for monitoring. This offers support if one environment goes down. The agent would essentially switch to another management group where the monitoring can continue.

Disaster recovery versus multihoming configuration

There are some differences between more traditional ways of performing a disaster recovery or high availability configuration and using multihoming to achieve this.

In Operations Manager, one form of disaster recovery/high availability would come from the resource pools, which can load balance between multiple management servers. On the other side, agents can have a primary management server and a secondary management server which acts as an active/passive type of parenting configuration.

So, if the primary management server were to be unavailable, then the assigned secondary management server would step in, and this would be within the same management group.

For multihoming, there are two separate Operations Manager environments where the management group entries are configured within the SCOM agent, therefore, two separate environments monitor that particular agent. In cases where both environments do not share a replicated setup, if one environment goes down, while it may still be monitored, there could be a gap in specific monitoring that could be missing. Since both environments would contain their own data warehouse the missing historical data also becomes a factor.

Azure Monitor

Azure Monitor is a solution that allows you to create monitors for your Azure environment. There are various areas of Azure Monitor to consider which we will go into to contribute to the planning of your overall monitoring solution.

Areas which can be monitored involve the following:

- Applications
- Virtual machines
- Guest Operating Systems
- Databases

System Center Operations Manager Managed Instance planning

For SCOM **Managed Instance (MI)** planning you need to consider the following:

- **Overview and prerequisites:** SCOM MI is a Cloud version of Operations Manager that allows you to have a SCOM instance within Azure. With this method of using Operations Manager, you can also look into the migration of your on-premise setup and transition everything into the Azure instance.

  In order for you to do so, you need an existing Azure infrastructure that will accommodate this and will include, but is not limited to, the following:
  - Entra ID
  - Azure resource groups
  - Azure networking
  - Azure SQL database (Operations Manager and DW databases)

  To expand further on Azure Networking, if you want to utilize a multihoming scenario or a connection between both on-premise and SCOM MI, then the networking for your Azure environment may desire a hybrid connection or **Virtual Private Network (VPN)** gateway, which would ensure that both the on-premise and SCOM environment will see the SCOM MI environment.

  In addition to looking at a summarized requirement of SCOM MI we also need to assess justifications for it being more beneficial to have a Cloud-based SCOM as opposed to an on-premise-based SCOM.

- **Cost factors**: If you are utilizing an environment that already contains enough resources, physical or virtual, then the most cost-effective way will be to have an on-premise environment.

  When it comes to using any form of an Azure-based environment then moving from a scenario that would endure no cost to a monthly cost is an important point to consider In the case of SCOM MI resources, which would utilize the most in pricing, would be around the Azure SQL databases in control of both SCOM databases (Operational DB and Data warehouse DB) and the Azure networking depending on the requirements you are looking at moving forward.

  To have a better understanding on what the price reflection would be, you can use the Azure pricing calculator here: https://azure.microsoft.com/en-au/pricing/calculator/?&ef_id=_k_EAIaIQobChMIxO72joisgQMVBkJBAh1EtwuyEAAYASACEgL3nvD_BwE_k_&OCID=AIDcmmiouhop3i_SEM__k_EAIaIQobChMIxO72joisgQMVBkJBAh1EtwuyEAAYASACEgL3nvD_BwE_k_&gad=1&gclid=EAIaIQobChMIxO72joisgQMVBkJBAh1EtwuyEAAYASACEgL3nvD_BwE

Log Analytics planning

Log Analytics is another Azure-based solution that allows you to obtain information by using workbooks that monitor query and inventory information from your Azure estate.

The language used within workbooks is known as **Kusto Query Language** (**KQL**). The idea behind this language is somewhat similar to the SQL language but the syntax is different. They work in a similar way, as they involve creating queries that you can run against objects to pull information from.

Planning consideration comes into play around the involvement of your on-premise managed agents and if you want to add this into your Log Analytics.

Integration with Operations Manager

You can expand the Azure Monitor into Operations Manager to have a single pane of glass for all your monitoring from on-premise and Azure.

You can register the Log Analytics and use this feature to collect the machine data from all your SCOM managed agents, as shown in the following figure:

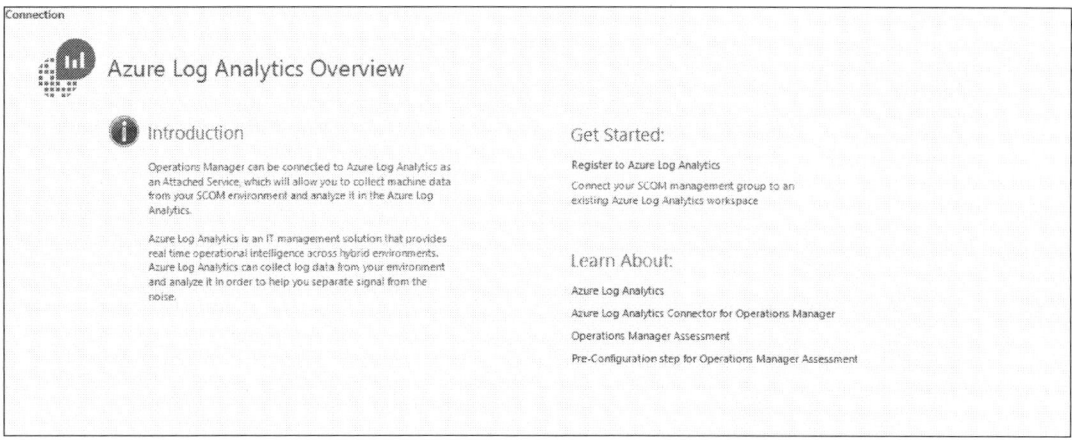

Figure 5.6: Azure Log Analytics Overview page in Operations Manager console

In addition to further integration with Log Analytics, the managed agents themselves can have the Log Analytics workspaces added to the agent configurations, as shown in the following figure:

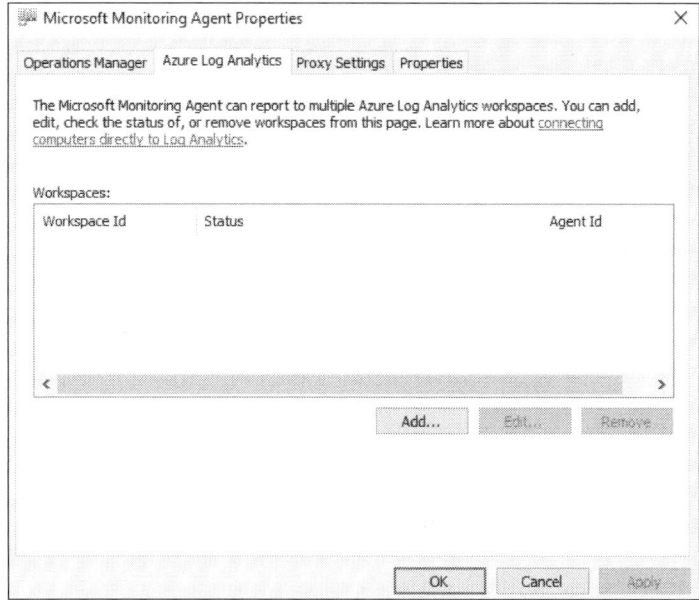

Figure 5.7: Operations Manager agent Azure Log Analytics tab

Operations Manager lab requirements

For the purpose of this book, the readers should understand the requirement levels for a lab, which will help them fully understand how the Operations Manager can work in different types of scenarios.

Here, we will outline the lab requirements for multiple scenarios. The first is the main structure to use as this will be seen as its foundational initial setup.

Single management server lab

With the most simplistic topology, it is useful for a quick deployment and understanding of how SCOM works.

The specifications listed are not necessarily specific in terms of suggestions for consolidated deployments where all roles fit on one server; they can either be split on different servers or have a consolidated deployment. The specifications detailed in the following table breaks down each role with its hardware and Operating System requirements:

Operations Manager role	CPU (Cores)	CPU (GHz)	Memory (GB)	Disk space (GB)	Operating System
Management server	4	2.66	8	10	Windows Server 2019/2022
Web console server	4	2.66	8	10	Windows Server 2019/2022
Reporting server	4	2.66	8	10	Windows Server 2019/2022

Table 5.5: Operations Manager agent Azure Log Analytics tab

Multi-management server lab

The next table shows how specifications would look when we have more than one management server within our lab. This is a great way of understanding resource groups and load-balancing between them when more are introduced.

This is traditionally the next step after deploying the first topology for a single management server for your solution. The following table shows the specifications:

Operations Manager role	CPU (Cores)	CPU (GHz)	Memory (GB)	Disk space (GB)	Operating System
Management server	4	2.66	8	10	Windows Server 2019/2022
Management server	4	2.66	8	10	Windows Server 2019/2022
Web console server	4	2.66	8	10	Windows Server 2019/2022
Reporting server	4	2.66	8	10	Windows Server 2019/2022

Table 5.6: Operations Manager agent Azure Log Analytics tab

Demilitarized Zone server lab

With this lab setup, it will be another step or extension of your monitoring solution if you want to explore how the gateway server contributes to your environment.

The gateway server requirements detailed in the following table is not specific to the platform of objects that you are looking to monitor. These can be for Windows, UNIX/Linux or network devices.

We have included an additional management server within this lab. This is optional but can widen the perspective for the reader or administrator to understand how the scalability progresses when we want to implement a solution that will help accommodate a DMZ type of scenario:

Operations Manager role	CPU (Cores)	CPU (GHz)	Memory (GB)	Disk space (GB)	Operating System
Management server	4	2.66	8	10	Windows Server 2019/2022
Management server	4	2.66	8	10	Windows Server 2019/2022
Gateway server	4	2.66	8	10	Windows Server 2019/2022
Web console server	4	2.66	8	10	Windows Server 2019/2022
Reporting server	4	2.66	8	10	Windows Server 2019/2022

Table 5.7: Operations Manager agent Azure Log Analytics tab

Multihoming server lab

For this type of structure, the following requirements would be looked at to duplicate for two labs. This would follow the following requirements; this way, the multihoming configuration can proceed.

The number of management servers can be by discretion:

Operations Manager role	CPU (Cores)	CPU (GHz)	Memory (GB)	Disk space (GB)	Operating System
Management server	4	2.66	8	10	Windows Server 2019/2022
Management server	4	2.66	8	10	Windows Server 2019/2022
Web console server	4	2.66	8	10	Windows Server 2019/2022
Reporting server	4	2.66	8	10	Windows Server 2019/2022

Table 5.8: Operations Manager agent Azure Log Analytics tab

Conclusion

The Operations Manager has evolved throughout the changes being brought in 2022. This has enabled it to reach scalability across the Cloud via Azure services, therefore showcasing the reader not just foundational understanding and requirements, but also the benefits of the Cloud scalable features.

Monitoring planning solutions is more complicated than people may realize due to the several areas of SCOM that must be accounted for. This includes not just requirements for hardware and software but also the considerations regarding what you want to monitor and its ability to monitor your environment.

Disaster recovery also plays an essential role within Operations Manager but can be extended through various means such as the multihoming processes outlined in the section *Multi Homing*. It can also detail the difference between a typical disaster recovery and the parts that the multihoming play.

The next chapter will put everything we have learned about the design points for the Operations Manager into practical usage when we look at how we perform the installation and implementation of Operations Manager.

Points to remember

- Every initial Operations Manager setup will begin as a single management server topology until scalability comes into play where multiple management servers are introduced.
- To manage devices which are untrusted/DMZ/workgroup-based, this can be extended using gateway servers in which the agents can use certificate-based authentication.
- Multihoming is a process in which a managed device is reporting to more than one management group.
- Planning for a monitoring solution involves various moving parts including, but are not limited to, management packs, Run-As accounts, overrides and Azure-based monitoring.
- Azure Monitor monitors your Azure infrastructure and extends to your on-premise managed devices.
- SCOM MI is an Operations Manager instance that is managed within your Azure environment.
- Log Analytics is an extension of Azure Monitor which allows for the creation of queries in KQL to query machine collected data.

Multiple choice questions

1. **What is the name of the server role that allows agents to connect using a certificate authentication from untrusted areas?**
    a. Management server
    b. Resource pool
    c. Web console server
    d. Gateway server

2. **What is the name of the logical container that allows for load-balancing between multiple management servers?**
    a. Management group

b. Resource pool

c. Log Analytics

d. Management pack

3. **What are the areas we need to consider before introducing any form of Azure Monitor features?**

    a. Cost

    b. Practicality

    c. On-premise integration

    d. All of the above

4. **Which language does Log Analytics use in order to prepare queries, whether individually or for creating workbooks?**

    a. KQL

    b. SQL

    c. WQL

    d. PQL

5. **What is the name of the process when a SCOM-managed agent has more than one management group assigned to them?**

    a. Run-As account

    b. Secondary management

    c. Multihoming

    d. Load balance

6. **What is the fundamental difference between a sealed management pack and an unsealed management pack?**

    a. An unsealed management pack can only be created in the Visual Studios

    b. An unsealed management pack is encrypted with a key.

    c. A sealed management pack can be an official Microsoft release only.

    d. A sealed management pack is encrypted with a key.

Answers

1. d
2. b
3. d
4. a

5. c
6. d

Key terms

- **Distribution content**: Represents the content within Configuration Manager that has been added to a distribution point where software library content is stored and can be distributed to managed devices.
- **WQL**: Known as the Windows Management Instrument Query Language. It is recognized in Configuration Manager as the language used to query the WMI SDK.
- **EULA**: End User License Agreement, which is to be assigned before using any software.
- **Cloud attach**: Cloud attach is the functionality that allows Configuration Manager devices to be uploaded to the Endpoint Manager
- **Microsoft Endpoint Manager**: Another term for the Intune portal.

Join our book's Discord space

Join the book's Discord Workspace for Latest updates, Offers, Tech happenings around the world, New Release and Sessions with the Authors:

https://discord.bpbonline.com

CHAPTER 6
Deployment and Administration of System Center Operations Manager

Introduction

This chapter will concentrate on the development and deployment of the **System Center Operations Manager** (**SCOM**). The importance of this chapter is to illustrate the setup of the Operations Manager and the overall deployment so we can ensure the design plan that we specified in the previous section allows us to have a healthy setup. There will also be some troubleshooting points to help the reader understand some common and uncommon issues that can arise during the development and deployment process.

It will also provide an in-depth look into the overall administration of SCOM as well as outlining its best practices. The administration is what will allow an engineer to perform their **Business As Usual** (**BAU**) tasks, but also within the administrative side, another area that would enrich the BAU tasks and overall **user interface** (**UI**), is where the best practices come in. Best practices are normally looked at as a professional and recommended level to what you should do and not do. We will explore this area so we can understand the real-world scenarios which can conflict and outline the differences between both.

Structure

This chapter will cover the following topics:
- Operations Manager single management server deployment
- Operations Manager multi-management server deployment
- Management resource pool health validation of deployment
- Administration of Operations Manager
- Best practices
- Real-world scenario

Objectives

In this chapter, you will be aware of the latest updates and versions available to System Center in general as well as per each product where we will cover how the latest versions are released. We will find out more about those updates in terms of what new features come along. We will also learn about the overall best practice to adopt in real scenarios when it comes to upgrading any System Center products within your organization.

Operations Manager single management server deployment

The initial deployment of the Operations Manager will consist of a topology that will contain a single primary management server.

However, before we proceed with the instructional breakdown of the steps to install Operations Manager, we first need to go into the prerequisites that are required to be installed onto the servers before we can move forward, which are as follows:

- **Windows Server prerequisites for management server**: The management server role in Operations Manager 2022 does not require any server roles or features to be added.
- **Windows Server prerequisites for Operations Console**: The management server role in Operations Manager 2022 does not require any server roles or features to be added.
- **Windows Server prerequisites for web console**: Some server roles and features are required to be configured before we install the Operations Manager.

As there are various roles that you can decide from in the initial installation, we will cover the requirements on a per role basis:
- **Server roles**: The following roles need to be installed:
  - Web Server (IIS)

- **Server features**: The following features need to be installed:
    - .NET Framework 3.5 features
    - .NET Framework 4.7 features

Windows Server Operating System installation media

Before you go ahead and follow the instructions, there are some other tasks you will need to complete first. Since one of the server features is .NET Framework 3.5, it can only be installed when you have the installation media of the Windows Server OS. You either have this mounted to the computer or copied locally to the system drive where you can point to the directory.

Installing server roles and features

To install the server roles, perform the following steps:

1. Click on the start menu.
2. Go to the **Server Manager** console.
3. In the top right-hand corner, select **Manage**: **Add Roles and Features**
4. **Before you begin:** Click **Next**.
5. **Select the installation type:** Ensure the **Role-based or feature-based installation** is selected, then click **Next**.
6. **Select destination server: Server selection**: Ensure that the **Select a server from the server pool** has your server selected, then click **Next**.
7. **Select server roles:** Select the following roles:
    a. Web Server (IIS)
    b. Click the **Add Features** button within the dialogs when they pop, then click **Next**.
8. **Select features:** Features | Select the following features:
    a. **.NET Framework 3.5 features**: .NET Framework 3.5 (includes .NET 2.0 and 3.0)
    b. **.NET Framework 4.8 features**: .NET Framework 4.8
    c. **.NET Framework 4.8 features**: ASP.NET 4.8
    d. **.NET Framework 4.8 features**: WCF Services | HTTP Activation
    e. **.NET Framework 4.8 features**: WCF Services | **Transmission Control Protocol (TCP)** Port Sharing
9. **Web Server Role (IIS):** Click **Next**.
10. **Select role services:** Select the following role services:

a. Web Server | Common HTTP features | Default Document
b. Web Server | Common HTTP features | Directory Browsing
c. Web Server | Common HTTP features | HTTP Errors
d. Web Server | Common HTTP features | Static Content
e. Web Server | Web Server Health and Diagnostics | HTTP Logging
f. Web Server | Web Server Health and Diagnostics | Request Monitor
g. Web Server | Performance | Static Content Compression
h. Web Server | Security | Request Filtering
i. Web Server | Security | Windows Authentication
j. Web Server | Application Development | .NET Extensibility 3.5
k. Web Server | Application Development | .NET Extensibility 4.8
l. Web Server | Application Development | ASP.NET 3.5
m. Web Server | Application Development | ASP.NET 4.8
n. Web Server | Application Development | ISAPI Extensions
o. Web Server | Application Development | ISAPI Filters
p. Web Server | Management Tools | IIS Management Console
q. Web Server | Management Tools | IIS 6 Management Compatibility
r. Web Server | Management Tools | IIS 6 Management Compatibility | IIS 6 Metabase Compatibility
s. Then, click **Next**.

11. **Confirm installation selections:** Click on the **Specify an alternate source path** link at the bottom of the window.
12. **Specify alternate source path:** Enter the path of the installation media to point to the following folder that is, `D:\Sources\SxS`. Then click **OK**.
13. **Confirm installation selections:** Click **Install**.

Reporting server: Windows Server prerequisites

The management server role in Operations Manager 2022 does not require any server roles or features to be added.

Structured Query Language server reporting services

Depending on where you will be installing this role, the targeted server needs to have a **Structured Query Language (SQL) Server Reporting Services (SSRS)** installed to be able to run reports, as well as the successful deployment of the reports throughout the installation of Operations Manager.

There are also some checks which you will need to complete to verify that your SSRS service is indeed working correctly. To view the post-installation steps visit: **https://learn.microsoft.com/en-us/system-center/scom/deploy-install-reporting-server?view=scom-2022**

Service account requirements

The Operations Manager contains various service accounts that are required for it to function properly.

The following table shows all the service accounts required to be set, along with an explanation to what each service account is for:

Name	Description	Local or domain
Management server action account	Used to run tasks on the management server or on SCOM agents	Both
System Center Configuration service and System Center Data Access service	Used to run the main SCOM services to run correctly	Both
Data reader account	Used as a read only account to read from the SCOM database	Domain
Data writer account	Used as an account with write permissions to write to the SCOM database	Domain

Table 6.1: Operations Manager service account table

> **Note: Although there is a choice with two service accounts to operate as a local system (Non-domain) account, it is however recommended to use a domain-based account. This will be covered further in the "Best Practices" section**

If using domain-based accounts, then you will need to have the appropriate service accounts created beforehand within your active directory to you to proceed into the Operations Manager installation.

Firewall requirements

The following table outlines the firewall requirements for you to operate the Operations Manager correctly.

In the following table, all the outlined roles and the directions in which the traffic will flow are shown:

Firewall direction	Port used	Protocol type	TCP or User Datagram Protocol (UDP)
Management server to Operations Manager database	1433/1434	Default **Structured Query Language** (**SQL**) Port	1433 (TCP) 1434 (UDP)
Management server to Operations Manager database	135 445	**Remote Procedure Call** (**RPC**)	TCP
Management server to Management server	5723 5724	SCOM ports	TCP
Management server to Network Device (Bi-directional)	161 162	SNMP ports	UDP
Gateway Server to Management server	5723	SCOM ports	TCP
Reporting Server to Management server	5723 5724	SCOM ports	TCP
Operations Console to Management server	5724	SCOM ports	TCP
Windows Agent to Management server/Gateway Server	5723	SCOM ports	TCP
Management server/Gateway Server to UNIX Agent	1270	Port for UNIX/Linux communication	TCP

Table 6.2: Operations Manager firewall table

The table outlines the important ports before you proceed with the installation, to view a full list of all of the ports required for Operations Manager this can be viewed here: **https://learn.microsoft.com/en-us/system-center/scom/plan-security-config-firewall?view=scom-2022**

Installing single management server

Once everything above has been verified and checked, we will proceed with the deployment of the Operations Manager.

This installation will set the foundation for you to look into the scalability and add additional roles to your topology.

> **Note: The installation of each role or component will be specified in this section, if you were to select all the components listed then you will see all the steps from each section.**

Installing management server

To begin the installation, perform the following steps:

1. Open the installation media and then double-click the **Setup.exe** file
2. When the splash screen launches, click the **Install** button.
3. **Getting Started: Select features to install.** Select the **Management Server** role, then click **Next**.
4. **Getting Started:** Select the location which you are looking to install the Operations Manager to, then click **Next**.
5. **Prerequisites:** Proceed with setup. Check that no prerequisites are showing, then click **Next** as shown in *Figure 6.1*:

> Note: Sometimes, you may see one as a warning for Pending Restart Check. Though you can still proceed, it is recommended to reboot and restart the installation again so any pending actions are resolved beforehand.

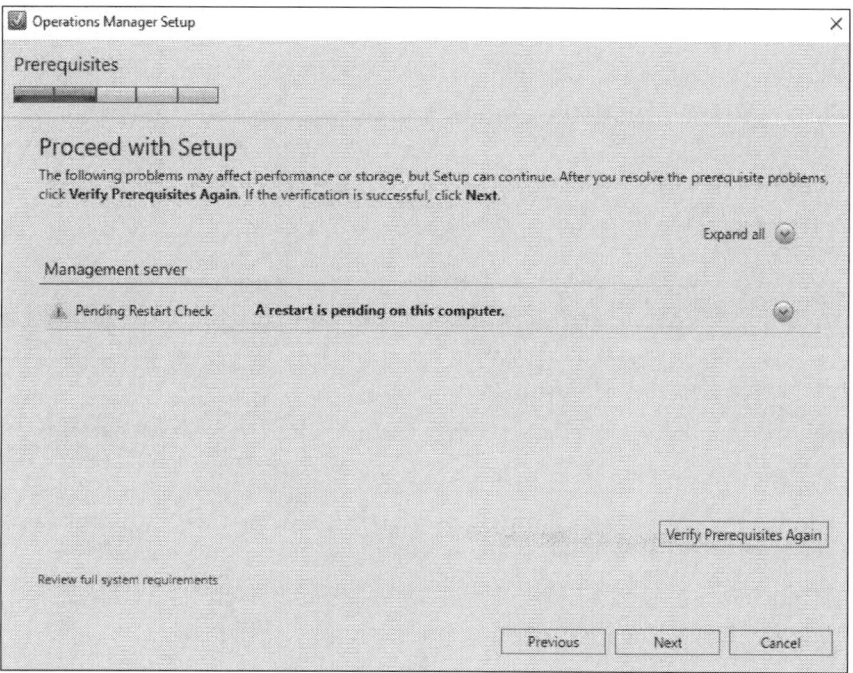

Figure 6.1: Pending restart check screen

6. **Configuration: Specify an installation option.** As this will be your first management server, you would select the first option **Create the first management server in a new management group**, then enter the name of the management group, then click **Next**.

7. **Configuration:** Please read the license terms. Click the **I have read, understood, and agree with the license terms** then click **Next**.
8. **Configuration: Configure the operational database**. Enter the name of the SQL Server and the instance name that connects to the SQL Server that you will use to configure the operational database. Once done, you will be able to accept the defaults or change the name of the database, size and the location of the database files. Now, click **Next**.
9. **Configuration**: **Configure the data warehouse database**. Enter the name of the SQL Server and instance that connects to the SQL server used to configure the data warehouse database. Once done, you will be able to accept the defaults or change the name of the database, size and the location of the database files. Now, click **Next**.
10. **Configuration**: **Configure Operations Manager accounts**. Enter the username and password for the service accounts depending on if you are utilizing domain accounts. Click **Next**.
11. **Configuration**: **Diagnostic and Usage Data**. Click **Next**.
12. **Configuration: Microsoft Update.** Click to decide if you want Microsoft Update to retrieve any updates for the Operations Manager. Then, click **Next**.
13. **Configuration: Installation Summary**. Review all the configurations you have done for your Operations Manager Management server. Then, click **Install**.

Installing Operations Console

In this section, we will go through how to install the Operations Manager console, note that this can be done either all at once alongside the rest of the server roles and components mentioned previously or if you simply want to install the console to which you will connect to a management server to view your monitoring:

1. Open the installation media and then double-click the `Setup.exe` file.
2. When the splash screen launches, click the **Install** button.
3. **Getting Started: Select features to install**. Select the **Operations Console**, then click **Next**.
4. **Getting Started:** Select the installation location. Select the location which you are looking to install the Operations Console to, then click **Next**.
5. **Prerequisites:** Proceed with setup. Check that no prerequisites are showing, then click **Next**.

> Note: Sometimes, you may see one as a warning for Pending Restart Check. Though you can still proceed it is recommended to reboot and restart the installation again so any pending actions are resolved beforehand.

6. **Configuration:** Please read the license terms. Click the **I have read, understood, and agree with the license terms,** then click **Next**.

7. **Configuration: Diagnostic and Usage Data.** Click **Next**.

8. **Configuration: Microsoft Update:** Click to decide if you want Microsoft Update to retrieve any updates for Operations Manager. Then, click **Next**.

9. **Configuration: Installation Summary**. Review all the configuration you have done for your Operations Console. If happy, click **Install**.

Installing web console

This section covers the installation of the Web Console for Operations Manager which is used to view your monitoring infrastructure through the web-based version of the Operations Manager console:

1. Open the installation media and then double-click the `Setup.exe` file.
2. When the splash screen launches, click the **Install** button.
3. **Getting Started: Select features to install.** Select the web console role, then click **Next**.
4. **Getting Started:** Select the installation location. Select the location which you are looking to install the web console to, then click **Next**.
5. **Prerequisites:** Proceed with setup. Check that no prerequisites are showing, then click **Next**.

> Note: Sometimes, you may see one as a warning for Pending Restart Check. Though you can still proceed, it is recommended to reboot and restart the installation again just so any pending actions are resolved beforehand

6. **Configuration:** Please read the license terms. Click the **I have read, understood, and agree with the license terms,** then click **Next**.
7. **Configuration: Specify a Management server.** Enter the management server that the web console will use. Wait until it resolves correctly, then click **Next**.
8. **Configuration: Specify a website for use with the web console**. Select which website to use on your IIS, and select if you wish to use Enable **Secure Socket Layer (SSL)**.

> Note: You will need to ensure that you have a valid SSL certificate created beforehand and ensure your IIS website is using HTTPS in order for you to use Enable SSL.

9. **Configuration: Select an authentication mode for use with the web console.** Select the authentication method to use for your web console. Click **Next**.
10. **Configuration: Diagnostic and Usage Data.** Click **Next**.

11. **Configuration: Microsoft Update:** Click to decide if you want Microsoft Update to retrieve any updates for Operations Manager. Click **Next**.
12. **Configuration: Installation Summary**. Review all the configuration you have done for your web console. If happy, then click **Install**.

Installing reporting server

This section covers the reporting server role installation used to view the native reports for the Operations Manager and provide the capability of adding additional reports when new management packs are installed. To do so, perform the following steps:

1. Open the installation media and then double click the `Setup.exe` file.
2. When the splash screen launches, click the **Install** button.
3. **Getting Started: Select features to install:** Select the reporting server role, then click **Next**.
4. **Getting Started:** Select installation location: Select the location which you are looking to install the reporting server to, then click **Next**.
5. **Prerequisites:** Proceed with setup: Check that no prerequisites are showing, then click **Next**.

> Note: Sometimes you may see one as a warning for Pending Restart Check. Though you can still proceed, it is recommended to reboot and restart the installation again so any pending actions are resolved beforehand

6. **Configuration: Specify a management server.** Enter the management server which the web console will use. Wait until it resolves correctly, then click **Next**.
7. **Configuration: SQL Server instance for reporting services**. Select the SQL Server instance which contains SSRS. Click **Next** to start the resolve of the discovered instance.
8. **Configuration**: **Configure Operations Manager accounts**. Enter the username and password for the service accounts depending on if you are utilizing domain accounts. Click **Next**.
9. **Configuration**: **Diagnostic and Usage Data**: Click **Next**.
10. **Configuration: Microsoft Update:** Click to decide if you want Microsoft Update to retrieve any updates for Operations Manager. Click **Next**.
11. **Configuration: Installation Summary**: Review all the configuration you have done for your Operations Console. If happy, then click **Install**.

Installing Audit Collection Services Collector

You will need to perform this installation on an existing management server which the following steps:

1. Open the installation media and double-click the **Setup.exe** file.
2. When the splash screen launches click the **Audit Collection services** option underneath where it says **Optional Installations**.
3. **Welcome to the Audit Collection Services Collector Setup Wizard:** Click **Next**.
4. **Microsoft Software license terms**: Select **I accept the license terms**, then click **Next**.
5. **Database on installation options: Choose a database option**. Select to create a new database, then click **Next**.
6. **Data source**: Enter the name of your audit collection services data source, then click **Next**.
7. **Database**: Enter the details of the database server. If using a remote SQL server then select **Remote database server** and enter the database name. Click **Next**.
8. **Database authentication: Connect using**. Select the authentication to use for your database, then click **Next**.
9. **Database creation options**: Select if you want to accept the default directories for both the database and log files, or alternatively you can click to specify directories and enter the appropriate locations. Click **Next**.
10. **Event retention schedule**: Configure the schedule to perform database maintenance, then click **Next**.
11. **Audit Collection Services (ACS) stored timestamp format**: Configure how you want the timestamps to be recorded whether based on local time or UTC time. Click **Next**.
12. **Summary:** Review the configuration of your ACS collector role. Once happy, click **Next**.

Operations Manager multi-management server deployment

Now that you have the first management server built and ready within your environment, to look into the scalability or even to expand the overall availability of your environment, you can add additional management servers to your environment.

Adding additional management servers

The process of adding additional management servers is very similar to the installation instructions outlined in the section. However, the options you select are quite different, which are outlined as follows:

1. Open the installation media and double-click the **Setup.exe** file.
2. When the splash screen launches, click the **Install** button.

3. **Getting started: Select features to install:** Select the management server role, then click **Next**.
4. **Getting started:** Select the location to you are looking to install Operations Manager, then click **Next**.
5. **Prerequisites:** Proceed with setup. Check that no prerequisites are showing, then click **Next**.

> **Note: Sometimes, you may see one as a warning for Pending Restart Check. Though you can still proceed, it is recommended to reboot and restart the installation again so any pending actions are resolved beforehand**

6. **Configuration: Specify an installation option**: Now, this time we already have a management group in place. So, for this option, we would select **Add a management server to an existing management group**. Click **Next**, as shown in the following figure:

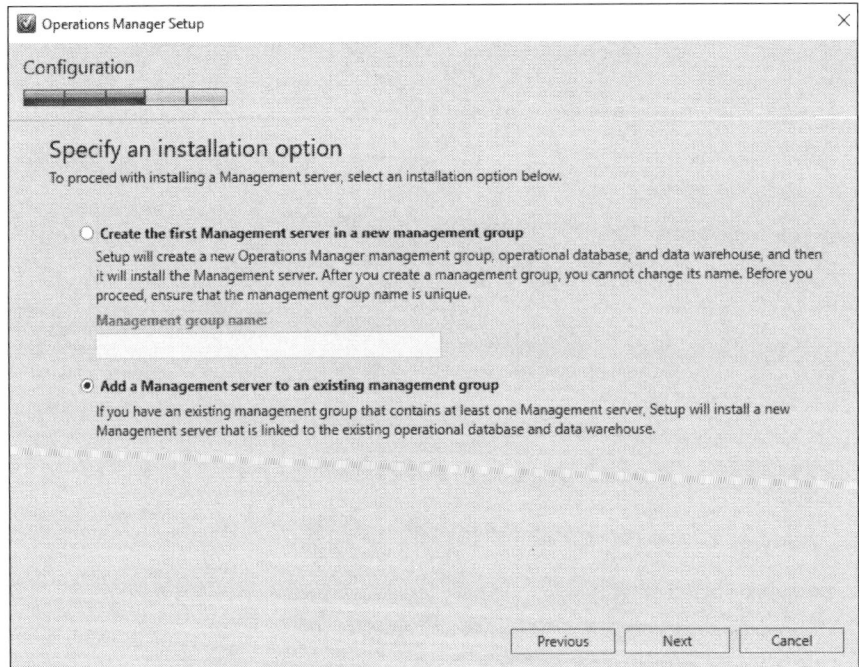

Figure 6.2: Configuration screen to add another management server

7. **Configuration:** Please read the license terms. Click the **I have read, understood, and agree with the license terms,** then click **Next**.
8. **Configuration: Configure the operational database**. Enter the name of the SQL Server and instance name which connects to the SQL server. Once this resolves you will then have the option to select the correct operational database to proceed. Click **Next**.

9. **Configuration**: **Configure Operations Manager accounts**. Enter the username and password for the service accounts depending on if you are utilizing domain accounts. Click **Next**.
10. **Configuration**: **Diagnostic and usage data**: Click **Next**.
11. **Configuration: Microsoft Update:** Click to decide if you want Microsoft Update to retrieve any updates for Operations Manager. Click **Next**
12. **Configuration: Installation summary**: Review all the configuration you have done for your Operations Manager Management Server. If happy, then click **Install**.

Installing Gateway Server

Another form of the scalability of Operations Manager is, evidently, to understand if you have any devices which are a part of the non-domain environments such as workgroups, **Demilitarized Zone** (**DMZ**) or areas in which Kerberos authentication may not be possible.

With these scenarios in mind, we would then need to introduce adding a Gateway Server to our environment.

The instructions for the installation are as follows:

1. Open the installation media and double-click the `Setup.exe` file.
2. When the splash screen launches, click the **Gateway Management Server** option underneath where it says **Optional Installations**, as shown in the following figure:

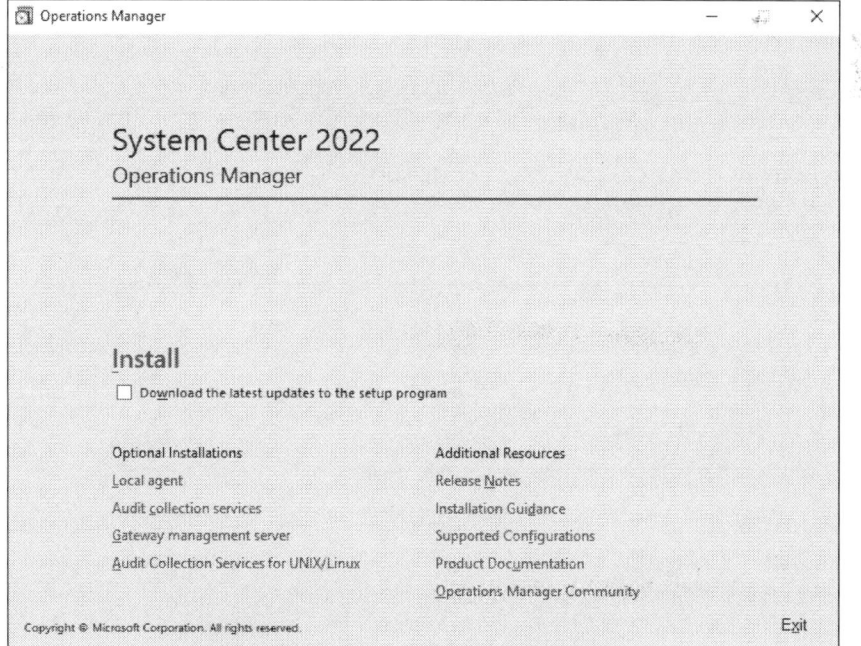

Figure 6.3: Operations Manager 2022 splash screen

3. **Welcome to the System Center Operations Manager Gateway Server Setup wizard.** Click **Next**.
4. **Important Notice: Microsoft Software license terms**: Click **I agree**.
5. **Destination Folder: Select the installation folder**. Select the destination where you will install the Gateway Server, then click **Next**.
6. **Management group configuration: Specify the management group information which is necessary for this computer to connect.** Enter the management group name and management server information for which the gateway will talk to, then click **Next**.
7. **Gateway Action Account: Specify which account should be used for the Gateway Action Account**, Specify the account which will be used to run actions for the Gateway Server, then click **Next**.
8. **Microsoft Update: Use Microsoft Update to help keep your computer secure and up to date.** Click to decide if you want Microsoft Update to retrieve any updates for Operations Manager. Click **Next**.
9. **Ready to install: Click Install to begin the installation of the System Center Operations Manager Gateway Server**. Review the details of the configuration you have specified for your Gateway Server. Once happy, click **Install**.

Management resource pool health validation of deployment

Once the Operations Manager installation has been completed, you will be able to open the Operations Console and connect to your management server and management group.

Here, we will make some validation checks of our environment to ensure that everything has gone through successfully.

Operations Manager services validation

The first step is to make a reference to the Windows services which allow for the Operations Manager to run. These services are as follows:

- System Center Data Access service.
- System Center Management configuration.

Now, the main service is the **System Center Data Access service**. Without this running, you will be unable to open the SCOM console to connect to your management group and management server.

The other service, System Center Management Configuration, looks after a main process known as the **MonitoringHost.exe**, which is responsible for running the main activities for SCOM. It is so that the monitoring can be done through the health services which operate within the agent from the management server connection, as shown in the following figure:

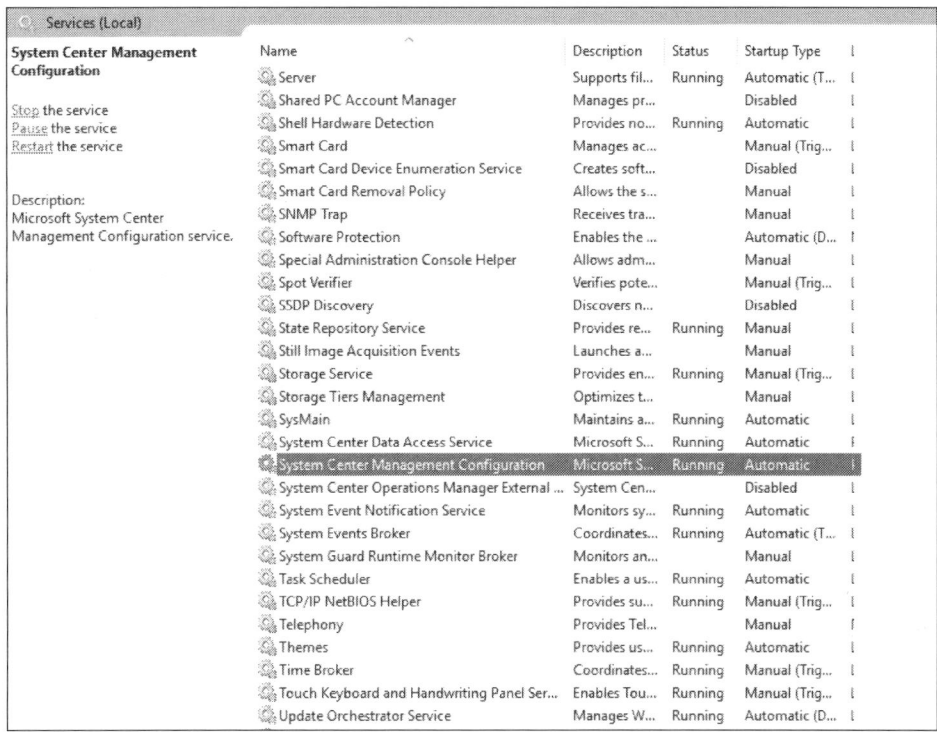

Figure 6.4: Windows services console showing the services

Resource pool validation within the Operations Console

The next part is then to look through the console and make the necessary checks to ensure that everything is working correctly. The steps for this are as follows:

1. Go to the start menu.
2. Search for Microsoft System Center Operations Console, then click the **Operations Console**.
3. You will then see a prompt box as outlined in *Figure 6.5*, which gives you the option to connect to your management server where you would put the **Fully Qualified Domain Name** (**FQDN**) of the management server, then click the **Connect** button:

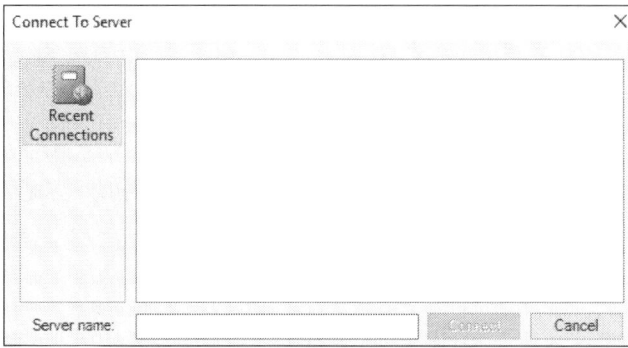

Figure 6.5: *Connect to Server box*

> Note: When opening the console on a server which has the management server, you may find that it will open automatically to the management group you had just created, if however, this is an additional management server or more than one management group, then you may get prompted with the above shown in *Figure 6.5*.

Once you have completed this, you should then see the console opened, as seen in *Figure 6.6*:

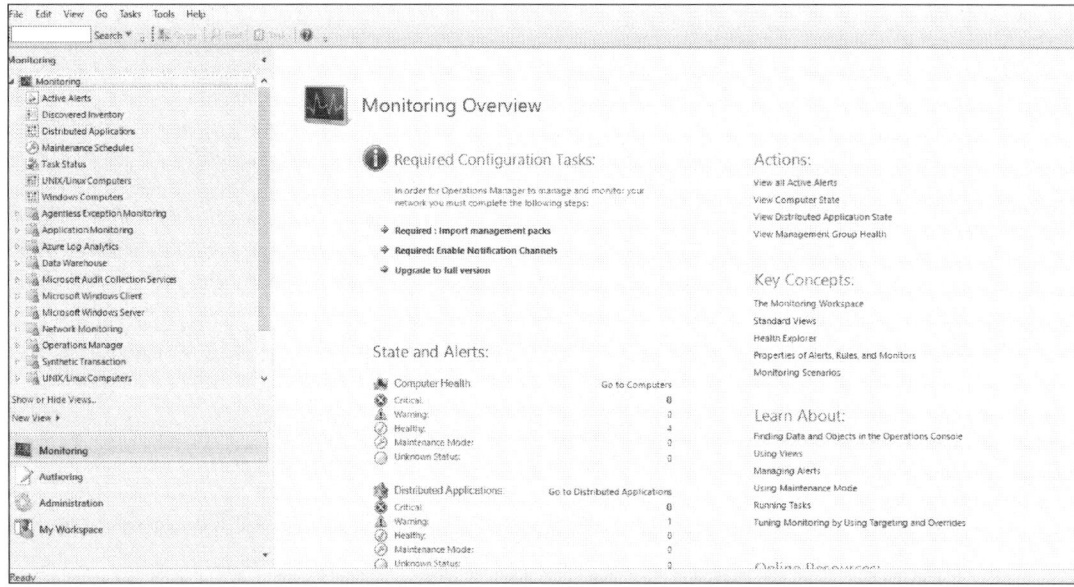

Figure 6.6: *Operations Manager console monitoring view*

The first initial parts you will see will be the overall health state of all the servers which are managed within Operations Manager. We will cover this further in the next topic *administration tasks*.

In this section we will focus on the actual resource pool health. We will go to the **Administration | Resource Pools** which will then provide you with a list of the default resource pools, as seen in *Figure 6.7*:

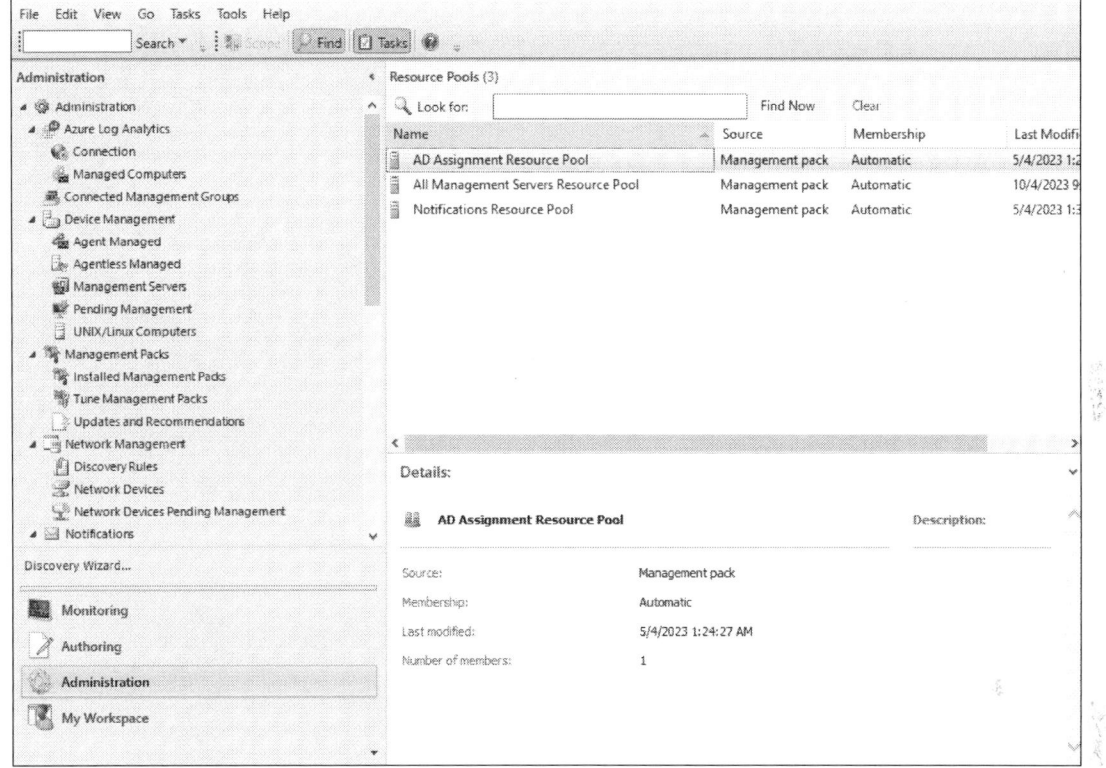

Figure 6.7: Resource pools view

These resource pools are created by default, but the one which we really want to be focused on is primarily around the **all-management servers resource pool**.

This contains all the management servers within your management group, and as the membership is automatic, any new management servers will be added on an incremental basis.

You can create new resource pools where the membership can be manual and allow the administrator to select the specific management servers. This is useful when you want to have a pool dedicated to a specific workflow which we can cover in more detail within the next topic.

If we want to view the resource pool health, we can switch to the **Monitoring** tab again and select the `Operations Manager` folder and the **Management Group Health** view which will give a **Single Pane Of Glass (SPOG)** look into the health state of your Operations Manager environment.

This folder represents the default management for Operations Manager and has various views which show the overall health of Operations Manager.

If any issues with this resource pool arise, we would not only see the health state turn to a critical symbol, but also see a new alert created within the Operations Manager outlining this. In *Figure 6.8*, we can see the state of the all management servers resource pool:

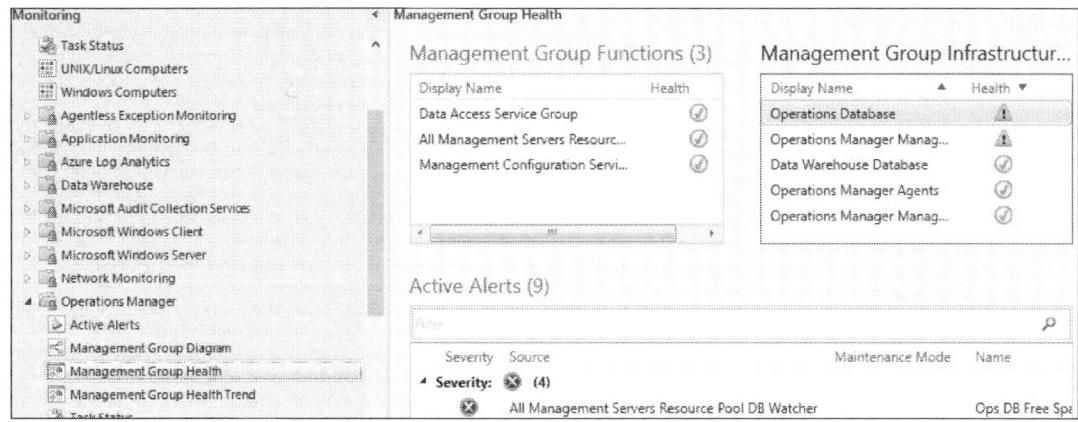

Figure 6.8: Management Group Health view

Administration of Operations Manager

In order for you to have the Operations Manager's environment fully up to speed, there are various administrative tasks you need to perform to build up the solution where your environment will be fully monitored.

These administrative tasks are common throughout most SCOM versions, but some optimizations will also be seen in features that are specific to the latest version of SCOM 2022.

Installing management packs

With the exception of default management packs which come with the Operations Manager, we may want additional management packs which will enhance the coverage of the monitoring for our environment.

In the previous chapter, we discussed the different types of management packs which are available.

> **Note:** *.MP are sealed management packs. *.MPB are management pack bundles which can contain more than one management pack or additional component, and *.XML are unsealed management packs.

In this section, we will cover the processes of how to install a management pack through the following steps:

1. Open the Operations Manager console.
2. Go to **Administration** | **Management packs** | **Installed management packs**.
3. Click the **Import Management packs** option in the right-hand tasks pane.
4. **Import management packs: Select Management packs** | Click the **Add** button and select **Add from disk** if importing a local management pack you downloaded. If you want to import directly from the internet, you can use **Add from catalog**, but you will need an internet connection to perform this.
5. Browse to the location where your management pack files are, then select.
6. Ensure the management pack has a green tick selected then click **Install**.

You should now see the management pack listed in the **Installed Management packs** view.

Troubleshooting

If you experience any red ticks to management packs you have in the import list or they fail, check the hyperlinks on them once they are flagged. They may have dependencies on other management packs to be imported first, which prevents them from being successfully imported.

Creating management packs

There are various steps to the administration of management packs and for situations when you are required to build a management pack. Hence, we will go through the various steps of its construction within the Operations Manager console.

Creating a new management pack

This part creates the logical container shell of a new management, which would then allow us to add different components to the management pack. All management packs created in this way are all unsealed management packs. The steps are as follows:

1. Open the Operations Manager console.
2. Go to **Administration** | **Management packs** | **Installed Management packs**.
3. Click the **Create Management Pack** option in the right-hand tasks pane.
4. **General properties: General properties:** Enter a Name, version number and description for your management pack, then click **Next**.
5. **Knowledge: Knowledge Article** | click **Create**.

Once this has been created, you can start to look through the authoring objects, which can be found in the **Authoring** tab of the Operations Manager console. In this exercise, we will cover adding a monitor to our new management pack container and how to configure an override for the same monitor.

Adding a new monitor

We will go through the process of adding a monitor focused on the Windows services to provide you with an idea of the authoring process. The process is as follows:

1. Open the Operations Manager console.
2. Go to **Authoring | Management Pack Templates**.
3. Select **Add Monitoring Wizard** from the right-hand tasks pane.
4. **Monitoring type: Select the monitoring type.** Select the **Windows Service** option, then click **Next**.
5. **General:** Enter a friendly name and description. Enter the name of your monitor and description. For the management pack, select the management pack that we created earlier, then click **Next**.
6. **Service details:** Click the ellipsis for the service name and select the service you want to monitor. Then select a targeted group for which the monitor will be applicable. You can choose **All Windows Computers** if you wish to apply the monitor for all windows devices. Toggle if you want to **Monitor only automatic service**, then click **Next**.
7. **Performance data**: **Set the performance data collection settings**. Select if you want to have additional monitoring which would include counters for CPU and Memory spikes caused by your service monitor, then click **Next**.
8. **Summary**: Review all the configuration for your monitor, then click **Create** to complete.

Configuring an override

With the management pack we have created, we can register overrides for existing monitors and rules if we decide we do not want them to run or if we want to change specific parameters. To do the same, perform the following steps:

1. Open the Operations Manager console.
2. Go to **Monitoring | Active Alerts** or **Monitoring | Windows Computers** or **Monitoring | Unix/Linux Computers**
3. Right click and select **Overrides | Override the Monitor | For the object:***** or if you are in a different view right-click and select **Open | Health Explorer**, then select the Overrides tab above.

Here, you will be presented with various parameters which you can override. To override any one of them, select the override tick box for the desired parameter then change the default value. Once happy, select the management pack you just created. Click **Apply**, then **OK**.

> Note: Too many overrides can cause issues so ensure to make necessary overrides where appropriate.

Creating resource pools

When a new resource pool is required, you can perform the following instructions:

1. Open the Operations Manager console.
2. Go to **Administration | Resource Pools**.
3. Click the **Create Resource Pool** option in the right-hand tasks pane.
4. **General Properties:** Enter a name and description for the resource pool, then click **Next**.
5. **Pool Membership:** Click the **Add** button to select the management servers you want in your resource pool. When done, click **Create**.

Creating a Run As account

Run As accounts can be required to be used in conjunction with the Run As profiles that are assigned to different classes belonging to particular management packs to ensure the right permissions are used to properly discover and monitor the desired objects.

Once the account is created, we then need to assign it to a Run As profile or create one if a custom monitoring solution is required.

To create a Run As account, perform the following:

1. Open the Operations Manager console.
2. Go to **Administration | Run As Configuration | Accounts**.
3. Click **Create Run As Account** from the right-hand task pane.
4. **Introduction:** Click **Next**.
5. **General Properties:** Select the type of account you want to create then specify the display name for your account, then click **Next**.
6. **Credentials:** Enter your credentials, then click **Next**.
7. **Distribution Security**: Select **More secure** so that you have full control over which managed devices can use the Run As account details. Then, click **Create**.
8. **Completion**: You will see a confirmation of your created account alongside a warning stating you will need to distribute the account to managed devices on completion.
9. After creating the account, right click the account you created and select properties.
10. Go to the **Distribution** tab, select the **Add** button and add the computers that you want to use the Run As account details on. These should ideally be computers

which will be utilized correctly within the management packs or monitoring you have configured.

Creating UNIX/Linux accounts

These have a similar purpose to the Run As accounts. However, these are more optimized for UNIX/Linux as they are also used to install the Linux agents. To create an account, perform the following steps:

1. Open the Operations Manager console.
2. Go to **Administration** | **Run As configuration** | **UNIX/Linux Accounts**.
3. Click **Create Run As Account** from the right-hand task pane.
4. Account Type: **UNIX/Linux Run As Account Type.** Select **Monitoring Account**, then click **Next**.
5. **General Properties: Name and Description:** Enter a name for your Run As account, then click **Next**.
6. **Account Credentials:** Enter the credentials for your account and select if this is a privileged account. Then, click **Next**.
7. **Distribution Security**: Select **More secure** so that you have full control of which managed devices can use the Run As account details. Then, click **Create**.
8. **Completion**: You will see the confirmation of your created account. Alongside a warning stating you will need to distribute the account to managed devices on completion.
9. After creating the account, right-click the account you created and select properties.
10. Go to the **Distribution** tab and select the **Add** button and add the computers that you want to use the Run As account details. These should be ideally computers which will be utilized correctly within the management packs or monitoring you have configured.

Creating Run As profiles

Once you have Run As accounts created, we can assign them to Run As profiles which will then be used within management packs to perform the necessary tasks with the correct permissions to monitor and discover targeted objects. This exercise covers the same process if you were to edit an existing Run As a profile, the steps for which are as follows:

1. Open the Operations Manager console.
2. Go to **Administration** | **Run As Configuration** | **Profiles**.
3. Click **Create Run As Profile** from the right-hand task pane.
4. **Introduction:** Click **Next**.
5. **General Properties**: Enter a name for your Run As profile, select the correct management pack to store the Run As profile, then click **Next**.

6. **Run As Accounts**: Click the **Add** button to get the additional window where you can select the Run As account that you have created. Here you will also select if the Run As account can be used to manage all targeted objects or you can filter this down to specific objects. Once done, click **OK**, then click **Save**.

> Note: All targeted objects mean every object that gets discovered/monitored will utilize it. If you want to further secure the usage of the Run As account, you can use a class, group or singular object. Run As profiles can be generic if created like previously or embedded in management packs where they are tied to specific classes.

Adding new agents

One of the first tasks to perform once your Operations Manager environment is fully installed is to be able to add new agents to Operations Manager so that they can be monitored.

The following types of agents that can be added are as follows:
- Windows
- UNIX/Linux
- Network devices

This is shown in *Figure 6.9*:

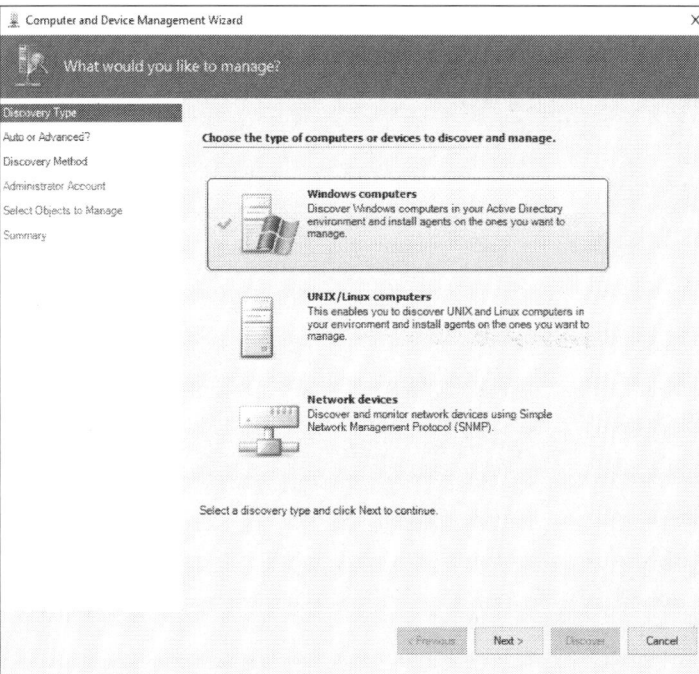

Figure 6.9: Computer and device management wizard

Another type of agent to take into account as part of a native option within SCOM is agentless monitoring. Agentless monitoring is for devices which are to receive a basic form of monitoring based on the uptime and performance of a device similar to a *Dr Watson* information.

> Note: *Dr Watson* is a legacy component that was used for debugging information on the Windows OS. For more information on the .exe this can be found here https://en.wikipedia.org/wiki/Dr._Watson_(debugger)

Adding a Windows Agent through Automatic discovery

To perform adding a Windows Agent to Operations Manager to be monitored, perform the following steps:

1. Open the Operations Manager console.
2. Go to the **Administration** tab and select the **Discovery Wizard** option at the bottom of the left-hand pane.
3. Choose the type of computers or devices to discover and manage - Select **Windows computers**, then click **Next**.
4. **Choose automatic or advanced discovery** | Select automatic discovery, then click **Next**.
5. Administrator account | Enter the name of an account which has sufficient permissions to the machine you are looking to discover or go with the management server action account.

> Note: The management server Action account must have permissions on the machine you are looking to discover in order for you to be able to discover and install the agent onto the machine.

6. **Select objects to manage: Discovery Results:** Select the devices you want to manage, then click **Next**.
7. **Summary:** Look through the details of where the agent installation directory is and select the account which will be used to perform agent actions. You also have the option to enable **Application Performance Monitoring** (**APM**) which we will cover in this topic. Click **Finish** for the agent to begin installation.

Adding a Windows Agent through Advanced discovery

To add a Windows Agent to the Operations Manager to be monitored, perform the following steps:

1. Open the Operations Manager console.
2. Go to the **Administration** tab and select the **Discovery Wizard** option at the bottom of the left-hand pane.
3. Choose the type of computers or devices to discover and manage. Select **Windows computers**, then click **Next**.
4. Choose automatic or advanced discovery. Select automatic discovery. Select if you want to find both servers and clients or just one specific and decide if you require contact validation when discovered, then click **Next**.
5. **Discovery Method:** How do you want to discover computers? Select if you want to **scan active directory** by a specific **organizational unit (OU)** or if you want to type in the names manually in **Browse for, or type-in computer names,** then click **Next**.
6. **Administrator account:** Enter the name of an account which has sufficient permissions to the machine you are looking to discover or go with the management server action account.

> Note: The Management server Action account must have permissions on the machine you are looking to discover for you to discover and install the agent onto the machine.

7. **Select objects to manage: Discovery Results** | Select the devices you want to manage, then click **Next**.
8. **Summary:** Look through the details of where the agent installation directory is and select the account that will be used to perform agent actions. You also have the option to enable the APM, which we will cover within this topic. When done, click finish for the agent to begin the installation.

Adding a Windows Agent through manual installation

The manual installation option uses the installation files on the installation media or the management server location. Refer to the following locations:

- **Installation media agent files:** `<Installation Media>\System Center Operations Manager\Agent\amd64\MOMAgent.msi`
- **Management Server agent files:** `<Program Files>\Microsoft System Center\Operations Manager\Server\AgentManagement\amd64\MOMAgent.msi`

This form of installation will require an additional task to approve the agent once the installation is completed which we will cover within the following instructions:

1. Open the installation media or management server agent files location and double-click `MOMAgent.msi`.
2. **Welcome to the Microsoft Monitoring Agent setup wizard.** Click **Next**.

3. **Important notice: Microsoft Software License Terms**. Click **I Agree**.
4. **Destination folder:** Select the installation folder. Select where you want the agent installation installed, then click **Next**.
5. **Agent setup options:** Specify setup options for this installation of Microsoft Monitoring Agent. Select the **Connect the agent to System Center Operations Manager** option, then click **Next**, as shown in the following figure:

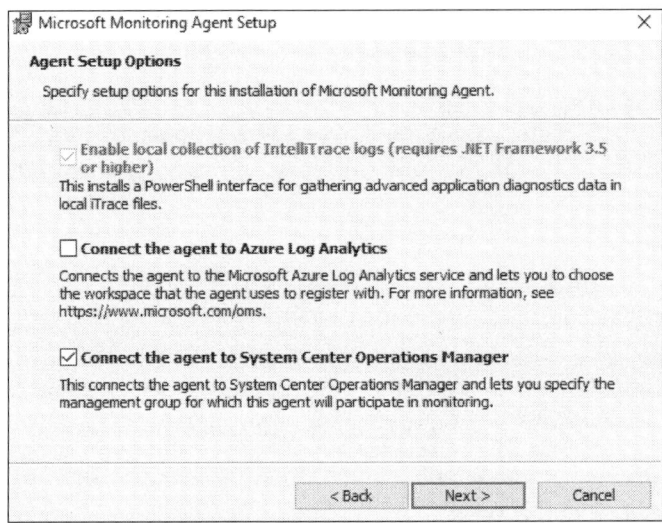

Figure 6.10: Agent Setup Options window

6. **Management group configuration:** Specify the management group information that is necessary for this computer to connect to. Enter the management group name and server you want to connect the agent to, then click **Next**.
7. **Agent action account:** Specify which account should be used for the agent action account. Select the type of account to use to perform agent-based actions, then click **Next**.
8. **Microsoft Update:** Use Microsoft Update to help keep your computer secure and up to date. Select if you want to receive Microsoft updates for your agent, then click **Next**.
9. **Ready to Install**: Click **Install** to begin the installation of the Microsoft Monitoring Agent..

Once this has been completed you need to approve this within the Operations manager console by performing the following instructions:

1. Open the Operations Manager console.
2. Go to **Administration | Device Management | Pending Management**.
3. Here you will see the device you just installed the agent on showing as a pending installation. Right click and select **Approve**.

Adding a UNIX or Linux Agent through automatic discovery

To perform adding a UNIX/LINUX agent to Operations Manager to be monitored, perform the following steps:

1. Open the Operations Manager console.
2. Go to the **Administration** tab and select the **Discovery Wizard** option at the bottom of the left-hand pane.
3. Choose the type of computers or devices to discover and manage. Select **UNIX/Linux computers**, then click **Next**.
4. **Discovery data:** Define the criteria for discovering UNIX/Linux computers. Select the resource pool to use, then click the **Add** button to get the **Discovery Criteria** window, as shown in the following figure:

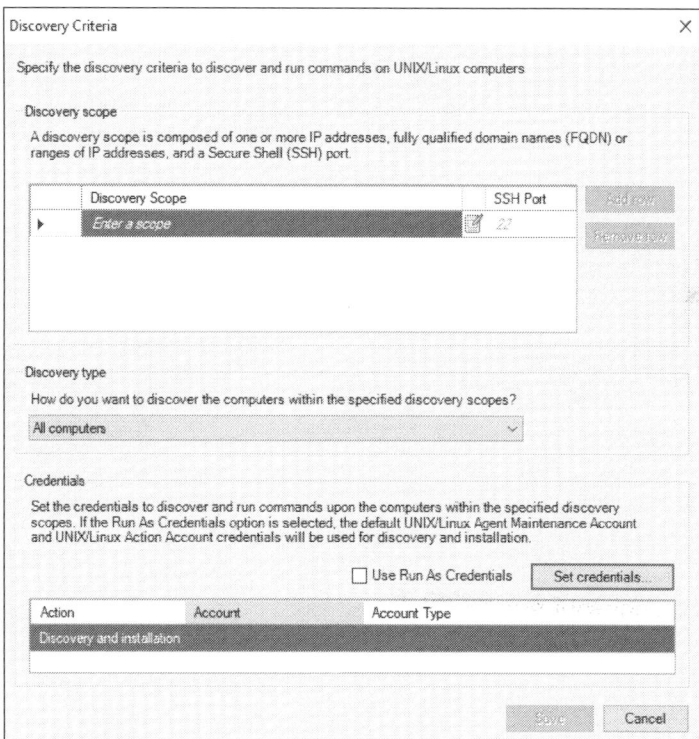

Figure 6.11: Discovery criteria window

5. **Discovery criteria:** Enter the DNS name or IP address of the UNIX/Linux device you want to discover. Then, proceed down to the credentials section. If your Run As account (see **Create Run As Accounts/Profiles** section) has permissions to the device, you can click the **Use Run As Credentials**. If not, then click **Set credentials,** as shown in the following figure:

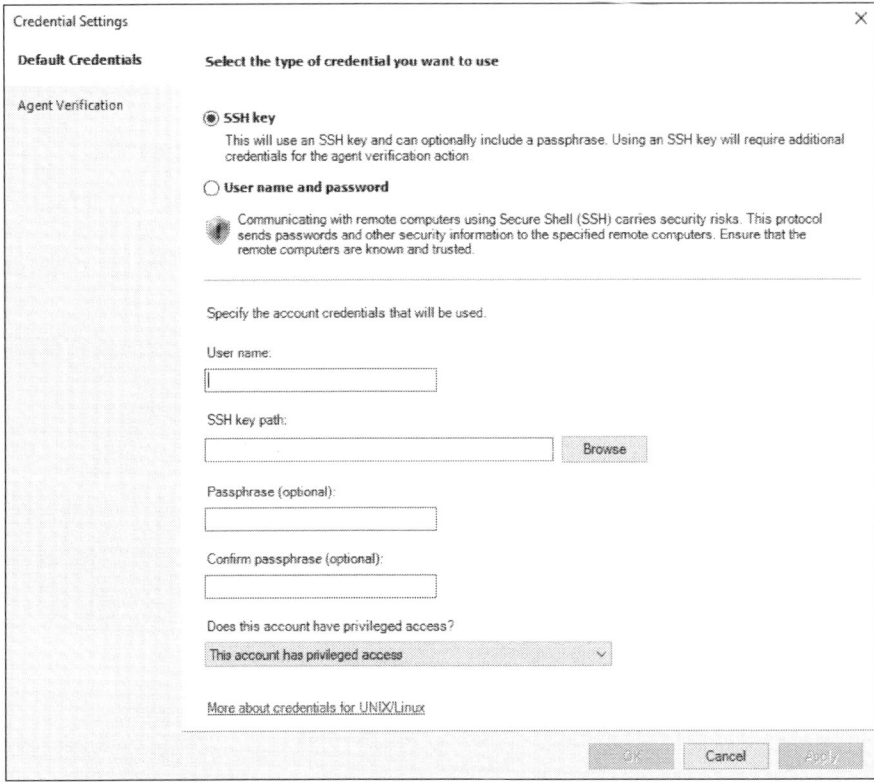

Figure 6.12: Credential settings

6. Enter the type of credentials required and confirm if it is a privileged account, then click **OK**.
7. Select the computers you want to manage. Select the devices you want to manage in the **manageable computers** tab, then select **Manage** to begin.

> Note: If your account does not use privileged access then you can select "This account doesn't have privileged access" which will then give you elevation tab to allow for "sudo" or "su" rights to perform the installation.

Azure Log Analytics setup

For all the devices which have a SCOM agent installed, they are capable of being attached to an Azure Log Analytics workspace which will allow them to be manageable from Cloud solutions such as Azure Monitor and Microsoft Sentinel.

You will require the following details before you can complete these instructions:
- Workspace ID
- Workspace key

These details can be found within your Log Analytics workspace settings.

To add a SCOM-managed device to your Log Analytics workspace, perform the following steps:

1. Open the **Control Panel**.
2. Go to **System and Security**.
3. Go to **Microsoft Monitoring Agent**.
4. Select the **Azure Log Analytics** tab.
5. Select the **Add** button, as shown in the following figure:

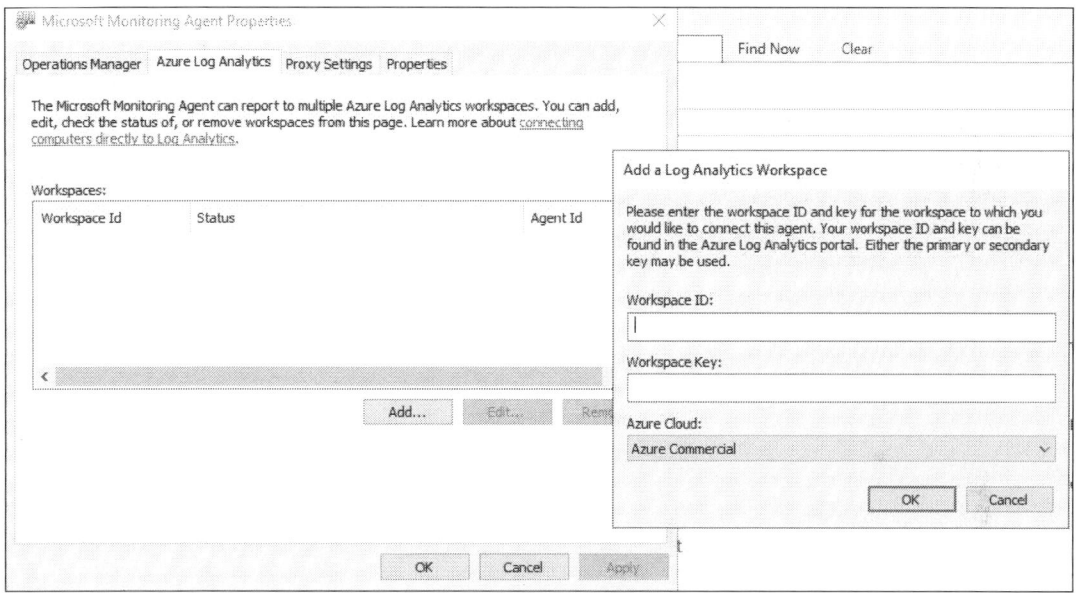

Figure 6.13: Azure Log Analytics SCOM agent settings

6. Enter the Workspace ID and Workspace key for your Log Analytics workspace, then click **OK**.
7. Click **Apply**.

At this point, the agent service will restart, and the status will change to check if your device has been successfully added to your workspace.

Upgrading Operations Manager

There are two important tasks to be performed when upgrading the Operations Manager. They are as follows:

- Hotfixes
- Upgrade from the lower version.

Here, we will cover the process for both.

Applying hotfixes to the Operations Manager must stick to the following order:
- Management servers
- Audit Collection Servers
- Web Console
- Gateway Server
- Operation Manager Console
- Reporting Server
- Agents

Once you have the files downloaded, they will be in a `.msp` format and will be for each individual component, as listed previously.

To install, perform the following. Double-click the corresponding `.msp` file for each component and follow the wizard, which will then upgrade the components.

In this example, we have Operations Manager 2022 UR1, so we would do the following:

1. Go to **https://support.microsoft.com/en-gb/topic/update-rollup-1-for-system-center-2022-operations-manager-3f5780c9-36d9-4bba-8361-d40ca7c7ae80**.
2. Browse to the end and find the Download the Operations Manager update package now link.
3. Here you will be taken to the Microsoft Update Catalog website which will show all the different components, as shown in the following figure:

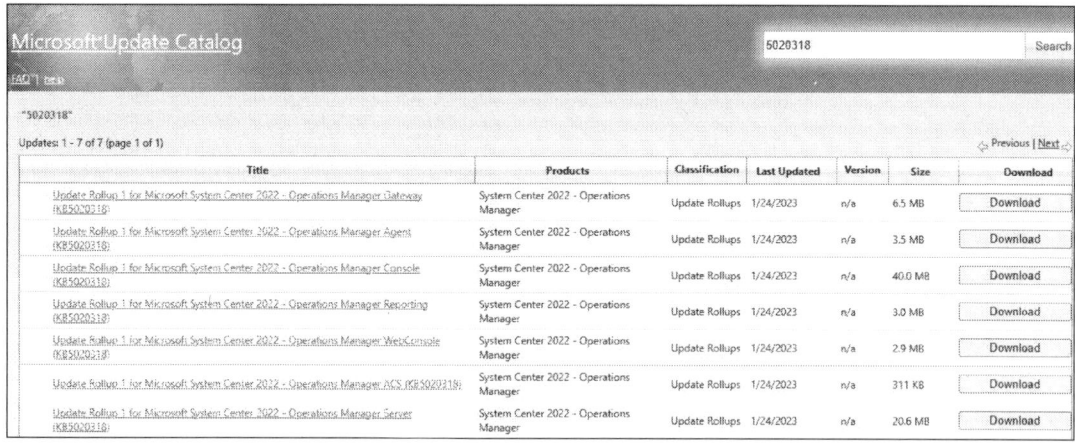

Figure 6.14: Microsoft Update for Operations Manager 2022 UR1

4. Select the **Download** button, then click the hyperlink to download the `.cab` file.
5. Open the `.cab` file and extract the `.msp` file.

To see a full instructional list on how to install a hotfix or update rollup, you can refer to the KB article, which represents the UR or hotfix right here: **https://support.microsoft.com/en-gb/topic/update-rollup-1-for-system-center-2022-operations-manager-3f5780c9-36d9-4bba-8361-d40ca7c7ae80**

Agents can be upgraded within the Pending Management section of the Operations Manager console, but you also have the option to manually deploy the agent to the machine.

Monitoring alerts

Now, you are ready to start looking through Operations Manager alerts. There are a few areas which you should be aware of when it comes to monitoring alerts and will help you navigate through them.

The first view to get yourself familiarized with is the Active Alerts view is shown in *Figure 6.15*, which shows a list of active alerts:

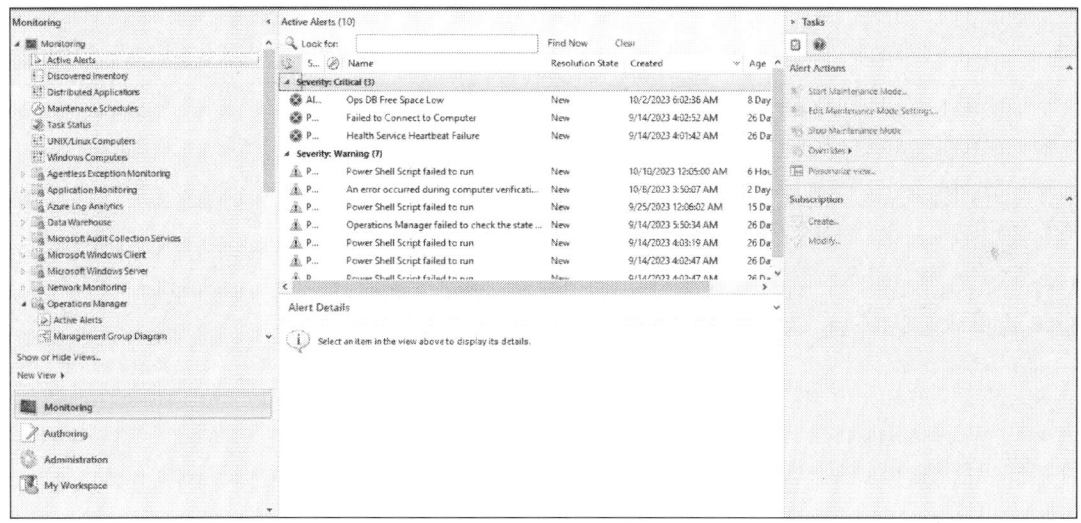

Figure 6.15: Active alerts view

You can see more information by selecting open alerts and can decide how to proceed with them. Most alerts can auto close, but in some cases, they are not configured this way, and therefore, may need to be manually closed. You can right click and **set resolution state** or **Close Alert**.

To investigate an opened alert further, you can right-click and select **Open | Health Explorer**. By default, when using the healthy explorer on an alert, it will filter down to the specific alert in question to showcase its knowledge base article and an additional tab named **State Change Events**, which shows a timestamp for when the health state changes. *Figure 6.16* shows a more detailed breakdown of the affected area:

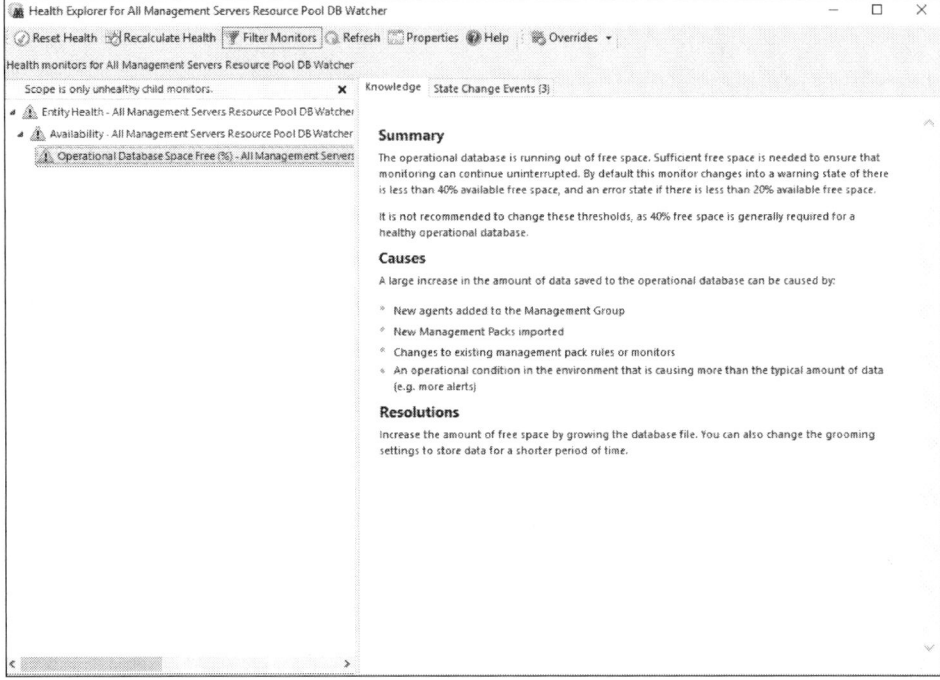

Figure 6.16: Health explorer view

Two options that you should familiarize yourself with are:

- Reset Health
- Recalculate Health

Reset Health basically forces the alert or monitor to go right back to healthy and will remain healthy until the next interval is reached to detect its health state. This must be used only in certain circumstances such as false positives, or for cases when health states may not have an auto-close, etc.

Recalculate health, however, works differently as this forces an immediate check using the healthy criteria of the monitor to check if the alert is now resolved or healthy.

Best practices

In this section, we have some of the best practices for Operations Manager.

Creating closed alerts view

When it comes to tracing alerts in Operations Manager, any closed alerts will no longer show in the default Active Alerts view, though you can enable it to show closed alerts but it is best to leave this untampered with.

Having a view of closed alerts is important when you want to further troubleshoot or keep track.

To create a view for this, perform the following steps:

1. Open the Operations Manager console.
2. Right-click the Monitoring node at the top and select **New** | **Alert View**.
3. Enter a name for the view, then for conditions select **with a specific resolution state,** then select the specific hyperlink defined in the criteria description and select the **Closed (255)** option.
4. Click **OK**, then click **OK** to create the view.

Tuning management packs

Config churn is a terminology which can cause very serious impact to your environment, and is usually caused by alert storms or too much data being processed for your Operations Manager to handle.

To stay on top of this, the best way is to not only check the alerts regularly but also run the following report named **Data Volume by Management** pack if you have the reporting role enabled, which can be found by doing the following steps:

1. Open the Operations Manager console.
2. Go to **Reporting** | **System Center Core Monitoring**.
3. Go to the **Data volume by management** pack.

Configure the parameters by selecting the management packs and the timeframe. This will show you all the data volumes per each management pack to give an indication of where the problems lie.

Another way is to go to the Tuning Management packs section of the Operations Manager console by going to **Administration** | **Management** packs | **Tune management** packs, which will show you the number of alerts being generated and will provide you with some options on automatic tuning.

Default management pack

The best practice part for this is to **never save** anything to this management pack. This is a default management pack that comes with the Operations Manager by default and if the Operations Manager were to go be inaccessible or more importantly trickier to administrate, any overrides or any saved authored objects can potentially be lost resulting in a single point of failure. So it is always encouraged to create a new management pack if wanting to add any changes.

Testing management packs

When importing any new management packs, it is best to test them first, preferably within a development environment so that you can monitor some data which comes out. The worst thing you can do is to import a management pack into a production environment and possibly cause a config churn or any other form of complications or corruptions. This is important to follow especially when you are importing any community-based management packs.

Real-world scenario

You will find a real- world scenario regarding monitoring with Operations Manager in this section. There is a bigger split between best practice and real-world scenario in this chapter, but the reality comes down to the preference of how constructing monitoring will go. This is the primary topic which will be talked about in this chapter.

Console versus Visual Studio in Management packs

This is a tricky area when it comes to real world scenarios. A lot of organizations tend to use more advanced methos of developing management packs which is either through Visual Studio in combination with the **Visual Studios Authoring Extensions (VSAE)** add-on or other third-party management pack development tools.

It is mostly because of the ability of utilizing PowerShell based monitoring which is not in Operations Manager by default. Other reasons are also around the integrity of the custom developed management pack where it can remain in house and more importantly sealed!

It is much more convenient to develop a management pack within Operations Manager, but the selection on which one you choose to develop with really does depend on the request at hand.

Conclusion

The Operations Manager has different types of topology deployments that can be rolled out to support your environment by having a sufficient monitoring solution. Combined with this chapter and the previous chapter, should help outlined the scale level you require to put together the right decision.

Even after the initial implementation there are various moving parts to consider especially around agent management depending on the platforms you want to support as well as having the correct level of permissions to not only configure the agents but also the correct monitoring that they should receive as well.

In the next chapter we will start to explore the next System Center product being Service Manager, and we will also be able to tie in the possible integrations with Operations Manager into this technology.

Points to remember

- Service accounts are required for the Operations Manager to work and preferably should be domain-based accounts.
- The reporting role for the Operations Manager must have SQL Server reporting services installed before this can be added.
- The ACS role should be installed on an existing management server role.
- Agent management can manage Windows, UNIX/Linux, and Network Devices.
- Azure Log Analytics can be configured on agents after they have been installed or during a manual installation of the agent.
- Management servers, by default, will fall into the All-management servers resource pool.
- Management packs created in SCOM are unsealed, whilst management packs created in Visual Studio have the option of being sealed.
- Overrides are used to change the default configuration of authored objects such as monitors, rules and run As accounts.

Multiple choice questions

1. **What type of account is required for you to be able to add an agent to a UNIX/Linux Machine?**
    a. Resource Pool
    b. Run As Account
    c. Management pack
    d. Config Churn

2. **What is the name of the term used when too much data is being produced from a management pack or from SCOM in general?**
    a. Health Explorer
    b. Resolution State
    c. Config Churn
    d. Alert Storm

3. **Name the option used to obtain a further look into an alert or health state?**
    a. Health Explorer

b. Tune Management packs

c. Active Alerts

d. Administration

4. How would you find out which management packs are producing the most data?

    a. Installed Management packs.

    b. Tuning Management packs.

    c. Data Volume by Instance Report.

    d. Data Volume by Management pack report.

5. Name the different types of platforms which SCOM can manage?

    a. Windows

    b. UNIX/Linux

    c. Network Devices

    d. All the above

6. Management servers are upgraded before Gateway Servers.?

    a. true

    b. false

Answers

1. b
2. c
3. a
4. d
5. d
6. a

Key terms

- **Active Alert**: An alert that is currently opened.
- **Agent**: A device that is managed from the installation of a SCOM agent.
- **Unsealed Management pack**: Management pack which has a *.XML file extension.
- **Sealed Management pack**: Management pack which has a *.mp or *.mbp file extension.
- **SSRS**: SQL Server Reporting Services.
- **MSP**: File extension for update rollups.

Chapter 7
Service Reporting and Analytics with System Center Service Manager

Introduction

In this chapter, we will look into the planning and design of the **System Center Service Manager** (**SCSM**). This area will be applicable for most versions of this technology as the same key areas have to be considered, especially when looking into how the solution will be used. Scalability is also a key area that we will analyze when planning a new design. We will also discover the upgrade paths that would need to be taken to be applicable for System Center 2022. For Service Manager, we will analyze the requirements for which Service Manager will be used and how we will design based on this.

Also included will be a minimum and recommended requirement level where the reader can develop a lab environment, which they can use to follow through with the next chapter so you can gauge practical and theoretical understanding.

Structure

This chapter will cover the following topics:
- Service Manager topology structure
- Product connector planning
- Information Technology Service Management planning
- Configuration Management Database design

- Disaster recovery
- Service Manager lab requirements

Objectives

The objectives of this chapter are to understand the role that the Service Manager plays and to observe all key areas in which planning is required for you to design and provide a solution where the Service Manager can benefit, enrich, and automate the processes within your environment.

Service Manager topology structure

SCSM does have some common role functions in Operations Manager, in fact, you will find some relations and native integrations between the both of them. This is why, in this topic, it is important to run through all the roles that the Service Manager has so that the reader can understand the significance of each role and understand the outlined Service Manager topologies.

Service Manager roles

The Service Manager roles are as follows:

- **Management server**: A management server for this technology will work slightly differently than the Operations Manager product, as there are no agents distributed from the Service Manager. A management server will process workflows run throughout the Service Manager.

  The first deployment of a management server will become the primary management server, thus requiring a definition of an initial management group, and in a similar fashion to Operations Manager, has a common service being the "System Center Management Service" which runs the process `monitoringhost.exe` to allow for the workflows to run.

  Additional management servers work autonomously as a load-balanced configuration when added to the same management group as the primary server.

- **Data warehouse server**: The data warehouse server role for the Service Manager allows for historical data to be stored. In addition, the data warehouse also contains several other roles, which include, native reporting and **Structured Query Language** (**SQL**) Server analysis functionalities, which run **several Data Warehouse jobs** (**DW Jobs**) that run on a regular interval to ensure that the data is correctly processed from the operational database to the data warehouse server.

  Unlike Operations Manager, this role does not come as a default option to be installed alongside the management server. This server has to be a separate to hold this role. The server is also connected to the management server via a connector, which we will discuss in further detail within the section *Product Connector Planning*.

> **Note:** Any defined server that has a Service Manager role, Operations Manager role or other system center roles, will not be able to hold multi-system center roles on one server.

- **Self-service portal**: The self-service portal allows users to connect and request work-related services which are presented as published. They can then be put through an automated workflow process to supply a user with the required outcome. For example, a user may want to request a specific piece of software that may require a license. A request could be published to the portal in which the user fills out a form and creates a request ticket, which then triggers a workflow that connects back into the internals of the Service Manager to initiate stages of the request such as approvals, etc. then providing a confirmation of the completed request.

Single management server topology

A single management server topology will be the foundational setup of the Service Manager. Now, there can be a few methods to a single management server topology, as outlined.

> **Note:** With the exception of the Service Manager console and self-service portal with a management server role, each role outlined in the following scenarios requires its own Windows server to install the specified roles.

The methods are presented through scenarios.

Scenario one

Representing the more simplistic structure which you can implement for Service Manager:

- Management server
- Service Manager console

You can indeed have a simplistic form where you do not need to have a data warehouse server if you do not want to introduce a data retention feature to your system. Scenarios such as these can be for simpler testing or technology exploration and are enough to develop the design out further and test out the product connectors that are available.

Scenario two

Specific for those who want to utilize the data warehouse feature within Service Manager:

- Management server

- Data warehouse server
- Service Manager console

In this case, we have added the data warehouse server which will now play a role in the data retention and the DW jobs to ensure data is historically captured.

Scenario three

For those who want to use the Service Manager at its full capability and have the self-service functionality for end users:

- Management server
- Data warehouse server
- Self-service portal
- Service Manager console

Now, we have a complete Service Manager topology introduced which has all the roles added and configured for this management group. Either scenario, starting from scenario 1, supports scalability to introduce further role additions and additional management servers into the fold.

Multi-management server topology

Introducing additional management servers into the existing management group would allow for a multi-management server topology for the Service Manager.

Here, there is a logical load-balance between each of the management servers, as each server will maintain its own "`monitoringhost.exe`" process to act on the workloads and workflows that run.

If you are using a self-service portal with additional management servers, you can select which management server will be the authoritative one for your self-service portal requests.

Hardware requirements

To support the topologies or scenarios outlined, we first need to take into account the requirements that are needed in order to build out the server roles. These requirements help us understand the recommended specification levels to understand not only what our design will be but also its overall scalability.

Table 7.1 shows the hardware requirements table, with all the roles that the Service Manager has and the requirements for each role:

Service Manager role	CPU (Cores)	CPU (GHz)	Memory (GB)	Disk space (GB)
Management server	4	2.66	8	10
Data warehouse management server	4	2.66	16	10
Self-service portal	8	2.66	16	80
Management server with self-service portal	8	2.66	32	80

Table 7.1: SCSM 2022 hardware requirements

Operating System requirements

The next part of the requirements is for the **Operating Systems (OS)**. The following tables, *Table 7.2* and *Table 7.3*, outline the OS requirements for both server roles and machines that would use the Service Manager console:

Service Manager role	Windows Server version	Windows Server edition	Windows Server GUI	Windows Server core
Management Server	2019/2022	Standard/Datacenter	Yes	Yes
Data warehouse management server	2019/2022	Standard/Datacenter	Yes	Yes
Self-service portal	2019/2022	Standard/Datacenter	Yes	Yes

Table 7.2: SCSM 2022 server OS requirements

The following table shows the SCSM 2022 Client OS and server OS requirements for SCSM console:

Service Manager role	Windows Server version	Windows Server edition	Windows Server GUI	Windows Server core	Windows Client OS version
Service Manager Console	2019/2022	Standard/Datacenter	Yes	Yes	Windows 10/Windows 11

Table 7.3: SCSM 2022 Client OS and server OS requirements for SCSM console

Structured Query Language Server requirements

Here are the SQL Server requirements for the Service Manager. As there are several parts to consider when planning your SQL Server environment, we have included a few tables to break down the overall requirements.

The first table shows the hardware requirements for the SQL Servers, and the further tables will show the SQL Server versions:

Service Manager role	CPU (Cores)	CPU (GHz)	Memory (GB)	Disk space (GB)
Database	8	2.66	32GB	10
Data warehouse database	4	2.66	32GB	10

Table 7.4: SCSM 2022 Database Hardware requirements

The following table shows the SQL Server versions:

SQL Server version	SQL cumulative update (Minimum level)	Service Manager database
SQL Server 2022	N/A	Operational/Data warehouse
SQL Server 2019	CU8	Operational/Data warehouse
SQL Server 2017	Latest	Operational/Data warehouse

Table 7.5: SCSM 2022 SQL Server version requirements

Product connector planning

In the previous section, we touched lightly on the features of connectors that the Service Manager has. We will dive further into the same.

Connectors are a functionality that the Service Manager has to form an integration with other Microsoft or third-party-based products.

The ones you can use by default are as follows:

- Data warehouse connector
- Active Directory connector
- Configuration Manager connector
- System Center Operations Manager **Configuration Item (CI)** connector
- System Center Operations Manager Alert connector
- System Center Virtual Machine Manager connector
- System Center Orchestrator connector

There are other connectors also, but first, we will break down each bullet pointed connector to outline its use and its purpose within Service Manager.

Figure 7.1 shows an idea of how the connectors options are displayed within Service Manager:

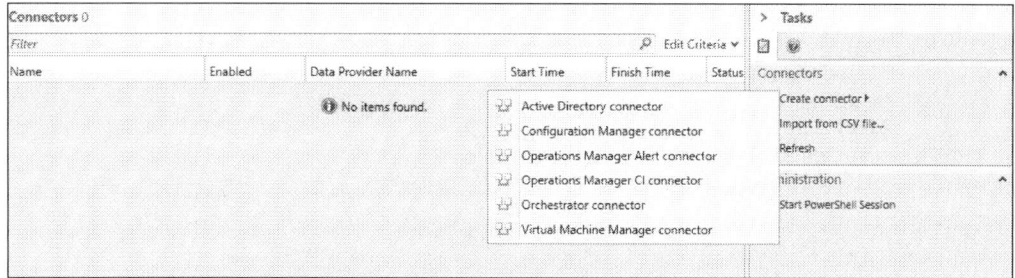

Figure 7.1: *Connectors screen in Service Manager console*

Data warehouse connector

One of the first connectors available for the data warehouse is via the data warehouse connector.

Once the connector has been configured to talk to your data warehouse server, the DW jobs will be created, and the deployment of the native Service Manager reports will start to be deployed.

Though this connector is one of the first wizards you will encounter once opening the Service Manager console, it is not a mandatory requirement as you are able to use Service Manager without a data warehouse depending on the design you have, which can be seen in *Figure 7.2*:

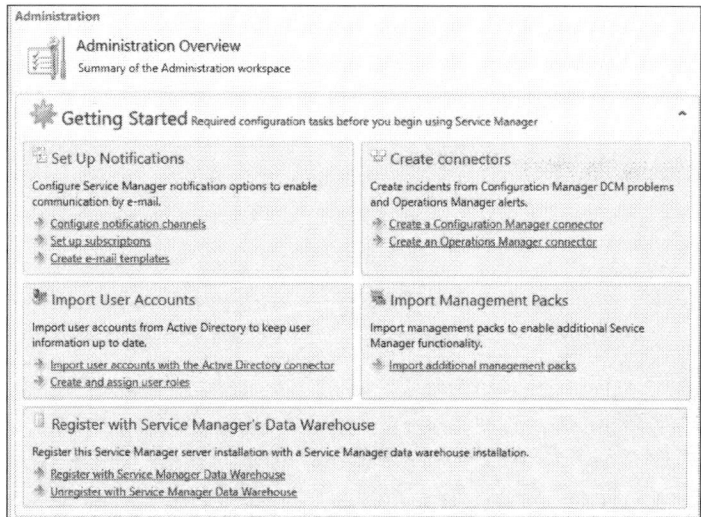

Figure 7.2: *Administration screen showing data warehouse registration*

Active Directory connector

The Active Directory connector allows you to synchronize all your AD objects into Service Manager to populate the **Configuration Management Database (CMDB)**.

The objects are:
- Computers
- Users
- Groups (Optional to include users of each group)

This would be considered somewhat of a base connector, as this has some foundational setups for your CMDB, which will allow you to have a pool of user accounts synced from Active Directory where other users can be related to workflows as CI reference points.

Configuration Manager connector

The Configuration Manager connector is used to pull various bits of information into the Service Manager, which includes, but is not limited to the following:
- Hardware inventory
- Software inventory
- Applications
- Packages
- Software updates

These help to populate the CMDB for Service Manager to enrich the forthcoming processes that will be developed to create meaningful **Information Technology Service Management (ITSM)** workflows.

The connector is able to recognize the legacy versions of Configuration Manager, and the latest versions and works by polling the device collections which are in the console and collects the information based on the devices which belong to that collection.

System Center Operations Manager CI connector

One of the two connectors for Operations Manager that focuses specifically on the CI in Operations Manager.

The connector will bring in all the inventoried data of devices that are managed in **System Center Operations Manager (SCOM)**, similar to the Configuration Manager connector. However, in this case the information which is brought in is dependent on the management packs that the Service Manager can recognize from SCOM.

For example, if you wanted to pull in data from the SCOM which carried information around the *Microsoft Hyper-V* platform, then you would need to have these management packs installed in SCOM as well as SCSM before you bring this information over.

> Note: When importing management packs for this connector, it is best to import only important ones that ideally have "Discovery" or "Library" or if it is a single management pack, not part of a bundle. These contain the classes and property attributes which hold the inventory data when discovered in SCOM.

System Center Operations Manager alert connector

The second connector for the Operations Manager is specifically around the alerts that are generated from SCOM.

The connector works by creating a workflow that allows you to synchronize alerts in SCOM and create individual instances for them within the Service Manager, which allows for them to be assigned to different users.

In addition, the connector can be configured to allow asynchronous processes which are able to detect the closure from each side. For example, if an alert in SCOM was to be closed, then essentially, this would close the open incident in Service Manager.

System Center Virtual Machine Manager connector

This connector works by synchronizing the virtual machine templates which are used within **System Center Virtual Machine Manager (SCVMM)**. For example, in Virtual Machine Manager you can create templates to build out virtual machines to a certain standard. These are objects stored within the library management that SCVMM uses and are brought into the fold of the Service Manager to be added to the CMDB. We will go into more detail later in this topic on how the planning would work for this connector.

System Center Orchestrator connector

This is an interesting connector due to the relationship between both the Service Manager and Orchestrator. We will go into detail further within this topic.

This connector synchronizes all the runbooks created in Orchestrator into the Service Manager but not just for the purpose of a CMDB function. The Service Manager can create workflows and processes; this can be enhanced further with the runbooks synchronized by the connector.

To provide an example, let us say we have a user who needs to be added to a specific Active Directory group. A ticket could be raised, which can have a runbook associated with that same ticket which would complete the request in an automated fashion from the triggering of the runbook to perform the requested action.

> Note: You will need an existing runbook which already has the Active Directory integration pack installed for this scenario to work.

Exchange connector

Though the connector itself is not on the Service Manager by default, it still plays an important function if it is required.

The Exchange connector allows mailboxes to be synchronized to detect incoming emails. They are filtered using specific criteria to determine if they need to be turned into a request in the Service Manager, which would be one of the work items such as Incidents, etc.

The connector is capable of obtaining mailboxes that are used by the Exchange Online and on-premise mailboxes.

Connectors via System Center Orchestrator

The System Center Orchestrator is also labeled as the official custom connector creator for the Service Manager and the internal connector available within SCSM.

How this works is mainly down to the integration packs that you would need to put together. The main one you need is the System Center Service Manager integration pack.

With this integration pack, you would establish a connection to your SCSM management server. Once you have this, you can create runbooks that can do read-and-write actions.

In the case of the connector, you have actions such as **Create CI** which allow you to create a new CI record for the Service Manager. Now, this particular action is the same process which the internal connectors use to synchronize data between the desired product and the Service Manager.

This option is because of various products and technologies, whether that be Microsoft or other third-party vendors, that most likely will not have a connector option natively in the Service Manager. If you want to extend what the Service Manager is able to store as a CI, then creating custom connectors in the way of Orchestrator runbooks would be a great way.

We discussed how runbooks can be synchronized into the Service Manager from the connector, but to use these runbooks as connectors, they do not need to be synchronized into SCSM in this way. The runbooks run solely on the Orchestrator whether on a manual, triggered basis or a scheduled interval that would be a replica of the internal connectors.

Planning for connector usage

Now that we have established what each connection does, we now need to plan about using these connectors. Here are some categories to define the plan of utilizing the Service Manager:

Connectors to use

We will evidently be limited to the products we have within our environment. Although, if there are other products from the System Center family, Microsoft or bespoke-based tools, this is going to make a difference in our plan on what connectors to use.

So, if we have the products that match the native connectors in the console, we can easily decide which ones would be utilized (more to be covered in the section *deciding on SCOM connector*). However, we also need to take into account if there will be any products that would require a custom connector to be developed.

Summarising it, you need to develop a plan that would fit the following scenarios:

- The products connect to that the Service Manager has a connector for.
- The products that will require a custom connector via the Orchestrator.
- If a custom connector from the Orchestrator is required, do we have the necessary integration packs for the Orchestrator?

Scheduling connector sync

All connectors have a sync schedule functionality by default. Whilst configuring, you may find that the default time is 03:00, which might be convenient. However, you will need to understand the importance of each connector configured to understand the best times.

The best way to look at this is through prioritising the connectors we have. We can assume that the Active Directory connector would be the most critical to planning your Service Manager effectively with the accounts that exist within your organization. Accepting the default would mean that by office hours you would have the latest information for all objects used within Active Directory.

Now, let us look into connectors that are around the System Center or the Configuration Manager connector. Depending on the many devices you manage and the database size will dictate how long this would take. You might not want connectors such as this to run concurrently with an Active Directory connector. The information is just as important, but understanding your environment beforehand will help to know your scheduling plans.

Deciding on System Center Operations Manager connectors

Two connectors belonging to the Operations Manager do not mean that you have to choose one or the other. It is bout deciding if one or both are going to be the most beneficial to you.

For the CI connector, you must understand if the inventoried information collected from the management packs in SCOM has vital information helpful to your synchronized Cis, as not all management packs may have relevant information. As there is a dependency of importing those same management packs into the Service Manager, it is even more important to understand what you want to do here.

Now, the alert connector can provide an entirely different scenario. Since we know that alert storms and configuration churns can occur in SCOM, you do not want to introduce the same issue into the Service Manager where thousands (hopefully not millions) of open alerts, which could turn out to create millions of tickets into SCSM. This will put you in a position to fight a bigger storm across two products.

Another side of the spectrum, when it comes to this connector, is the monitors used in SCOM. A lot of monitoring can have auto-resolution. If you were to allow for asynchronous closure for both products, for agents which may be more prone to the same alerts being created, could cause a different kind of configuration churn. So, in short you will need to ensure that you maintain a clean SCOM environment as well as a clean SCSM environment.

Information Technology Service Management planning

The next part of planning consideration is around the ITSM side; this is where you will see all the work items being processed when you start to generate processes. Now, there are several categories of work items in which the Service Manager can organize. They are as follows:

- Activity management
- Change management
- Incident management
- Problem management
- Release management
- Service request

Before we get into other areas of ITSM management planning, we will first go through each work item type to build an understanding of what each does, which will aid the planning process:

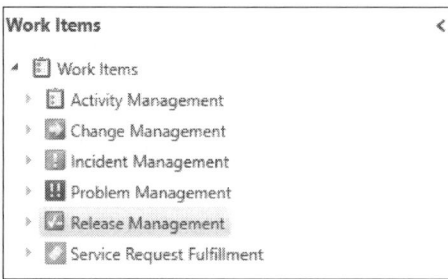

Figure 7.3: Work Items list in Service Manager console

Activity management

Activity management contains work items that consist of actions performed either manually or automatically. There are various activities listed here, with one being an approval activity for approvals required by another user, and a manual activity that waits for a user to action something and confirms the action when completed. Another example is a runbook activity where an Orchestrator runbook is attached to the activity that would perform an automated function within a request or work item.

Change management

Change management contains work items for change requests. These would be the same change requests you would typically see within a **Change Advisory Board** (**CAB**) setting.

Incident management

Incident management contains work items for Incidents that would be raised within your environment if any technical issues were to arise.

Incidents have various forms of having work items generated which are not limited to, the following:

- E-Mail Incidents
- Operations Manager (Alert connector)
- Portal Incidents (Generated from the self-service portal)

Incidents can have **Service Level Agreements** (**SLAs**) attached to them to manage the response times and when any open tickets are overdue and awaiting resolution or closure.

Problem management

Problem Management contains work items for problem requests generated. Following the definition of ITSM classes problems is the reason why Incidents would keep generating; hence some default views of the problem management section within the Service Manager detail a category such as "Active Known Errors"..

Release management

Release Management contains work items used for release requests. There are some bits discussed within CMDB that may help to understand this section more. Going by its ITSM definition, these items are handy for managing the release of certain processes whether that be environmental basis, that is, development release to pre-production, or even software releases, etc.

Fulfilling service request

Service Requests contain work items that are used for service request management. These work items have a bit of ambiguous use due to the nature of how these can be used.

Not only can these be requested through the Service Manager console, but they also have an integration into the self-service portal. This help to tie the service request templates to service requests made available to users within the self-service portal.

Developing templates

Templates are related to each category of ITSM requests mentioned in the preceding section. You can have as many as you require, whether that be from cloning an existing template or creating one from scratch.

This area is very important depending on your design, as you may want to have specific requests that require different types of information to be entered by the end user.

Let us take the Service Requests for example, you may have an idea of a request which would allow a user to have their password reset. Now, take into account that the person who requires this request is unable to do this because their account is locked out due to too many tries; therefore, someone would have to request this on their behalf.

We could, of course, just enter this in a default template for a service desk team to read, but would that be enough in reality? It may be better to have some activities attached to a request, which would allow for some checks and approvals. This is where a template would kick in.

Here, we could create a service request and name it something like "Reset User Password". With this request filled out, it would have several activities within its process, which would call on the user manager to observe the request and approve it. It would then detail the approval to the service desk team to grant the user to be provided with a temporary password which they can use to reset within the next login.

Overall, the example detail areas to consider are:
- The most common user requests.
- Requirement of defined change request templates for BAU and project-based requests.
- Availability of sandpits and pre-production environments to require release management?
- Service requests are eligible for publication in a self-service portal.

The bullet points help to give an idea of how to approach a template model for your Service Manager environment.

To take the customization further, you can create a template within a new SCSM management pack which would contain custom fields used by the user to enter more specific information. This would require you to have other tools such as the Visual Studio VSAE extension or the SCSM management pack authoring tool.

> Note: The SCSM management pack authoring tool now comes with SCSM as an additional installation program. You can use either this or Visual Studio VSAE, but there is still a dependency on Visual Studio on either one if you choose to create a management pack from scratch.

Once imported, you will then see your template in the Service Manager, which would then have an additional tab detailing the new fields you have entered.

Development of workflows

The workflows in the Service Manager determine the default behavior regarding certain work items. These can be determined by the name of the work item, the person who raised the ticket, and even to who the ticket is assigned to.

With this in mind, this is where we would need to define criteria for how our workflow or workflows would be designed.

To give an idea, let us create an example version of an Incident workflow, which is as follows:

- An object is created.
- Service Desk is assigned to user.
- A support group Incident template is applied.
- Notify the service desk group that a new Incident has been created.

The preceding bullet points represent the conditions of the workflows that can be defined. With various properties for each section of a work item, it can allow the administrator to formulate different kinds of workflows based on the structure of the specific work items that it is based on.

Configuration Management Database design

With all the topics collated, it helps us form how the CMDB will be designed. Let us go over some of the key areas around the design of this.

Up-to-date information

As we discussed previously, the information to populate the CMDB will primarily come from all the connectors defined in the Service Manager, whether those are the native connectors or outside connectors developed within the System Center Orchestrator.

In order to run an effective Service Manager, the Ci within the CMDB would need to be accurate. Old information could start to hinder the overall workflows, making the gap of accuracy much bigger to the point where the CMDB would not hold much business purpose.

This part of the design holds a dependency on the connectors working and correct scheduling.

Views for custom Configuration Item classes

The Service Manager contains custom views used to show the CI that have been synchronized as seen in *Figure 7.4*.

The views can also be created, and are vital to be created, if you want a visual look into the different types of CI objects captured within SCSM.

To provide another example of how this would go, let us look at the default CI views that we have, such as computers, which contain a summarized hardware and software inventory view. Now, we know certain computers can hold more specific role functions, let us say they are SQL Servers part of a cluster or AlwaysOn.

If we have configured the Operations Manager CI connector and allowed for the SQL Server information to be captured, this would now be within the Service Manager databases. It is evidently not visible. This is where the views come in.

This area now has a dependency on connectors to bring in the information, but to have it as a visual and registered CI, which could be added as a related item within an ITSM work item, you will need a custom view to at least view the information, validate its accuracy from how it is synchronized and have the ability to update where needed and we can see an example of this within *Figure 7.4*:

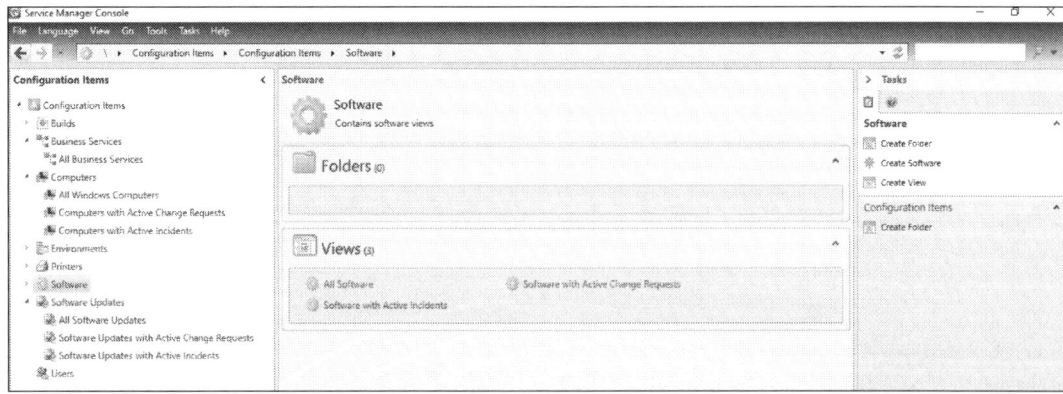

Figure 7.4: *CI view in Service Manager console*

Disaster recovery

The options for disaster recovery within the Service Manager can be somewhat limited, with the exception of server backups, SQL server backups, and high availability methods for both Windows and SQL perspectives. Let us explore other areas where we can provide disaster recovery.

Additional management servers

Service Manager has some advantages regarding disaster recovery, where management servers are concerned, to provide a load-balanced functionality when other management servers are introduced into the management group.

Secure storage backup

After installing the Service Manager product, you have the secure storage backup application, which contains an encryption key. This key can be backed up and used in the future and without this key, you cannot recover the original Service Manager setup if the systems go down. You will be unable to retrieve this information again and, therefore, will need to start from scratch.

It is best to ensure that you make a backup of this key and store it in a safe area quickly before proceeding with any further configuration, as shown in the following figure:

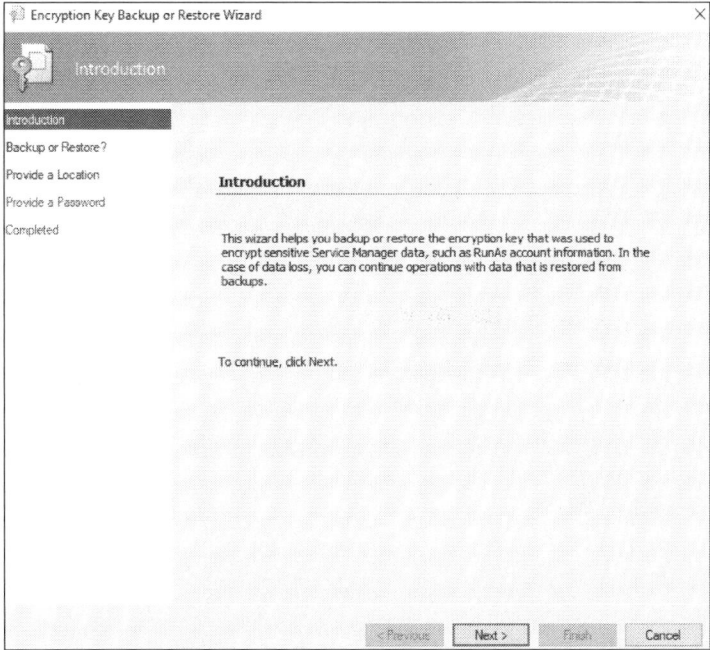

Figure 7.5: Encryption key backup or restore wizard screen

Service Manager lab requirements

Now, when designing a Service Manager lab there are two scenarios that you can use to test to understand SCSM better, as seen in the following table.

The easiest and simplest topology you can use that does not have to use a data warehouse or self-service portal in this scenario.

Single management server

This type of lab works for the more simplistic and consolidated setup which allows you to get up and running with the Service Manager much quicker to be able to explore the product further:

Service Manager role	CPU (Cores)	CPU (GHz)	Memory (GB)	Disk space (GB)
Management server	4	2.66	8	10
Service Manager role	Windows Server version	Windows Server edition	Windows Server **Graphical User Interface (GUI)**	Windows Server ore
Management server	2019/2022	Standard/Datacenter	Yes	Yes

Table 7.6: Single Management server requirement table

Single management server and data warehouse

Now, take another scenario in which you want to have a data warehouse brought into the lab. The specifications would look as follows:

Service Manager role	CPU (Cores)	CPU (GHz)	Memory (GB)	Disk space (GB)
Management server	4	2.66	8	10
Data warehouse management server	4	2.66	16	10

Table 7.7: Single management and data warehouse management requirement table

The specifications are as follows:

Service Manager role	Windows Server version	Windows Server edition	Windows Server GUI	Windows Server core
Management server	2019/2022	Standard/Datacenter	Yes	Yes
Data warehouse management server	2019/2022	Standard/Datacenter	Yes	Yes

Table 7.8: Single management and data warehouse management OS requirements table

Multi management server and data warehouse

The most comprehensive topology to have a full-Service Manager structure includes all roles, and with an additional management server so you can now utilize the self-service portal role effectively, as shown in the following table:

Service Manager role	CPU (Cores)	CPU (GHz)	Memory (GB)	Disk space (GB)
Management server	4	2.66	8	10
Data warehouse management server	4	2.66	16	10
Self-Service Portal	8	2.66	16	80
Management server with Self-service portal	8	2.66	32	80

Table 7.9: Multi management server and data warehouse hardware requirements table

The multi-management server requirements are shown in the following table:

Service Manager role	Windows Server version	Windows Server edition	Windows Server GUI	Windows Server core
Management server	2019/2022	Standard/Datacenter	Yes	Yes
Data warehouse management server	2019/2022	Standard/Datacenter	Yes	Yes
Self-Service Portal	2019/2022	Standard/Datacenter	Yes	Yes

Table 7.10: Multi management server requirements tables

Conclusion

The Service Manager has an integral role but perhaps a complicated one as it sits in a centralized area within the System Center suite where its integrations with its family counterparts to make the Service Manager product much more powerful.

This product is here to keep the ITSM side of your environment held together and performing a function which helps and benefits the business and allows for the service desk teams or any BAU functions within an organization to be able to effectively manage all kinds of different requests from general service, project and incidents.

This can only happen when Service Manager is designed correctly with its core processes defined out very early on. Service Manager is indeed a product where spontaneous add-ons can potentially throw the framework it provides out of whack, and as it contains a CMDB role it is very important to ensure that the information is accurate as well as enriched to provide a core business function.

The next chapter will focus on how we install and configure Service Manager, and also how we are able to administer the technology efficiently.

Points to remember

- Connectors are used to integrate with other System Center and core Microsoft products within your environment.
- The data warehouse registration is a default connector provided at the beginning of opening the console to integrate the server that holds this role.
- Operations Manager contains two connectors which are used to integrate between itself and the Service Manager.
- System Center Orchestrator is known as the official product used to create custom connectors for further integration methods.
- ITSM management is used to manage work items which belong to several categories within the ITSM stack
- CMDB information is stored with records listed as CIs, which hold a dependency to the connectors, which are in the Service Manager console.
- Additional management servers are needed if you want to utilize the self-service portal in the most proficient way.
- Management servers are a way to increase availability within the Service Manager process to provide a load-balanced method across workflows created.
- Workflows can be tied into work items which follow a specific process to achieve an overall outcome.

Multiple choice questions

1. **What tool is required to create management packs from scratch to be imported into the Service Manager for custom form templates?**
   a. Visual Studio
   b. VSAE
   c. VS Code
   d. Service Manager Management pack authoring tool

2. **Which connector is not available by default but provides a function that allows you to connect to mailboxes?**
   a. Exchange connector
   b. Orchestrator
   c. Runbook
   d. Configuration Manager connector

3. **How does the Orchestrator utilize its runbooks to be attached to work item template processes?**
   a. Workflows
   b. Incident management
   c. Orchestrator connector
   d. Custom runbook created via the Orchestrator

4. **In order to show Ci that have been brought into the Service Manager, that do not fit the default views, how do we make these visible within the Service Manager console?**
   a. Custom template
   b. Custom management pack
   c. Custom view
   d. Administration tab

5. **In case of a disaster recovery, what is important to have before proceeding to recover any existing Service Manager structure during a disaster recovery event?**
   a. Reset this PC
   b. SQL AlwaysOn
   c. Additional management server
   d. Secure storage backup key

6. When adding additional management servers to the Service Manager, you will add a function that allows for more custom classes to be created.

    a. True

    b. False

Answers

1. d
2. a
3. c
4. c
5. d
6. b

Key terms

- **ITSM**: Information Technology Service Management
- **CMDB**: Configuration management database
- **CI**: Configuration Item
- **Workflow**: A process which has more than one activity that follows a step by step to provide a desired result
- **Integration**: A relationship between both products where synchronous or asynchronous communication can begin
- **Data warehouse**: A data retention storage mechanism that is used to cover data from an operational database to be backed up and stored to provide historical results.

Join our book's Discord space

Join the book's Discord Workspace for Latest updates, Offers, Tech happenings around the world, New Release and Sessions with the Authors:

https://discord.bpbonline.com

CHAPTER 8
Deployment and Administration of System Center Service Manager

Introduction

This chapter will concentrate on the development and deployment of the **System Center Service Manager** (**SCSM**). The importance of this chapter is to illustrate the setup of the Service Manager and the overall deployment, so we can ensure the design plan that we specified in the previous section allows us to have a healthy setup. There will also be some troubleshooting points to help the reader understand the common and uncommon issues that can arise during the development and deployment process.

You will also get an in-depth look into the overall administration of the System Center Service Manager, as well as its best practices. The administration side is what will allow an engineer to perform their **business as usual** (**BAU**) tasks, but also within the administrative side, another area that would enrich the BAU tasks and the overall UI, is where the best practices come in. Best practices are normally looked at as professional and recommended levels of what you should and not do. Although, we understand that a real-world scenario can conflict with best practices, hence we will look to outline the differences between both.

Structure

This chapter will cover the following topics:
- Service Manager installation
- Connector configuration
- Self-Service configuration
- Administrator of the Service Manager
- Best practices
- Real-world scenarios

Objectives

The reader, at this point, would have understood the usage of the Service Manager and will be able to move onto the next step and structure the design they require through learning to perform the installation of various roles of the Service Manager infrastructure.

To develop a full picture of how a typical environment is implemented and administrated, some points around best practices and real-world scenarios will be given to paint a more realistic picture of the experience you will obtain from the Service Manager.

Service Manager installation

Before getting into the installation of the Service Manager, we first need to understand the prerequisites required to install any core roles.

These prerequisites can range from the Windows OS specific to the prerequisites which the installation media requires before proceeding.

Management Server

As there are various roles you can decide from in the initial installation, we will cover the requirements on a per role basis. The following server roles and features are required to be configured before installing the management server role:

- **Server features**: The following feature needs to be installed:
  - .NET Framework 3.5 Features
- **Server roles:** No additional server roles are required.

Data warehouse server

As there are various roles you can decide from in the initial installation, we will cover the requirements on a per role basis. The following server roles and features are required to be configured before we install the management server role:

- **Server features**: The following features need to be installed:
    - .NET Framework 3.5 Features
- **Server roles**: No additional server roles are required.

Self-Service Portal

As there are various roles that you can decide from in the initial installation, we will cover the requirements on a per role basis. The following server roles and features are required to be configured before we install the management server role:

- **Server roles**: The following features need to be installed:
    - Web Server (IIS)
- **Server features**: The following features need to be installed:
    - .NET Framework 3.5 Features

Self-Service Portal Internet Information Services installation

The instructions on how to correctly perform the installation of the Self-Service Portal in Service Manager are:

1. Click on the start menu.
2. Go to the **Server Manager** console.
3. In the top right-hand corner, select **Manage: Add Roles and Features**.
4. **Before You Begin:** Click **Next**.
5. **Select Installation Type:** Ensure the **role-based or feature-based installation** is selected, then click next.
6. **Select destination server: Server Selection**: Ensure that the **Select a server from the server pool** has your server selected, then click **Next**.
7. **Select server roles: Server roles**: Select the following roles:
    a. Web Server (IIS)
8. **Select features: Features:**
    a. .NET Framework 3.5 Features | .NET Framework 3.5 (includes .NET 2.0 and 3.0)
    b. .NET Framework 4.8 Features | .NET Framework 4.8
    c. .NET Framework 4.8 Features | ASP.NET 4.8
    d. .NET Framework 4.8 Features | WCF Services | HTTP Activation
    e. .NET Framework 4.8 Features –| WCF Services | TCP Port Sharing

9. **Select role services**: Select the following role services:
   a. Web Server | Common HTTP Features | Default Document
   b. Web Server | Common HTTP Features | Directory Browsing
   c. Web Server | Common HTTP Features | HTTP Errors
   d. Web Server | Common HTTP Features | Static Content
   e. Web Server | Web Server Health and Diagnostics | HTTP Logging
   f. Web Server | Performance | Static Content Compression
   g. Web Server | Security | Request Filtering
   h. Web Server | Security | Basic Authentication
   i. Web Server | Security | Windows Authentication
   j. Web Server | Application Development - .NET Extensibility 4.8
   k. Web Server | Application Development - ASP
   l. Web Server | Application Development - ASP.NET 4.8
   m. Web Server | Application Development | ISAPI Extensions
   n. Web Server | Application Development | ISAPI Filters

   Then click **Next**
10. **Confirm installation selections:** Click on the **Specify an alternate source path** link at the bottom of the window.
11. **Specify an alternate source path**: Enter the path of the installation media to point to the following folder that is, `D:\Sources\SxS`. Then, click **OK**.
12. **Confirm installation selections: Confirmation** | Click **Install**.

Service Manager console

As there are various roles that you can decide from, in the initial installation, we will cover the requirements on a per-role basis. The following server roles and features are required to be configured before we are able to install the management server role:

- **Server features**: The following features need to be installed:
  - .NET Framework 3.5 Features
- **Server roles:** No additional server roles required.

Windows Server OS installation media

Before following the instructions, there are some other tasks you need to perform first. Since one of the server features is .NET Framework 3.5, it can only be installed when you have the installation media of the Windows Server OS. You either have this mounted to the computer or copied locally to the system drive, where you can point to the directory.

Installation of server roles and features

To install the server roles, perform the following instructions:

1. Click the start menu.
2. Go to the **Server Manager** console.
3. In the top right-hand corner, select **Manage** | **Add roles and features**.
4. **Before you begin:** Click **Next**.
5. **Select installation type: Installation Type** | Ensure the **Role-based or feature-based installation** is selected, then click **Next**.
6. **Select destination server: Server Selection** | Ensure that the **Select a server from the server pool** has your server selected, then click **Next**.
7. **Select server roles:** Click **Next**.
8. Click the **Add Features** button within the dialogs when they pop, then click **Next**.
9. **Select features:** Select the following features:
   a. .NET Framework 3.5 Features - .NET Framework 3.5 (includes .NET 2.0 and 3.0)

   Then click **Next**.
10. **Confirm installation selections: Confirmation** | Click on the **Specify an alternate source path** link at the bottom of the window.
11. **Specify an alternate source path**: Enter the path of the installation media to point to the following folder that is,. **D:\Sources\SxS**. Then, click **OK**.
12. **Confirm installation selections: Confirmation** | Click **Install**.

Service Manager prerequisites

Though there many Windows Server OS requirements, there are however two prerequisites that must be installed before you proceed further into the installation, as per *Figure 8.1*.

The following softwares are required:

- Microsoft **Structured Query Language** (**SQL**) Server Analysis Management Objects
- Microsoft OLE DB Driver for SQL:

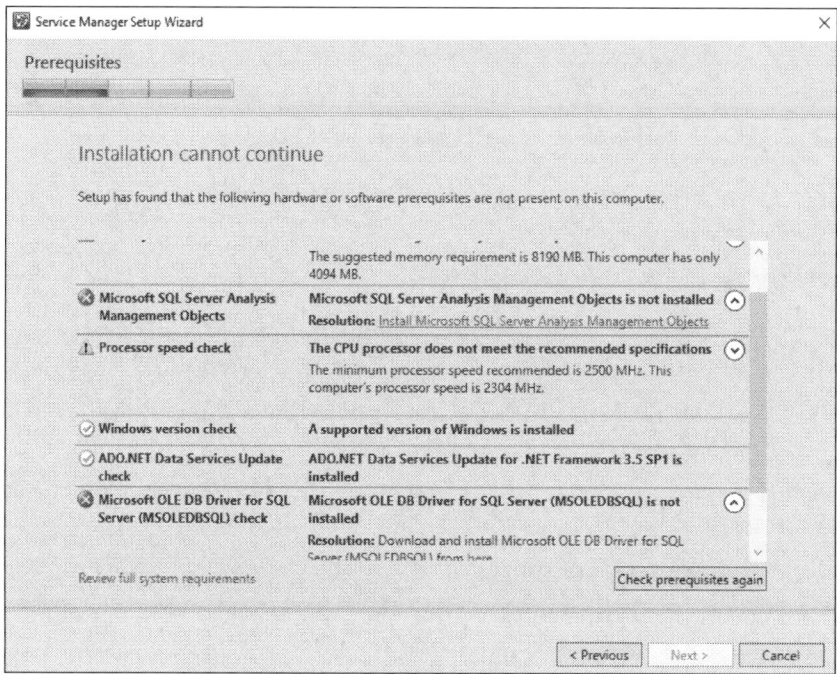

Figure 8.1: Service Manager Prerequisites screen

Installing Microsoft SQL Server Analysis Management Objects

The installation files for this prerequisite can be found in the installation media of Service Manager in the Prerequisites folder.

To install, perform the following:

1. Open the Installation media for Service Manager.
2. Browse to the Prerequisites folder and double-click the `SQL_AS_AMO.msi` file.
3. **Welcome to the Installation Wizard for Microsoft Analysis Management Objects** | Click **Next**.
4. **License agreement**: Select "I accept the terms in the license agreement", then click **Next**.
5. **Ready to Install the Program**: Click the **Install** button to complete the installation.

Installing Microsoft OLE DB Driver for SQL

While the previous prerequisite is available within the installation media, the OLE DB driver has to be downloaded in order to get the file.

The download can be found here **https://go.microsoft.com/fwlink/?linkid=2168853**.

To install, perform the following:
1. Download the installation file from the link above.
2. Double-click the `msoledbql.msi` file.
3. **Microsoft OLE DB Driver for SQL Server Setup** | Click **Next**.
4. **License Agreement**: Select "**I accept the terms in the license agreement**", then click **Next**.
5. **Feature Selection** | Click **Next**.
6. **Ready to install the program**: Click the **Install** button to complete the installation.

Service account requirements

The Service Manager contains service accounts that are required to run correctly.

The following table shows all the service accounts required to be set up, along with an explanation about what each service account is for:

Name	Description	Local or domain
Service Manager services	Used to run the main services on the management server for SCSM	Domain
Service Manager workflow account	Used to run any workflows that are created within SCSM	Domain
Reporting account	Used for reporting data sources and generating native reports for Service Manager	Domain
Analysis Services account	Used to communicate with the data marts for the Data Warehouse role	Domain
Self Service Portal account	Used for the application pool for SMSelfServicePortal	Local/Domain

Table 8.1: Service Manager service account table

Firewall requirements

The following firewall requirements table shows the required ports which need to be opened. This is in reference to the official documentation **https://learn.microsoft.com/en-us/system-center/scsm/ports?view=sc-sm-2022**. The table is as follows:

Firewall direction	Ports used	Protocol type	TCP or UDP
Service Manager console to Service Management server/Data warehouse management server	5724	SCSM Port	TCP
Service Management server to SQL Server	1433	SQL Port	TCP
Data warehouse management server to SQL Server	1433	SQL Port	TCP
Service Management Server to Operations Manager connectors	5724	SCSM Port	TCP

Table 8.2: Service Manager firewall requirements

Management server installation

Once these prerequisites have been installed, we can perform the installation for a management server.

To install the management server, perform the following instructions:

1. Open the installation media to Service Manager 2022.
2. Double-click the **setup.exe** file.
3. Select the Service Manager management server under the Install section of the splash screen.
4. **Getting Started: Product Registration** | Enter the name and organization you will be registering the product on and enter a product key for the product, unless you are choosing to install the evaluation version that lasts for 180 days. Select the **I have read, understood, and agree with the terms of the license terms** tick box, then click Next.
5. **Getting Started: Installation Location** | Select where you want to install the product, then click **Next**.
6. **Prerequisites: System check results** | Ensure that there are no critical errors or warnings upon the prerequisite check before proceeding, then click **Next**.
7. **Configuration: Configure the Service Manager database** | Enter the name of the SQL Server and instance name you will be creating the operational database for. Wait for the connection check to be successful and verify the location of the database and log files. Then, click **Next**.

> Note: You may see a notification pop-up informing you of the SQL collation being used on the instance if you are using the default SQL_Latin1_General_CP1_CI_AS. This is fine if you are not planning on having a multi-lingual environment. You can see the notification for reference in *Figure 8.2:*

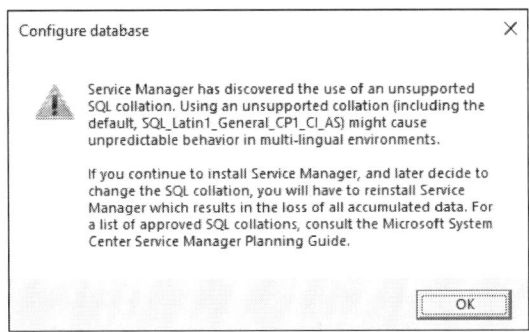

Figure 8.2: *Configure database notification*

8. **Configuration: Configure the Service Manager management group** | Enter the name of the management group name which this management server will be using. Select a user or group that will have administrative rights to your Service Manager environment, then click **Next**.

> Note: The Administrator account cannot be used for this, so you will need to pick a domain-based user or group.

9. **Configuration: Configure the account for Service Manager services.** Enter the details of the domain account which will be used to run the Service Manager service. Test credentials to ensure it has the correct permissions, then click **Next**.

10. **Configuration: Configure the Service Manager workflow account.** Enter the details of the domain account which will be used to run the workflow service. Test credentials to ensure it has the correct permissions, then click **Next**.

11. **Configuration: Diagnostic and usage data** | Click **Next**.

12. **Configuration: Use Microsoft Update to help keep your computer secure and up-to-date**. Select if you want the product to use Microsoft Update to check for updates for Service Manager, then click **Next**.

13. **Configuration**: **Installation Summary** | Review the configuration for the management server, then click **Install** to begin:

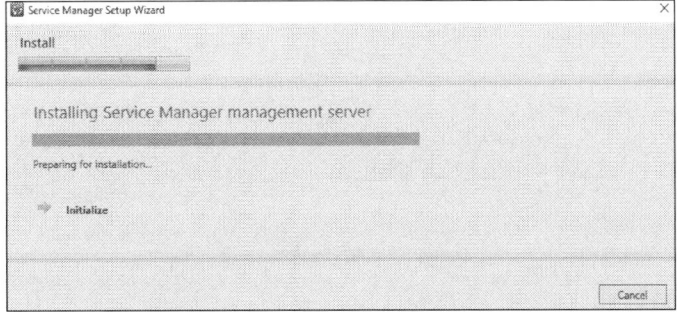

Figure 8.3: *Installation of Service Manager 2022*

> Note: To further look into the installation progress or even if the installation has failed, you can review the log files in the %temp% folder which contain .log files such as SCSMSetup, SCSMSetupWizard, SCSMPrereqCheck and SCSMInstall.

Management Server encryption key backup

Upon finishing the installation, you will have a box ticked which will allow you to back-up the encryption key, which is used in a disaster recovery scenario. After the **Finish** button has been clicked, it will launch the wizard.

Alternatively, you can go to the installation media and `Tools\SecureStorageBackup\SecureStorageBackup.exe` to bring up the same wizard.

To back-up the key, perform the following:

1. **Introduction: Introduction** | Click **Next**.
2. **Backup or Restore: Select Action** | Select **Backup the Encryption Key,** then click **Next**.
3. **Provide a Location**: Specify the location of the backup file | Enter the path of the backup file key, which will use a `.bin` file extension.

> Note: It is best to make a back-up of this key and store it in a secure network location. You can, of course, create the key and then move the key to a secure network share afterward.

4. **Provide a Password:** Specify the password that will authorize the back-up or restore. Enter the password to be used with the encrypted key. Click **Next**.
5. **Secure Storage Backup Complete** | Click **Next**.

Additional Management Server installation

The procedure is very similar to the first management server installation, but the steps may vary slightly.

The instructions on how to add additional management servers to your SCSM environment is aa follows:

> Note: In order for the installation of additional management servers to work, you must be logged into an account that has administrative rights within your SCSM environment.

1. Open the installation media to Service Manager 2022.
2. Double-click the `setup.exe` file.

3. Select the Service Manager management server under the Install section of the splash screen.

4. **Getting Started: Product Registration** | Enter the name and organization you will be registering the product on and enter a product key for the product, unless you are choosing to install the evaluation version which lasts for 180 days. Select the **I have read, understood, and agree with the terms of the license terms** tick box, then click **Next**.

5. **Getting Started: Installation Location** | Select where you want to install the product, then click **Next**.

6. **Prerequisites**: **System check results** | Ensure that there are no critical errors or warnings on the prerequisite check. Then, click **Next**.

7. **Configuration**: Configure the Service Manager database. Enter the name of the SQL Server and the instance name for where you will be using the existing operational database for. Wait for the connection check to be successful and then select **Use an existing database.** Select the Service Manager database. You will see a notification confirming a similar detail as made in the note above regarding the account used to make this connection. Click **Next**.

8. **Configuration**: **Configure the Service Manager management group** | Here, you will see the details for the management group name, and the management group administrators have been greyed out but prefilled. If these details are indeed correct, then click **Next**.

9. **Configuration:** Configure the account for Service Manager services. Enter the details of the domain account which will be used to run the Service Manager service. Test the credentials to ensure it has the correct permissions, then click **Next**.

10. **Configuration: Diagnostic and usage data** | Click **Next**.

11. **Configuration:** Use Microsoft Update to help keep your computer secure and up-to-date. Select if you want the product to use Microsoft Update to check for updates for Service Manager, then click **Next**.

12. **Configuration**: **Installation Summary** | Review the configuration for the management server, then click **Install** to begin.

Data warehouse reporting prerequisites

Before you use the reporting function correctly, you will need to prepare the **SQL Server Reporting Services** (**SSRS**) instance that you will use to handle the reporting for the Service Manager first, before going through the installation.

In your installation media, you will notice that in the Prerequisites folder, you will see a file called `Microsoft.EnterpriseManagement.Reporting.Code.dll`. This file is required to be copied over to the SSRS instance to allow for remote communication between the data warehouse and the Service Manager; this can be seen in *Figure 8.4:*

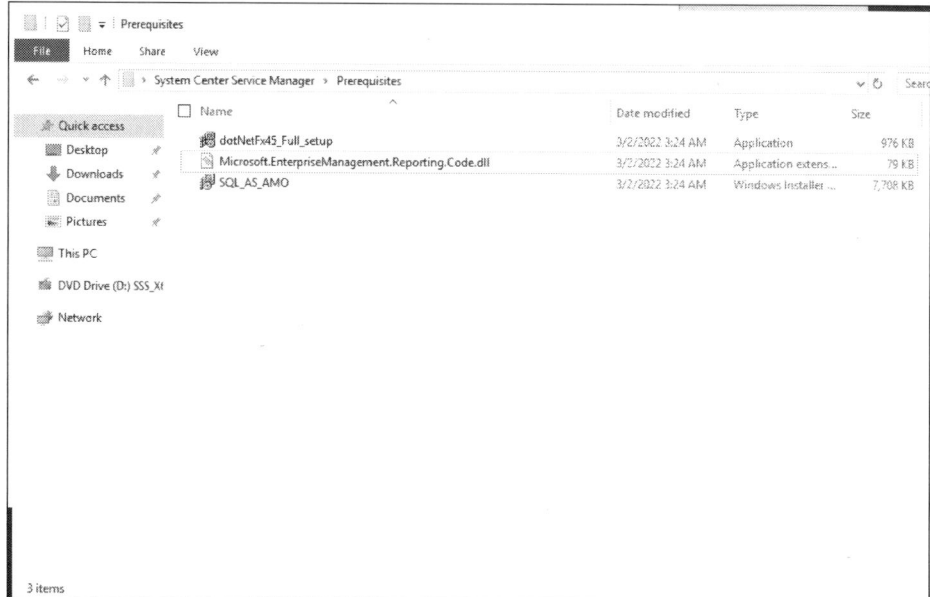

Figure 8.4: Prerequisites folder

We will go through the process of how to prepare this part, which is also in reference to the following official Microsoft documentation **https://learn.microsoft.com/en-us/system-center/scsm/prepare-remote-ssrs?view=sc-sm-2022. The process is as follows:**

1. **Copy the installation media to your SQL Server SSRS instance machine.**
2. **Open the installation media for the Service Manager.**
3. **Go to the prerequisites folder and copy the `Microsoft.EnterpriseManagement.Reporting.Code.dll` file.**
4. **Browse to the location `%Program Files%\Microsoft SQL Server Reporting Services\SSRS\ReportServer\bin`.**
5. **Copy the file to this location.**
6. **Open the following file `%Program Files%\Microsoft SQL Server Reporting Services\SSRS\ReportServer\rsreportserver.config` in the notepad.**
7. **Search for the XML line with `<Data>` where you will find a list of extension lines created, and then paste the following line in:**

    `<Extension Name="SCDWMultiMartDataProcessor" Type="Microsoft.EnterpriseManagement.Reporting.MultiMartConnection, Microsoft.EnterpriseManagement.Reporting.Code" />`

8. **Save the file, then close.**

Your `rsreportserver.config` should look like how it is displayed in *Figure 8.5*:

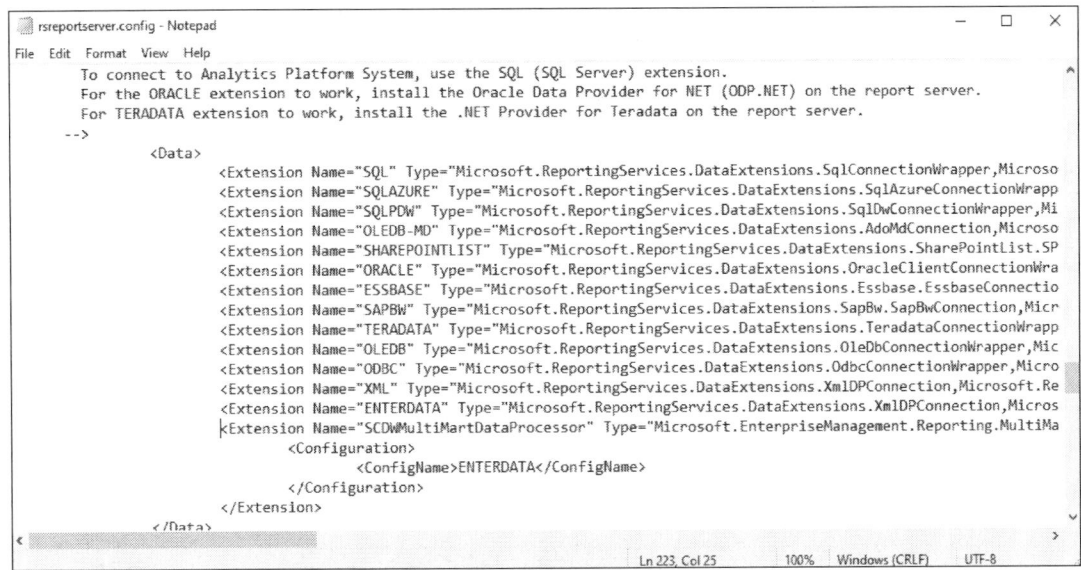

Figure 8.5: Rsreportserver with additional extension added

Data warehouse server installation

To install the data warehouse role, perform the following instructions:

1. Open the installation media to Service Manager 2022.
2. Double-click the `setup.exe` file.
3. Select the Service Manager data warehouse management server under the **Install** section of the splash screen.
4. **Getting Started: Product Registration** | Enter the name and organization of the person who will register the product and enter a product key for the product unless you are choosing to install the evaluation version, which lasts for 180 days. Select the **I have read, understood, and agree with the terms of the license terms** tick box, then click **Next**.
5. **Getting Started: Installation Location** | Select where you want to install the product, then click **Next**.
6. **Prerequisites: System check results** | Ensure that there are no critical errors or warnings upon the prerequisite check. Then, click **Next**.
7. **Configuration**: Configure the data warehouse database. To do so enter the name of the SQL Server and the instance name where you will be creating the data warehouse databases. Wait for the connection check to be successful and then select then confirm the details for both the **Staging and Configuration** and **Repository** databases. You will also need to repeat the same step for the **Data Mart** database below. When ready click **Next**.

8. **Configure additional data warehouse datamarts:** Enter the name of the SQL Server and instance name for where you will be creating the **Operations Manager (OM)** Data mart and **Configuration Manager (CM)** Data Mart databases on. Wait for the connection check to be successful, and then select. Confirm the details for both, then click **Next**.

9. **Configuration**: Configure the data warehouse management group. Here, you will see the details for the management group name. The management group administrators have been greyed out but prefilled. If these details are indeed correct, then click **Next**.

10. **Configure the reporting server for the data warehouse:** Enter the name of where the SQL Server Reporting Services instance is. Then, select the **Report server** instance and web service URL. Select the **I have taken the manual steps to configure the remote SQL Server Reporting Services as described in the Service Manager Deployment Guide** tick box, then click **Next**.

Note: Follow the data warehouse prerequisites section before confirming the preceding step, as you will face significant issues if this part is not completed correctly.

11. **Configuration:** Configure the account for Service Manager services. Enter the details of the domain account which will be used to run the Service Manager service. Test the credentials to ensure it has the correct permissions, then click **Next**.

12. **Configuration: Configure the reporting account** | Enter the details of the domain account that will be used to run the reporting service. Test credentials to ensure it has the correct permissions, then click **Next**.

13. **Configuration: Configure Analysis Services for Online Analytical Processing (OLAP) cubes** | Enter the name of the SQL Server that has the SQL Server Analysis Services installed. Wait for the verification check to finish. Confirm the details, then click **Next**.

14. **Configuration: Configure Analysis Services Credential** | Enter the details of the domain account which will be used to run the analysis services. Test the credentials to ensure it has the correct permissions, then click **Next**.

15. **Configuration: Diagnostic and usage data** | Click **Next**.

16. **Configuration:** Use Microsoft Update to help keep your computer secure and up-to-date. Select if you want the product to use Microsoft Update to check for updates for Service Manager, then click **Next**.

17. **Configuration**: **Installation Summary** | Review the configuration for the management server, then click **Install** to begin:

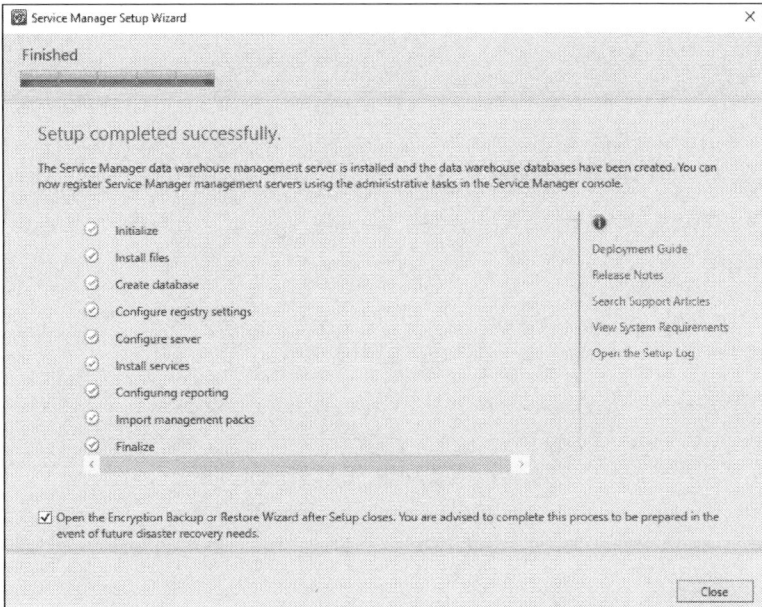

Figure 8.6: Data warehouse management server installation complete

Connector configuration

Now that we have built the initial management server and data warehouse server, we can start to formulate the connectors which are available. This is a mandatory task if you want to have a data warehouse management server as a part of your SCSM environment.

Setting up the data warehouse connector

To configure the data warehouse connector, perform the following instructions:

1. Open the Service Manager console.
2. On the Administration Overview page, go to the **Register with Service Manager's Data Warehouse** window. Then select **Register with Service Manager Data Warehouse**.
3. **Before You Begin: Register with the Service Manager Data Warehouse** | Click **Next**.
4. **Data Warehouse: Specify the data warehouse management server name** | Enter the name of the data warehouse management server and then click **Test Connection** to verify the connectivity. Then, click **Next**.
5. **Credentials**: Provide credentials for the data warehouse. Enter the credentials which will be used to make the connection. Then, click **Next**.

6. **Summary**: Confirm Connection Settings | Click **Create** to finish the connector setup.

Once this has been completed, you will see a notification advising you of the reporting functionality being set up. From then on, the Service Manager console will show two additional tabs, which are as follows:

- Data warehouse
- Reporting

The **Data Warehouse** tab will be the first tab to show up instantly, as this is where the data warehouse jobs take place to setup the reporting function.

Figures 8.7 and *8.8* give a breakdown of how this process works:

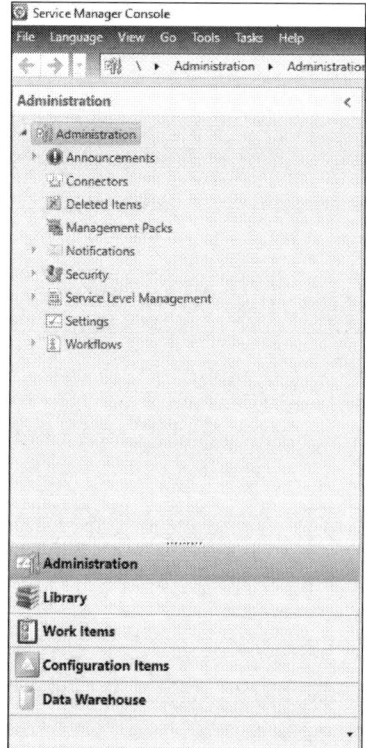

Figure 8.7: *Data Warehouse tab in Service Manager console after data warehouse connection*

To see a further breakdown of the process, refer to the following figure:

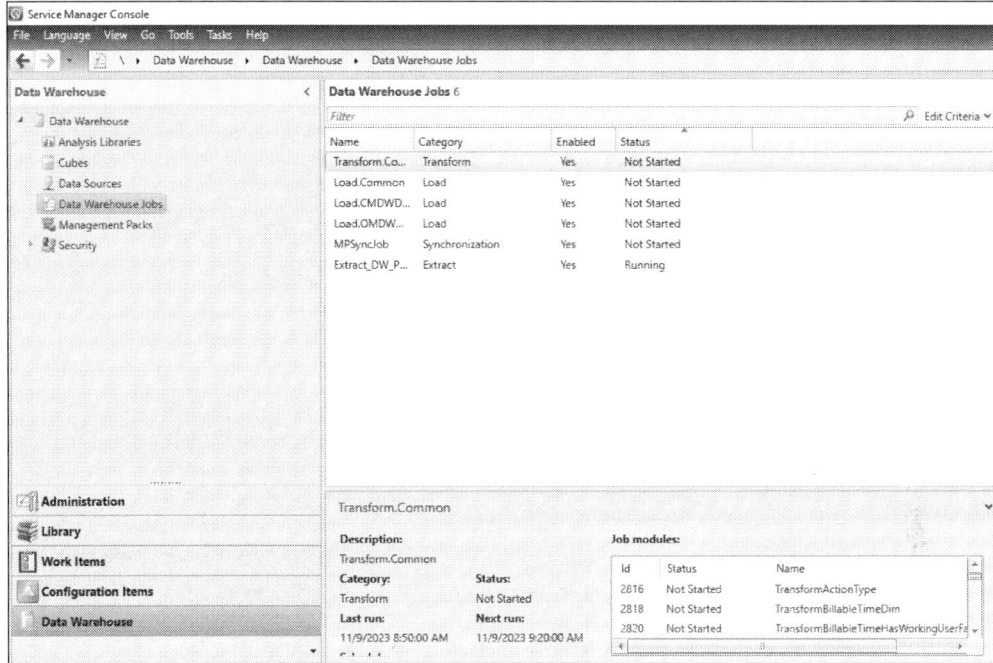

Figure 8.8: Data warehouse jobs

Setting up the Active Directory connector

To setup an integration sync between your Active Directory domain and your Service Manager environment, perform the following:

1. Open the Service Manager console.
2. On the **Administration** tab select **Connectors**.
3. Right-click in the **Connectors** window and select **Create Connector** | **Active Directory Connector**.
4. **Before You Begin: Create an Active Directory connector** | Click **Next**.
5. **General: Enter a name and description for the connector** | Enter a name for your connector. You can toggle if you want the connector to be enabled right after the creation. Click **Next**.
6. **Domain or organization unit: Select a domain or organizational unit** | Select the domain and/or **Organizational Unit (OU)** you specifically want to synchronize from. Select the credentials you wish to use to make the connection, or click **New**. If you want to define new credentials to be used specifically with your connector, click **Next**.
7. **Select objects:** Select the type of objects you want to synchronize from the Active Directory or you can accept the default to sync all objects. Then click **Next**.

8. **Schedule: Create a schedule** | Create a schedule to where the connector will synchronize with your Active Directory, then click **Next**.
9. **Summary: Confirm connector settings** | Review the configuration of your connector, then click **Create**.

Setting up the Configuration Manager connector

To set-up an integration sync between your Configuration Manager environment and your Service Manager environment, perform the following:

1. Open the Service Manager console.
2. On the **Administration** tab, select **Connectors**.
3. Right-click in the **Connectors** window and select **Create Connector** | **Configuration Manager Connector**.
4. **Before You Begin: Create a new connector** | Click **Next**.
5. **General: Enter a name and description for the connector** | Enter a name for your connector. You can toggle if you want the connector to be enabled right after the creation. Click **Next**.
6. **Management Pack: Select a management pack where this connector will be stored** | Select the **System Center Configuration Manager 2012 Connector Configuration**. Click **Next**.

> Note: The Service Manager contains two options for this step. The 2012 option is for all preceding versions, 2012 including Current Branch. The first option is for legacy options such as 2007.

7. **Database: Enter database and credential information for the connector** | Enter the name of the SQL Server and the database name, then select the credentials or create new ones with permissions to the Configuration Manager environment. Then, click **Next**.
8. **Collections**: Choose the collections you want to synchronize. Select the collections you want to synchronize into the Service Manager. Then, click **Next**.
9. **Schedule: Create a schedule** | Create a schedule to where the connector will synchronize with your Configuration Manager, then click **Next**.
10. **Summary: Confirm connector settings** | Review the configuration of your connector, then click **Create**.

Setting up the Operations Manager Alert connector

The first Operations Manager connector allows you to bring your alerts into your Service Manager environment to translate them into Incident tickets. To configure this connector, perform the following:

1. Open the Service Manager console.
2. On the **Administration** tab, select **Connectors**.
3. Right-click in the **Connectors** window and select **Create Connector | Operations Manager Alert** connector.
4. **Before You Begin: Create a connector |** Click **Next**.
5. **General: Enter a name and description for the connector |** Enter a name for your connector. You can toggle if you want the connector to be enabled right after the creation. Click **Next**.
6. **Server details: Enter the server name and credentials for the Operations Manager server:** Enter the name of the SCOM Server and then select the credentials or create new ones with permissions to the Operations Manager environment. Then, click **Next**.
7. **Alert routing rules:** Specify the routing rules for incoming alerts. Here, you can decide that all SCOM alerts can be assigned a default Operations Manager Incident Template, or you can click **Add** to create a custom rule for specific SCOM alerts to get a certain template, as seen in *Figure 8.9*. Then, click **Next**.
8. **Schedule**: Create a schedule to where the connector will synchronize with your Operations Manager. Then, click **Next**.
9. **Summary**: **Confirm connector settings |** Review the configuration of your connector, then click **Create**.

Click **Add** to create a custom rule for specific SCOM alerts to get a certain template, as seen in *Figure 8.9*:

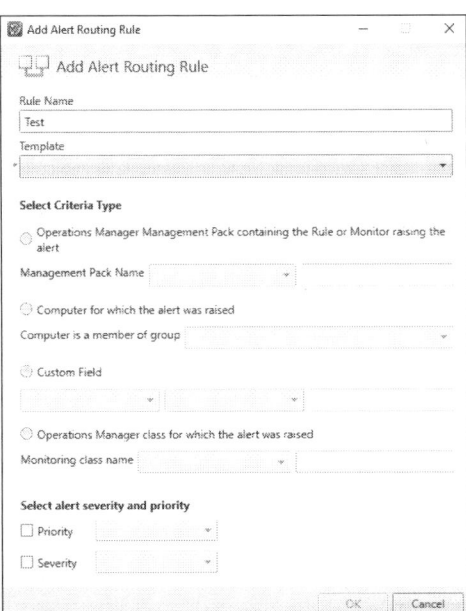

Figure 8.9: Add alert routing rule

Setting up the Operations Manager CI connector

The other Operations Manager connector allows you to bring discovered class instances into your Service Manager environment to populate your **Configuration Management Database (CMDB)**. To configure this connector, perform the following:

1. Open the Service Manager console.
2. On the **Administration** tab, select **Connectors**.
3. Right-click in the **Connectors** window and select **Create Connector** | Operations Manager **Configuration Item (CI)** connector.
4. **Before You Begin: Create a connector** | Click **Next**.
5. **General: Enter a name and description for the connector** | Enter a name for your connector. You can toggle if you want the connector to be enabled right after the creation. Click **Next**.
6. **Server Details: Enter the server name and credentials for the Operations Manager server** | Enter the name of the SCOM Server and select the credentials or create new ones with permissions to the Operations Manager environment. Then, click **Next**.
7. **Management packs:** Select the configuration items to import or reconcile with the Operations Manager. Select the management packs that you want to pull **CIs** from in the Operations Manager. Then, click **Next**.
8. **Create a schedule**: Create a polling schedule where the connector will check for alerts with the Operations Manager. You can also configure the asynchronous methods of alerts and incident closure between SCOM and SCSM. Then, click **Next**.
9. **Summary**: **Confirm connector settings** | Review the configuration of your connector, then click **Create**.

Setting up the Orchestrator connector

The first Operations Manager connector allows you to bring your alerts into your Service Manager environment to translate them into incident tickets. To configure this connector, perform the following:

1. Open the Service Manager console.
2. On the **Administration** tab, select **Connectors**.
3. Right-click in the **Connectors** window and select **Create Connector** | **Orchestrator Connector**.
4. **Before You Begin: Create a System Center Orchestrator connector** | Click **Next**.
5. **General: Enter a name and description for the connector** | Enter a name for your connector. You can toggle if you want the connector to be enabled right after the creation. Click **Next**.

6. **Connection: Provide the URL and credentials for the Orchestrator web service** | Enter the web service URL of your Orchestrator server, then select the credentials or create new ones with permissions to the Orchestrator environment. Then, click **Next**.
7. **Sync folder**: Select the folder you are looking to synchronize the runbooks from. If you select all then you can select the root. Then, click **Next**.
8. **Web console URL:** Enter the Web console URL of your Orchestrator server then select the credentials or create new ones with permissions to the Orchestrator environment. Then, click **Next**.
9. **Create a schedule**: Create a schedule where the connector will synchronize with your Orchestrator. Then, click **Next**.
10. **Summary**: **Confirm connector settings** | Review the configuration of your connector, then click **Create**.

Setting up the Virtual Machine Manager connector

The first Operations Manager connector allows you to bring your alerts into your Service Manager environment to translate them into incident tickets. To configure this connector, perform the following:

1. Open the Service Manager console.
2. On the **Administration** tab, select **Connectors**.
3. Right-click in the **Connectors** window and select **Create Connector** | **Virtual Machine Manager** connector.
4. **Before You Begin: Create a connector** | Click **Next**.
5. **General: Enter a name and description for the connector** | Enter a name for your connector. You can toggle if you want the connector to be enabled right after the creation. Click **Next**.
6. **Connection:** Please provide the server name and credentials. Enter the name of the Virtual Machine Manager server and then select the credentials or create new ones with permissions to the Virtual Machine Manager environment. Then, click **Next**.
7. **Create a schedule**: Create a schedule where the connector will synchronize with the Operations Manager. Then, click **Next**.
8. **Summary**: **Confirm connector settings** | Review the configuration of your connector, then click **Create**.

Self-Service configuration

The Self-Service Portal is the optional part of the Service Manager installed onto a management server. You can have an additional management server to add the Self-Service Portal if you do not want to install onto the single management server.

To configure the Self-Service Portal, perform the following:

1. Open the installation media to Service Manager 2022.
2. Double-click the `setup.exe` file.
3. Select the Service Manager Self-Service Portal under the **Install (Optional)** section of the splash screen.
4. **Getting Started: Product Registration** | Enter the name and organization of the person who will be registering the product and enter a product key for the product unless you are choosing to install the evaluation version, which lasts for 180 days. Select the **I have read, understood, and agree with the terms of the license terms** tick box, then click **Next**.
5. **Getting Started:** Select where you want to install the product, then click **Next**.
6. **Prerequisites**: **System check results**: Ensure that there are no critical errors or warnings upon the prerequisite check. Then, click **Next**.
7. **Configuration: Configure the Self-Service Portal server** | Enter the name if you want to change the default and configure if you want to use the **Secure Socket Layer** (**SSL**) encryption. When ready, click **Next**.
8. **Configure the account for the Self-Service Portal:** Enter the name of the credentials for the Self-Service Portal account. Then, click **Next**.
9. **Configuration: Diagnostic and usage data** | Click **Next**.
10. **Configuration:** Use Microsoft Update to help keep your computer secure and up-to-date. Select if you want the product to use Microsoft Update to check for updates for the Service Manager, then click **Next**.
11. **Configuration**: **Installation Summary** | Review the configuration for the management server, then click **Install** to begin.

Administration of the Service Manager

During your task of administrating your Service Manager environment, there are various administrative tasks that you may undertake at certain points, whether that be on a regular basis or a per-case basis.

Following are a series of different, as well as common, tasks which you may come across.

Management packs

Management packs are required in order for you to carry out monitoring of your environment, and management packs can also be used to expand your monitoring.

Following are sections that provide instructions on how you can manage and administer them.

Adding management packs

You may undertake adding management packs at some point, whether that be adding additional features derived from third party providers, custom management packs, or if you are looking to enrich the Operations Manager CI connector.

To add management packs to the Service Manager, perform the following:

1. Open the Service Manager console.
2. Go to **Administrator** | **Management Packs**.
3. Go to the right-hand pane, and under the **Management Packs** section, select **Import**.
4. Select the management pack you wish to import. You will need to select from the dropdown list to change the file format selection of the management pack you want. Click **Open**
5. Review the management packs listed in the **Import Management Packs** Then, click **Import**.

Creating new management packs

To create a new management pack where you can store templates and other Service Manager objects, perform the following:

1. Open the Service Manager console.
2. Go to **Administrator** | **Management Packs**.
3. Go to the right-hand pane, and under the Management Packs section, select **Create Management Pack**.
4. **Create Management Pack: Management pack general properties** | Enter a name and description for your management pack, then click **OK** to create.

Creating new templates

If servicing ITSM tickets for your environment, you might need specific templates that cater to the needs of your BAU, project-specific tasks, or various types of templates that can accommodate all types of specific requests.

The instructions on how to develop a new template from the Service Manager console are as follows:

1. Open the Service Manager console.
2. Go to the **Library** tab.
3. Select **Templates**.
4. On the right-hand pane under the **Templates** section, select **Create Template**.

5. **Creating template:** Enter a name and description for your new template. Next, click on the **Browse** button to select the class in which the template will be based around, that is, selecting the incident class if you want to create an incident based template. Once selected, you can choose which management pack you want to store the template in. You can use a custom management pack created earlier or select a new one and go through the same wizard as the previous section. Once completed, click **OK**.

After creating the template, you should see it listed in the **Templates** window with an incremental number change to the number of templates shown.

Creating workflows

The workflows help in structuring how new objects or updated objects are handled within the Service Manager, and the workflows are each split into different ITSM categories. To create a workflow, perform the following:

1. Open the Service Manager console.
2. Go to **Administration** | **Workflows** | **Configuration**.
3. Right-click one of the workflow configuration templates, then select **Properties**.
4. **Configure workflows:** Click **Add** to add a workflow configuration.
5. **Before You Begin: Before you Begin** | Click **Next**.
6. **Workflow information:** Enter the name for your workflow. Select the type of workflow you want to create if it is based on whether new objects are created or updated. Select which management pack the workflow will be stored in, then click **Next**.
7. **Specify event criteria**: Select the conditions of the class, if any. Accepting the default means that any object created as an Incident, for example, would be a part of this workflow. If you want to add criteria by filtering specific properties of the class, you can do this. Then, click **Next**.
8. **Select Incident template**: Select if you want to add a specific template to the object. Click **Next**.
9. **Select people to notify**: Select if you want to allow specific people to be notified of the created object. Then, click **Next**.
10. **Summary**: Review the information in the change, then click **Create** to create the workflow.

Publishing to Self-Service Portal

There are two parts of the Self-Service Portal required to be done to show your service requests allowing users to utilize the portal for service requests.

New request offering

A request offering is mainly the service request which is made publicly available for the user to see when they access the Self-Service Portal, as seen in *Figure 8.10* and *Figure 8.11*:

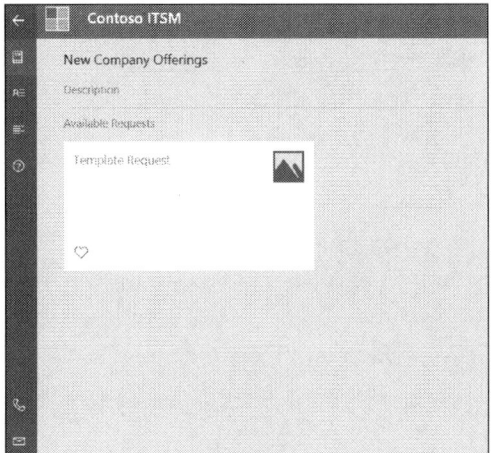

Figure 8.10: Template request offering in Self-Service Portal

Request offering is shown in the following figure:

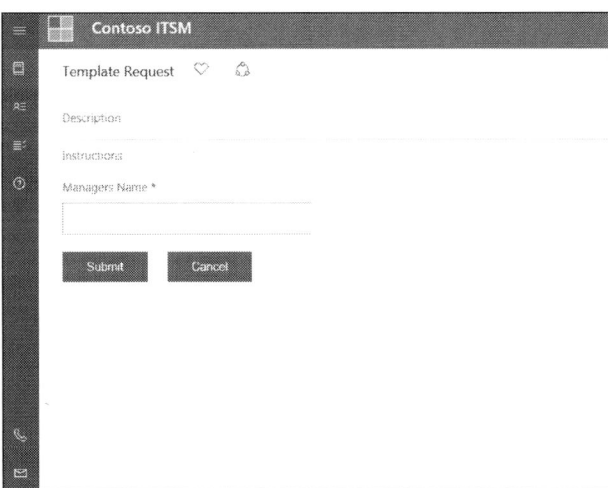

Figure 8.11: Request Offering with user prompt

To create a request offering, perform the following:
1. Open the Service Manage console.
2. Go to the **Library** tab.
3. Go to **Service Catalog | Request Offerings**.
4. On the right-hand tasks pane, select **Create Request Offering**.

5. **Before You Begin: Create a new request offering** | Click **Next**.
6. **General: Specify the information for this offering** | Enter a name for the service request you will create. Select a template to attach. If you do not have a custom service request template, you can create one using the instructions on the **Create a Custom Template** section. Click **Next**.
7. **User prompts: Enter the prompts or information text** | Use the buttons to add prompts for the user to complete when they are presented with the form. For example, you can have a field called Managers Name where you will enter details, and utilize a Query Results prompt type, so you can pull this information from your CMDB. Click **Next**.
8. **Configure user prompts:** Select the **Configure** button to configure the options from the previous step further. To this to set up the information that can be used for your user prompts.
9. **Map prompts to properties:** Here, you can choose which properties within your service request you map the user prompts to. For example, if you want to add the username of the person who made the request, you could map **Token: Portal User Name** to the Title property of your request. Click **Next**.
10. **Knowledge Articles: Select the knowledge articles that are related to this offering** | Add any knowledge articles you need to this section. Click **Next**.
11. **Specify publishing information:** Offerings must be set to Published in order for them to appear on the portal | Select if you want the offering to be available on the portal. You can do this by using the offering status drop-down to decide if it will remain in draft or be published. Then click **Next**.
12. **Summary**: **Please confirm the settings of this offering** | Review the configuration outlined, then click **Create**.

New service offering

The service offering is the overall parent offering, which has a list of the request offerings added to it, so when a user accesses the Self-Service Portal, they would first see the service offering, which then allows for the request offerings to be made visible as shown in *Figure 8.12*:

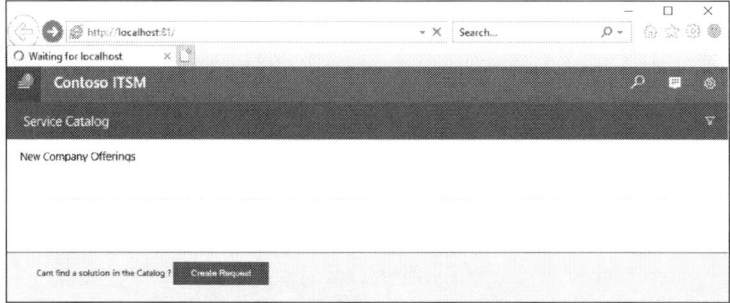

Figure 8.12: *Service Offering in Self-Service Portal*

To create a new service offering within Service Manager, perform the following:

1. Open the Service Manage console.
2. Go to the **Library** tab.
3. Go to **Service Catalog | Service Offerings**.
4. On the right-hand tasks pane, select **Create Service Offering**.
5. **Before You Begin: Create a new service offering** | Click **Next**.
6. **General: Specify the information for this offering** | Enter a name for the service request you will create. Select a category for your service offering and provide an overview of what the service offering entails. Click **Next**.
7. **Detailed information: Specify the information for this offering** | Enter additional detailed information where necessary. Click **Next**.
8. **Related services: Select the services that are related to this offering** | Click on the add button to add any additional services that are related to this service offering. If none, then you can keep it as default. Then click **Next**.
9. **Knowledge Articles: Select the knowledge articles that are related to this offering** | Add any knowledge articles you need to this section. Click **Next**.
10. **Request Offering: Select the request offering that users will see grouped under this service offering** - Click the add button so you can add the request offering that was created in the previous step. Then click **Next**.
11. **Publish:** Specify publishing information. Offerings must be set to Published in order for them to appear on the portal. Select if you want the offering to be available on the portal. To this by using the offering status drop-down to decide if it will remain in draft or be published. Then click **Next**.
12. **Summary**: **Please confirm the settings of this offering** | Review the configuration outlined, then click **Create**.

Now, when we go to the Self-Service Portal, the default should be **https://localhost:81**. You should now see the Service Catalog and offerings below.

These now allow users to utilize the Self-Service Portal to create requests directly from the Self-Service Portal.

Creating custom views for Configuration Management database

Custom views help to show the additional CIs not visible natively within the CIs view.

To create custom views, perform the following:

Creating folder

To create a new folder, perform the following steps:

1. Open the Service Manager console.
2. Go to the **Configuration Items** tab.
3. Go to the right-hand tasks pane and select **Create Folder**.
4. **Create Folder** - Enter a name for the folder, then select the management pack to store the view. Click **OK** to create.

Creating view

To create a custom view, perform the following:

1. Open the Service Manager console.
2. Go to the **Configuration Items** tab.
3. Go to the folder you just created. Right-click and select **Create View**.
4. **Create View:** Enter a name for the view. Go to the criteria section and select browse to choose the class you want to show CIs for. For example, if you brought in devices from Configuration Manager, you can select the class from this view. Once selected, go to the display view and select the properties you want to show, then click **OK** to create.

Upgrading the Service Manager

When new hotfixes or update rollups are available for the Service Manager, you need to apply the latest updates to your environment at the earliest convenience.

The order of the installation is as follows:

1. Data warehouse server
2. Primary management server
3. Secondary management server
4. Self-Service Portal
5. Service Manager consoles

To install an **Update Rollup** (**UR**)or hotfix, perform the following steps:

1. Once downloaded you need to close all Service Manager consoles or Self-Service Portal sessions.
2. Double-check if the Service Manager data warehouse jobs have been completed and synchronized.
3. Run the installation as an administrator detailed in the order shown previously.

To see a full guide on applying Update rollups, visit the following link: **https://support.microsoft.com/en-gb/topic/update-rollup-2-for-system-center-2022-service-manager-631042ca-f36d-4716-898c-6a4d4856f353**

Best practices

Following are some best practices for the Service Manager:

- **Management packs for different functions**: Different types of objects, whether that be views, workflows, or templates of any sort, should be kept in a management pack that will keep track of all the changes.

  Preferably, the naming of the management packs should fit with the custom objects that you develop. Though the Service Manager does not have a default management pack as such, like the Operations Manager, there are however, default management packs which can belong to certain areas of the ITSM requests such as Incidents, Service Requests, etc.

- **Run As account max permissions**: Though the course of developing connectors or workflows will depend on a Run As account to allow this to be operational, you want to ensure that the accounts you use do not have an overbearing amount of permissions. You will need a domain-based account that has administrative privileges within the product, but you also do not want to share the same credential with multiple connectors or workflows.

  This type of scenario can end up making a single point of failure if, for whatever reason, something happens to the account, such as a password expiration, locked out, etc.

Real-world scenarios

Following are some real-world scenarios for the Service Manager:

- **Custom management packs:** Most Service Manager environments you will find can be vastly complicated, depending on the amount of customization that has been configured within it. Management packs can be created in the console, but you will find that more customizations happening overtime will prompt the Service Manager Authoring Console to develop a management pack in a way that the Service Manager console cannot do.

  These can also be used to develop a new type of CI class, template form structure as well as developing objects, which you are not able to do within the Service Manager console such as list objects.

  The authoring tool can be found here **https://www.microsoft.com/en-us/download/details.aspx?id=105032**

- **Exchange connector:** The exchange connector is not a native connector in Service Manager, but is heavily used in the real-world scenarios to be able to monitor for specific emails which come into a mailbox which can then be translated into a ticket, very similar to the workflows which you can develop in the Service Manager console.

- **Third-party Self-Service Portals:** Further customization is likely to go into the Self-Service Portal in order to introduce much more heavier company branding to provide the users with a much better feel and user experience when using the portal to make requests or raise tickets.

    One popular third-party solution for this is with Cireson **https://cireson.com/products/service-management/analyst-portal/** which allow for much more advanced features to enhance the Self-Service Portal visual interface and ways to organize the service requests which hold your customized templates structured for various BAU uses.

Conclusion

Service Manager does have some ways in which building a logical load balanced setup isn't as complicated as some of the other products within the System Center family. With everything outlined you can see that the connectors and integrations it shares within its System Center family counterparts as well as core Microsoft products, it will help to enrich the entire experience of how you manage your environment.

It must be understood that this product can be as complicated as you want to as basic as you require depending on the role it will play in aiding the ITSM management and CMDB management of your environment.

The next chapter will focus on the next product within the System Center suite which is Orchestrator, where we will cover the planning and design for this product.

Points to remember

- Additional management servers can be added to your Service Manager environment by adding to the existing operational database.
- The data warehouse server role is optional, but you need to be aware of the prerequisites before deployment.
- Connectors play an integral role in the enrichment of your CMDB environment.
- The use of templates and workflows help to personalize and standardize the environment to help address the regular BAU tasks to be managed by the ITSM framework.
- Understand the importance of adding new management packs to the Service Manager environment.
- The Self-Service publishing portal is an alternative for users to create tickets if not going through the main Service Manager console.

- The connector has to be configured to get the data warehouse server to talk to the management server.
- Use the best accounts with the maximum permissions required to connect to the relevant servers through your connectors.
- Custom views help to display further extended CIs list once more configurations have gone into the Service Manager.

Multiple choice questions

1. How do we enrich the data we pull in from the Operations Manager CI connector?
   a. Publishing a new service request
   b. Custom views
   c. Create new management pack
   d. Importing management packs

2. What is the main prerequisite when it comes to data warehouse management server?
   a. Reporting DLL
   b. Editing the rsperortserver.config file
   c. Adding a new line in the extension area
   d. All the above

3. If you want to extend the Cis within your Service Manager utilizing the Operations Manager CI connector, how do we do this?
   a. Visual Studios
   b. Installing management packs in the Service Manager
   c. Installing management packs in the Service Manager and Operations Manager
   d. Creating new management packs

4. Select all the methods which can be used to develop a new incident template?
   a. Duplicating an existing template
   b. Creating a new template
   c. Creating a new management pack and add a template
   d. Creating a connector

5. A primary management server must be upgraded before the data warehouse management server?
   a. True

b. False

6. Where can we find the prerequisite files for the Service Manager?

    a. Installation media

    b. Download from Microsoft

    c. Windows updates

    d. Microsoft support

Answers

1. d
2. d
3. c
4. a,b,c
5. a
6. a

Key terms

- **ITSM**: Information Technology Service Management
- **CMDB**: Configuration Management Database
- **CI**: Configuration Item
- **Workflow**: A process which has more than one activity that follows a step by step to provide a desired result
- **Integration**: A relationship between both products where synchronous or asynchronous communication can begin
- **Data warehouse**: A data retention storage mechanism that is used to cover data from an operational database to be backed up and stored to provide historical results.
- **AD**: Active Directory
- **SCSM**: System Center Service Manager
- **SCOM**: System Center Operations Manager

Chapter 9
Building Scalable and Resilient Orchestration Environments

Introduction

In this chapter, we will look into the planning and design for the System Center Orchestrator. This area will be applicable for most versions of this technology as the same key areas have to be taken into consideration, especially when looking into how the solution will be used. Scalability is also a key area that we will want to analyze when planning a new design. We will also discover the upgrade paths that would need to be taken to be applicable for System Center 2022. For Orchestrator, we will look into the planning of the areas and technologies which we want to form an integration with, to paint the picture of how our automation and workflows will run.

Also included will be a minimum and recommended requirement level the reader can develop a lab environment till, which they can use to follow through with the next chapter so you can gauge a practical and theoretical understanding.

Structure

This chapter will cover the following topics:
- Orchestrator topology structure
- Product integration planning
- Service Management Automation

- Service Manager connectors
- Disaster recovery
- Orchestrator lab requirements

Objectives

The reader will understand the overarching product regarding Orchestrator being the first product to upgrade within the System Center, its topologies, requirements, and the key areas when it comes to future planning and highlighting new areas and features introduced to the product since its 2012 debut.

Orchestrator topology structure

Orchestrator contains quite a few roles that make up the overall solution. We will explore this in further detail so the reader has a clearer understanding of how each role is used and its scalability features.

Orchestrator roles

The roles of the Orchestrator are:

- **Management server**: Following with the tradition of other System Center products, Orchestrator uses a management server role to run the main services. This is done to allow the Orchestrator infrastructure to function.

    While it does have a management server role, there are no *clients* as such, like the other System Center products, that use agent installations.

- **Runbook server**: A Runbook server plays allows the Runbook workflow processes to be run on the device. The management server holds the communication of the Runbook servers being able to run these processes, and also maintain their own services to function.

    Adding additional Runbook servers helps provide the scalability that you require and also helps you control the affinity for which the Runbook servers workflow processes can run on.

- **Runbook designer**: The Runbook Designer is the GUI console, used for Orchestrator which allows you to connect into the Orchestrator, where the administrator is able to create Runbooks, edit and view any existing Runbooks.

- **Web console**: The console connects to the management server services to form a connection, where the importance of the management server role comes into play. The web console has two parts to it; the first being the web console itself, which looks close to the Runbook designer console that you would install onto a server.

- **Web API Service**: The other part is the web service, which can be used to make API calls to Orchestrator to action commands or to pull information such as Runbook activities, etc.

  To see more on Orchestrator web service API integrations please take a look here for further reading: https://github.com/openark/orchestrator/blob/master/docs/using-the-web-api.md

Single Runbook server topology

Orchestrator can sometimes be viewed as an experimental or quick solution to automate BAU processes better than other tools used, such as Microsoft Configuration Manager. So, we can use a popular topology like having all the Orchestrator server roles installed on a single server.

This consists of all roles like:
- Management server
- Runbook server
- Runbook Designer
- Web console

This type of topology is fine if you are not utilizing the product as a business-critical service. Though it is the most simplistic and convenient type of structure to have, it offers little in terms of future scalability as well as a single point of failure.

Technically, more Runbook servers can be added to increase the scalability, but you want to distribute the workload of the Runbooks used in a controlled manner, and this is where the next topology comes into play, which may be better suited.

Multi-Runbook server topology

Multiple Runbook servers in your environment help the load-balancing between the servers to ensure that Runbook activities can be split evenly, as multiple Runbooks with multiple instances can cause lag if this is all being actioned on one server.

Another side to this structure is also the benefit of being able to control the affinity of which Runbooks can actually be used on each Runbook server.

> **Note: Each Runbook server has its own services dedicated to the function of the server, so when this goes down, you are in a better position to distribute the load to another Runbook server in this case.**

Hardware requirements

To support any of the topologies or scenarios outlined, we first need to take into account the requirements that are needed to build out the server roles. These requirements help us understand the recommended specification levels to understand not only what our design will be, but also its overall scalability.

Table 9.1 shows all the roles that Orchestrator has and its requirements for each role:

Orchestrator role	CPU (Cores)	CPU (GHz)	Memory (GB)	Disk space (MB)
Management server	2	2.1	2	200
Runbook server	2	2.1	2	200
Runbook Designer	2	2.1	2	200
Web console	2	2.1	2	200

Table 9.1: Orchestrator 2022 hardware requirements

Operating System requirements

The next part of the requirements is for the Operating Systems. Table 7.2 and Table 7.3 outline the Operating System requirements for both server roles and machines that would use the Service Manager console:

Service Manager role	Windows Server version	Windows Server edition	Windows Server GUI	Windows Server core
Management server	2019/2022	Standard/Datacenter	Yes	Yes
Runbook server	2019/2022	Standard/Datacenter	Yes	Yes
Runbook Designer	2019/2022	Standard/Datacenter	Yes	Yes
Web console	2019/2022	Standard/Datacenter	Yes	Yes

Table 9.2: Orchestrator 2022 server Operating System requirements

Structured Query Language Server requirements

Here are the **Structured Query Language (SQL)** Server requirements for the Orchestrator. As there are several parts to consider when planning your SQL Server environment, we have included a few tables to breakdown the overall requirements.

The first table shows the hardware requirements for the SQL Servers:

Service Manager role	CPU (Cores)	CPU (GHz)	Memory (GB)	Disk space (GB)
Database	8	2.66	32GB	10

Table 9.3: Orchestrator 2022 database hardware requirements

SQL Server versions:

SQL Server version	SQL cumulative update (Minimum level)
SQL Server 2022	Latest
SQL Server 2019	Latest
SQL Server 2017	Latest

Table 9.4: Orchestrator 2022 SQL Server version requirements

Product integration planning

The powerful part of Orchestrator is the integration options that it brings to your environment. This is not just limited to Microsoft-based products but also to other big third-party products which might in your data center.

In this topic, we will explore all the technologies that can be integrated in better detail.

Integration packs

Integration packs are the management packs of the Orchestrator, similar to how management packs are to its other System Center counterparts such as **System Center Operations Manager (SCOM)** and **System Center Service Manager (SCSM)**.

Integration packs contain activities that relate to a task that can be performed according to the technology that the integration pack is made for.

There are some important fundamentals that the reader must understand when adding any integration pack to plan correctly:

- Do you already have the product?
- Do you have a user account with the correct permissions to make a connection with the correct instance?
- Have you analyzed the **Business As Usual (BAU)** tasks performed within the technology that Orchestrator can help enrich or fully automate?

Orchestrator runs a powerful automation solution but is equally as dangerous if a Runbook has not been constructed correctly. Anything automated and running on schedule or for period of time when not managed, could end up being a problem, and these must be considered before using any integration pack. Here, we will discuss the planning and understanding of each available integration pack, so the reader is aware of the activities within them.

The following figure depicts the integration packs available for Orchestrator at the time of writing this book:

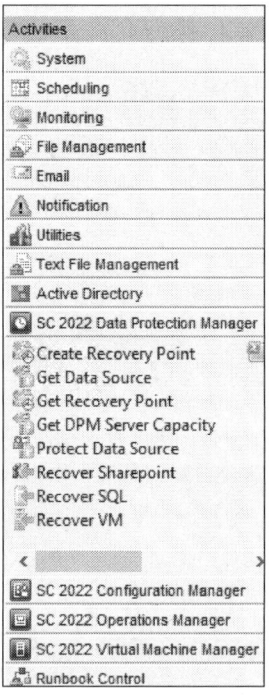

Figure 9.1: Integration packs with activities within the Runbook Designer application

Native integration packs

Without any integration packs added to the Orchestrator to integrate with other products, there are a few native integration packs, which are as follows:

- System
- Scheduling
- Monitoring
- File Management
- Notification
- Utilities
- Runbook Control

These contain base activities that help to develop a Runbook, which can be triggered by default steps that help integrate with other products and generalist type Runbooks.

For example, the Runbook Control integration pack contains an activity called **Initialize Data**. This is the most common first step of any Runbook and can be used to set out template fields that have to be answered before a Runbook proceeds to other steps, which can be seen in *Figure 9.2*:

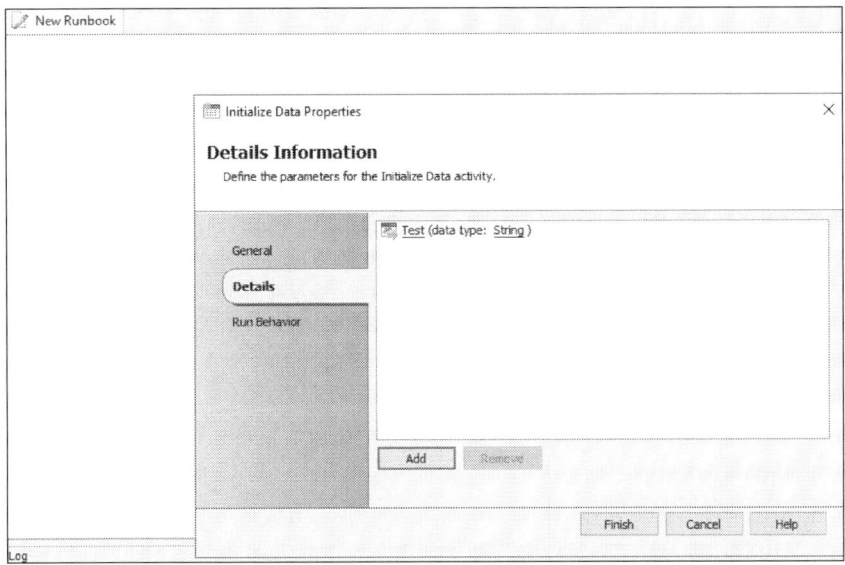

Figure 9.2: Initialize data step and parameter in Runbook Designer

If this step is left blank, it will simply complete and go to the next steps.

If we had one with fields such as first name and last name, these would need to be filled before the Runbook continues.

Overall, this activity is known as a trigger step, when integrated with other products which are able to push/initiate a specific Runbook that would pass along the data that this activity requires.

Other common activities that can be used to trigger Runbooks are the ones based on Schedule, such as the Schedule integration pack that contains activities based on running at a specific time, a specific date, or monitoring a specific date.

Microsoft-based integration packs

There are several other integration packs which exist for native integration packs such as Sharepoint and Microsoft Exchange, but we will cover the fundamental and more popular integration packs to provide examples of the activities they contain.

Planning for Active Directory integration

Arguably the main integration pack to configure when it comes to building any automation solutions around your environment, based on the importance of the Active Directory in general.

Constructing automated tasks with Active Directory allows you to tie in several workflows that are specific or tied to an Active Directory object, which helps greatly in deciding how to deal with specific users/computers or for a specific state of users/computers such as new starters, leavers, etc.

The activities for this integration pack are as follows:
- Add Computer to Group
- Add Group to Group
- Add User to Group
- Create Computer
- Create Group
- Create User
- Delete Computer
- Delete Group
- Delete User
- Disable Computer
- Disable User
- Enable Computer
- Enable User
- Get Computer
- Get Group
- Get Organizational Unit
- Get User
- Move Computer
- Move Group
- Move User
- Remove Computer From Group
- Remove Group from Group
- Rename Group
- Rename User
- Reset User Password
- Unlock User

- Update Computer
- Update Group
- Update User

Planning for Configuration Manager integration

Orchestrator allows for an integration with the Configuration Manager by utilizing an integration pack.

This allows for a connection to your Configuration Manager environment by connecting to the SQL database of the Configuration Manager site which you are looking to connect to.

When it comes to planning integration with the Configuration Manager environment, there are fundamentals that are specified within this topic but are more specific to Configuration Manager. You need to take into consideration the impact of automated Runbook tasks with the Configuration Manager, as improper configurations of automated tasks can cause huge impact:

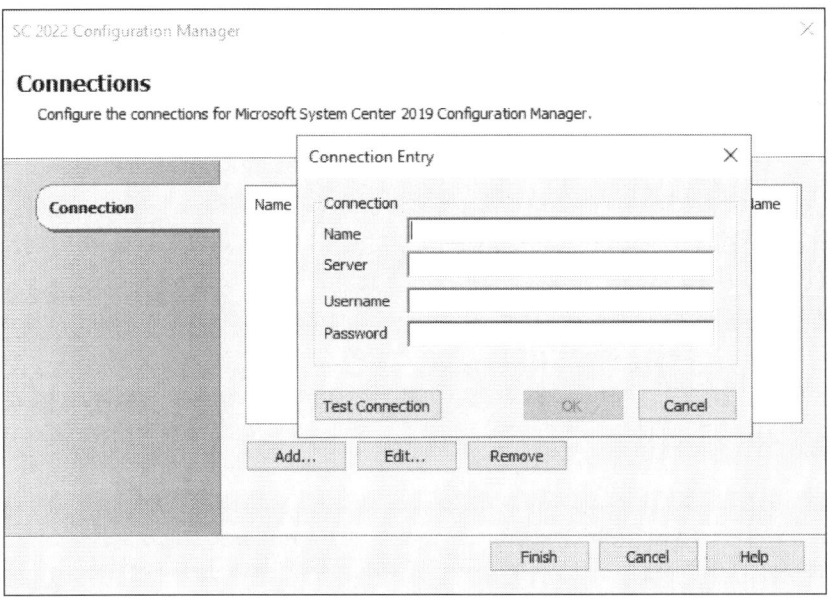

Figure 9.3: Connection entry for the Configuration Manager integration pack

Primarily, the activities available evolve around the collection management and the deployment of an object to a collection. Now, when you perform these actions manually within the Configuration Manager, there is more careful consideration as well as testing before making an advertisement available to anything within your environment. Bearing in mind the dangers of what a Task Sequence can do, you have an activity called *Deploy Task Sequence*. So, you will need to ensure that thorough testing has been done before you start considering the preparation of this product integration.

The activities for this integration pack are as follows:
- Add Collection Rule
- Create Collection
- Delete Collection
- Delete Collection Rule
- Deploy Application
- Deploy Configuration Baseline
- Deploy Program
- Deploy Software Update
- Deploy Task Sequence
- Get Collection Members
- Get Deployment Status
- Perform Client Action
- Query ConfigMgr
- Update Collection Membership

Planning for Operations Manager integration

The activities within this integration are quite limited and based more around creating alerts and understanding more of a specific alert.

When it comes to SCOM itself, everything is monitored based on everything the managed objects can discover from a management pack that has been installed. When it comes to an integration with the Orchestrator, you will need to understand some questions, such as:
- Are there specific alerts that may need to be created?
- Do we require specific actions once alerts enter into a specific state?
- What to do if an alert gets created?

Orchestrator helps to build an overall workflow to help respond to alerts in your Operations Manager environment which a management pack may not have. This integration can help and be less complicated than trying to develop a mechanism within your custom management pack made for SCOM.

Tasks in SCOM, such as recovery and diagnostic tasks, can perform close to this, but where your integration with Orchestrator is concerned, you can build a precise response to your SCOM environment.

The activities for this integration are as follows:
- Create Alert.
- Get Alert.

- Get Monitor.
- Monitor Alert.
- Monitor State.
- Start Maintenance Mode.
- Stop Maintenance Mode.
- Update Alert.

Planning for Service Manager integration

Service Manager integrations have more options than others, which we will discuss further in the section *Service Manager connector*.

In the integration pack itself are activities to help further extend the capabilities of detecting the state of certain **Information Technology Service Management** (**ITSM**) tickets or workflows that you have in your Service Manager environment.

The activities for this integration pack are as follows:

- Create Change with Template.
- Create Incident with Template.
- Create Object.
- Create Related Object.
- Create Relationship.
- Delete Relationship.
- Get Activity.
- Get Object.
- Get Relationship.
- Monitor Object.
- Update Object.
- Upload Attachment.

Planning for Virtual Machine Manager integration

The **System Center Virtual Machine Manager** (**SCVMM**) integration pack has the most activities within it, which aim to help with virtual machine automation.

Though you will be able to configure the Runbooks however you need, when automating any form of your virtual estate, you will need some diligent planning to increase the number of virtual machines when you take into account the data stores you keep to ensure that you have enough space to perform any of these activities.

Being able to control the **virtual machine** (**VM**) states for starting, stopping, and suspending provides interesting options here. However, this also incurs the same type of risk as the space issue, where you will need to plan ahead to ensure the impact of certain virtual machines which are part of these activities and make sure it does not cause any issues to business critical services.

The integration pack works by connecting to your main **Virtual Machine Manager (VMM)** management server.

The activities for this integration pack are as follows:
- Apply Pending Service Update.
- Configure Service Deployment.
- Check Checkpoint.
- Create New Disk.
- Create New Disk from VHD.
- Create Network Adapter
- Create User Role
- Create VM From Template
- Create VM from VHD
- Create VM from VM
- Deploy Service
- Get Checkpoint
- Get Cloud
- Get Disk
- Get Network Adapter
- Get Service
- Get Service Configuration
- Get Service Template
- Get Tier
- Get User Role
- Get User Role Quota
- Get VM
- Get VM Host
- Get VM Network
- Get VM Subnet
- Manage Checkpoint
- Move VM
- Remove User Role
- Remove VM

- Repair VM
- Resume VM
- Run VMM PowerShell Script
- Scale Tier In
- Scale Tier Out
- Set Pending Service Update
- Shut Down VM
- Start VM
- Stop Service
- Stop VM
- Suspend VM
- Update Disk
- Update Network Adapter
- Update User Role Property
- Update User Role Quota
- Update VM

Planning for Data Protection Manager integration

Given the importance of backup and disaster recovery strategies for your environment, this integration pack helps to provide you with activities around creating recovery points as well as being able to recover certain points.

The recovering side would need some more testing before building an automated workflow around this.

The integration pack works by connecting to the **Data Protection Manager** (**DPM**) management server.

The activities for this integration pack are as follows:

- Create Recovery Point
- Get Data Source
- Get Recovery Point
- Get DPM Server Capacity
- Protect Data Source
- Recover Sharepoint
- Recover SQL
- Recover VM
- Run DPM PowerShell Script

Third-party integration packs

Third-party integration packs are available for various technologies that may not have an official one released for them, as well as alternatives for integration packs, that may already exist but may contain more activities that are on offer.

For example, the Configuration Manager integration pack might not contain an activity to create an application. This is where a third-party could contain an activity for this.

> Note: One of the known creators of third-party integration packs are a company called *Kelverion*, which more information can be found at https://www.kelverion.com

Service Management Automation

Orchestrator has an additional counterpart of itself, known as the **Service Management Automation (SMA)**.

This is used to create Runbooks similar to the Orchestrator. However, in this case, activities are defined by the PowerShell script language in order to perform an action and can be run specifically on Cloud endpoints or on-premise endpoints.

To understand SMA more, it will be useful for the reader to be familiar with the various components which SMA has, to see its similarity to the architecture of Orchestrator.

Figure 9.4 shows the setup screen for Service Management Automation:

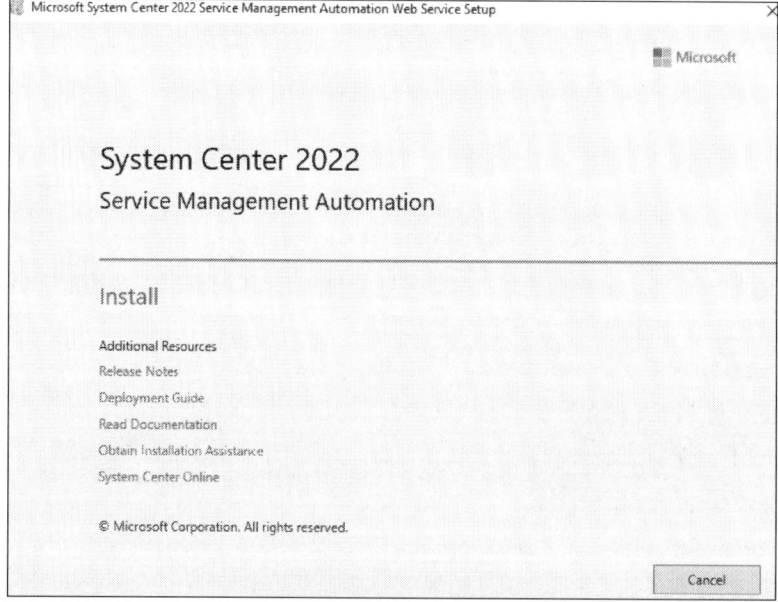

Figure 9.4: Service Management automation installation splash screen

Web service

The web service has a similar role to how the management server in the Orchestrator operates but there are some fair differences. The web service uses the Microsoft Azure integration pack t setup a connection to your Azure tenancy.

Runbook Worker

Runbook Workers work quite identically to how Runbook servers work in Orchestrator and are used for the Runbooks to be able to run. Similar to the Orchestrator, the more Runbook Workers you introduce into the architecture, the better your load balancing will be.

PowerShell module

The PowerShell module is used to not only connect to your SMA instance but also to author the Runbooks are written in the PowerShell.

> **Note:** An additional PowerShell Integrated Scripting Environment (ISE) add-on is also available for further and more complex Runbook editing, which can be found on the following link: https://www.powershellgallery.com/packages/SMAAuthoringToolkit/1.0

Choosing Orchestrator, Service Management Automation or both

This decision is more dependent on the requirements at hand as well as the overall preference.

The best way to outline this is to focus on the PowerShell side of the technologies. So, let us analyze the Orchestrator itself when it comes to the PowerShell. Within the native Runbook system, the main activity used for PowerShell is the Run .NET Script, which you can toggle to use PowerShell. While this step is indeed helpful, its drawbacks are mainly around the fact that it uses a 64-bit PowerShell, which could be an issue if you want to use the 32-bit specific PowerShell. This also may prove to be tricky when you want to use specific PowerShell commands not recognized due to the version gaps, and ultimately the importing of modules could also be a problem.

Workarounds have been established for this, such as using the Run Program activity from the same native Runbook, where you have more control over where to call the PowerShell from and even specify a specific script or command to run. However, you run into an issue where it comes to error handling and knowing if something has run successfully.

Other alternatives have been also to use third-party integration packs which help address a lot of these issues, but they come with a cost.

This is perhaps where SMA will its appeal from. If you are a heavy PowerShell user and need to maneuver with less restrictions, rather than using a specific action in an integration pack, then SMA might be the better option for you, where you can write a Runbook in 100% PowerShell.

There can also be justifications to where both products are sufficient, in not just supporting multiple requirements applicable to both products, but also to take into account the scalability of SMA where you can utilize these some Runbooks within your Azure tenancy.

Service Manager connectors

Alongside the initial integration pack which allow you to connect to your Service Manager environment, Orchestrator is officially labelled as the product which is able to provide additional connectors.

In the previous chapter, we discussed the native connectors which are a part of the Service Manager that help you populate the CMDB with your CIs. However, if an organization has other products, bespoke or wants to enrich existing CIs, Orchestrator would then be able to create additional connectors in the form of Runbooks to allow for this to work.

Custom connectors

Custom connectors are formed by using activities within the Service Manager integration pack. Now, when it comes to where you pull or read data from, these can come from any activity within an integration pack, but ultimately the last step in the Runbook would most likely be an activity named **Create Object** or **Update Object**.

Let us outline an example of this first. Say we wanted to pull data from the Configuration Manager, which held information for Linux-based computers (though this is not supported in the Configuration Manager anymore, it may exist in some cases) which, by default, the Configuration Manager connector would not populate your SCSM with. With that, we could create a Runbook that uses a PowerShell script to obtain information and then the last steps would be to locate the object we are looking to update and use **Update Object** to update the information.

In cases where a class does not exist, and if we were to create a custom class from a newly created management pack, we could then create a Runbook which would be able to connect to a form of repository that keeps information such as a SQL database, PowerShell Module or even a file. We could then create a Runbook capable to pull this information and then with its last step being Create Object, it would create a new CI within your CMDB for the new class you have created for the Service Manager.

This essentially is how a custom connector would work when utilizing Orchestrator.

Syncing Orchestrator Runbooks to the Service Manager

Another form of integration between both products is the connector which can pull the Runbooks from Orchestrator and synchronize them into objects for your Service Manager environment.

These Runbooks can then be assigned to ITSM templates which can perform automated tasks on behalf of ITSM tickets created against the template.

This is where steps such as "Initialize Data" are important so that you can easily trigger a Runbook to run from the Service Manager or use the string parameters you define within this step on your Runbook. These can then be used to enter from an ITSM ticket to allow for the Runbook to process the data and complete the task.

Disaster recovery

Orchestrator has different areas of how disaster recovery can work, from balancing the loads of workflows to recovering from situations that causes downtime.

More Runbook servers

Multiple Runbook servers help to distribute the load of Runbooks run on each server. This helps to ensure that there is no single point of failure where important Runbooks play business critical or important BAU processes.

Data Store Configuration

There are times when either performing an upgrade, moving a database or any form of maintenance can sometimes cause an issue regarding where your Orchestrator management server might lose connection to its database.

This normally can be resolved by using the Data Store Configuration utility app, which gets installed by default on management server roles for you to point to the location of your database, so that you can reform a new connection or restore the same connection again.

Orchestrator Data Protection Manager integration

Orchestrator and DPM can form an integration where DPM can look after backing up the Orchestrator information and its SQL database.

This topic will be broken down in further detail in the chapters focusing on DPM.

Orchestrator lab requirements

Now that we are at the final topic, we can outline what we think the appropriate specification for your Orchestrator Lab will look like.

The lab requirements can follow a similar pattern to the requirements outlined in the first section, *Orchestrator topology structure*, as well as, previous chapters for other products, but the aim is to ensure the specification fits to sustain a healthy environment.

Consolidated topology

The easiest topology to deploy is where all the roles sit on one server. It is the perfect structure if you want to learn the technology or a non-business critical service:

The following tables show the requirements for this lab:

Orchestrator role	CPU (Cores)	CPU (GHz)	Memory (GB)	Disk space (MB)
All server roles	2	2.1	2	200

Table 9.5: Orchestrator 2022 hardware requirements

The following table represents the OS requirements:

Orchestrator role	Windows Server version	Windows Server edition	Windows Server GUI	Windows Server core
All server roles	2019/2022	Standard/Datacenter	Yes	Yes

Table 9.6: Orchestrator 2022 Server OS requirements

The next table represents the hardware requirements for the SQL database:

Orchestrator role	CPU (Cores)	CPU (GHz)	Memory (GB)	Disk space (GB)
Database	8	2.66	32GB	10

Table 9.7: Orchestrator 2022 database hardware requirements

The following table represents the SQL version requirements in the consolidated topology:

SQL Server version	SQL cumulative update (Minimum level)
SQL Server 2022	Latest
SQL Server 2019	Latest
SQL Server 2017	Latest

Table 9.8: Orchestrator 2022 SQL Server version requirements

Scalable topology

The next topology is what you want to be going forward with, where you can have more than one Runbook server to provide load balancing and support more Runbooks and activities for your business critical and BAU tasks.

The following tables show the requirements needed for this lab:

Orchestrator role	CPU (Cores)	CPU (GHz)	Memory (GB)	Disk space (MB)
Management server	2	2.1	2	200
Runbook server x2	2	2.1	2	200
Runbook Designer	2	2.1	2	200
Web console	2	2.1	2	200

Table 9.9: Orchestrator 2022 hardware requirements

The following table represents the OS requirements for the scalable topology:

Service Manager role	Windows Server version	Windows Server edition	Windows Server GUI	Windows Server core
Management server	2019/2022	Standard/Datacenter	Yes	Yes
Runbook server	2019/2022	Standard/Datacenter	Yes	Yes
Runbook Designer	2019/2022	Standard/Datacenter	Yes	Yes
Web console	2019/2022	Standard/Datacenter	Yes	Yes

Table 9.10: Orchestrator 2022 Server Operating System requirements

The following table represents the hardware requirements for the SQL database:

Service Manager Role	CPU (Cores)	CPU (GHz)	Memory (GB)	Disk Space (GB)
Database	8	2.66	32GB	10

Table 9.11: Orchestrator 2022 database hardware requirements

The following table represents the SQL version requirements in the scalable topology:

SQL Server version	SQL cumulative update (Minimum level)
SQL Server 2022	Latest

SQL Server version	SQL cumulative update (Minimum level)
SQL Server 2019	Latest
SQL Server 2017	Latest

Table 9.12: Orchestrator 2022 SQL Server version requirements

Conclusion

Orchestrator plays a role with an apt name, as it is able to orchestrate the whole of its System Center counterparts and other native Microsoft productions. This can allow users to construct an automated workflow which can cross-reference with different streams in order to enhance regular or specific tasks.

Though it has its limitations, where workarounds are required, in reference to its PowerShell capabilities, this is where SMA can step in and aid for a more fitting and preferred solution, alongside supporting the topology of having both to be used in the same environment.

A product labeled as the preferred solution for developing connectors for the Service Manager, also promotes a bigger user case where the enhancement of another System Center product has a dependency for further solution scalability. Orchestrator is a good choice to have with its multi-purpose usage.

The next chapter will put everything we have learned here into practice for the installation of Orchestrator, as well as how to administer and configure the product.

Points to remember

- Orchestrator does not use any agents to manage clients like its other System Center counterparts.
- Multiple Runbook servers help to provide a load-balanced configuration for your Orchestrator environment.
- Integration packs are used to install the Orchestrator to allow activities for other technologies to be used to create Runbooks with
- Runbook Designer application is used as the GUI to be able to develop Runbooks.
- The web service allows for REST API integration and the web console is used for a web version of the Runbook Designer application.
- **Service Management Automation (SMA)** is an alternative solution within the Orchestrator product that allows you to create Runbooks solely in the PowerShell.
- Service Manager can use or integrate with the Orchestrator by synchronizing Runbooks to Service Manager, and be used to develop custom connectors to pull additional CMDB information into the Service Manager.

Multiple choice questions

1. You can add more than one Runbook server to your Orchestrator topology.
   a. True
   b. False

2. Orchestrator is known as the official product to create custom connectors for Service Manager.
   a. True
   b. False

3. What is the name of the files installed to create Runbooks using different activities?
   a. Management Packs
   b. Integration Packs
   c. Solution Packs
   d. Runbooks

4. Which application is used to create and develop Runbooks?
   a. Runbook Designer
   b. SMA
   c. Data Store Configuration
   d. Deployment Manager

5. SMA allows us to create Runbooks in XML language only.
   a. True
   b. False

6. Runbook server is a component of the Orchestrator. What is the equivalent of this role in SMA?
   a. Runbook Designer
   b. PowerShell
   c. Management Server
   d. Runbook Worker

Answers

1. a
2. a

3. b
4. a
5. b
6. d

Key terms

- **SMA**: Service Management Automation
- **ITSM**: Information Technology Service Management
- **CMDB**: Configuration Management Database
- **SCSM:** System Center Service Manager
- **SCORCH:** System Center Orchestrator
- **Workflow**: A process that has more than one activity that follows a step by step to provide a desired result

Join our book's Discord space

Join the book's Discord Workspace for Latest updates, Offers, Tech happenings around the world, New Release and Sessions with the Authors:

https://discord.bpbonline.com

Chapter 10
Deployment and Administration of System Center Orchestrator

Introduction

This chapter will concentrate on the development and deployment of the System Center Orchestrator. The importance of this chapter is to illustrate the setup of Orchestrator and the overall deployment, so we can ensure the design plan that we specified in the previous section allows us to have a healthy setup. There will also be some troubleshooting points to help the reader understand some common and uncommon case issues which can arise during the development and deployment process.

This chapter will provide an in-depth look into the overall administration of System Center Orchestrator as well as outline its best practices. The administration side is what will allow an engineer to perform their **Business As Usual (BAU)** tasks, but also within the administrative side another area which would enrich the BAU tasks and overall **user interface (UI)** is where the best practices come in. Best practices is normally looked at as a professional and recommended level to what you should and not do, but we can also understand that a real-world scenario can conflict with this, so we will look to outline the differences between both.

Structure

This chapter will cover the following topics
- Orchestrator: Single runbook server deployment
- Orchestrator: Multi-runbook server deployment
- Administration of Orchestrator
- Best practices
- Real-world Scenarios

Objectives

Following on from the previous chapter, which went into the detail of the various topologies which can be created for Orchestrator depending on the business criticality it plays, the objectives for this chapter is for the reader to not only be proficient in the installation of Orchestrator, but also be able to comfortably administer the technology.

This chapter aims to cover all aspects of the Orchestrator deployment and administration so the reader is fully aware of each area to know the best way forward when wanting to introduce Orchestrator as a viable solution for the environment.

Single runbook server installation

Starting off with the initial installation of Orchestrator, it involves the base installation of a consolidated structure deployment where all of the roles are installed, and the management server would also contain the runbook server role.

Before going further into the installation steps, we must first analyse the prerequisites needed for each role to be installed. Once established this will set the foundation for the second topic which will illustrate on how to expand the runbook servers within your Orchestrator environment.

Installing splash screen

In order to launch the splash screen to install the Orchestrator, you first need to install the prerequisite of the following files:
- Microsoft Visual C++ 2015-2022 Redistributable (x86)
- Microsoft Visual C++ 2015-2022 Redistributable (x64)

The prerequisite files mentioned can be found here for the latest versions: **https://learn.microsoft.com/en-us/cpp/windows/latest-supported-vc-redist?view=msvc-170**

The roles and prerequisites which are needed to be able to install them are:
- **Management server**: There are no prerequisites required in order for you to install the management server role.
- **Runbook server**: There are no prerequisites required in order for you to install the runbook server role.
- **Runbook Designer**: There are no prerequisites required in order for you to install the Runbook Designer role.
- **Web API service**: To install the Web API service you will need the following prerequisites:
    - IIS CORS Module: https://www.iis.net/downloads/microsoft/iis-cors-module
    - .NET Core 5.0.50 SDK: https://dotnet.microsoft.com/en-us/download/dotnet/thank-you/sdk- 5.0.202 -windows-x64-installer
    - .NET Core 5.0.5 Runtime Hosting Bundle: https://dotnet.microsoft.com/en-us/download/dotnet/thank-you/runtime-aspnetcore-5.0.5-windows-hosting-bundle-installer
    - .NET Core 5.0.5 Runtime: https://dotnet.microsoft.com/en-us/download/dotnet/thank-you/runtime-5.0.5-windows-x64-installer

Note: Normally, you would install the latest versions of .NET Core libraries and the version listed above is out of support, but the latest versions have not been successful in passing prerequisites, therefore you need to ensure that the 5.0.5 versions are installed and all match the versioning in order to proceed.

- **Orchestration console**: To install the Orchestration console, you will need the following prerequisites:
    - IIS URL Rewrite Module: https://www.iis.net/downloads/microsoft/url-rewrite

.NET Framework 3.5 Installation Media

Before you go ahead and follow the instructions, there are also some other tasks you will need to complete first. Since one of the server features, .NET Framework 3.5, can only be installed when you have the installation media of the Windows Server OS, you either have this mounted to the computer or copied locally to the system drive, where you can point to the directory.

To install the server roles, then perform the following instructions:
1. Click the start menu.
2. Go to the **Server Manager** console.

3. In the top right-hand corner, select **Manage | Add Roles and Features**
4. **Before you begin:** Click **Next**.
5. **Select the installation type: Installation Type** - Ensure the **Role-based or feature-based installation** is selected, then click **Next**.
6. **Select destination server: Server Selection** | Ensure that the **Select a server from the server pool** has your server selected, then click **Next**.
7. **Select server roles:** Click **Next**.
8. Click the **Add Features** button within the dialogs when they pop, then click **Next**
9. **Select features:** Select the following features
    a. **.NET Framework 3.5 Features**: .NET Framework 3.5 (includes .NET 2.0 and 3.0)
    b. Then click **Next**.
10. **Confirm installation selections: Confirmation** | Click on the **Specify an alternate source path** link at the bottom of the window.
11. **Specify Alternate Source Path:** Enter the path of the installation media to point to the following folder i.e. `D:\Sources\SxS`. Then click **OK**.
12. **Confirm installation selections: Confirmation** | Click **Install**.

Orchestrator account requirements

Orchestrator uses service accounts for services to run, which control the running of the runbooks created within Orchestrator.

The following table shows all the service accounts required to be setup, along with an explanation of what each service account is for:

> **Note: Ensure that any of the service accounts have the "Log On as a Service" right in the local policy of the server in which will hold Orchestrator roles.**

Name	Description	Local or domain
Orchestrator Management Service	Used to enable the management capabilities of Orchestrator	Doman
Orchestrator Remoting Service	Used to deploy runbooks through to Orchestrator	Local
Orchestrator Runbook Server Monitor	Used for reporting on the health state of the runbook server.	Domain
Orchestrator Runbook Service	Used to allow for running of runbooks	Domain

Table 10.1: Orchestrator service account table

It is also worth mentioning that when going through the initial installation of Orchestrator, you will only be prompted for one service account login, which will prefill the same login details for the following accounts:

- Orchestrator Management Service
- Orchestrator runbook server monitor
- Orchestrator runbook service

Firewall requirements

The following firewall requirements table shows the required ports which need to be opened. This is in reference to the official documentation **https://learn.microsoft.com/en-us/system-center/orchestrator/tcp-port-requirements?view=sc-orch-2022**

The firewall requirements table is as follows:

Firewall direction	Ports used	Protocol Type	Transmission Control Protocol (TCP) or User Datagram Protocol (UDP)
Runbook Designer to Management server	135, 1024-65535	**Remote Procedure Call (RPC)**	TCP
Management server/ runbook server/Web Service to database	1433	**Structured Query Language (SQL)** Port	TCP
Internet Browser to Web API service	81	HTTP (Alternate Port)*	TCP
Internet Browser to Orchestration console	82	HTTP (Alternate Port)*	TCP

Table 10.2: Orchestrator firewall requirements

* Indicates the HTTP alternate ports shown. The default port is generally port 80, but with the assumption that this port is already in use from the default website within IIS, 81 and 82 are the default assumed ports to be used when using the Web API service and Orchestration Console.

Orchestrator installation

Once these prerequisites have been installed, we can proceed to perform the installation for a management server.

To install the management server, perform the following the instructions:

1. Open the installation media to Orchestrator 2022.

2. Double-click the **SetupOrchestrator.exe** file.
3. Select the **Install** button on the System Center 2022 Orchestrator splash screen.
4. **Getting Started: Product registration** | Enter the name and organization of whom will be registering the product and enter a product key for the product unless you are choosing to install the evaluation version which lasts for 180 days. Select the **I have read, understood, and agree with the terms of the license terms** tick box, then click **Next**.
5. **Getting Started: Please read this License Term**s. Read through the license terms and then select **I accept the license terms,** then click **Next**.
6. **Getting Started: Diagnostic and Usage Data**. Read through the page, then click **Next**.
7. **Getting Started**: **Select features to install** | By default, all of the features are selected to install with the Management Server role greyed out as the assumed preselected role. Click **Next**.
8. **Prerequisites: System check results** | Ensure that there are no critical errors or warnings upon the prerequisite check. Then, click **Next**.
9. **Configure the service account:** Enter the details of the domain account which will be used to run the orchestrator service. Test credentials to ensure it has the correct permissions, then click **Next**.
10. **Configure the database**: Enter the name of the SQL Server and the instance name for where you will be creating the operational database for. Wait for the connection check to be successful and verify the location of the database and log files. Then, click **Next**.
11. **Configure the database:** Enter the name of the database which you will use. By default, this will be Orchestrator. Click **Next**.
12. **Configure the Orchestrators users group:** Select a group to use which will maintain a list of whitelisted users which are able to access the Runbook Designer console. By default, this will be the **OrchestratorUsersGroup** and select the **Grant remote access to the Runbook Designer** option, then click **Next**.
13. **Configure the ports of the Web API:** Check the default port selected and the URL used to access the Web API, then click **Next**.
14. **Configure the ports for the Web console**: Check the default port selected and the URL used to access the web console, then click **Next**.
15. **Configuration: Select the installation location**. Confirm the installation location, then click **Next**.
16. **Configuration: Use Microsoft Update to help keep your computer secure and up-to-date** | Select if you want the product to use Microsoft Update to check for updates for Orchestrator then click **Next**.

17. **Configuration**: **Installation Summary** | Review the configuration for the management server, then click **Install** to begin, as shown in the following figure:

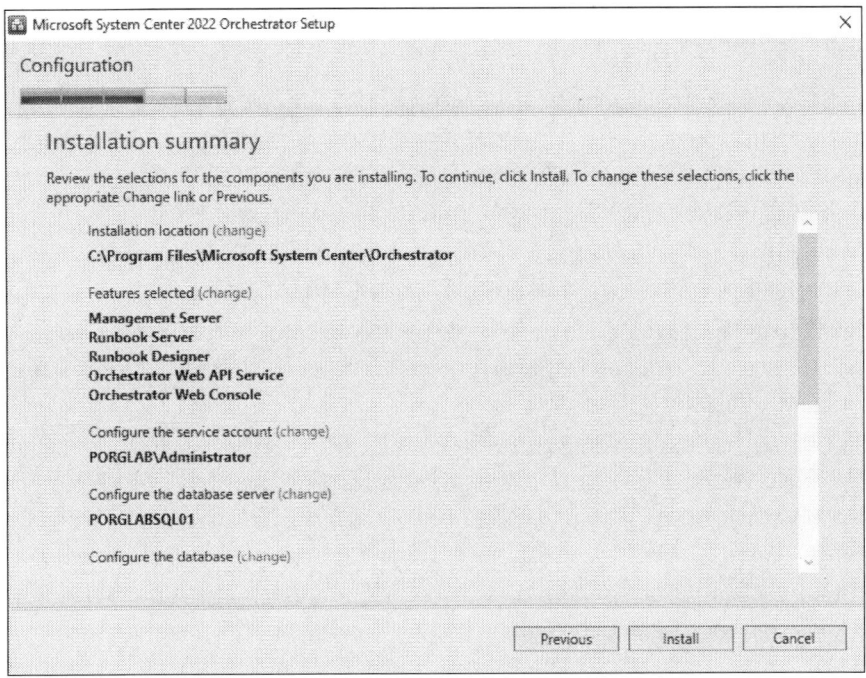

Figure 10.1: Installation summary of Orchestrator 2022

Multi-runbook server installation

Now that we have built the initial management server and data warehouse server, we can now start to formulate the connectors which are available. This is a mandatory task if you want to have a data warehouse management server as part of your **System Center Service Manager** (**SCSM**) environment.

Installing additional runbook

To install an additional runbook server, perform the following instructions:

1. Open the installation media to Orchestrator 2022.
2. Double-click the `SetupOrchestrator.exe` file.
3. Select the runbook server under the Standalone installations section of the System Center 2022 Orchestrator splash screen.
4. **Getting Started: Product Registration** | Enter the name and organization of the individual for whom you will be registering the product and enter a product key for the product, unless you are choosing to install the evaluation version which

lasts for 180 days. Select the **I have read, understood, and agree with the terms of the license terms** tick box, then click **Next**.

5. **Getting Started: Please read this License Terms** | Read through the license terms and then select **I accept the license terms,** then click **Next**.

6. **Getting Started: Diagnostic and Usage Data** | Read through the page, then click **Next**.

7. **Getting Started**: **Select features to install** | By default, all the features are selected to install, excluding the Management Server role. Click **Next**.

8. **Prerequisites**: **System check results** | Ensure that there are no critical errors or warnings upon the prerequisite check. Then, click **Next**.

9. **Configure the service account** | Enter the details of the domain account which will be used to run the orchestrator service. Test credentials to ensure it has the correct permissions then click **Next**.

10. **Configure the database:** Enter the name of the SQL Server and the instance name for where you will be creating the operational database for. Wait for the connection check to be successful and verify the location of the database and log files. Then, click **Next**.

11. **Configure the database:** Select the existing database for which we did the initial installation for, then click **Next**:

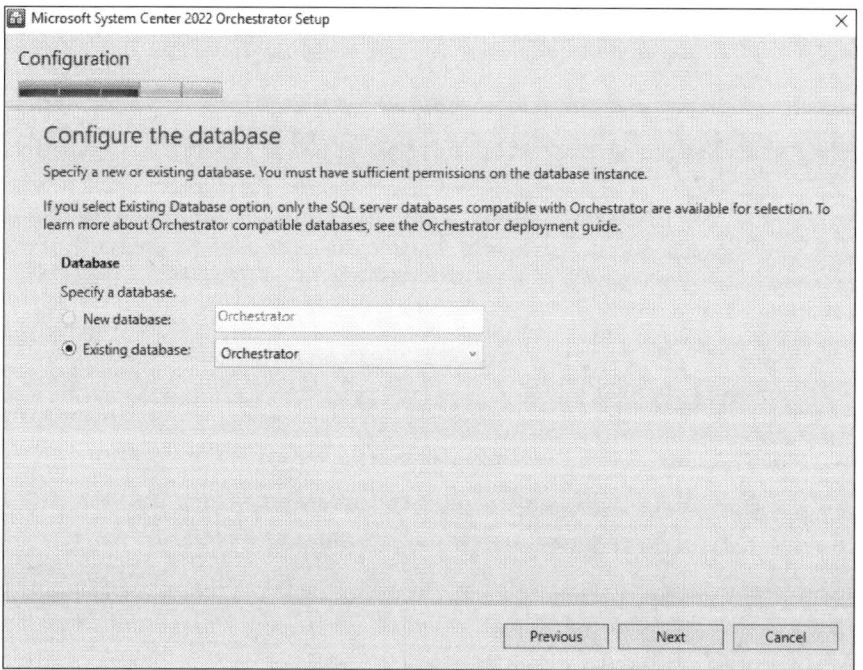

Figure 10.2: *Existing database selection for runbook server in Orchestrator 2022*

12. **Select the installation location**: Confirm the installation location, then click **Next**.

13. **Use Microsoft Update to help keep your computer secure and up-to-date**: Select if you want the product to use Microsoft Update to check for updates for Orchestrator, then click **Next**.
14. **Installation summary:** Review the configuration for the management server, then click **Install** to begin:

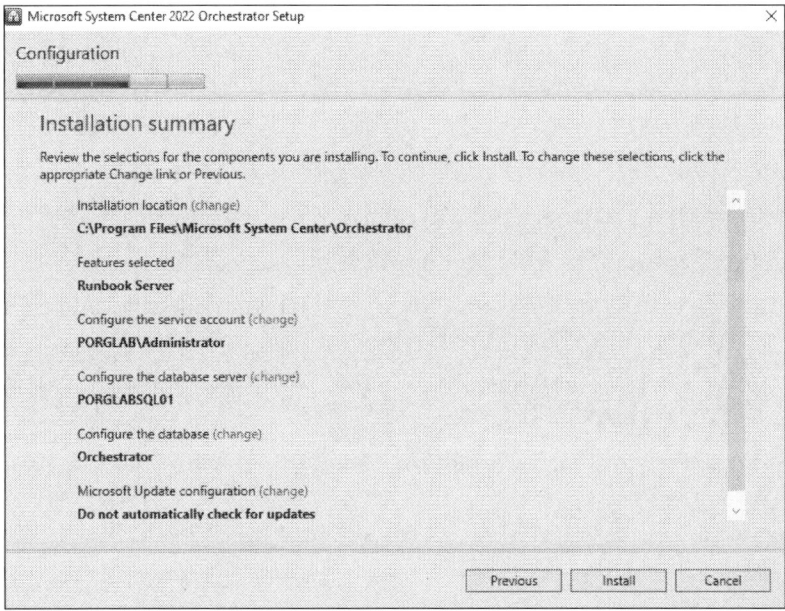

Figure 10.3: Installation summary of runbook server installation in Orchestrator 2022

Administrating Orchestrator

After you have completed the installation of Orchestrator, you can start the post installation and the various administrative tasks to fully utilize Orchestrator.

Deploying manager tasks

The deployment manager application is responsible for managing integration packs within Orchestrator. Some sections which will explain how administrative tasks are carried out to manage the integration packs.

Register integration packs

> **Note: Ensure that you close the Runbook Designer application and where possible stop any runbooks that are running that are related to an older version of the integration pack which you are looking to upgrade.**

Though you will have native integration packs within the Runbook Designer, there will be various official Microsoft integration packs that you may want to install to start further integration with other Microsoft products, such as Active Directory or Configuration Manager or to initiate other integration paths with the System Center counterparts, such as Virtual Machine Manager, Operations Manager, Service Manager, and Data Protection Manager.

The application used to install integration packs is called deployment manager, which is a part of the Orchestrator installation for when you install the Orchestrator Management server role.

To register integration packs, perform the following steps:

1. Click the start menu and go to **Microsoft System Center**.
2. Select the **Deployment Manager** application.
3. Right click the **Integration Packs** folder in the left-hand pane as seen in *Figure 10.4*, then select **Register IP with the Orchestrator Management Server…**
4. **Integration Pack Registration Wizard: Welcome to the Integration Pack Registration Wizard** | Click **Next**.
5. **Integration Pack or Hotfix Selection:** Select **Integration Packs or Hotfixes** | Select the **Add** button and choose the integration packs that you want to register to your Orchestrator. Once selected you will see this listed outlining its product name, version and file path. Click **Next**.
6. **Completing Integration Pack Registration Wizard: Completing the Integration Pack Wizard** | Click **Finish**.
7. Read through the software license terms and select **Accept** to allow for the registration to begin.

Once you have completed this, you will see the integration pack listed as seen in *Figure 10.4* but you will also see some updated log entries within the deployment manager console indicating that it has been successfully registered. This process means that the integration pack is officially listed and ready to be deployed to a runbook server/Runbook Designer machine.

Deploy integration packs

To deploy the integration pack next, perform the following:

1. Click the start menu and go to **Microsoft System Center**.
2. Select the **Deployment Manager** application.
3. Right-click the `Integration Packs` folder in the left-hand pane as seen in *Figure 10.4*, then select **Deploy IP with the Orchestrator Management Server**.
4. **Integration Pack Deployment Wizard: Welcome to the Integration Pack Deployment Wizard** | Click **Next**.

5. **Integration Pack or Hotfix Deployment: Deploy Integration Packs or Hotfixes** | Select the Integration Pack or packs which you want to deploy, then click **Next**.
6. **Computer selection:** Computer Selection Details | Enter or add the computer or computers to which the integration packs will be deployed to, then click **Next**.
7. **Installation Options:** Installation Configuration | Select if you want to have a schedule to deploy the integration packs against, default will allow for these to be installed immediately. You also have the option to select if you want to stop all runbooks during the process of the installation of the integration pack, or you can allow them to keep running but may have to reboot the server after successful installation. Click **Next**.
8. **Completing Integration Pack Deployment Wizard: Completing the Integration Pack Deployment Wizard** | Click **Finish**.

Once completed, you will then see some log entries confirming of a successful deployment of the integration pack.

Deploy Runbook Designer servers via deployment manager

The deployment manager is also able to deploy the Runbook Designer application to different servers. A similar method is used to install the Runbook Designer application through the installation wizard:

1. Click the start menu and go to Microsoft System Center.
2. Select the **Deployment Manager** application.
3. Right-click the Runbook Designers folder in the left-hand pane, then select **Deploy new Runbook Designer**.
4. **Runbook Designer Deployment Wizard: Welcome to the Runbook Designer Deployment Wizard** | Click **Next**.
5. **Computer Selection Details**: Type in or add the computer in which you wish to deploy the Runbook Designer application to, then click **Next**.
6. **Integration Pack or Hotfix Deployment: Deploy Integration Packs or Hotfixes** - Select the integration packs to deploy to the server then click **Next**.
7. **Completing Runbook Designer Deployment Wizard: Completing the Runbook Designer Deployment Wizard** – Click **Finish** to complete the deployment.

Deploy runbook servers via deployment manager

The deployment manager application is also capable of deploying the runbook server role to additional servers as well to save from performing this task using the installation media for Orchestrator.

To deploy runbook servers utilizing this method, perform the following steps:
1. Click the start menu and go to **Microsoft System Center**.
2. Select the **Deployment Manager** application.
3. Right-click the `Runbook Designers` folder in the left-hand pane, then select **Deploy new Runbook Server**.
4. **Runbook Server Deployment: Welcome to the Runbook Server Deployment Wizard** | Click **Next**.
5. **Runbook Server Selection: Service Information** | Enter the computer details of the server which you want to have the Runbook Server role, then enter the service account username and password.
6. **Integration Pack or Hotfix Deployment: Deploy Integration Packs or Hotfixes** | Select the integration packs to deploy to the server, then click **Next**.
7. **Completing Runbook Server Deployment Wizard: Completing the Runbook Server Deployment Wizard** | Click **Finish** to complete the deployment.

Configuration of integration packs

Once the integration packs have been deployed, open the Runbook Designer application. You should then see them listed on the right-hand side of the console under the **Activities** pane, as seen in *Figure 10.4*:

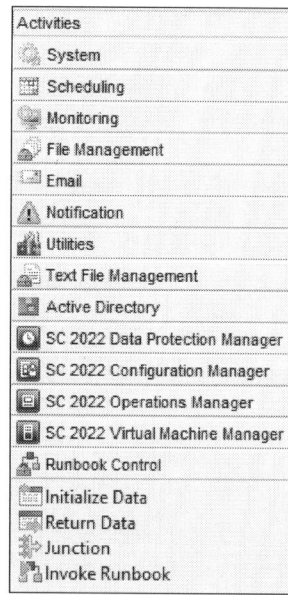

Figure 10.4: Activities pane in Runbook Designer console

Even though the integration packs have been deployed, they will still need to be configured to point to the servers that hold the correct product corresponding to the integration pack installed.

Integration packs can vary from requiring a connection to the server which hosts the primary or management services, to servers which hold the SQL Server databases.

To configure integration pack connections, perform the following instructions:

1. Open the Runbook Designer application.
2. In the toolbar pane at the top of the application, select **Options** where you will be presented a list of the integration packs which require configuration.

Note: You will only see integration packs that had to be installed to Orchestrator, where you will be required to configure the integration packs. No native integration packs or activities are required for further connections.

In this example, we will look at two integration packs as they both have different forms of connections. We want to show the vast differences between different connections.

Active Directory Integration Pack Configuration

Let us explore how a connection for this integration pack is created:

1. From the **Options** menu, select **Active Directory**.
2. **Add Configuration**: Select the **Microsoft Active Directory Domain Configuration**.

Once selected, you will then see the following fields to fill out to make a successful connection to your Active Directory domain, as seen below in *Figure 10.5*:

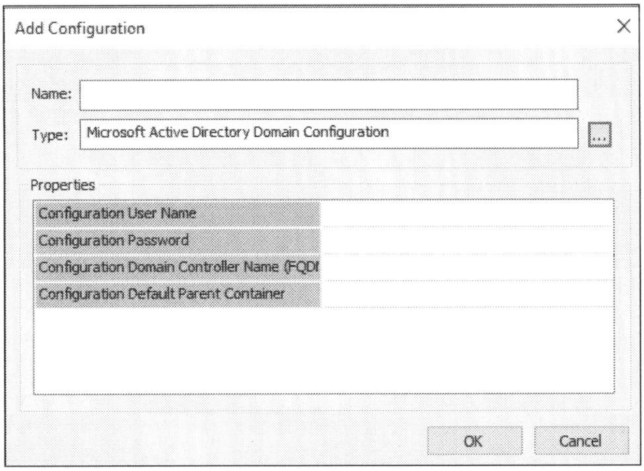

Figure 10.5: *Active Directory Integration Pack Configuration*

As you can see, this configuration requires an account with permissions to read from Active Directory including the **Fully Qualified Domain Name (FQDN)** of your domain controller and a parent container if you are looking to limit the scope of where you will pull the Active Directory objects from.

System Center 2022 Operations Manager

This integration pack, alongside its other System Center products and Configuration Manager, the Operations Manager configuration has vastly different options of fields to fill out to create the configuration.

To configure the Operations Manager integration pack, perform the following steps:

1. From the **Options** menu, select **SC2022 Operations Manager**.
2. **SC 2022 Operations Manager: Microsoft System Center Operations Manager Connections** | Select **Add**.

In *Figure 10.8*, you will see the connection details required for you to make a connection to your Operations Manager server:

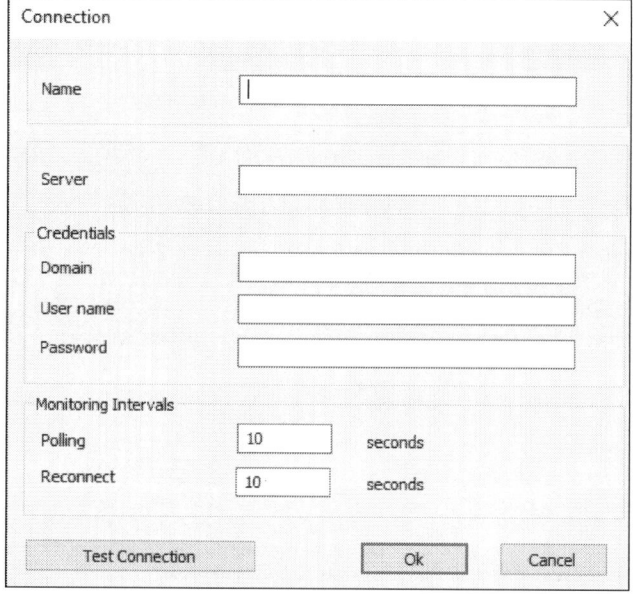

Figure 10.6: SC 2022 Operations Manager Integration Pack Configuration

> **Note:** Products such as System Center, Configuration Manager or any other products, which have a GUI console, may require the console of that application to be installed onto the runbook server to effectively run activities from the integration pack relating to that product.

Creating runbooks

Now that everything is in place, we are now ready to start creating runbooks for Orchestrator. What we will do here is go through the general steps and processes on how to formulate a simple runbook to provide the reader with an understanding on how each component works all the way through to a successful running or triggering of the runbook.

New runbook

First, we will need to create a new runbook template, which will provide us with the canvas where we will be able to use activities from the integration packs in the orchestrator.

To do this, perform the following steps:

1. Open the **Runbook Designer** application.
2. Right-click **Runbooks** and select **New | Runbook**.

This will then provide the blank canvas, which we can see in *Figure 10.7*:

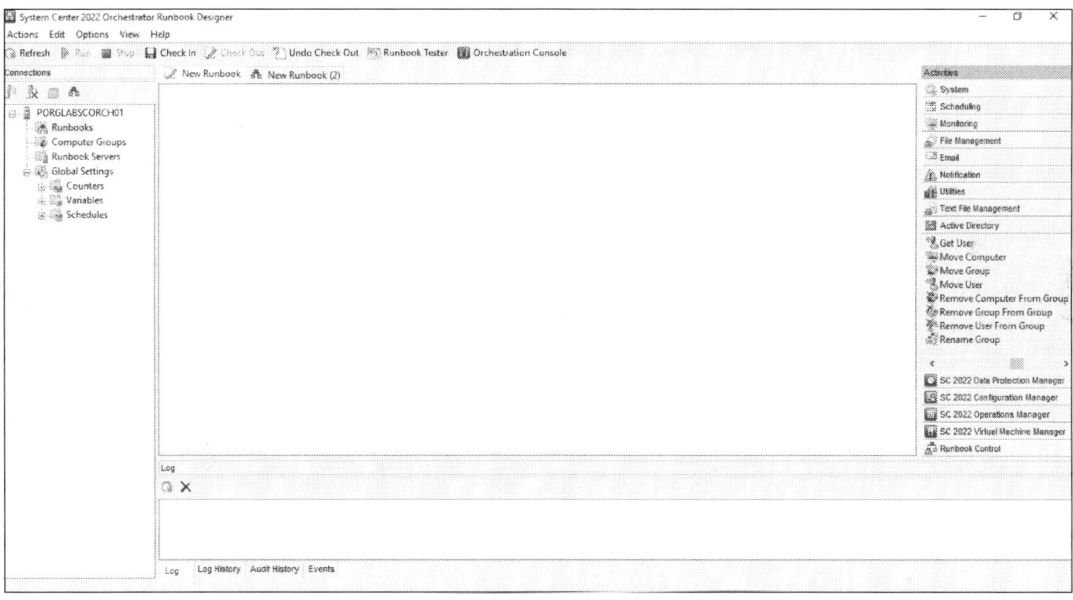

Figure 10.7: New runbook in Runbook Designer

Edit runbook

In order for us to further develop a runbook or to simply edit an existing one, we first need to be familiar with the different states of a runbook.

In *Figure 10.7*, you will see two runbooks which have the name **New Runbook** but you will notice that the icons on the left-hand side of each runbook are quite different, which we will explain.

If we start by looking at the new runbook we created called **New Runbook (2)** this is a state called **Checked In**. The **Checked In** state means that the runbook is locked from any further edits and is ready to be ran or triggered to perform its designated use. All new runbooks, when created are in this state by default.

If we want to edit a runbook, we perform an action called **Check Out** which then changes the icon on the runbook to exactly what you see in the **New Runbook** tab in *Figure 10.7* where you can make all the changes you need until you are ready to Check In the runbook.

> Note: If any runbooks are running, then when wanting to check out, it will essentially stop the runbook from running.

Creating runbook workflows

With the runbook template created, we can now look at how to create runbook workflows.

This can be a few simple steps, from activities spread across various integration packs, or much more complex depending on what we are trying to achieve. We will explore the variants of basic to complex and analyze the different components and properties of activities which will help to understand its purpose.

Runbook activity basics: Initialize data

Though we touched on this in the previous chapter, we will cover this again to provide you a better understanding of the basics.

The most important step or activity within a runbook is essentially the very first step, which is what allows the runbook to be effectively triggered. In order to provide a good example, we will show three different examples of basic runbooks that detail the basics and how the first step and additional steps work.

The first common step to kick off a runbook is the **Initialize Data** activity within the Runbook Control section of the activities pane in the Runbook Designer console. This is usually left either blank or with field parameters, which someone can enter in depending on where it might be triggered from. In *Figure 10.8*, we can see an example of two steps, in which we have the Initialize Data step and have added another one, which derives from the Active Directory Integration pack, which is an activity named **Get User.**:

Deployment and Administration of System Center Orchestrator ■ 249

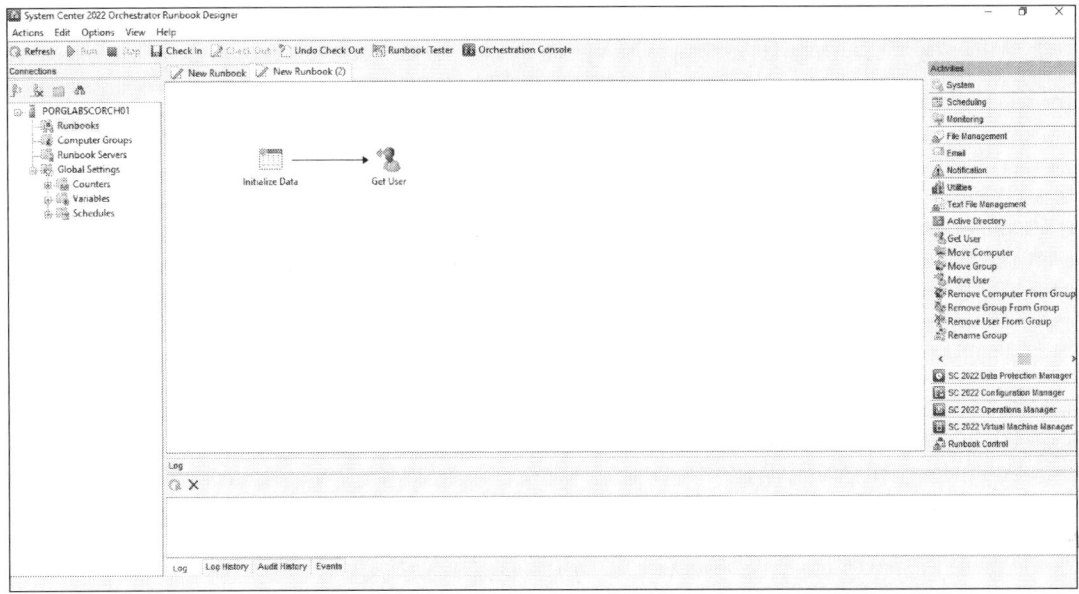

Figure 10.8: Example runbook in Runbook Designer

When the runbook is started with this step (if blank), then the next step would be to get a user from Active Directory as a high-level explanation. Let us break this down in a lower level to understand these components better.

The initialize data step we explained can be left blank if you want a simple step trigger. However, if we want to add parameters to it, which a user would enter information into, as seen in *Figure 10.9*, we have a parameter named **username**, which would be used to represent the user and its datatype. In this case, it is a string, but this can be changed to other types if we want to be more specific:

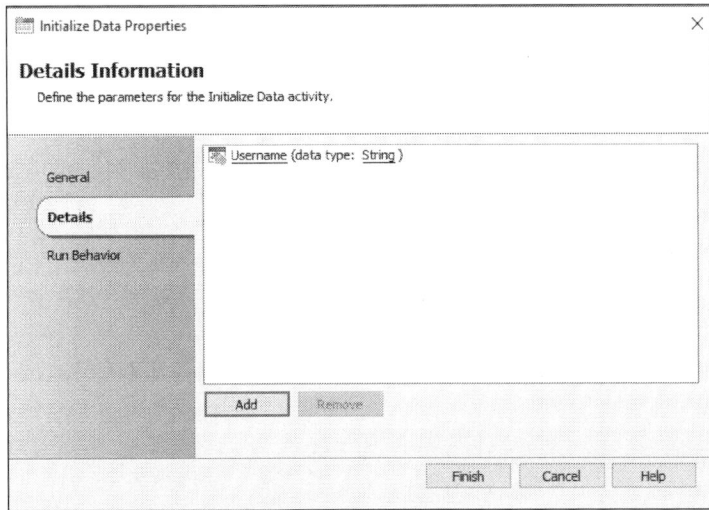

Figure 10.9: Initialize step properties

So, instead of being a blank step trigger, this will be a prerequisite for information when triggered to go onto the next step; however, before going to the next step, there is a logical component in between, called a **link**, which is represented by the arrow in between both steps as seen in *Figure 10.8*. Links control the condition of what criteria must be met before proceeding to the next step. By default, it is normally based on the successful running of the previous step, but we may not want this. For example, if we want the next step to run if the previous step failed or if it met a specific string pattern or value. This is where we can make further edits by right-clicking the arrow icon and selecting its properties so we can see our options, as shown in *Figure 10.10*:

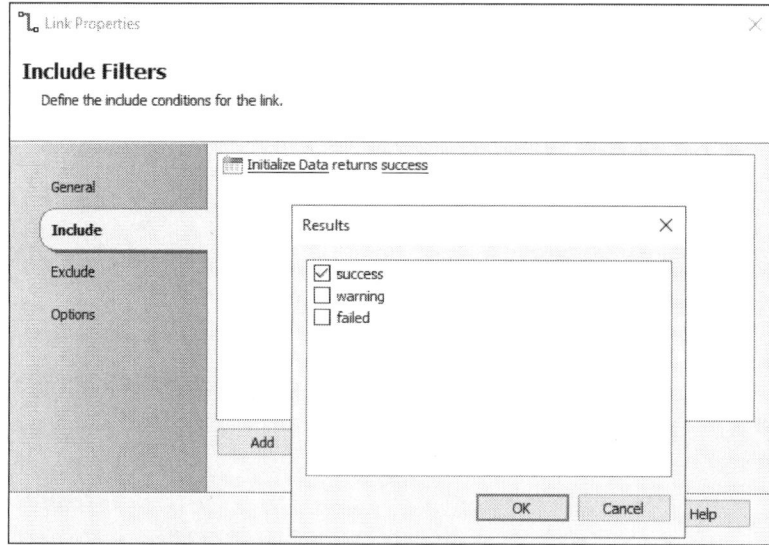

Figure 10.10: Link properties

The exclude option is used to not proceed with any entries that may represent the same three listed results.

Then, we move onto the **Get User** step. As this is an integration pack that had to be installed, we would need to ensure we have a configuration setup as shown in *Figure 10.5*. Once this is done, we can then select the configuration as shown in *Figure 10.11*, which would then allow us to have further options for filtering our results:

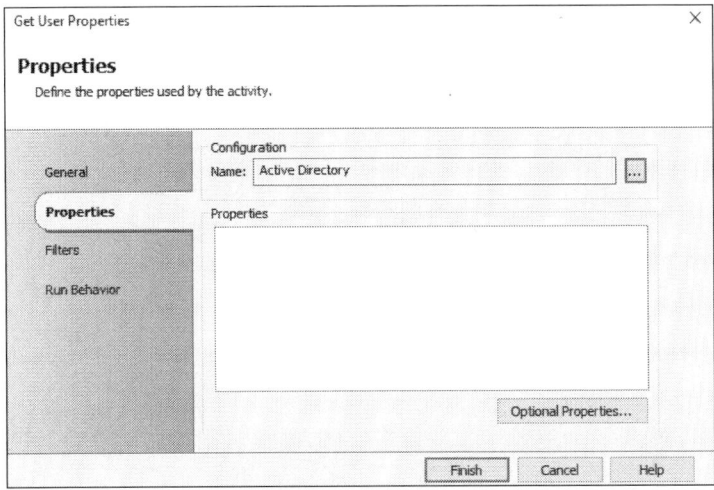

Figure 10.11: Get user properties

As this step is very broad, it will grab every user account in the Active Directory, but for the purpose of our workflow, we want to limit it only to what we specifically provided within the previous step, **Initialize Data**. So, for us to do that, we would go to the filters section and click **Add** to get a filter settings window, as shown in *Figure 10.14*, then specify what we want to filter to the User Principal Name, for example. Then, for the value, we right-click and select **Subscribe | Published Data**:

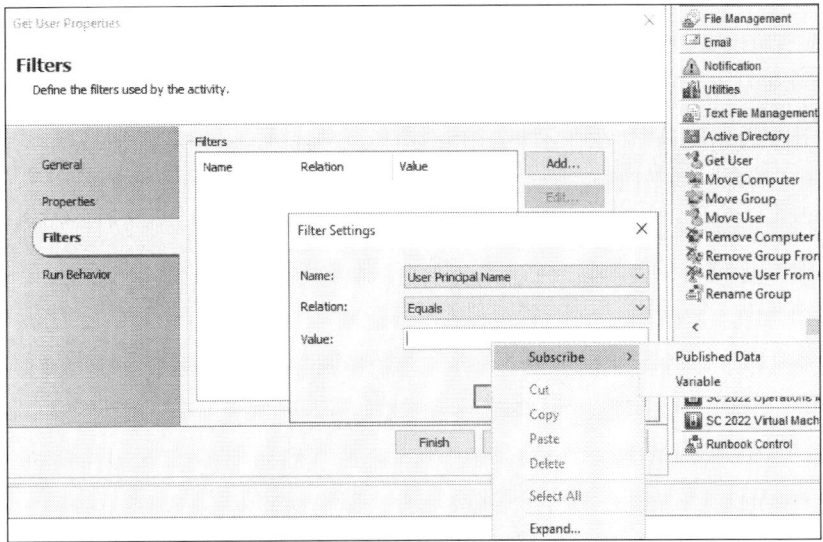

Figure 10.12: Subscribe to published data options

This option allows us to select the username parameter that we specified in the previous step. To use other published data, we can select the **Show common Published Data** option, which will give us some more generic parameters to use if needed, as shown in *Figure 10.13*:

252 ■ Windows System Center 2022

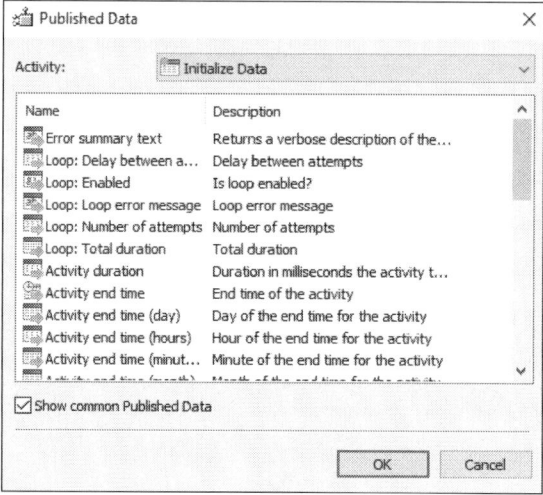

Figure 10.13: Published data window

At this point, we have a runbook that is considered ready to work. Hence, we would select the **Check In** button which would allow us to run the runbook as needed.

Runbook activity basics: Monitor trigger

Another form of a runbook for triggering is having an activity based on monitoring for a specific outcome or status. Once triggered, the runbook would commence.

Let us take *Figure 10.14*, where we use an activity like **Monitor Service** which comes from the **Monitoring** activity section. This is where we can configure the activity to monitor the status of a particular service. Here, we can enter the computer name as well as the name of the service to refer to, as shown in the following figure:

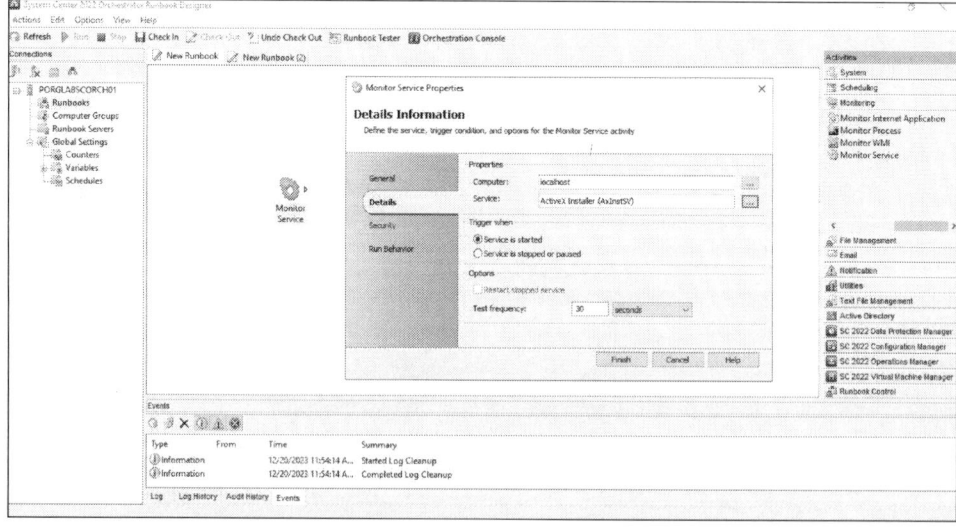

Figure 10.14: Monitor Status activity

We can also toggle if we want to trigger if it started or stopped. Once the condition is met, the next step of the runbook will proceed.

Runbook activity basics: Another runbook trigger

Another method of a triggering process is an activity which involves triggering another runbook to run. This can be seen in *Figure 10.15* with a step called "Invoke Runbook", which allows the administrator the ability to select another runbook to trigger.

A great part of this step is that it allows us to wait for the completion of that process before proceeding with the current runbook.

We can see these options referenced in *Figure 10.15*:

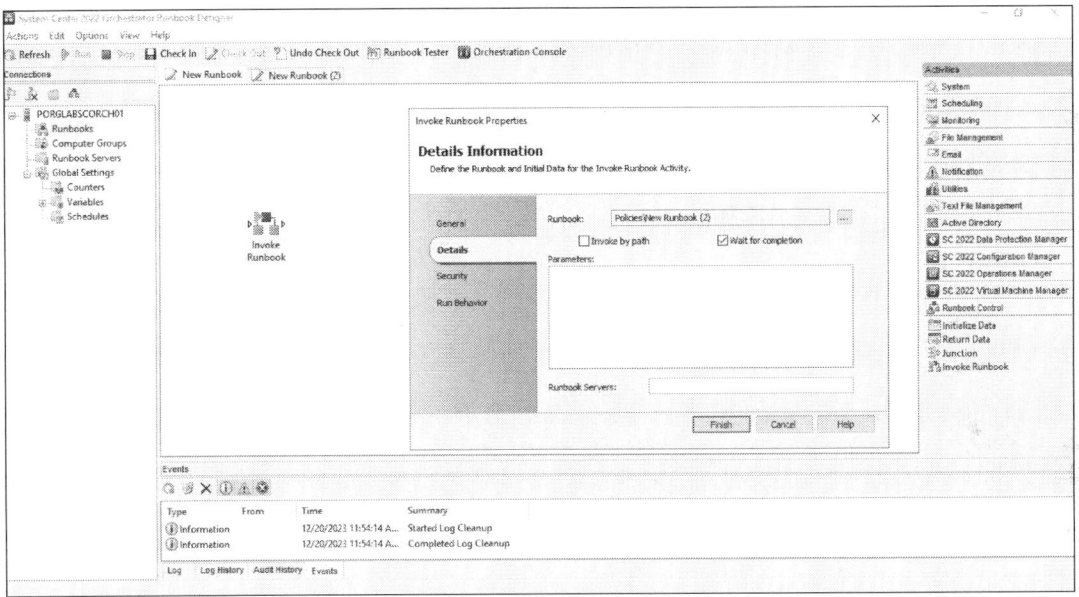

Figure 10.15: Invoke runbook activity

Global settings

Global settings are variables which allow for constant values to be stored and used within different runbook activities and help with passing definitive values across runbooks as well.

There are three different forms of global settings:
- Counters
- Variables
- Schedules

These variables are with different data types. So, for example, the "Counters" global settings are integer-based variables defined by using a numerical default value and primarily used with activities that utilize these, such as Modify Counter, Monitor Counter, etc. The purpose of this could be to have a runbook that may execute a process that may go through a looping process and count the number of times it has been executed and using a counter would establish a maximum to set a limit. Overall, it is another way of enriching a process by utilizing these steps.

Variables have more of a string data type, similar to how a variable uses, in all programming languages to use a definitive value. For example, if we had a SQL server named test.contoso.com, this variable would contain this as a value and be labeled as "SQL Server". While building a runbook that has to execute something specific on an SQL Server, we could use this variable in the Published Data. Another benefit is that the variable can be changed so that there are no additional edits within an existing runbook.

The schedules global settings is defined by using configuration to state when a schedule can be applied in certain days, occurrences, months, and even as hours. These global settings work in conjunction with activities defined within the **Scheduling** activities section, more specifically, the **Check Schedule** activity. Once you define a schedule that the runbook can run, you could join it to a step like **Monitor Date/Time**, which would allow for a trigger to execute once the correct date/time has been reached.

Testing runbooks

Testing runbooks is a crucial practice to make sure that what we have created works exactly as intended, or it can also be used to troubleshoot a certain workflow if any issues occur.

Runbook Designer contains another tool called the "Runbook Tester" which allows us to perform such tests. There has been some discrepancies of the usage of the tool, as essentially, it just runs the runbook the same as just running a runbook in general where what we want to potential action just does it anyway.

This is true, however, the tool does provide a better GUI breakdown of how its configured and also provides an option where you can have a step through which allows you to manually go through a runbook step by step and only move to the next activity, until you press step.

To access this tool within the Runbook Designer, go to the toolbar and select Runbook Tester. This then gives us another window showing the same runbook but within a different setting.

So, if we select the Step through option as an example, you will see it enter the first step but with a pause. When ready we select step to initiate the first step.

> Note: The Runbook Tester tool, when used with runbooks that contain the Initialize Step option, allows for you to be prompted with the parameters specified, so you can test what happens once you enter the required information

Once stepping through and testing the runbook, you may see a similar result, shown in *Figure 10.16* which shows the results of trying to find all user accounts in Active Directory:

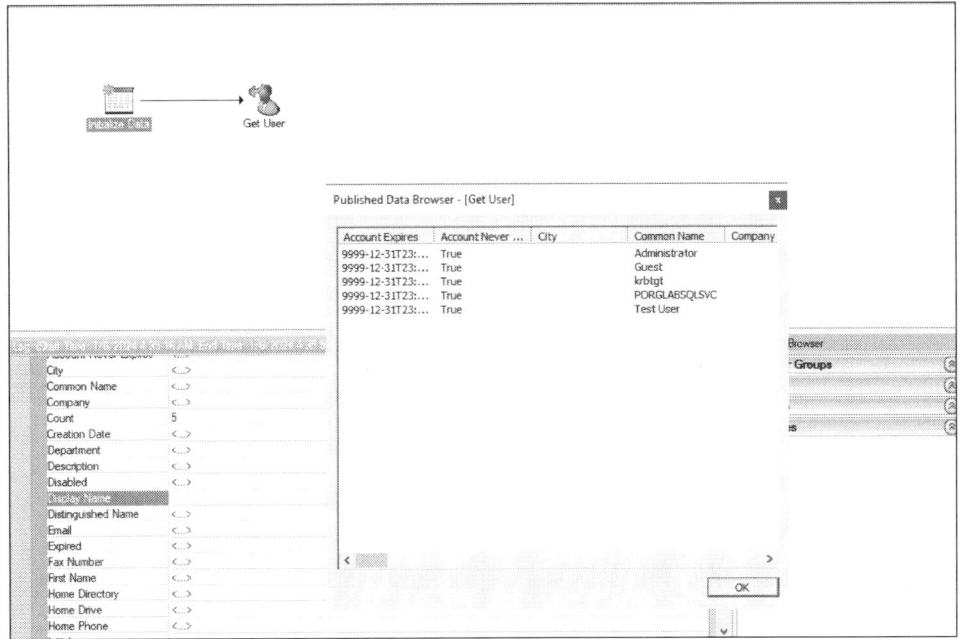

Figure 10.16: Runbook Tester results

Update Orchestrator (Update Rollups)

Orchestrator, like the other products, has the same process when it comes to applying update rollups where there is an update specific for each role that orchestrator has.

Though there is not a specific order in which the updates would apply in, it would be best practice to follow a similar structure to other System Center products that have multiple roles, such as:

- Management server
- Runbook server
- Runbook Designer
- Web console
- Web API

The updates can generally be found in the Microsoft Update catalog to obtain the update for each component.

Currently, the latest UR for Orchestrator 2022, at the time of writing this book, is UR2, which can be found here: **https://support.microsoft.com/en-gb/topic/update-rollup-2-for-system-center-2022-orchestrator-c43fd5ad-3e40-4ea0-8586-4c5c5901aae0**

Best practices

Here are some of the best practice points for Orchestrator to keep in mind when going through any administration tasks.

Multiple integration pack connections

The section *Administrating Orchestrator* showed how we can create a connection for an integration pack, which requires a connection to a server. This represents that with technology, you have the ability to create more than one connection. This can be handy if you have an environment which may contain multiple environments, that is, development, pre-production or if you have different servers for each product. The benefit of this is that where certain disaster recovery situations happen, you can then have the ability to change the configuration scope within the activity to use a different configuration to avoid downtime or even to develop a runbook that may use multiple connections in case one went down which will enter as a great segway into the next section below.

Effective error handling

Error handling in Orchestrator is very important, especially for your runbooks when you want to troubleshoot or highlight any processes which fail:

- **Link properties:** Examples of this would be, let us say, your link properties. Now, depending on how complex your runbook is, you may have conditions that handle success, warning, and failures. If you want to illustrate this process much clearer, you could color code links to refer to the conditions. For example, a green link would represent success, yellow for warning, and, of course, red for failure. This can be done within the link properties and the options section, and you will see how it displays in your Runbook Designer. Another way of further enhancement could be to go into the toolbar and select **Options | Configuration**, where you can have an option to show link labels. This will give you the opportunity to provide a meaningful name to the link property to state what it represents; that is, the name of the link could be "Success Link" just to indicate not only the color coordination but also to clearly show the route of your workflow when successful. The link option properties are shown in the following figure:

Deployment and Administration of System Center Orchestrator   257

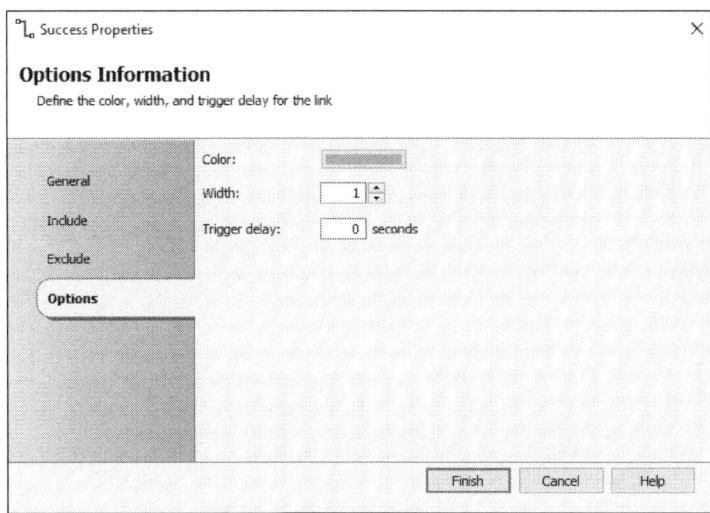

Figure 10.17: Link option properties

Figure 10.18 shows how we can then make link labels visible to where we can add text to show meaningful data, that is, whether it is the successful route or failure route:

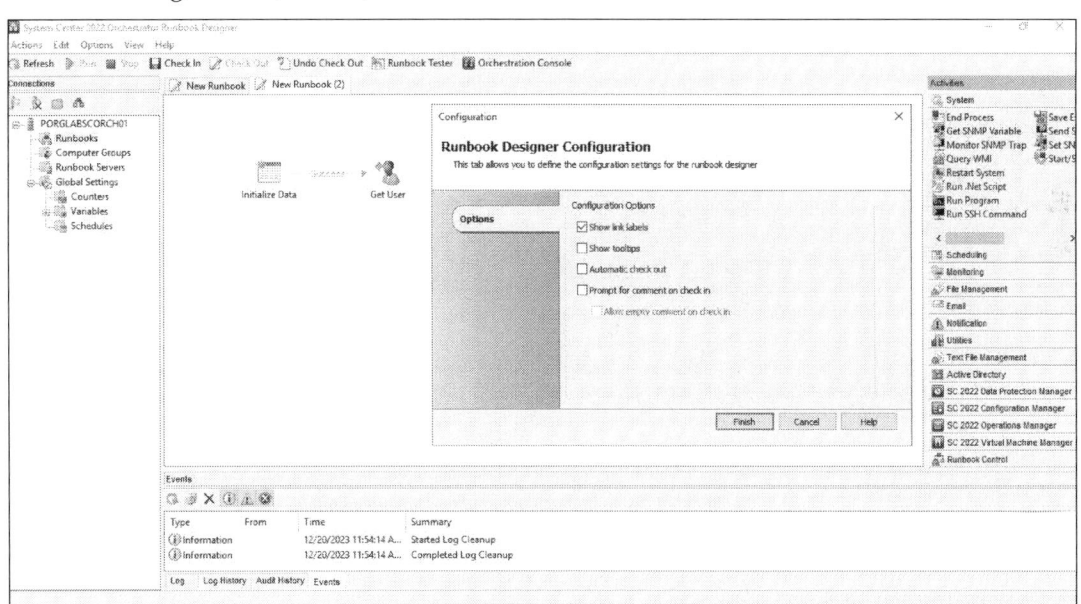

Figure 10.18: Link Properties options

- **Notification activities:** The utilization of these activities can be even more key to highlighting any issues. One great activity, that can be used is the "**Send Platform Event**" activity in the "**Notification**" activities section. Say, we have a failure in a certain part of your runbook. If you had a link property which clearly showed the path of if a process failed, the next step could be to create a platform event which would allow you to see this in the Events section, in the bottom of your Runbook Designer.

Consoles for integration packs

When you want to enrich your runbooks to incorporate some coding that may not be covered within the default activities, you will need these consoles on your runbook servers in order for them to refer to the right modules correctly.

PowerShell handling

Orchestrator, by default, possesses two activities that allow you to use PowerShell. The preferred one being the **Run .NET Script** activity due to its ability to create and forward variables.

The alternative activity is the **Run Program** activity. There can be cases when you may need to refer to a script and change the architecture version of where PowerShell refers to, if you need to run a script in 32-bit or 64-bit, as well as use correct permission elevation. The only real drawback to this step is the error handling, where you cannot easily know the outcome of the program ran. Hence, there would have to be some error handling and testing to go into this.

Other handy third-party integration packs exist that provide some more flexible options for handling PowerShell.

Real-world scenarios

The following are some of the real-world scenarios for Orchestrator to keep in mind when going through any administrative tasks.

Upgrading to Orchestrator 2022

Before proceeding to upgrade to Orchestrator 2022, you will need diligently check the compatibility of the integration packs that you are using.

You will find a definitive list here that shows all the available integration packs for Orchestrator 2022: **https://techcommunity.microsoft.com/t5/system-center-blog/system-center-2022-orchestrator-integration-packs/ba-p/3564571**

If you are utilizing any older versions of the products or using third-party integration packs, you will need to check with the vendor to see if they have one compatible within 2022 or you will face compatibility issues and errors when trying to deploy these through the deployment manager tool.

Clearing authorization cache

A common task you may run into, depending on how many runbooks you are running, is Orphaned Runbooks. This is basically when processes are stuck and do not finish or progress and remain within your log history for an undetermined period of time, causing a lot of lag and confusion.

Clearing the authorization cache is known as a workaround to get things back to normal where you need to stop all runbooks at first and execute a SQL truncate command on the `[Microsoft.SystemCenter.Orchestrator.Internal].AuthorizationCache` table. This helps to clear the orphaned processes and to start fresh again. This can also be a workaround for Service Manager if using an integration between it and Orchestrator to use runbooks.

Runbook limits

By default, Orchestrator allows 50 runbooks to be ran simultaneously However, where an environment scales in reality, this may not be possible to stick to. Though this can be changed, you will need to have the server resources to support this change.

Making changes to this area is known as runbook throttling. To find the process on how to do this, visit the following link: **https://learn.microsoft.com/en-us/system-center/orchestrator/how-to-configure-runbook-throttling?view=sc-orch-2022**

Distributed Component Object Model permission issues

Issues around the **Distributed Component Object Model (DCOM)** can lead to a lot of access denied errors, especially for accounts that are either local administrator, domain administrator, or even have membership of the Orchestrator administrator's group. These tend to happen around the Runbook Designer application and can happen if certain changes on the system, whether migration or some account changes, can cause issues around DCOM. There is a process that can allow you to troubleshoot and fix these issues which can be found here: **https://learn.microsoft.com/en-us/troubleshoot/system-center/orchestrator/runbook-designer-access-denied-error**

Conclusion

In this chapter, we learned about Orchestrator which has the ability to create complex processes which can address everything from BAU to business critical processes, but what comes with a product, such as Orchestrator, with regular use, is a lot of in-depth understanding of your workflow purposes, handling of errors and to be able to showcase this in a clear and decisive way which we understood.

We learned that it is a small product that has a tremendous ability to integrate with all the System Center products to form automated solutions across your environment is how we would conclude this product.

In the next chapter, we will explore the next product within the System Center suite which is Virtual Machine Manager, where we will look at the planning and design of the product.

Points to remember

- Orchestrator allows for multiple runbook servers and Runbook Designer servers to be added which can be done from the installation wizard or from the deployment manager console.
- Integration packs which are installed in addition may require a configuration to establish a connection to the server which represents the same technology.
- Integration packs may require the GUI console to be installed on the runbook servers in order to understand the DLLs or commands which the activities may have embedded.
- Best practices and real-world scenarios for Orchestrator are more crucial when it comes to regular administrative tasks.
- Runbooks can be either simple or complex processes depending on your requirements. Ensure to use global settings where possible to ease editing of runbooks whilst they are still running.

Multiple choice questions

1. **What is the name of tool which Orchestrator uses for you to test runbooks?**
   a. Runbook Designer
   b. Runbook Tester
   c. Web Console
   d. Deployment manager

2. **What is the name of the tool used to register and deploy integration packs to your runbook servers?**
   a. Deployment manager
   b. Data store configuration
   c. Runbook tester
   d. Runbook Designer

3. What type of global setting would you need to create in order to have a string value that can be used in multiple runbooks or activities?

   a. Global settings
   b. Counters
   c. Variables
   d. Schedules

4. When it comes to testing runbooks, what is the main drawback of using this method?

   a. Will still perform the actions of a running runbook.
   b. Cause logging issues.
   c. Cannot be stopped.
   d. Turns off main orchestrator services.

5. Integration packs can allow for more than one configuration.

   a. True
   b. False

6. Name the activities that can be used in Orchestrator to allow for the running of PowerShell Scripts?

   a. Run Program, Run .NET Script
   b. Run .NET Script, Run PowerShell Script
   c. Monitor Date/Time, Run Program
   d. Run Program

Answers

1. b
2. a
3. c
4. a
5. a
6. a

Key terms

- **SCORCH**: System Center Orchestrator
- **Activity**: A step that is part of an integration pack

- **Integration Pack**: A logical object that contains a family of activities which relate to the specific purpose or technology which it was designed for
- **Workflow**: A process that has more than one activity that follows a step by step to provide a desired result
- **Integration**: A relationship between both products where synchronous or asynchronous communication can begin
- **Data warehouse**: A data retention storage mechanism that is used to cover data from an operational database to be backed up and stored to provide historical results
- **AD**: Active Directory
- **SCSM**: System Center Service Manager
- **SCOM**: System Center Operations Manager
- **API**: Application Programming Interface
- **SC**: System Center

Join our book's Discord space

Join the book's Discord Workspace for Latest updates, Offers, Tech happenings around the world, New Release and Sessions with the Authors:

https://discord.bpbonline.com

CHAPTER 11
Virtualization with System Center Virtual Machine Manager

Introduction

In this chapter, we will understand the planning and design for **System Center Virtual Machine Manager** (**SCVMM**). This area will be applicable for most versions of this technology as the same key areas have to be considered, especially when looking into how the solution will be used. Scalability is also a key area that we will want to analyze when planning a new design. We will also discover the upgrade paths that would need to be taken in order to be applicable for System Center 2022. For **Virtual Machine Manager** (**VMM**), we will explore the virtual platforms that are in use and plan how we will design around the baseline requirements for virtual machine management.

Also included will be a minimum and recommended requirement so the reader can develop a lab environment they can use to follow through with the next chapter, to gauge practical and theoretical understanding.

Structure

This chapter will cover the following topics:
- Virtual Machine Manager topology structure
- Virtual environment management planning
- Virtual environment template design

- Disaster recovery
- Virtual Machine Manager lab requirements

Objectives

The objective for the reader is to understand how this product looks after the centralization of your virtual environment. You will also learn how the product can vastly help with the true scalability of your virtual environment and with different areas, which will allow you to add full automation to your virtual infrastructure.

Recommended specifications of the product will allow the user to understand all the design decisions to be made and assess how a sandpit lab can be developed to further understand how VMM works and the roles it uses.

Virtual Machine Manager topology structure

The VMM is a product that, compared to other counterparts, does not contain other additional roles from an installation wizard perspective, but there are indeed a few more roles we will discuss that add to the fabric of the VMM technology.

> **Note:** The term "fabric" is used to describe an area in VMM that contains all the VMM-based infrastructure and neighboring components like networking and storage.

Virtual Machine Manager roles

The roles within VMM are as follows:

- **Management server:** The main role and perhaps the only role that can be installed is the management server role. It is responsible for agents to respond to in order to receive the latest policies and be in sync with the rest of the fabric within VMM.
- **VMM console**: Though this is not a role, this is the GUI interface for VMM, which can be toggled within the installation wizard. Note that if you do choose to install the management server role, then it will be installed automatically.

Virtual Machine Manager post-installation roles

When fully installed, VMM then contains roles that can be added to the following existing or new servers:

- **Library server:** A library server is a role that can be deployed to additional servers after the installation has been completed. By default, a library server can be set up during the initial installation.

A library server is a repository role that allows the storage of various logical components such as templates, profiles, and other relevant objects. These help to build out virtual machines such as ISOs and virtual machine disks such as **Virtual Hard Disk/Virtual Hard Disk v2 (VHD/VHDX)** for virtual machine template usage.

The role is similar to how you would view a distribution point role within the Configuration Manager. However, in this case, the library server operates from just a share which allows the VMM server role and library server to correspond with.

- **PXE server**: The **Pre-boot execution (PXE)** environment servers are responsible for building out new virtual machine hosts from bare metal by applying an Operating System and making them a new host within the Hyper-V framework.

  To draw comparisons with the Configuration Manager or a native role in Windows such as **Windows Deployment Services (WDS)** where they can hold the PXE role to build machines via bare metal, but for VMM, the roles are native for the product itself to be able to build out new hosts and add them to the correct cluster if these are available.

- **Update server**: Another comparison to the Configuration Manager, where the software update role would perform patch deployment to its managed agents. In VMM's case, the update server is used to patch the managed Hyper-V hosts as well as the VMM fabric.

Single management server topology

There are various areas to be considered for the topology of VMM, like the VMM side and the fabric/cluster/host management side that can make this area quite complex. We will discuss these further in next section.

For this side of the topology, we will focus more on the VMM side, which is for a single management server in the topology. It emphasizes having a small to medium environment of hosts to manage or containing an environment that may not be considered business-critical.

This would not stop you from managing an environment that would have business-critical virtual servers. This topology will always be key in the initial deployment of VMM where you can start to scale larger beneficial to have more than one management server, which will also be covered in more detail in the *Disaster recovery* section.

Virtual environment management planning

The planning for your virtual environment management can be rather complex due to the vast number of options for your entire virtual infrastructure.

The areas to look into for further planning are given.

Hardware requirements

Table 11.1 contains all the hardware requirements for the main roles within the VMM:

> Note: For the full requirements for VMM 2022 you can find them here: https://learn.microsoft.com/en-us/system-center/vmm/system-requirements?view=sc-vmm-2022

VMM role	CPU (Cores)	CPU (GHz)	Memory (GB)	Disk space (GB)
Management server	16	2.8	16	10
Library server	4	2.8	4	*Based on size amount/stored files
VMM console	2	2.00	4	10

Table 11.1: System Center Virtual Machine Manager hardware requirements table

The disk space, in this case, is dependent on all the files stored within your library server, so you will need to ensure you have a sufficient amount of GB to be able to accommodate current and scalable file storage.

As there are other infrastructure fabric servers to consider, we will also include the hardware requirements for those specified in the next table under *table 11.2* which covers the requirements for VMware ESXi hosts that can be managed:

VMM VMware infrastructure role	Version supported	Update Rollup required
ESX	6.5/6.7/7.0/8.0	7.0 upwards requires UR1
vCenter	6.5/6.7/7.0/8.0	7.0 upwards requires UR1

Table 11.2: Virtual Machine Manager VMware support requirements

Operating System requirements

The **Operating System (OS)** requirements for the main VMM server roles are as follows:

VMM role	Windows Server version	Windows Server edition	Windows Server GUI	Windows Server core
Management server	2022	Standard/Datacenter	Yes	Yes
Library server	2022	Standard/Datacenter	Yes	Yes
VMM console	2022	Standard/Datacenter	Yes	No

Table 11.3: VMM Operating System requirements

In addition, there is another table that gives the requirements of the OSs that can be managed within the fabric:

VMM role	Hyper-V	Scale Out File Server (SOFS)	Update server	PXE server
Windows Server 2016 Core (Standard/Enterprise)	Yes	Yes	No	No
Windows Server 2016 GUI (Standard/Enterprise)	Yes	Yes	Yes	Yes
Windows Server 2019 Core (Standard/Enterprise)	Yes	Yes	No	No
Windows Server 2019 GUI(Standard/Enterprise)	Yes	Yes	Yes	Yes
Windows Server 2022 (Standard/Enterprise)	Yes	Yes	Yes	Yes

Table 11.4: Virtual Machine Manager Operating System fabric requirements

Structured Query Language requirements

The **Structured Query Language (SQL)** requirements for VMM 2022 are:

SQL version	SQL cumulative update (Minimum)
*SQL Server 2022 – Standard/Enterprise	Latest
SQL Server 2019 – Standard/Enterprise	Latest
SQL Server 2017 – Standard/Enterprise	Latest
SQL Server 2016 – Standard/Enterprise	Latest

Table 11.5: System Center Virtual Machine Manager 2022 SQL server requirements

* SQL Server 2022 is supported once VMM 2022 has Update Rollup 1 applied.

Virtual Machine Manager limitations

The following table shows a list of all the maximum limitations in VMM to indicate how many can be created/added to the fabric:

Object type	Maximum
Physical hosts	1000
Virtual Machines	25000

Object type	Maximum
Services	1000
User roles	1000
Clouds	20
Virtual networks	2000
Logical networks	20
Library resources	1000
Library objects (Templates)	100

Table 11.6: VMM limitations

Hypervisor platform management decisions

Before implementing VMM, the first thing you need to do is understand all the hypervisors you are running in your environment.

If you are primarily using Hyper-V hosts for your virtual environment, then a standardized Microsoft environment will make your design plans much less complex, as these will just need to have the VMM agent installed in order to communicate with the VMM management host.

If you primarily have a VMware-based environment, this can also involve slightly less complexity, assuming that this is your only hypervisor platform. In this case, you would need to add a vCenter server to your VMM fabric to manage ESXi hosts and clusters within your environment.

Where you have a multi-platform hypervisor environment, although it is possible to manage both platforms with VMM, you will find that the topology will indeed need to scale if you are using a single management server. In this scenario, more than one management server would be the ideal minimum requirement to effectively manage both hypervisor environments to ensure you do not end up with a single point of failure.

Infrastructure role planning

In the section *Virtual Machine Manager topology structure*, we have covered all the various roles that can be added to your VMM environment. Now that we have those established, we need to assess each role again and look into the planning of each to understand the relevance and requirements for your environment and see if these are needed.

Library servers

When thinking of library servers, there are a few points or questions one should ask. They are:

- Will one library server be enough?
- Can it be consolidated with the VMM management server or separated?
- Storage space for the library server requirements.
- Host group assignment consideration.

So, regarding the first point, with the amount of library servers, this would be dependent on factors like the network structure you have and how accessible the library server is across the network.

In the case in which you have different geographical locations or split data centers, if your library server is not in a centrally accessible location for all to communicate with, then you need to understand if you would require an additional library server to serve that particular location. With consideration to the various profiles, templates, and software stored, you will want to ensure that bandwidth does not become an issue when needing to deploy these to your fabric. Once you can add more to your fabric in the network section, then you have the option of adding the VM networks to your library server, as seen in *Figure 11.1*:

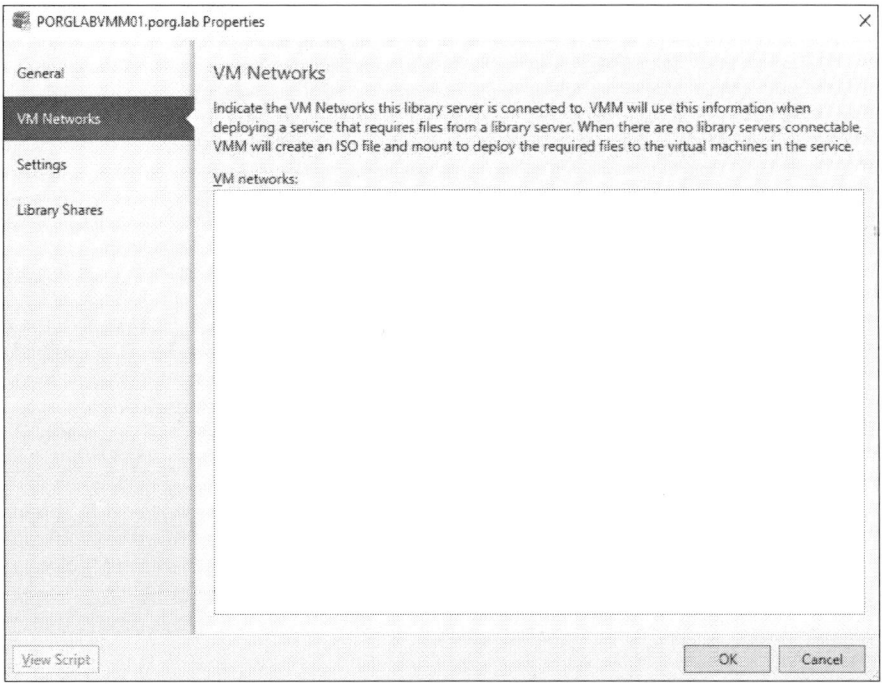

Figure 11.1: Library server VM network options

Now we take the second point on addressing the consolidated setup from the initial installation. This might be fine depending on the scenario you have, where you have a simplified one hypervisor platform (being Hyper-V), all on the same network subnet where this can be feasible, of course, if you want to avoid the single point of failure scenario again, then perhaps, having a dedicated library server will be much better in the long run.

You will need to remember your virtual machine storage and profile/templates and how much you will expect these to grow to ensure that you do not run into space issues along the way.

Then lastly, would be the host group association. By default, the library server is applicable for all hosts managed in VMM, but if you have a case in which your single library server or multiple library servers fit the scenario mentioned in the first point, then you will have a better idea of how these can be allocated as seen in *Figure 11.2*:

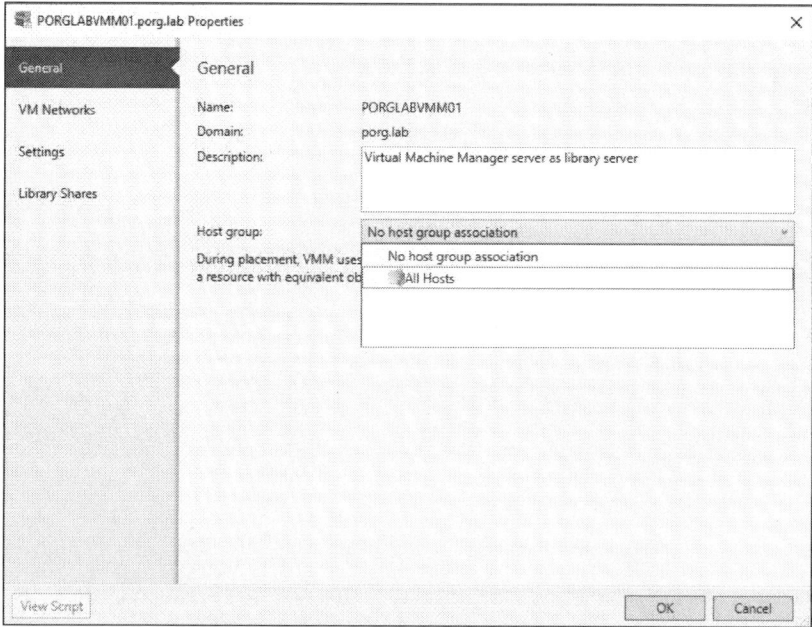

Figure 11.2: Library Server Host Group options

PXE servers

PXE server planning can have similar questions to the library servers; that being said, you will need to understand whether you need to onboard new hosts from bare metal autonomously, which PXE servers are able to do, or if you will be manually provisioning them through other means of PXE server deployment which can derive from products, such as:

- **Configuration Manager**: PXE deployments via the distribution point roles, which can deploy a server OS task sequence
- **Windows Deployment Servers (WDS)**: OS images (`.wim` format) used to deploy the OS image over the network
- **Microsoft deployment toolkit**: An alternative PXE deployment solution to Configuration Manager that utilizes task sequence deployments

Though, there are alternatives that can build bare metal servers, as well as applying the VMM agent to the host to be managed by your management server, the internal PXE infrastructure server is configured to do this natively.

> Note: To reiterate this feature is specifically for Hyper-V hosts fabric and not for ESXi host fabric. For the ESXi hosts, you would either have to use the templates within your VCenter, datastores or even the alternative methods mentioned above.

Update servers

Patching is an essential aspect to ensure that vulnerabilities are managed correctly. Again, the same points for both the PXE server and library servers will apply, but in this case, we need to understand the overall effects when it comes to patching your VMM estate:

- Patching your VMM infrastructure servers, such as management servers, library servers, and other roles, will cause downtime for overseeing the management of your hosts and VMs
- Patching of the clusters or hosts will cause downtime for any virtual machines or critical services hosted within them

The second point is perhaps the most important here. As unexpected or unplanned downtime can cause serious issues for your environment, and keeping into account an environment that uses an ITSM framework, you could raise a lot of incidents where critical **Business As Usual** (**BAU**) services go down in a forceful fashion.

This is where you would need to consider your planning of servicing windows and maintenance windows, that prevent you in causing any unexpected alerts when hosts and virtual machines require any patching.

If you were to use an alternative method for patching, such as **Windows Server Update Services** (**WSUS**) or Configuration Manager via a Software Update Point, you then have the addition of using the maintenance windows for managed devices within Configuration Manager.

> Note: If you are using both VMM and the Configuration Manager, ensure that you do not cause any overlaps by applying two different sets of maintenance windows. This can lead to confusion in patching windows where hosts or VMs either miss patching deployments or even get caught in patching deployments unexpectedly.

Storage planning

Next would then be for setting up the storage within your fabric.

There are various elements to consider here, which is whether you will depend on the storage directly attached to your hosts or will use additional storage servers to scale your storage, such as:

- Windows File servers
- iSCSI connections
- **Storage Area Network (SAN) / Network Attached Storage (NAS)** servers
- Fiber Channel fabric connections

Direct storage on your hosts allow your VMs to be created, utilizing the local storage disks, which the hosts have directly attached if you are using physical servers. Here, you can define if your disks will be as follows:

- **Fixed**: The size you set it as will be exactly this. It can also be referred to as a fat drive.
- **Dynamic**: You set a base size and the disk size will increment on usage which is also known as a thin drive.

Network planning

The next part is then around your networking fabric, which allows your hosts or clusters to create virtual machines that can communicate on the desired network.

Logical networks

These are the network connections that you create to define to which network your VMs will be connected to, where you have multiple different network connection options, as seen in *Figure 11.3*:

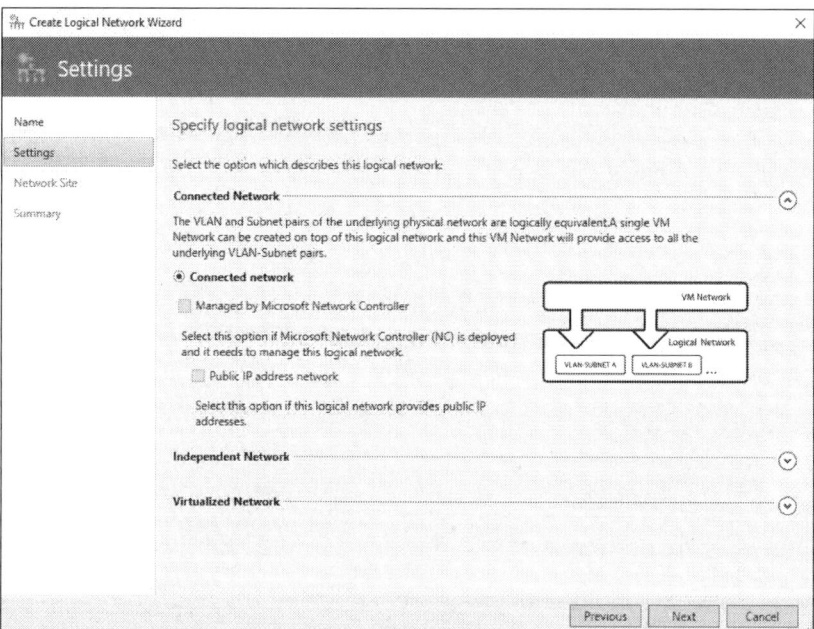

Figure 11.3: Create logical network Wizard

Logical networks can automatically be set up once you have added a host to your VMM fabric, whether that be through onboarding with a VMM agent or if you have onboarded a Hyper-V host by using a bare metal deployment through a PXE server.

Overall, you have the option to have these automatically created or you can define these manually which involves defining a static IP pool that can then be assigned to a specific host or host group, as seen in *Figure 11.4*:

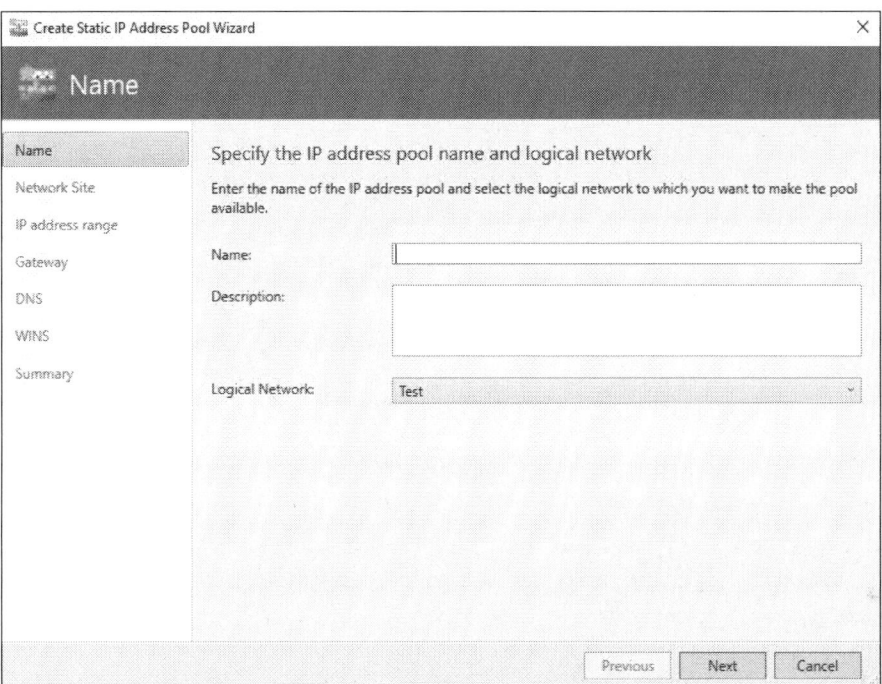

Figure 11.4: Create Static IP Pool wizard

Virtual environment template design

After the previous section, where we investigated the design of our fabric, it is time to start looking at our template portfolio.

These templates and profiles help to build baseline-level virtual machines or hosts which are required to help scale our virtual environment and remove the need to manually define configurations when they are encapsulated within different templates and profiles.

Here, we will explore the common types of templates and profiles and discuss the design thoughts of each one.

Physical host profile design

If you are going with bare metal provisioning of new hosts via a PXE server, then starting with the physical computer profiles would be a good place to start initial designs.

The general configuration of these profiles contains the following categories:
- OS image version
- Hardware configuration
- OS configuration
- Host settings

Now, when it comes to the planning of these profiles there are some areas to take into consideration.

Operating System of host server

For example, let us take the host OS that will be used, depending on the mixture of OS flavors you have in your environment. If you have multiple OS out there, then you need to base your physical computer profile needs to bear this in mind.

If your licensing can accommodate this, you can use the latest Windows OS- Windows Server 2022, which can manage your virtual machines on the same OS level or lower.

Remember that within your VMM fabric, the lowest version of a Hyper-V host will be a minimum of **Windows Server 2016,** as shown in the *Table 11.3* detailing the Hyper-V host OS requirements.

Hardware configuration

The configuration here evolves around the network adapters that it will utilize and if these will connect to a logical switch that you have within your fabric.

In addition, it will include the storage for how the disks will be formatted and if using a local drive or from your storage fabric.

These configurations add an additional layer of planning where different network and storage requirements for Hyper-V servers may be vastly different. Hence, if you have very specific configurations then you may need to consider splitting the number of profiles you have, to be able to accommodate both or multiple scenarios.

Operating System configuration

Here is where the defining of the base OS configuration, such as:
- Domain to join
- Local administrator password

- Time zone
- Product Key
- Pre and post-deployment scripts

To break down each preceding point mentioned for domain details, if you are planning to have hosts that are split into multiple domains or forests, then you again need to work on the scaling of each profile to accommodate each type of host you are looking to provision. This bullet point is perhaps the most dividing factor when it comes to how many physical computer profiles you will decide to have.

Another point to pick out design considerations would be the pre and post deployment scripts. The first type is an answer file which is used to help pre-configure the OS settings.

> Note: Answer files are in an *.XML format and normally have a name such as Unattend.xml. The best way to create one is to use a tool such as Windows System Image Manager (WSIM) to develop an answer file. For more information on this area, you can view it here: https://learn.microsoft.com/en-us/windows-hardware/manufacture/desktop/update-windows-settings-and-scripts-create-your-own-answer-file-sxs?view=windows-11

For post-deployment scripts, they are run once the OS has been installed, configured and available during the phase in which either a user can log in or has completed the initial installation.

The part where you need to consider design configuration planning evolves around a *company standard* set of pre-configurations which all servers within your environment have to be at. These are:

- Applications
- OS configurations
- Security settings
- GPO policies

This is where you can define within your profile, how these hosts will be built once they are going through the process of being onboarded.

Virtual machine profile design

Virtual machine profiles have different types to consider for your template planning, which contain profiles, such as:

- Application profiles
- Azure profiles
- Capability profiles
- Guest OS profiles

- Hardware profiles
- SQL Server profiles

These profiles enrich the template portfolio you will have in VMM to scale with your virtual environment fabric.

Starting with the Guest OS profiles It is similar to the OS configurations category in the physical computer profile section, depending on the flavor of OS in your environment, is going to determine how many of these profiles in which you will need.

If you have a standardized environment where all the OS levels are the same, then this can be a simplified design decision that applies well to the hardware profiles defining the virtual machine hardware configuration. Different guest OS will have different minimum and recommended requirements, as well as, predefined organization roles, which the hardware profile will also have to accommodate.

In *Figure 11.5*, we get an idea of how the hardware profile wizard looks, which is reminiscent of building a virtual machine within Hyper-V or other hypervisor platforms:

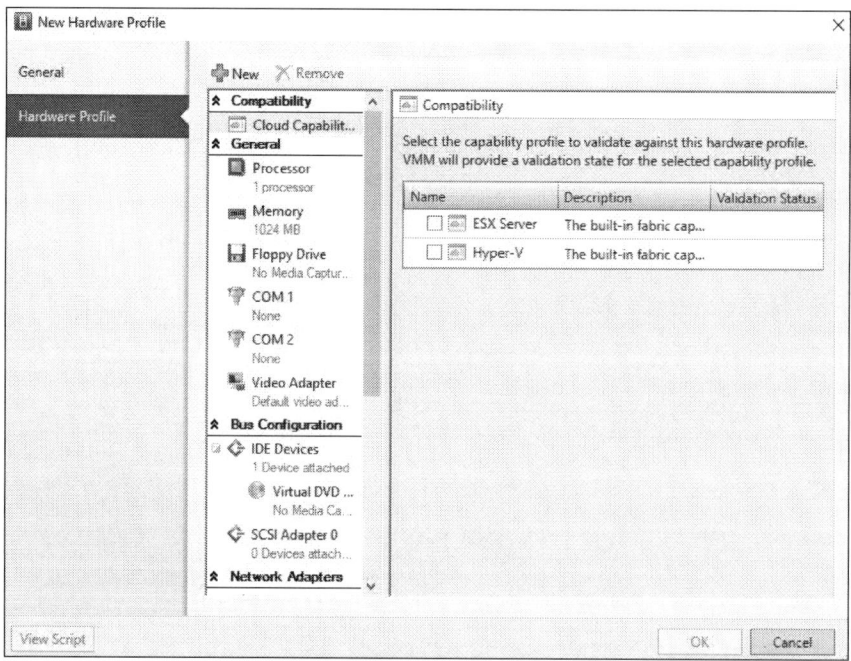

Figure 11.5: *VMM hardware profile*

Capability profiles, on the other hand, are a slightly different function. By default, there are two pre-defined profiles that relate to both hypervisor fabrics, Hyper-V and VMware (ESX server). They allow for a baseline that the virtual machines have to meet before they can be created on a host representing the respective fabric. You can add additional ones if you want to make tougher conditions to the capability. This could work well if you have any hosts that are more security restrictive or lower on resources than other hosts within your fabric.

More specialized profiles, such as SQL Server profiles or application profiles, to help enrich deployments for virtual machines, which require a specific optimized role. SQL Server profiles help to deploy and configure a SQL instance for a virtual machine, so that they are a ready built SQL Server which can start to manage databases.

Application profiles allow applications or script packages to be deployed to virtual machines which can be used for SQL Server-based applications or web-based applications. Script packages work well if you are looking to extend the function of a similar role that the Guest OS profiles play when it comes to utilizing additional tools, such as an answer file or post-deployment scripts.

Templates design

After all the profiles we have discussed, we are lead to the final stage where we can consolidate everything to have a full-fledged VM template.

Rather than discussing the design points of each, it will be better to give an overview of each one, as all design decision points in the previous sections will apply here as well.

VM templates are ultimately used to build out the virtual machine onto a host or cluster. After all the virtual machine profiles which we discussed, these can be used inside of the VM template to form a parent object to consolidate a full working VM solution.

Service templates, on the other hand, are more over-arching where they can utilize VM templates, profiles, and defined objects within your fabric to develop one tier, two tier or multi-tier application models.

Say, for example, we wanted to build out a Configuration Manager environment- a simple one with just a primary server, distribution point and management point. We could have something to the tune of the following:

- 1 VM template to build the primary server
- 1 VM template to build the management point
- 1 VM template to build the distribution point
- 1 VM template with a SQL Server profile for your SQL Server

Figure 11.6 shows this design to provide an idea of how this can be designed and how you foresee a solution being fully deployed:

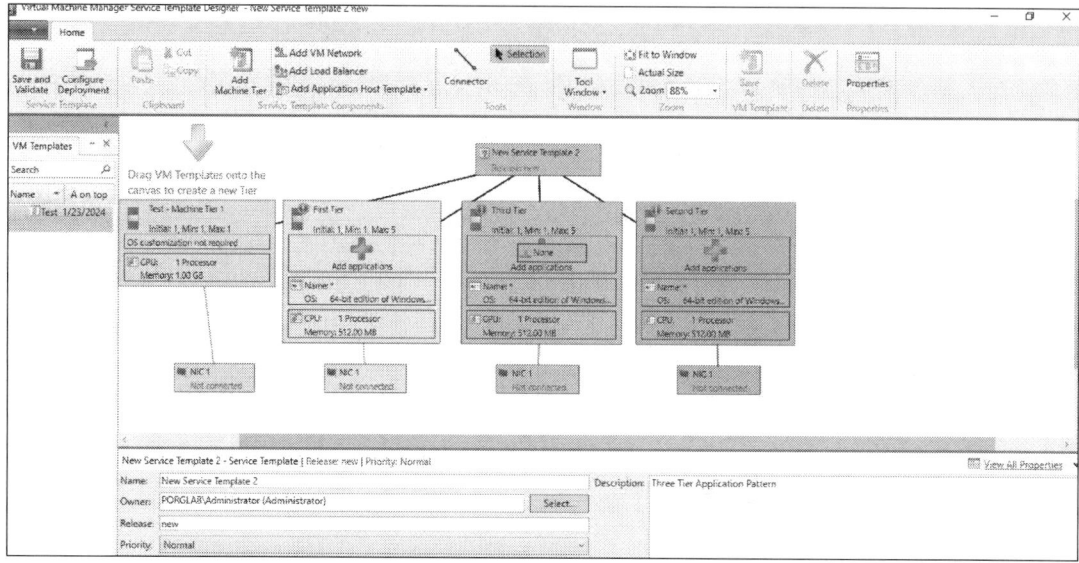

Figure 11.6: Virtual Machine Manager service template

Disaster recovery

VMM has different options for implementing configurations that help disaster recovery. We have broken this down per the infrastructure role type to provide more detail:

- **Management server**: Multiple management servers help in balancing the number of hosts, and clusters are managed within your fabric to help with single point of failure scenarios.

    High availability options for VMM management servers to be clustered also provide better options for disaster recovery.

- **Library server**: Though library servers have the benefit of multiples, you also need to take into consideration the backup of the content which resides on the library servers.

    The objects stored within VMM are essentially file shares, so high availability is even more important to ensure your library objects are backed up.

    Shared storage or **Distributed File System (DFS)** functionality to ensure the uptime of your files can definitely help towards any disaster recovery scenarios.

- **Virtual machines**: With multiple hosts in clusters, you can allow for virtual machines to be highly available so that if anything happens with the host which the virtual machine resides on then you can allow for the virtual machine to be migrated to another host.

Virtual Machine Manager lab requirements

Now, we are ready to look at the designs for our virtual lab, which can be used as a test lab, **Proof Of Concept (POC)**, or possibly a pre-production environment.

Single management server

All initial installations may have this topology to start off with, and it is great if you have a base lab in order to learn the technology much better. This can be a consolidated setup that all works on one server, or this can be looked at as a specification for each server that has to fit the recommended requirement:

VMM Role	CPU (Cores)	CPU (GHz)	Memory (GB)	Disk space (GB)
Management server	16	2.8	16	10
Library server	4	2.8	4	*Based on size amount/stored files
VMM console	2	2.00	4	10

Table 11.7: Single management server hardware requirements table

Next table shows the OS requirements:

VMM Role	Windows Server version	Windows Server edition	Windows Server GUI	Windows Server core
Management server	2022	Standard/Datacenter	Yes	Yes
Library server	2022	Standard/Datacenter	Yes	Yes
VMM console	2022	Standard/Datacenter	Yes	No

Table 11.8: Single management server lab

High availability or mixed hypervisor environment configuration

A high-availability configuration would consist of at least two VMM management servers, and where you might have a mixture of vCenter and Hyper-V hosts to manage, you will want to ensure you have availability for the management of both environments.

The first table outlines the hardware requirements for the high availability/mixed hypervisor topology:

VMM role	CPU (Cores)	CPU (GHz)	Memory (GB)	Disk space (GB)
Management server	16	2.8	16	10
Library server	4	2.8	4	*Based on size amount/stored files
VMM console	2	2.00	4	10

Table 11.9: VMM hardware requirements table for high availability/mixed hupervisor

The next table shows the OS requirements for this topology:

VMM role	Windows Server version	Windows Server edition	Windows Server GUI	Windows Server core
Management server	2022	Standard/Datacenter	Yes	Yes
Library server	2022	Standard/Datacenter	Yes	Yes
VMM console	2022	Standard/Datacenter	Yes	No

Table 11.10: VMM OS requirements for high availability/Mixed Hypervisor topology

The following table shows the details of the high availability lab:

VMM VMware infrastructure role	Version supported	Update Rollup required
ESX	6.5/6.7/7.0/8.0	7.0 upwards requires UR1
vCenter	6.5/6.7/7.0/8.0	7.0 upwards requires UR1

Table 11.11: High availability lab

Conclusion

VMM once is another powerful product within the System Center family stack. Though its roles are not as many as the other products, the native roles which you can assign can really shape how much control you can have in the management and scalability of your environment.

Templates and profiles can be developed for a multitude of uses, which can then be consolidated into other parent templates to help aid with decision-making on the designs of your hosting and virtual machine placement.

You also have ability to enrich your environment with VMM by being expanding the fabric resources.

With this conclusion, we can now proceed into the next chapter which will go through how we will install and configure VMM according to the requirements outlined in this chapter that provides the understanding of how to plan and design the VMM product.

Points to remember

- VMM consists of two base roles- the management server and the library server.
- Library servers are responsible for the storage of templates, profiles, and virtual machine VHD/VHDX templates.
- Profiles are used as logical containers that have settings which can be used as templates for both physical hosts and virtual machines.
- The fabric allows you to add additional storage servers and networking for additional virtual networks, logical switches, and load balancers.
- Native roles after installation range from PXE servers, to update servers.
- VMM allows the management of Hyper-V and VMware hypervisor virtual environments.

Multiple choice questions

1. **Which role is used to allow for Hyper-V hosts to be built from bare metal?**

    a. Management server

    b. Update server

    c. Library server

    d. PXE server

2. **Which role is used to provide updates across the Hyper-V hosts and infrastructure servers within VMM?**

    a. Management server

    b. Update server

    c. Library server

    d. PXE server

3. **Which role is used to store templates and profiles to be used for building virtual machines?**

    a. Management server

    b. Update server

    c. Library server

    d. PXE server

4. What is the name of the template used to help create SQL Server virtual machines?

    a. SQL Server profile

    b. Application profile

    c. Capability profile

    d. Hardware profile

5. How can the VMM help to manage virtual environments within the VMware stack?

    a. Bare metal deployment.

    b. Installing agent onto ESXi host.

    c. Adding a V-center server.

    d. Additional library server.

6. Library servers use file shares to allow for virtual machine object storage.

    a. True

    b. False

Answers

1. d
2. b
3. c
4. a
5. c
6. a

Key terms

- **VMM**: Virtual Machine Manager
- **Profile**: Logical container for settings
- **Template**: Logical container for setting and profiles.
- **VHD**: Virtual Hard Disk
- **WSIM**: Windows System Image Manager
- **PXE**: Pre-boot Execution Environment

Chapter 12
Deployment and Administration of System Center VMM

Introduction

This chapter will concentrate on the development and deployment of **System Center Virtual Machine Manager** (**SCVMM**). The importance of this chapter is to illustrate the setup of Virtual Machine Manager and its overall deployment so we can ensure the design plan specified in the previous section allows us to have a healthy setup. There will also be some troubleshooting points to help the reader understand the common and uncommon issues which arise during the development and deployment process.

This chapter will also provide an in-depth look into the overall administration of SCVMM as well as outlining its best practices. The administration side allows an engineer to perform their **Business As Usual** (**BAU**) tasks, but within the administrative side, another area that would enrich the BAU tasks and overall **user interface** (**UI**) is where the best practices come in. Best practices are normally looked at as a professional and recommended level of what you should and should not do. We can also understand that a real-world scenario can conflict with this, so we will look to outline the differences between both.

Structure

This chapter will cover the following topics:
- Virtual Machine Manager single management server deployment
- Virtual Machine Manager multi-management server deployment
- Administration of Virtual Machine Manager
- Best practices
- Real-world scenarios

Objectives

The objective for the reader is to understand how this product looks after the centralization of your virtual environment and how the product can vastly help with the true scalability of your virtual environment with different areas allowing you to go up towards full automation of adding to your virtual infrastructure.

Recommended specifications of the product will also allow the user to understand all the design decisions to be made and assess how a sandpit lab can be developed to further understand how **Virtual Machine Manager** (**VMM**) works and the roles it uses.

Virtual Machine Manager single management server deployment

The first deployment will focus on the single management sever deployment which will work as a base and initial deployment before we are able to scale up further to the deployment topology within the next topic.

First, we will analyze the prerequisites needed before we can start the installation process.

Management server

The management server contains various prerequisites for the role to be successfully installed. Some requirements needed to be installed are as follows.

Windows Assessment Deployment Kit

This is the primary prerequisite you will need to install for the management server role.

At the time of writing this book, the latest version of the Windows **Assessment Deployment Kit** (**ADK**) would be applicable for the Windows Server 2022 10.1.25398.1 (September 2023) and the download location can be found here **https://learn.microsoft.com/en-us/windows-hardware/get-started/adk-install** which will contain all the information needed to help locate the applicable and latest version you need to install the Virtual Machine Manager 2022.

You will need to install both the ADK and the ADK WinPE Add-on to fulfill the requirements of the prerequisites.

To install the ADK, please perform the following steps:

1. Double-click the **adksetup** file.
2. **Specify Location:** Select **Install the Windows ADK to this computer,** then click Next.
3. **Windows Kits Privacy**: Read through and then select if you want to **Allow Microsoft to collect insights for the Windows Kits,** then click **Next**.
4. **License Agreement**: Read through the license agreement, then click **Accept**.
5. **Select the features you want to install**: Click **Install**.

> Note: The Windows ADK installs the Windows System Image Management tool (WSIM for both AMD64 and ARM64, which points to C:\Program Files (x86)\Windows Kits\10\Assessment and Deployment Kit\Deployment Tools\WSIM. When doing the VMM installation, you may experience an error on installation as it tries to find the files in the amd64 folder, as a work around, you may need to copy the files inside the AMD64 folder into the WSIM folder for the installation to complete.

Next, we will install the ADK WinPE add-on:

1. Double-click the **adkwinpesetup** file.
2. **Specify Location:** Select **Install the Windows ADK Windows Preinstallation Environment Add-ons to this computer,** then click **Next**.
3. **Windows Kits Privacy:** Read through and then select if you want to **Allow Microsoft to collect insights for the Windows Kits,** then click **Next**.
4. **License Agreement**: Read through the license agreement then click **Accept**.
5. **Select the features you want to install**: Click **Install**.

Structured Query Language Server Command Line Utilities

You will need to obtain the **Structured Query Language (SQL)** Server Command Line utilities for the SQL version you are looking to use, which can be found here **https://learn.microsoft.com/en-us/sql/tools/sqlcmd/sqlcmd-utility?view=sql-server-ver16&tabs=go%2Cwindows&pivots=cs1-bash**

Virtual Machine Manager console

There are no prerequisites required for you to install the VMM console.

Virtual Machine Manager service accounts

VMM does not have an extensive use of service accounts but one main service account to be used.

> Note: For high availability, which will be covered in the section *Virtual Machine Manager multi Manager server deployment*, will require you to use a domain account for the service account.

Table 12.1 shows the service account requirements for VMM:

Name	Description	Local or domain
VMM service account	Used to enable the management capabilities of VMM	Both

Table 12.1: VMM service accounts

Firewall requirements

VMM does have an extensive list of ports that need to be allowed to use the product effectively, but we will use a summarized breakdown within the following table to outline the key ports to be used to provide the reader with enough information to proceed.

The full firewall requirement list can be found here **https://learn.microsoft.com/en-us/system-center/vmm/plan-ports-protocols?view=sc-vmm-2022**

The following table shows the firewall requirements:

Firewall direction	Ports used	Protocol type	Transmissions Control Protocol (TCP) or User Datagram Protocol (UDP)
Management Server to VMM agent	80	HTTP WinRM 135 - RPC 139 - RPC 445 - SMB	Mixed	TCP
Management server to VMM guest agent	1433	SQL port	TCP

Firewall direction	Ports used	Protocol type	Transmissions Control Protocol (TCP) or User Datagram Protocol (UDP)
Management server to SQL Server	81	HTTP (Alternate port)*	TCP
Management server to Hypervisor Hosts (Hyper-V/vCenter)	82	HTTP (Alternate port)*	TCP
Library server to Hyper-V Hosts			

Table 12.2: VMM firewall requirements

Virtual Machine Manager installation

With the prerequisites having been addressed, we can now proceed with the initial installation of the VMM product, which will consist of the following:

- Management server
- VMM console

To start the installation, perform the following steps:

1. Open the installation media, then double-click the **setup.exe**.
2. On the installation splash screen, click the **Install** option.
3. **Getting Started: Select features to install.** Select the **VMM management server** which in turn will select the **VMM console** option automatically, then click **Next**.
4. **Getting Started: Product registration information.** Enter the name, organization and product key for the product, then click **Next**.
5. **Getting Started: Please read this license agreement** | Read through the license agreement, then tick **I have read, understood, and agree with the terms of the license agreement,** then click **Next**.
6. **Getting Started: Diagnostic and Usage Data** | Click **Next**.
7. **Getting Started: Microsoft Update** | Select if you want Microsoft Update to check for updates for VMM, then click **Next**.
8. **Getting Started: Installation Location** | Select the location where VMM will be installed, then click **Next**.
9. **Prerequisites: Please review these prerequisite warnings.** Check the prerequisites flagged and ensure they are all addressed. Once done, click the **check prerequisites again** button until they are all clear, then click **Next**.

10. **Configuration: Database Configuration** | Enter the name of the SQL Server you wish to use to install the VMM database. Once entered, it will check to see if the connection is valid and will show the new database name. Once happy, click **Next**.
11. **Configuration: Configure service account and distributed key management** | Enter the account details that will be used to run the service account, or alternatively, you can use a group-managed service account. Then, select if you want to store encryption keys in Active Directory or the local machine, then click **Next**.

> **Note:** Group managed service accounts are accounts that can be used with automatic password management for better security for the Windows accounts. More information on this area can be found here https://learn.microsoft.com/en-us/windows-server/security/group-managed-service-accounts/group-managed-service-accounts-overview

12. **Configuration: Port configuration** | Check the default ports and check they are all **OK**, then click **Next**.
13. **Configuration: Library Configuration** | Decide the name of the library server share, then click **Next**.
14. **Configuration: Installation Summary** | Review the installation configuration, then click **Install** to begin.

To validate further on successful installation, you can open the VMM console which will show the server name being the local host, as seen in *Figure 12.1*:

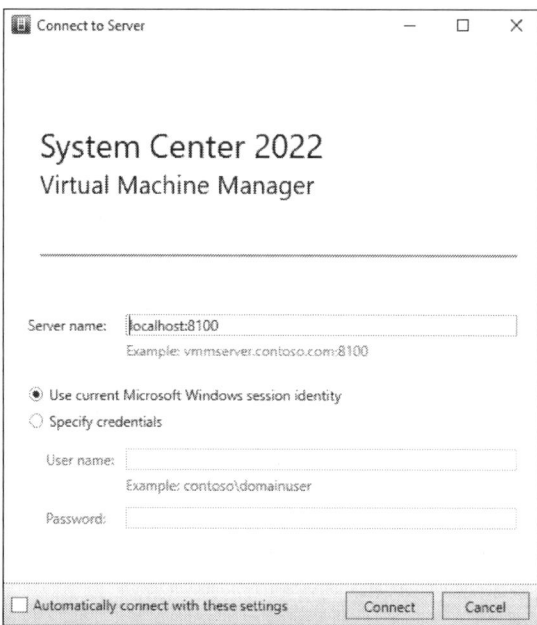

Figure 12.1: VMM console

Virtual Machine Manager multi-manager server deployment

When wanting to provide scalability, you will want to consider adding to your VMM infrastructure, specifically more management servers which help to provide a logical load balance.

Adding additional management servers

After you have placed your first management server into your fabric, you may want to scale your environment by adding additional management servers.

To do so, perform the following:

1. Open the installation media, then double-click the `setup.exe`.
2. On the installation splash screen, click the **Install** option.
3. **Getting Started: Select features to install** | Select the **VMM Management Server** which will select the **VMM console** option automatically, then click **Next**.
4. **Getting Started: Product registration information** | Enter the name, organization and product key for the product, then click **Next**.
5. **Getting Started: Please read this license agreement** | Read through the license agreement, then tick **I have read, understood, and agree with the terms of the license agreement**, then click **Next**.
6. **Getting Started: Diagnostic and Usage Data** | Click **Next**.
7. **Getting Started: Microsoft Update** | Select if you want Microsoft Update to check for updates for VMM, then click **Next**.
8. **Getting Started: Installation Location** | Select the location where VMM will be installed, then click **Next**.
9. **Prerequisites: Please review these prerequisite warnings** | Check the prerequisites flagged and ensure they are all addressed. Once done, click the **check prerequisites again** button until they are all clear, then click **Next**.
10. **Configuration: Database Configuration** | Enter the name of the SQL Server you wish to use to install the VMM database. Once entered it will check to see if the connection is valid and will show the new database name. It should detect this time that there is an existing database named **VirtualManagerDB**. Ensure that this is selected and click **Next**.
11. **Configuration: Configure service account and distributed key management** | Enter the account details used to run the service account, or alternatively, you can use a group managed service account. Then, select if you want to store encryption keys in Active Directory or the local machine, then click **Next**.

12. **Configuration: Port configuration** | Check the default ports and check they are all **OK**, then click **Next**.
13. **Configuration: Library Configuration** | Decide the name of the library server share. Then, click **Next**.
14. **Configuration**: **Installation Summary** | Review the installation configuration, then click **Install** to begin.

Administration of the Virtual Machine Manager

Now that we have the VMM installed, before we start getting to onboarding any hypervisor hosts to manage, we first want to go through the process of adding to our fabric, so that we are ready to start adding the hosts.

> **Note:** Any of the sections done here for administration regarding VMM will have a jobs window that will show the progress of any actions done. Typically, they can progress in stages of 33% increments until 100% completion as shown in the following figure:

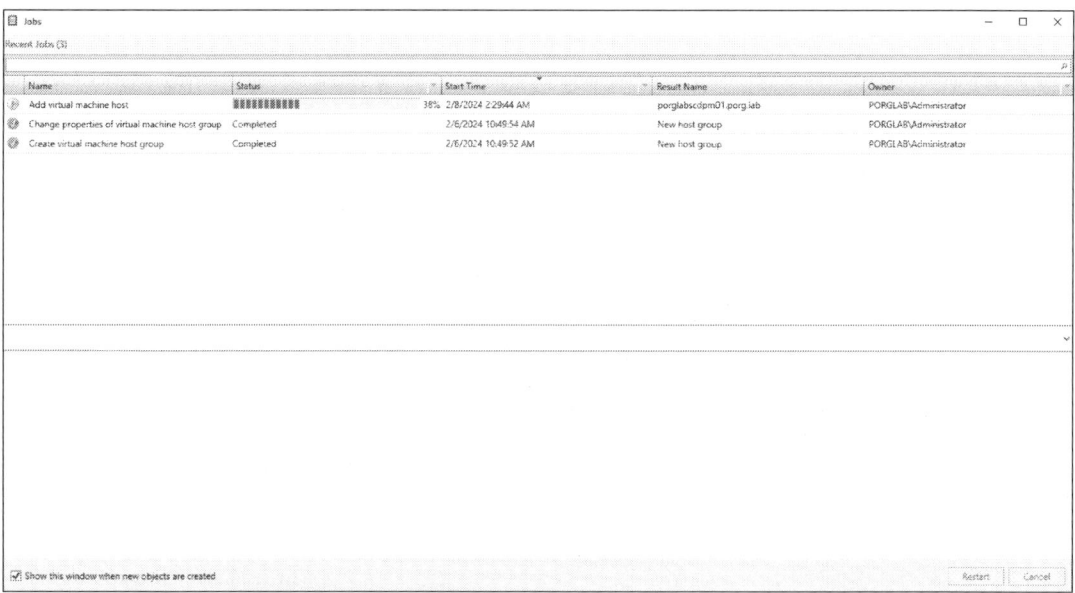

Figure 12.2: VMM jobs window

Adding infrastructure servers

We will go through each infrastructure server that can be added.

> Note: Each infrastructure server will have a button where you can view the PowerShell script used to add the object into the fabric.

Library server

Upon the first initial installation of the VMM management server, we would have set up the library server at this point, but if you need to add an additional library server, then you can perform the following:

1. Open the SCVMM 2022 console.
2. Go to the **Fabric** tab.
3. Go to **Servers | Infrastructure | Library Servers**.
4. Right-click and select **Add Library Server**.
5. **Enter Credentials:** Select the **Enter a username and password** if you need to enter credentials to set up the server role correctly.
6. **Select Library Servers:** Enter the domain and computer name which you are looking to add as a library server, then click the search button to find the designated server. Once selected, click **Next** as seen in *Figure 12.3*:

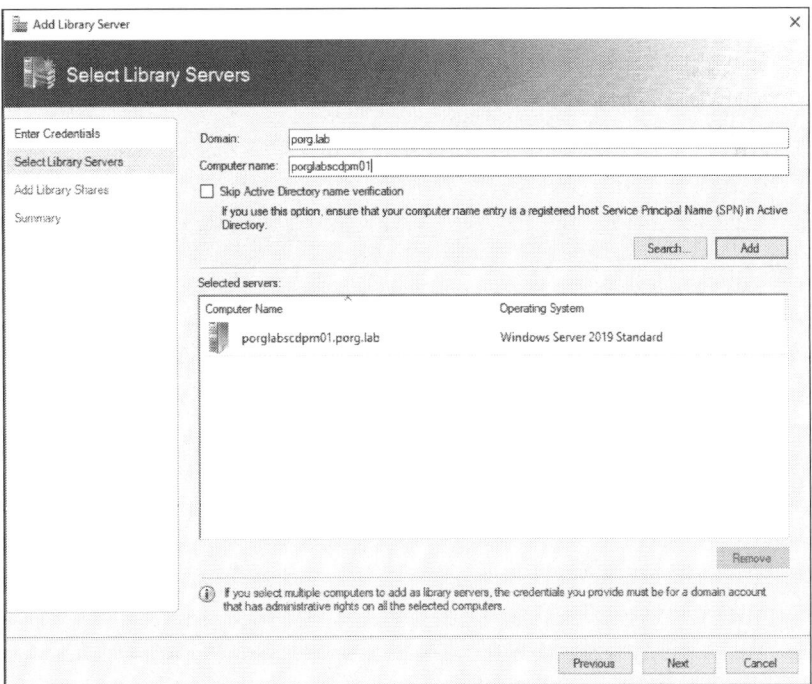

Figure 12.3: *Selecting the library servers window*

7. **Add Library Shares**: Add the shared folders available on the server, then click **Next**.

8. **Summary**: Review the configuration of your library server, then click **Add Library Servers**.

Pre-boot Execution Environment server

To add **Pre-boot Execution Environment (PXE)** servers to your environment, perform the following:

1. Open the SCVMM 2022 console.
2. Go to the **Fabric** tab.
3. Go to **Servers** | **Infrastructure** | **PXE Servers**.
4. Right-click and select **Add PXE Server**.
5. **Add PXE server:** Enter the computer name and the Run As account which will be used to prepare and add the PXE server. When ready, click **Add**.

Update server

To add an update server to your environment, perform the following:

1. Open the SCVMM 2022 console.
2. Go to the **Fabric** tab.
3. Go to **Servers** | **Infrastructure** | **Update Server**.
4. Right-click and select **Add Update Server**.
5. **Add Windows Server Update Services Server:** Enter the computer name and the port used to communicate with the update server and select the Run As account which will be responsible for the adding of the update server. Then, click **Add**.

Adding Storage

When adding hosts, the storage and data locations will already be available when you are creating virtual machines.

If you want to extend storage capabilities by utilizing file servers and fibre channel storage, then perform the following steps:

1. Open the SCVMM 2022 console.
2. Go to the **Fabric** tab.
3. Go to Storage, then right-click and select **Add Storage Devices.**
4. **Select provider type: Select a storage provider type** | Select the appropriate option for the file server you require, then click **Next**.
5. **Specify discovery scope:** Specify the IP address or **Fully Qualified Domain Name (FQDN)** of the Windows-based file server | Enter the IP address of FQDN of your

file server and select a Run As account which will be used to add the file server, then click **Next**.

6. **Gather information: Discover and import storage device** information | Wait for the discovery to complete, then click **Next**.

7. **Select storage devices:** Select the storage devices found on your file server, then click **Next**.

8. **Summary: Confirm the settings** | Review your configuration, then click **Finish**.

Adding networking

When adding hosts, you will find that the network adapters and logical networks will appear in the list of networks you can select from which can be seen in the Logical Networks list within the **Fabric** tab.

Logical Networks

If you are required to add additional networks or even switches, then perform the following:

1. Open the SCVMM 2022 console.
2. Go to the **Fabric** tab.
3. **Go to Networking**: Logical Networks and right-click, then select **Create Logical Network**.
4. **Name:** Enter the name and description of your logical network, then click **Next**.
5. **Settings:** Select the type of network you wish to configure, then click **Next**.
6. **Network sites:** Here, you can more logical objects for your logical network which can be based on a specific network site or a specific IP range. Add the necessary objects, then click **Next**.
7. **Confirm the settings:** Review your configuration, then click **Finish**.

Logical Switches

To add logical switches, perform the following:

1. Open the SCVMM 2022 console.
2. Go to the **Fabric** tab.
3. Go to **Networking** and right-click it, then select **Create Logical Switch.**
4. **General: Enter name and description for the logical switch** | Enter a name and description for your switch, then select the uplink mode required, then click **Next**.
5. **Settings: Specify logical switch settings** | Configure the bandwidth mode, then click **Next**.

6. **Extensions**: **Choose the extensions you want to use with this logical switch** | Select the virtual switch extensions you want to use, then click **Next**.
7. **Virtual port: Specify the port classifications for virtual ports part of this logical switch.** Here, you will add any port classifications you have in VMM. If you have not created any custom ones, then you can select a default one. However, this can be changed after creation when in the console to create a port classification profile.
8. **Uplinks:** Create an uplink profile for your switch, then click **Next**.
9. **Summary: Confirm the settings** | Review your configuration, then click **Finish**.

Adding hosts

Now, that we have some servers ready, we can look into the adding of the hypervisor hosts so that we can manage the virtual machines as well as their parent hosts or clusters within the fabric.

Host groups

Just before we start to look at the adding of hosts, we should first understand the host groups section. Typically, if you add a hypervisor host directly to the "All Hosts" folder, this will then place it in the default parent container.

The idea for these logical containers is to simply allow for a better way of managing the hosts. These can be split up by form of the following:

- Domain
- Geographical location

Just as examples, depending on the scale you grow to you may want to start looking at this early. You can, of course, do this later which we will go through further in this chapter.

To create a new host group, perform the following:

1. Open the SCVMM 2022 console.
2. Go to VMs and **Services** tab.
3. Right-click the `All Hosts` folder and select **Create Host Group**.

Though this procedure is a very simple one, the configuration going forward will matter much more.

Hyper-V hosts: Domain network

This option is to add a Hyper-V host or cluster which is on a trusted domain network. The process involves the installation of the VMM agent which will communicate to the assigned management server which it will refer to.

To add a Hyper-V host or cluster, please perform the following:
1. Open the SCVMM 2022 console.
2. Go to VMs **Virtual Machines (VMs)** and **Services** tab.
3. Right-click either the All Hosts group or your preferred host group container and select **Add Hyper-V Hosts and Clusters**.
4. **Resource Location: Indicate the Windows computers location** | Select the **Windows Server Computers in a trusted Active Directory domain** option, then click **Next**.
5. **Credentials: Specify the credentials to use for discovery** | Select an existing Run As account or manually enter a Run As account to be used for executing the host addition.
6. **Discovery Scope: Specify the search scope for virtual machine host candidates** | Enter the names of the Hyper-V servers you want to add or you can create an AD query to discover them. Once the AD verification has been completed, click **Next**.
7. **Target Resources: Select the computers that you want to add as hosts** | Select the hosts which are in the active directory domain then click **Next** as seen in *Figure 12.4*:

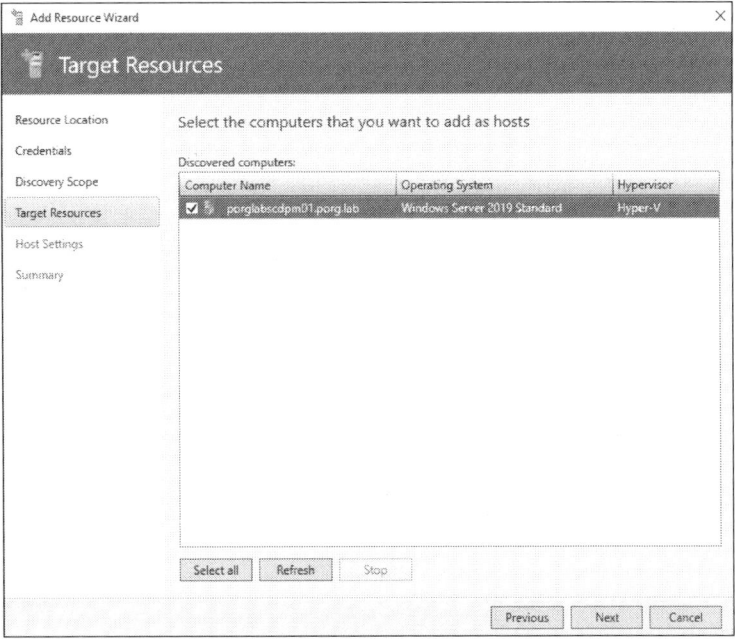

Figure 12.4: Target resources window

8. **Host Settings: Specify a host group and virtual machine placement path settings for hosts:** Select the host which the Hyper-V server or cluster will be added to. If you have completed the steps before to have additional host groups, this will be the best time to add them in.

9. Click **Next**.
10. **Summary: Confirm the settings** | Review the configuration you have specified for your host, then click **Add** to start the host being added.

Untrusted domain Hyper-V Hosts

There is not much difference in this process other than the import of a certificate with the VMM agent install to initiate a more secure communication between the managed host and the VMM server.

To do this, perform the following:

1. Open the SCVMM 2022 console.
2. Go to VMs and **Services** tab.
3. Right-click either the All Hosts group or your preferred host group container and select **Add Hyper-V Hosts and Clusters**.
4. **Resource Location: Indicate the Windows computers location** | Select the **Windows Server Computers in an untrusted Active Directory domain** option, then click **Next**.
5. **Credentials: Specify the credentials to use for discovery** | Select an existing Run As account to be used for executing the host addition, then click **Next**.
6. **Target Resources: Specify the Windows Hyper-V candidate computers** | Select the hosts which are in the Active Directory domain, then click **Next**.
7. **Host Settings: Specify a host group and virtual machine placement path settings for hosts:** Select the host which the Hyper-V server or cluster will be added to the host group. If you have completed the steps before to have additional host groups this will be the best time to add them in.
8. Click **Next**.
9. **Summary: Confirm the settings** | Review the configuration you have specified for your host, then click **Add** to start the host being added.

Perimeter network Hyper-V Hosts

For the perimeter network, though the process is somewhat the same, what is different in this specific exercise is that you will need to ensure that the VMM agent is installed on the server beforehand before adding the server within the add host wizard, and this is specific to the perimeter network scenario.

So first, we install the VMM agent by performing the following:

1. Open the VMM 2022 installation media.
2. Select the `setup.exe` file.
3. On the splash screen, select the **Local Agent**.

4. **Welcome to the Microsoft System Center Virtual Machine Manager Agent (x64) Setup Wizard:** Click **Next**.
5. **Microsoft software notice terms** | Read through the terms and then select **I agree with the terms of this notice,** then click **Next**.
6. **Destination folder**: Select the location of the installation, then click **Next**.
7. **Security file folder:** Tick the box This host is on a perimeter network and type in a code you will use for your security file encryption key. Alternatively, if you are using a CA-signed method, you will need to know the thumbprint of the certificate you are using for the authentication. Then, click **Next**:

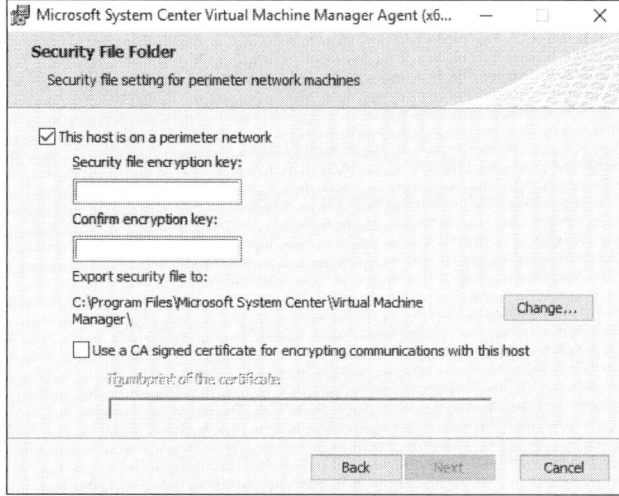

Figure 12.5: Security file window

8. **Host network name**: Enter the IP address of the VMM management server it will communicate to, then click **Next**.
9. **Configuration settings**: Confirm the ports used to communicate with the VMM management server, then click **Next**.
10. **Ready to install Microsoft System Center Virtual Machine Manager Agent**: When ready, click **Install**.

Once this has been installed, you will need to copy the security file made in *step 7* over to where the VMM management server is, which you can find in the default location of `C:\Program Files\Microsoft System Center\Virtual Machine Manager`. You will need it for the next steps to add the host.

Next, we will go through how to add the perimeter network-based host to VMM by doing the following:

1. Open the SCVMM 2022 console.
2. Go to VMs and **Services** tab.

3. Right-click either the All Hosts group or your preferred host group container and select **Add Hyper-V Hosts and Clusters**.
4. **Resource Location: Indicate the Windows computers location** | Select the **Windows Server Computers in a perimeter network** option, then click **Next**.
5. **Target Resources: Select the computers that you want to add as hosts** | Enter the computer name of the server which you manually installed the VMM agent on, and upload the security file alongside entering the key. Select the host group you wish to place the computer then click **Next**.
6. **Host Settings: Specify a host group and virtual machine placement path settings for hosts:** Select the host which the Hyper-V server or cluster will be added to. If you have completed the steps before to have additional host groups, this will be the best time to add them in.
7. Click **Next**.
8. **Summary: Confirm the settings** | Review the configuration you have specified for your host, then click **Add** to start the host being added.

VMware ESXi Hosts

Before we can add any of the ESXi hosts, we first need to add a vCenter server to the fabric which is done in a similar fashion to the *Infrastructure Servers* section earlier in this section.

So first, let us look into adding the VMware vCenter server:

1. Open the SCVMM 2022 console.
2. Go to the **Fabric** tab.
3. Go to **Servers** | **Infrastructure** | **vCenter Servers**.
4. Right-click and select **Add VMware vCenter Server**.
5. **Specify the vCenter Server that you want to add** | Enter the computer name of the vCenter server you wish to add and select the **Run As** account which will be used to connect to the vCenter server, and select if you wish to communicate with the ESX hosts in secure mode. When ready, click **Finish**.

> **Note: You may see a notification to import a self-signed certificate. Click to accept then wait until you see the jobs window to monitor the progress.**

Once this has been done, we can now move onto adding ESXi hosts. To do this, perform the following:

1. Open the SCVMM 2022 console.
2. Go to VMs and **Services** tab.

3. Right-click either the All Hosts group or your preferred host group container and select **Add VMware ESX Hosts and Clusters**.
4. **Credentials: Specify the credentials to use for accessing the ESX server host** | Select the **Run As** account to use with permissions to add this host, then click **Next**.
5. **Target Resources: Select ESX computers to add to your environment** | Select the vCenter server which you added and then select the host/s which you wish to add then click **Next**.
6. **Host Settings: Add one or more virtual machine paths or defaults** | Select the host profile which you will add the hosts to then click **Next**.
7. **Summary: Confirm the settings** | Review your configuration then click **Finish** to add the ESXi host.

Note: Using secure mode requires you to have an existing PKI setup to where you have a certificate and public key configured.

Profiles creation

From discussions in the previous chapter, we know that there are indeed several profiles that can be created within VMM, and though these are extremely helpful to build out VMs, they are not necessary in order to deploy a virtual machine.

However, where you require templates for specific virtual machines to be spun up on the fly these will be very handy. Hence, we will go through the creations of some of the profiles to illustrate how we are able to tie them together in order to form a potential VM template which will be able to enhance the deployment of a VM on a host that has a specific requirement ASAP.

Hardware profiles

The main profile you would want to use if creating virtual machines using a standard blank virtual disk template would be the hardware profile, which details out the specification VM will use.

To create one, perform the following:
1. Open the SCVMM 2022 console.
2. Go to the **Library** tab.
3. Go to **Profiles** | **Hardware Profiles**.
4. Right-click and select **Create Hardware Profile,** as shown in the following figure:

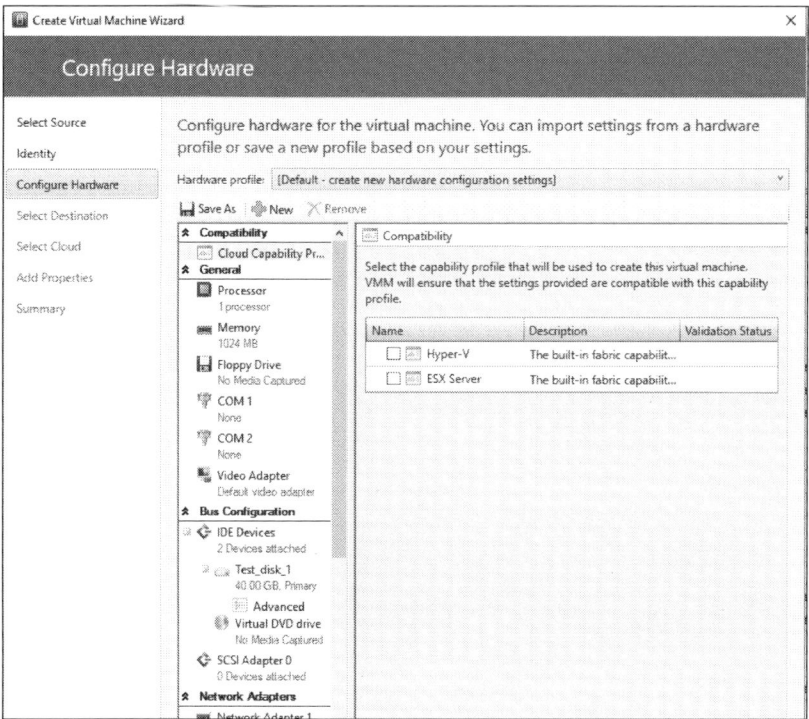

Figure 12.6: Hardware profile

5. **General:** Enter a name and description for the profile and select to which virtual machine generation type the VM will be, then click **Next**.

> **Note:** Hyper-V Virtual Machines have 2 generations, where the 1st generation applies to more legacy features and the 2nd generation allows for the use of Unified Extensible Firmware Interface (UEFI). To see more information on virtual machine generations, you can find this here https://learn.microsoft.com/en-us/windows-server/virtualization/hyper-v/plan/should-i-create-a-generation-1-or-2-virtual-machine-in-hyper-v.

6. **Hardware profile:** Add/remove or change any of the hardware specifications for your virtual machine in order to define the preset configuration. Then, when ready, click **OK** to complete.

This now completes the profile creation and will allow you to adapt this to the following process for creating new virtual machines.

Guest Operating System profiles

This profile works with the configuration of the OS which is being deployed onto the virtual machine. This particular profile is used more when creating an actual VM template which we will discuss in the *Creating virtual machines with virtual machine templates* section.

To create a guest OS profile, perform the following:
1. Open the SCVMM 2022 console.
2. Go to the **Library** tab.
3. Go to **Profiles** | **Guest OS** profiles.
4. Right-click and select **Create Guest OS Profile.**
5. **General:** Enter a name and description for the profile and select which OS platform the profile will be applicable, then click **Next**.
6. **Guest OS Profile** | Configure the Guest OS profile according to the requirements that you need and click **OK** to create the profile.

Creating Virtual Machines

Once we have hosts and clusters added into our fabric, we can now start creating virtual machines and placing them on the desired hosts.

In this part of the administration guide for VMM, we will illustrate how we create a new virtual machine just using a standard blank virtual disk. We will cover how we can create virtual machines using profiles and templates later on within this topic.

To perform the action of creating a virtual machine, perform the following:
1. Open the SCVMM 2022 console.
2. Go to VMs and **Services** tab.
3. Right-click either the All Hosts group or your preferred host group container and select **Create Virtual Machine**.
4. **Select the source for the new virtual machine:** Select the **Create the new virtual machine with a blank virtual hard disk**, then click **Next**.
5. **Identity: Specify Virtual Machine** Identity | Enter the name of the virtual machine and select the appropriate generation for your virtual machine, then click **Next**.
6. **Configure hardware: Configure hardware for the virtual machine. You can import settings from a hardware profile based on your settings**. Here, you can configure the hardware settings of your virtual machine, which in fact, is very similar to how you see this when creating a VM in Hyper-V. You also have an option where you can use a hardware profile to apply here, which will use a preset configuration that we discussed earlier. Once done, click **Next**.
7. **Select destination:** Choose whether to deploy or store the virtual machine. Select if you want to store the virtual machine on a host which you have added, or alternatively, you can store this within your library server for later use if you want to deploy to a host or a cloud. Click **Next**.
8. **Select host: Select a destination for the virtual machine** | Select the host on which you will place the VM. You will see a rating list indicating which is the most appropriate host to place the VM on. Click **Next**.

9. **Configure Settings: Review the virtual machine settings.** Here you will see the settings which will be configured for the VM. You can change these where necessary, then click **Next**.

10. **Select networks: Specify which virtual switches to use for the virtual machine** | Select the VM network details the VM network adapter will use, then click **Next**.

11. **Add Properties**: Select how the VM will react when its host is turned on, the action it will take the server stops, and to what OS your virtual machine will use, then click **Next**.

12. **Summary: Confirm the settings** | Review everything configured, then click **Create** to start the process.

Create Virtual Machines with Virtual Machine templates

VM templates allow you to spin up a virtual machine creation and placement on a host, almost instantaneously, without having to specify any configurations with the help of consolidating various profiles within VMM to have one parent template.

To create a VM template, perform the following:

1. Open the SCVMM 2022 console.
2. Go to VMs and **Services** tab.
3. Right-click ON either the All Hosts group or your preferred host group container and select **Create Virtual Machine**.
4. **Identity: VM Template Identity** | Enter a name and description for your template, then click **Next**.
5. **Configure Hardware: Configure hardware for the virtual machine. You can import settings from a hardware profile or save a new profile based on your settings.** Here, you can select your hardware profile that you created earlier or you can also define one here. Then, click **Next**.
6. **Configure OS: Configure identity, network settings, and scripts for the new virtual machine. You can import settings from a guest OS profile or save a new profile based on your settings.** Select an existing Guest OS profile or you can define one here for your VM template. Then, click **Next**.
7. **Summary: Before you create the new VM template, review the settings that you chose** | Review your configuration, then click **Create**.

Now, once you have this created, you can now use this to start creating new VMs utilizing this template by performing the following:

1. Open the SCVMM 2022 console.
2. Go to VMs and **Services** tab.

3. Right-click either the All Hosts group or your preferred host group container and select **Create Virtual Machine**.
4. **Select Source: Select the source for the new virtual machine** | Select the **use an existing virtual machine, VM template, or virtual hard disk** to select the template which you created, then click **Next**.
5. **Identity: Specify Virtual Machine Identity**. Enter the name of the virtual machine and select the appropriate generation for your virtual machine, then click **Next**.
6. **Configure hardware:** Configure hardware for the virtual machine. You can import settings from a hardware profile based on your settings. Here, you can configure the hardware settings of your virtual machine which, in fact, is very similar to how you see this if creating a VM in Hyper-V. You also have an option where you can use a hardware profile to apply here which will use a preset configuration which we discussed earlier. Once done, click **Next**.
7. **Select destination:** Choose whether to deploy or store the virtual machine. Select if you want to store the virtual machine on a host which you have added, or alternatively, you can store this within your library server for later use which you can later decide if you want to deploy to a host or a cloud. Click **Next**.
8. **Select host: Select a destination for the virtual machine** | Select the host which you will place the VM on. You will see a rating list indicating which is the most appropriate host to place the VM on. Click **Next**.
9. **Configure settings**: **Review the virtual machine settings**. Here, you will see the settings that will be configured for the VM. You can change these where necessary then click **Next**.
10. **Select networks: Specify which virtual switches to use for the virtual machine** | Select the VM network details that the VM network adapter will use, then click **Next**.
11. **Add properties**: Select how the VM will react when its host is turned on, the action it will take the server stops and to what OS your virtual machine will use, then click **Next**.
12. **Summary: Confirm the settings** | Review everything configured, then click **Create** to start the process.

Importing resources to the library server

The library server can be used to store **Virtual Hard Disks** (**VHDs**) and virtual machines that have been opted not to be deployed to hosts amongst various profiles.

There might be occasions you wish to make other resources available to be used directly from the library server such as installation media, ISO files, or even **Windows Image** (**WIM**) files, to provide an example.

To be able to import resources to your library server, perform the following:
1. Open the SCVMM 2022 console.
2. Go to the **Library** tab.
3. Go to **Library Servers** then go to the toolbar and select **Import Physical Resource**.
4. **Physical Resources to import:** Select **Add Resource,** then select the file/s which you wish to import, then click open. Here, you can select the exact folder which you want to import the files. Once ready, click **Import** to confirm the importing.

Bare metal deployment hosts

Bare metal deployments allow you to deploy Hyper-V hosts to your VMM, where they are provisioned and built with an OS, and then essentially added to VMM with the agent installed and ready for VM placement.

In order for us to do this, we need to have the following things in place:
- PXE server
- Physical computer profile

We have outlined the instructions on how to add a PXE server to our fabric, but what is currently outstanding is the physical host profile which we will go into.

Physical computer profile

This type of profile allows for the configuration of the physical host, similar to the hardware profile defined earlier.

To create a profile, perform the following:
1. Open the SCVMM 2022 console.
2. Go to the **Library** tab.
3. Go to **Profiles | Hardware Profiles**.
4. Right-click and select **Create Physical Computer Profile.**
5. **Profile Description:** Provide a name for the physical computer profile. **To do so** enter a name and description for the profile and specify that the role will be a **VM Host,** then click **Next.**
6. **OS Image: Select a virtual hard disk with an operating system image** | Select a virtual hard disk that contains a Windows Server OS, then click **Next**.
7. **Hardware configuration**: Enter the hardware details for your physical computer profile, then when ready, click **Next**.
8. **OS configuration**: Configure the OS settings for your profile, then click **Next**.
9. **Host settings: Specify virtual machine placement paths on the host**. Enter any specific paths you want to use to add virtual machine placement.

> Note: Adding paths for virtual machine placement is dependent on the number of disks you have configured. If only one disk, then essentially you will have C:\, the amount of disk drives is done in the Hardware Configuration part of the wizard.

10. **Summary: Confirm the settings** | Review your configuration, then click **Finish** to create the profile.

Adding host for provisioning

Now with a profile in place, we are ready to start to add hosts for being deployed as bare metal devices.

To do this, perform the following:

1. Open the SCVMM 2022 console.
2. Go to VMs and **Services** tab.
3. Right-click either the All Hosts group or your preferred host group container and select **Add Hyper-V Hosts and Clusters**.
4. **Resource Location: Indicate the Windows computers location** | Select the **Physical computers to be provisioned as virtual machine hosts** option, then click **Next**.
5. **Credentials and protocol: Specify the account and protocol to be used for discovery** | Select a **Run As** account to use to add the host and select the correct protocol to use for out of band, then click **Next**.
6. **Discovery scope: Specify the discovery scope for baseboard management controllers** | Enter the IP address, IP subnet or range to discover the host/s, then click **Next**.
7. **Provisioning options** | Select the host group to which you will assign the physical host to, then click **Next**.
8. **Deployment customization:** Enter the name of the host and select the host profile to use, then click **Next**.
9. **Summary:** Review your configuration, then click **Finish** and look at the job window to see the progress of the bare metal deployment.

Managing hosts and Virtual Machines

Other parts of general administration for VMM can be performed. For this section, we will cover some of the general tasks that can be done to manage these objects.

Managing checkpoints

To create a checkpoint for a virtual machine, please perform the following:

1. Open the SCVMM 2022 console.

2. Go to the VMs and the **Services** tab.
3. Go to **All Hosts**, then right-click the VM you require. Select **Manage Checkpoints**.
4. Click **Create**.
5. Provide a meaningful name for your checkpoint alongside description, then click **Create**.

> Note: You can also right-click the VM and select create checkpoint to get the same option, but the preceding direction is good if you want to asses any existing checkpoints which you want to manage first before creating another one.

Maintenance mode

Whenever you have any work that is to be carried out on a host that may cause some downtime, you will need to use maintenance mode in order to make sure that the host as well as virtual machines do not let off any unwanted alerts during the maintenance.

To do this, perform the following:

1. Open the SCVMM 2022 console.
2. Go to the VMs and **Services** tab.
3. Go to **All Hosts** and right-click the host you require, then select **Start Maintenance Mode**.
4. **Start Maintenance Mode: Select the action to perform when starting maintenance mode on <Hostname>** - Select if you wish to move VMs to another host or if you want to place the VMs in a saved state during the maintenance mode, then click **Finish**.

> Note: Saved state means that the machine will have its state saved at the exact point where it was at, similar to a paused state. If you want to take a host out of the maintenance mode, then you repeat the same instructions and select to Stop Maintenance Mode.

Upgrading the Virtual Machine Manager

At the time of writing this book, the latest version of the Update Rollup for the VMM 2022 is Update Rollup 2, applicable to the System Center suite which can be found here **https:// support.microsoft.com/en-us/topic/update-rollup-2-for-system-center-2022-0cfcf8c0-69d3-46ff-bd91-7813330ffac9**.

The package for the Update Rollups comes in the form of an .msu file extension, which means that they are applicable similarly to the other System Center products, which contain an update for specific roles within the technology.

To install the update, perform the following:
1. **Download the Update Rollup 2 for VMM 2022.**
2. **Extract the .msu from the CAB file downloaded.**
3. **Open a command prompt with administrative privileges.**
4. **Run the following command** `msiexec.exe /update kb5032369_vmmsrver_amd64.msu`

Best practices

Here, we will look at the best practices which are ideal to apply when managing and administrating VMM.

PRO tips for System Center Operations Manager integration

Performance and Resource Optimization (PRO) tips is an integration that can be created between both the Operations Manager and the VMM used to advise on recommendations for your virtual environment, such as VMs and hosts placement and warnings of resources which might be getting exhausted in certain areas, etc.

If you do have an Operations Manager environment, it may be best practice to have this enabled to achieve full optimization for your VMM environment.

This can be done within the settings of VMM where you have the System Center Settings section, which has an entry for Operations Manager.

Monitoring Virtual Machine Manager

Another part of the **System Center Operations Manager (SCOM)** integration with the VMM is the actual monitoring the Operations Manager has with the management packs that VMM contains.

Performing the part specified in the PRO tips section also does this. However, you may also be required to import these same management packs into your Operations Manager environment, where these can be found in `C:\Program File\Microsoft System Center\Virtual Machine Manager\Management Packs`.

Real-world scenarios

While there are best practices and recommended ways of carrying out tasks, there are also real-world scenarios that have to be taken into consideration. Here, we will explore those real-world scenarios within VMM.

Managing vCenter servers

Though there is the option to manage ESXi hosts within your VMM environment, typically in real world scenarios, you would prefer to use vCenter on its own rather than fulfilling an integration with VMM.

VMM is perhaps more the convenience of being able to manage both hypervisor platforms if licensing is perhaps an issue or if you do not have a large amount of ESXi hosts to manage. This is not to say that there are no benefits to managing VMware hosts within VMM, but many may prefer to keep both hypervisor platforms separate, or in fact may just be using only one hypervisor standard within their environment.

Conclusion

VMM, on the administration perspective, is also a very huge task when it comes to populating your fabric as well as the overall administration and management of the VMM product.

The reader must understand all common areas of administration to have and understanding of what they want to achieve when it comes to the management of their hypervisor environment, considering the different types of hypervisors that can be managed and the virtual machine/host placements.

Templates are vastly used to help customize and set a company standard foundation on how to structure the correct structure for not just hosts if using a bare metal deployment method, but especially for your virtual machines configuration and overall parental host placement.

In the next chapter, we will look at the final product within System Center, Data Protection Manager where we will understand its role within the infrastructure to provide a backup solution for your environment.

Points to remember

- VMM contains one base role, that is, the management server role. After installation, there are various roles that can be configured, which are not limited to library servers, PXE servers, and update servers.
- More than one management server can be added to VMM to provide options for high availability for your managed VMM estate.
- Library servers help keep a repository of your virtual machines for later deployment, templates and also other important objects which are used to help configure and build out your virtual environment.
- To add VMware ESXi hosts, you first need to add a vCenter server in order to enable this option.

- Hosts can be added to your VMM fabric based on different scenarios whether that be domain, untrusted domain or non-domain-based hosts.
- Maintenance mode has an effect on not just the host, but also all of the virtual machines that sit under that host and they can either be migrated across to another host or placed within a saved state.

Multiple choice questions

1. Which profile is used in order to allow you to create bare metal deployments for new hosts
    a. Guest OS profile
    b. Hardware profile
    c. SQL Server profile
    d. Physical computer profile

2. What is the name of the feature that allows you to integrate with SCOM to provide additional information on what the administrator can do to optimize VMM?
    a. PRO tips
    b. VMM management packs
    c. Alerting
    d. SCOM agent

3. What type of host requires a manually installed agent before it can be added to the VMM fabric?
    a. Untrusted domain host
    b. Perimeter Host
    c. Domain host
    d. Bare metal host

4. What is the name of the role which is required to deploy bare metal hosts?
    a. Library server
    b. PXE server
    c. Update server
    d. VMM server

5. Which of these objects is not possible to upload into your library server?
    a. ISO files
    b. VHDX

c. Templates

d. None of them

6. Which profile is used to help build virtual machines and required within a VM template?

   a. Hardware Profile

   b. Guest OS Profile

   c. VM Template

   d. Service Template

Answers

1. d
2. a
3. b
4. b
5. d
6. c

Key terms

- **VMM**: Virtual Machine Manager
- **Profile**: Logical container for settings
- **ESXi**: Elastic Sky X Integrated
- **PROTips**: Performance and Resource Optimization
- **MSU**: Microsoft Update Standalone Package
- **Template**: Logical container for setting and profiles.
- **VHD**: Virtual Hard Disk
- **PXE**: Pre-boot Execution Environment

Join our book's Discord space

Join the book's Discord Workspace for Latest updates, Offers, Tech happenings around the world, New Release and Sessions with the Authors:

https://discord.bpbonline.com

CHAPTER 13
Creating and Managing Backups with System Center DPM

Introduction

This chapter will look into the planning and design for the **System Center Data Protection Manager (SCDPM)**. This area will be applicable for most versions of this technology as the same key areas have to be considered, especially when looking into how the solution will be used. Scalability is also a key area that we will analyze when planning a new design. We will also discover the upgrade paths that would need to be taken in order to be applicable for System Center 2022. For the Data Protection Manager, we will take a look into all of the existing System Center technologies as well as other core Windows server areas in which we will plan how our centralized backup solution will move forward.

Also included will be a minimum and recommended requirement level to where the reader can develop a lab environment which they can use to follow through with the next chapter so you can gauge a practical as well as a theoretical understanding.

Structure

This chapter will cover the following topics:
- Data Protection Manager topology structure

- Product integration planning
- Backup scheduling design
- Disaster recovery
- Data Protection Manager lab requirements

Objectives

Understanding perhaps the most underused product within the System Center suite and the role that it plays within the organization. This chapter will explore the roles the product has, shaping out a strategy for how you will construct your backup design and how you will be able to conduct a recovery in a **disaster recovery** (**DR**) situation.

The reader will gain knowledge on what to consider and what to take into account when it comes to the planning of how your infrastructure can recover from any DR situation.

Data Protection Manager topology structure

Data Protection Manager (**DPM**) plays an integral role for not just the backup solution for your System Center suite products, but also for the key Microsoft product elements within your environment. We want to use this topic to outline some of the topology examples that can be used to help structure your DPM design from a foundation setting while showing its scalability when your environment and backup requirement needs to grow.

However, first, we will take a look into the roles which you can implement first to understand the whole structure of the product.

Data Protection Manager roles

Here are all the server roles which can be configured for DPM:

- **Management server**: DPM only contains one role, which is the management server that allows for client-managed machines to communicate into DPM in order to have DPM actions sent to perform the backup tasks.
- **Central console**: The central console is used as the **graphical user interface** (**GUI**) to be able to administer DPM which requires an active connection to the management server.

Single management server topology

For the topology of DPM, a single management server remains its only parental top-level topology. With a single role for this product, the management server remains a simple topology structure.

Creating and Managing Backups with System Center DPM • 313

A way in which this can be split out is by not using the conventional consolidated setup in which you would be required to use a separate server to act as your **Structured Query Language** (**SQL**) Server, or for another server to utilize the DPM central console to connect to your DPM management server.

Requirements for structuring your topology from outside the consolidated setup will be explained in the final topic for your DPM lab requirements.

Hardware requirements

Table *13.1* contains all the hardware requirements for the main roles within DPM.

> **Note: For reference of the full requirements for Data Protection Manager 2022 you can find them here: https://learn.microsoft.com/en-us/system-center/dpm/prepare-environment-for-dpm?view=sc-dpm-2022**

The hardware requirements for the main roles within DPM are:

DPM role	CPU (Cores)	CPU (GHz)	Memory (GB)	Disk space (GB)
Management server	4	3.3	8	3

Table 13.1: System Center DPM hardware requirements table

Operating System requirements

The operating system requirements for DPM are given in the following table:

Data Protection Manager role	Windows Server version	Windows Server edition	Windows Server GUI	Windows Server core
Management server	2022	Standard/Datacenter	Yes	Yes (2019 is supported)

Table 13.2: Data Protection Manager Operating System requirements

Structured Query Language requirements

The SQL requirements for DPM 2022 are given in the following table:

SQL Version	SQL cumulative update (Minimum)
*SQL Server 2022 – Standard/Enterprise	Latest
SQL Server 2019 – Standard/Enterprise	Latest
SQL Server 2017 – Standard/Enterprise	Latest

Table 13.3: System Center Data Protection Manager 2022 SQL Server requirements

* SQL Server 2022 is supported once DPM 2022 has Update Rollup 1 applied.

Product integration planning

With DPM, you have the ability to recognize Microsoft-based products that exist on protected devices, allowing integrations to take place where you have the ability to backup specific parts of that technology.

We will go through all the technologies recognized in this format as well as the exploration of further integrations.

Product recognition

So, the product recognition side of DPM comes from being able to identify either specific roles or Microsoft products. This then provides you with some options which allow for backups to be performed not only more granular, but also key areas within those products.

Here are some examples which are fundamentally recognized:

- File services
- SQL Server
- Microsoft Exchange
- SharePoint
- Hyper-V

To further expand on these points, we can take a look at *Figure 11.1* which shows a protection group wizard allowing the administrator to select the areas they can add to the backup protection group (will cover this more within in the next section):

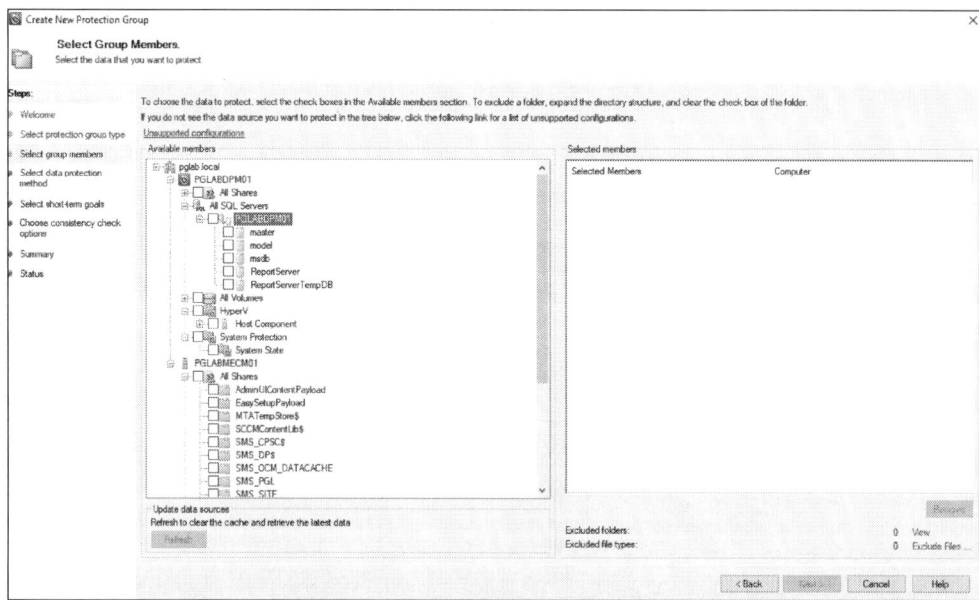

Figure 13.1: *DPM 2022 protection group view*

If we take some time to analyze the preceding figure, we can see a section for the DPM server, which shows the SQL Server. Now at this particular level, if we were to select the SQL Instance, this would essentially backup all the databases, including the system databases alongside it. However, with the product recognition, you can select if you want to backup individual databases.

Where file shares are concerned, within *Figure 11.1*, we have the **Microsoft Endpoint Configuration Manager** (**MECM**) server protected as well, and here we can see the share folders around the primary site as well as its DP shares.

Typically, the Configuration Manager would perform a site maintenance step to back up the site configuration and, optionally, the database along with it where you can centralize these backups. With DPM involved, you have the ability to perform the same and under a protection group which you can select all some of the Configuration Manager-created folders.

Managing VMware

DPM can also manage VMware, and this functionality is a native integration. Similar to the Windows servers, you can manage them to be able to back up the VMware **virtual machines** (**VMs**) however, in this case, an actual DPM agent is not used.

VMware estates are managed by using specified credentials which are used to connect to either the vCenter Server or directly to an ESXi host. There, you can add either all or the individual VMware servers which reside on them.

Figure 11.2 shows the credential management that is used for the VMware estate management:

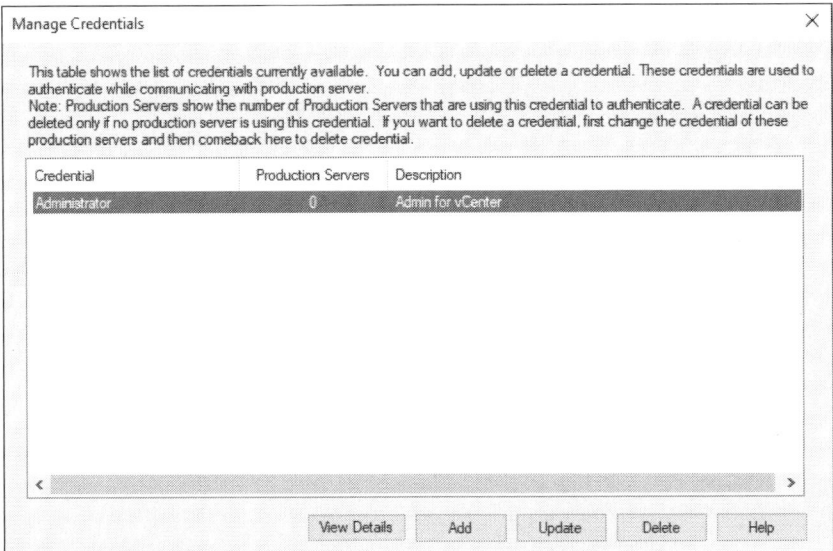

Figure 13.2: DPM 2022 manage credentials view

System Center Orchestrator

DPM 2022 can be integrated with System Center Orchestrator 2022 utilizing the DPM 2022 integration pack.

The connection to DPM uses a PowerShell remoting type, where you need to add the details of the DPM administrator console, server and login details to formulate the connection between Orchestrator and DPM.

The integration pack allows you to involve steps to action administrative tasks, such as:

- Create recovery point
- Get data source
- Get recovery point
- Get DPM server capacity
- Protect data source
- Recover SharePoint
- Recover SQL
- Recover VM
- Run DPM PowerShell script

The integration pack for DPM 2022 can be found here: **https://www.microsoft.com/en-us/download/details.aspx?id=104334**

System Center Operations Manager

Similar to the Orchestrator, the **System Center Operations Manager** (**SCOM**) has a management pack that allows for effective monitoring of the DPM server functionality.

The download for the DPM 2022 management pack can be found here: **https://www.microsoft.com/en-us/download/details.aspx?id=56560**

Backup scheduling design

Here, we will look through the design of the backup scheduling, as well as investigate the different structures we can use for our backup solution with DPM.

The backup scheduling itself is handled from the creation of protection groups, which contain the managed servers, objects to backup, and the scheduling of when backups take place.

First, let us look at the process from top to bottom to understand how we design this.

Protection group structuring

As the protection group is the overall parent, we first need to understand *how* we will decide the protection groups.

A great idea to understand the planning is to look at it by the environment we have and know the layers of how we would group this. A list to provide an example of the layers we would use to decide the protection groups is as follows:

- **By technology**: For example, we could create a protection group based on the product itself. Let us take, for example, Configuration Manager. Depending on the type of design you have, it may already have reached a certain point of growth to where you may have a server for each designated role. A protection group, in this manner, could help centralize backups for this product, which could be key, especially if it is a business-critical service.
- **By geographical site**: While this is a great way of grouping, this particular strategy may come at more expensive on storage. This type of method would assume a full backup of an entire server (or at least the file shares).
- **By environment:** This is aimed more at environments which may use multiple environment types, such as development, pre-production, and production environments. This type of strategy is perhaps better suited for development and pre-production environments, in which, these areas might be less intensive on storage as well as the volatility of them where *breaking the environment* and rebuilding is more of a regular occurrence. However, having some form of backups for certain parts could be handy when carrying out further **User Acceptance Testing (UAT)** testing with thoughts of proceeding into the next stages.
- **By client and server separation**: DPM allows you to backup client machines as well as server clients but is very similar to how the Operations Manager works. While you have the ability to manage client OS devices, you have to think of the reality of where that can go; depending on the size of the business, client machines multiply overtime. So, you will have to consider if you can recognize any important client machines that may benefit from being within a protection group.

Data retention planning scheduling

Here is where we plan the actual schedule of when we will perform these backups. The things you will need to consider first, are as follows:

- **Retention range**: These are specified in days for how old you want to keep data for before you were to perform another backup.

    Firstly, you will need to ensure that no matter which level of retention range you have, you need to have the correct amount of storage to accommodate any form of backups. The higher the retention range the more backups you will be holding in the short term.

Another rule of thumb here, is if you are looking to backup something that would be deemed business-critical and any form of downtime can cause serious issues, then you might want to look at reducing the number of days for your retention, you could drop this down to one day but you would need to be careful on the amount of data that will be backed up as this could mimic more of an incremental backup option which can be very resource intensive.

However, if you have a solution you wish to backup where the retention period could have some flexibility, that is, where information does not constantly change and would have little to no impact if it had to be recovered with the same information, then having a higher or default level of retention could work.

- **Backup schedule**: The express full backups are performed here, and to coincide with the retention range above, this is set at 20:00 daily.

    Depending on how you structure your retention range, you must allow for your schedule to accommodate this as well. You can change the time in half hour intervals and select to which days of the week you want to perform the backups on.

    If you have a higher retention range, then you can space out your scheduling to something like once a week, on a day and time that is suited for something convenient like out of hours, or at a time which is suitable within the day so that an administrator can observe the progress of the backup being performed.

- **Replica scheduling:** Another part to consider is the replica creation done to prepare the backup to the disk storage destination. In order for this to be done, the replica is created within the DPM server, so you will need to ensure you have sufficient space for this to work.

    Replicas can be performed either straight away or can be done on a schedule that works better.

    While having two different schedules for the replica and the initial backup, you could essentially use the default "Now" for the replica and structure the backup schedule to fit around where you have more control on the preparation of the start time.

> **Note: If using local storage on the DPM server to backup to with the protection group, then ensure you have enough space to accommodate for both the replica as well as the backup itself.**

Disaster recovery

With the protection groups design in place, we would need to set out our strategy for how we would look to recover data in a DR scenario.

When relating back to the previous topic on how we structure our data retention and scheduling, this will define how we are about to view the recovery points for our backed-up data residing from the protection groups.

Let us take a look at *Figure 11.3*, where we can see the recovery points for the Configuration Manager database:

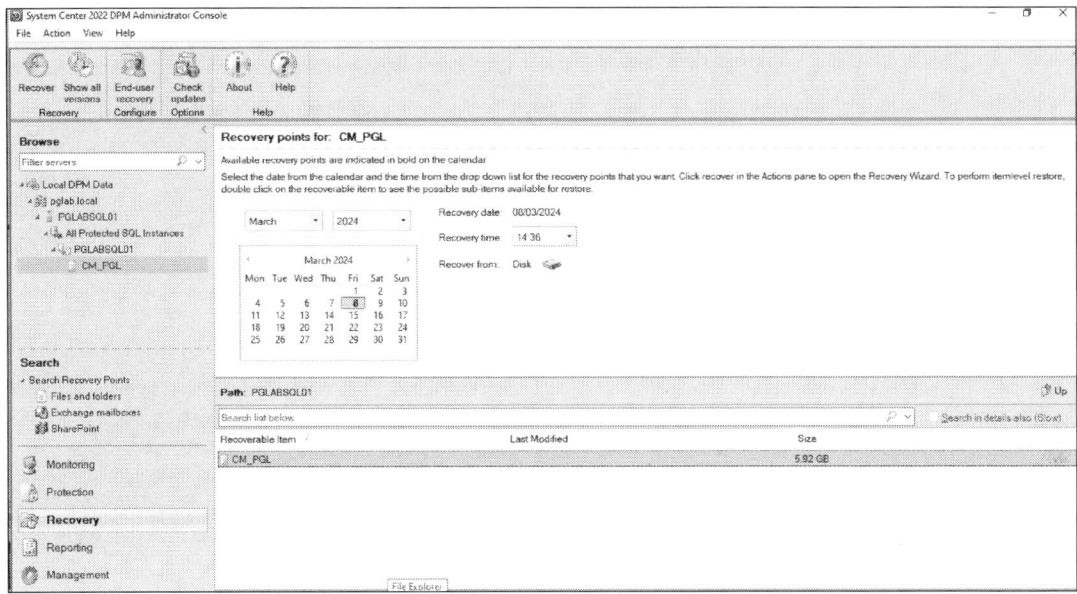

Figure 13.3: DM 2022 recovery tab

In a case of a technology such as Configuration Manager, the most up-to-date backup will be crucial in order to minimize **Business As Usual (BAU)** downtime, and consider understanding the recovery steps of the technology you are using DPM for.

This means that though we are backing up the database and have the ability to recover it, it does not necessarily mean that it is the *only* thing we have to do to get out of a situation where a DR scenario applies. DPM 2022 will work to perform backups of critical components but you will still need to have a defined process overall.

Another scenario could be where you are looking to have an SQL migration (in this scenario with the SQL recovery) where you want to recover to another SQL Server infrastructure or instance. This is indeed something which DPM has the capability to do as well.

Data Protection Manager lab requirements

With the uncomplicated nature of the infrastructure that DPM has, there are not many types of lab requirement scenarios to detail and to carry out with the initial requirements specified in the section *Data Protection Manager topology structure*. Having said that, we will add some additional tables to outline some ideal lab requirements where you can practice the protection group backup process.

Data Protection Manager 2022 lab setup table

The base requirements you can use for your DPM 2022 lab are as follows:

Lab configuration type	Lab configuration value
Roles to implement	DPM 2022 management server
CPU requirement	4 Cores at 3.3GHz
Memory requirements	8GB
Disk space	3GB
Additional Disk space	Up to 100GB
Operating System	Windows Server 2022
SQL version	SQL Server 2022

Table 11.4: Lab requirement table for DPM 2022

Although, you can bounce around on the SQL Server and Windows OS requirements defined within the section *Data Protection Manager topology structure*, the reader may get a better understanding with utilizing the latest versions of the software, so it coincides much better with the 2022 version of DPM.

> **Note:** The additional disk space is really to account for if you are looking to try backing up to a disk drive which may be local on the DPM server to take into account the replica as well as the actual backup file. This is also an illustration for if you are wanting to use disk drives on other servers as well, the demonstration on how to add disk storage will follow within the next chapter.

Conclusion

DPM 2022 plays a vital role which is required to structure a plan on how to not only backup your environment on a parental or granular level, but also a method on how you will be able to fully recover your environment also.

By default standards, your OS may contain Windows Backup, or even something further, such as **Volume Shadow Copy (VSS)** or other forms of backup around the DR planning for your virtual infrastructure where you could recover your virtual machines. In such cases, DPM can accommodate all of these scenarios as well as the integration with your selected hypervisor.

Groupings of servers make it possible to have a logical denominator to allow for the administrator to be able to put together a schedule that suits the business as well as the technical environmental needs.

In the next chapter, we will focus on the installation and configuration of DPM, where we will put the planning and design knowledge to practical use.

Points to remember

- DPM has a simple topology in which, the only role is the management server role, with a GUI console that can be used to connect to the environment.
- DPM uses an agent-based management system that allows servers or client OS devices to be managed and allows for its files, folders, and critical components to be eligible for backup.
- A product recognition mechanism exists for recognizing core Microsoft components used, such as SQL Server, Hyper-V, SharePoint, and Files and folder services, to allow for more granularity in backup component selection.
- A logical container is used in DPM known as protection groups where servers or client OS devices can be placed into for management.

Multiple choice questions

1. **What has to take place before a backup is created on the destination backup location? (Select all which apply)**
   a. DPM Agent has to be installed.
   b. Replica must be created on the DPM management server.
   c. Protection group must be created.
   d. Scheule must be put in place.

2. **DPM uses an agent-based management structure that can be installed on clients other than just servers.**
   a. True
   b. False

3. **DPM is able to manage VMware servers to be controlled within the protection groups.**
   a. True
   b. False

4. **Name two technologies which DPM can be directly integrated with to perform additional tasks?**
   a. SCOM and MECM
   b. MECM and SQL

c. SCVMM and SCOM

d. SCOM and System Center Orchestrator (SCORCH)

5. **How are you able to add Servers or Clients into a protection group?**

   a. Creating a protection group.

   b. Install DPM Agent.

   c. Install SCOM Agent.

   d. Adding servers or clients directly into the protection group.

6. **What are some of the ways in which you would want to create a protection group for specific backup purposes?**

   a. By technology

   b. By geographical location

   c. By network

   d. All the above

Answers

1. a,b,c,d
2. a
3. a
4. d
5. d
6. d

Key terms

- **DPM**: Data Protection Manager
- **DR**: Disaster Recovery
- **MECM**: Microsoft Endpoint Configuration Manager
- **SQL**: Structured Query Language
- **SCOM**: System Center Operations Manager
- **UAT**: User Acceptance Testing
- **SCORCH**: System Center Orchestrator
- **VM**: Virtual Machine

Chapter 14
Deployment and Administration of System Center DPM

Introduction

This chapter will concentrate on the development and deployment of the **System Center Data Protection Manager (SCDPM)**. The importance of this chapter is to illustrate the setup of the **Data Protection Manager (DPM)** and the overall deployment so we can ensure the design plan that we specified in the previous chapter allows us to have a healthy setup. There will also be some troubleshooting points to help the reader understand some common and uncommon issues that can arise during the development and deployment process.

This chapter will provide an in-depth look into the overall administration of SCDPM as well as outlining its best practices. The administration side is what will allow an engineer to perform their **Business As Usual (BAU)** tasks, but also within the administrative side, another area that would enrich the BAU tasks and overall **user interface (UI)** is where the best practices come in. Best practices are normally looked at as a professional and recommended level to what you should do and not do, but we can also understand that a real-world scenario can conflict with this, so we will look to outline the differences between both.

Structure

This chapter will cover the following topics:
- Data Protection Manager deployment
- Technology backup configuration
- Administration of Data Protection Manager
- Best practices
- Real-world scenarios

Objectives

In this chapter the reader will utilize everything they learnt within the previous chapter and apply the same when it comes to the deployment and administration of DPM.

Understanding its many administrative tasks will help the reader understand how to technically construct backup schedules with DPM and how to recover them in a disaster recovery scenario.

Data Protection Manager deployment

We are now ready to proceed with the deployment of DPM. Before we proceed to install the core components, we must first address any prerequisites which are required to be installed or configured before we able to successfully install any components from DPM.

Management server

Some prerequisites required before you can install the management server are as follows.

Structured Query Language Server management tools

The main prerequisite required for the DPM management server is the installation of the SQL management studio beforehand.

You will need to ensure that the SQL management studio application matches the correct version of the SQL Server you have installed, whether this is a local SQL or a remote SQL Server.

The latest version can be found here https://learn.microsoft.com/en-us/sql/ssms/download-sql-server-management-studio-ssms?view=sql-server-ver16#previous-versions and, alternatively, if you require an older version, if you are not using SQL Server 2022, then you can find the previous versions of SQL Server Management Studio (SSMS) here: https://learn.microsoft.com/en-us/sql/ssms/release-notes-ssms?view=sql-server-ver16#previous-ssms-releases

Once you have this downloaded, you will need to perform the following instructions:
1. Double-click the **SSMS-Setup**.
2. Check the installation path of the SSSMS. Click the **Install** button to begin

You might be required to reboot the server after you have performed the installation.

Structured Query Language Server

Let us look at the prerequisites required before you can setup a SQL Server to host your DPM database and reporting functions.

Reporting services

Most SQL Servers may have an instance of reporting services depending on the infrastructure and the SQL Server role, but in the case of DPM 2022, reporting services is a mandatory prerequisite to have.

The newer versions of SQL Server, starting from 2017, is now an add-on as opposed to being part of the native SQL Server installation files.

The same condition applies where you would need to have an **SQL Server Reporting Services** (**SSRS**) which corresponds to the correct version of your SQL Server.

The latest version can be found here **https://www.microsoft.com/download/details.aspx?id=104502 where you can change the filtering of the article to select the appropriate version for your SQL Server, as well as the latest version.**

> Note: SSRS has to be setup where the instance has a new database and functioning reportserver and reports link in order for you to have a non-interrupted installation of DPM.

Data Protection Manager 2022 support files

If you are using a remote server as your SQL server, you will need to prepare this server by installing the support files which will help with the prerequisite step changes.

To install this, perform the following:
1. Open the installation media.
2. Double-click the `setup.exe`.
3. On the splash screen, select **DPM Remote SQL Prep**
4. **Microsoft Software license terms:** Click **OK** to accept the agreement once this has been read through.

Once completed you should get a confirmation stating the successful installation of the support files.

> Note: In the Programs and Features you may see this listed as "Microsoft System Center 2019 DPM Support Files" but this is indeed the correct support files which comes from the DPM 2022 installation media.

Data Protection Manager service accounts

DPM does have services, but not specifically a requirement to configure them to use service accounts as they run under the local system by default. In order to provide an understanding of the services that allow DPM to run, we will explain each in more detail in the following table:

Name	Description	Local or domain
DPM	Implements and manages synchronization and shadow copy creation for protected file servers.	Local
DPM AccessManager service	Manages access to DPM.	Local
DPM agent coordinator	Manages the installation, uninstallation and upgrade of protection agents to remote servers.	Local
DPM CPWrapper service	Dpm Cmd Proc **Distributed Component Object Model (DCOM)- Windows Communication Foundation (WCF)** Bridge Service	Local
DPM writer	Manages backup shadow copies of DPM replicas, and manage backups of the DPM and DPM report databases for purposes of data archival.	Local
Data Protection Manager Library Agent (DPMLA)	DPM library agent service	Local
Data Protection Manager Recovery Agent (DPMRA)	Helps back up and recover file and application data to the DPM	Local
DPM **Virtual Machine Manager (VMM)** Helper Service	DPM VMM interaction service	Local

Figure 14.1: SCDPM 2022 service accounts

Firewall requirements

Table 14.2 contains the firewall requirements in order to install and administer DPM.

For the full list of firewall requirements, this can be found here **https://learn.microsoft.com/en-us/system-center/dpm/configure-firewall-settings-for-dpm?view=sc-dpm-2022**

Firewall rule type	Ports used	Protocol type	Transmission Control Protocol (TCP) or User Datagram Protocol (UDP)
DPM Server and DPM agent communications	135	RPC	TCP
DPM data channel	5718 5719	TCP	TCP
Protection group	6075	TCP	TCP
DNS	53	DNS	TCP
Kerberos	88	Kerberos	Both
Lightweight Directory Access Protocol (LDAP)	389	LDAP	Both
NetBios	137/138 - UDP 139/445 - TCP	Server Message Block (SMB)	Both

Table 14.2: SCDPM 2022 firewall requirements

Data Protection Manager installation

As DPM has a very simplified topology compared to the other products, the main and only installation is of the DPM Management Server role and the DPM console.

1. Open the installation media.
2. Click the **Setup.exe** file.
3. **Microsoft Software license terms**: Click the **Accept** button once you have read through the license terms.
4. **Welcome: Prerequisites check** | Click **Next**.
5. **Prerequisites check:** Enter the details of the SQL Server which you will use to perform the installation. This will then check and install the prerequisite components on the server, as shown in the following figure:

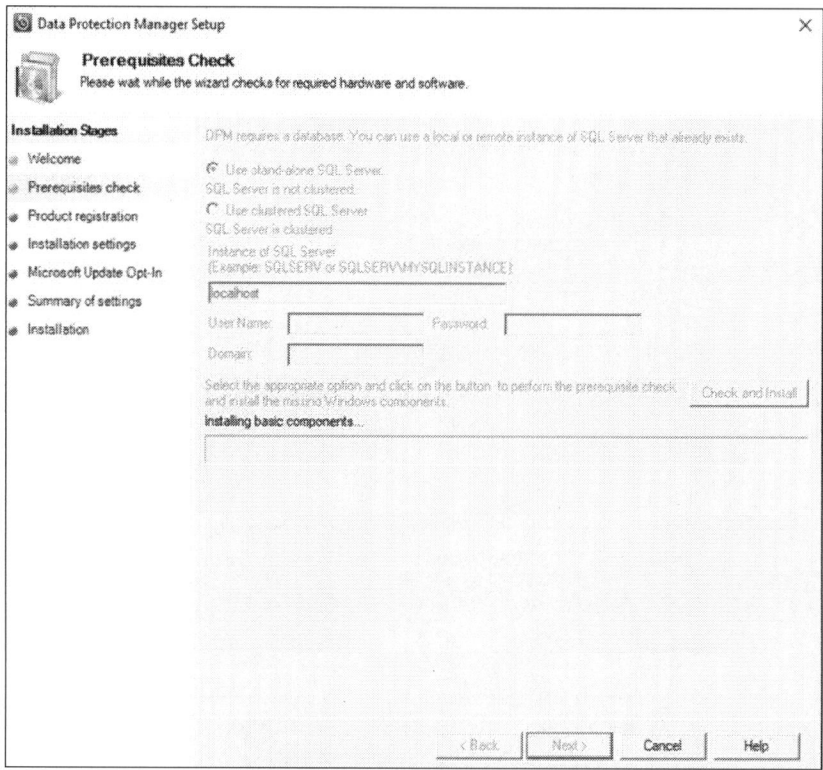

Figure 14.1: *DPM prerequisites check*

6. **Product registration:** Enter the username and company name, then click **Next**.

7. **Product registration: Installation Settings** | Confirm the installation path for DPM 2022 and double-check the disk space requirements to ensure you have a sufficient amount to proceed, then click **Next**.

8. **Microsoft update opt-in:** Select if you want to opt into the Microsoft update to check for updates for your DPM environment, then click **Next**.

9. **Microsoft update opt**-in: **Summary of settings** | Confirm the configuration you have done for your DPM 2022, then click **Install** to begin the installation:

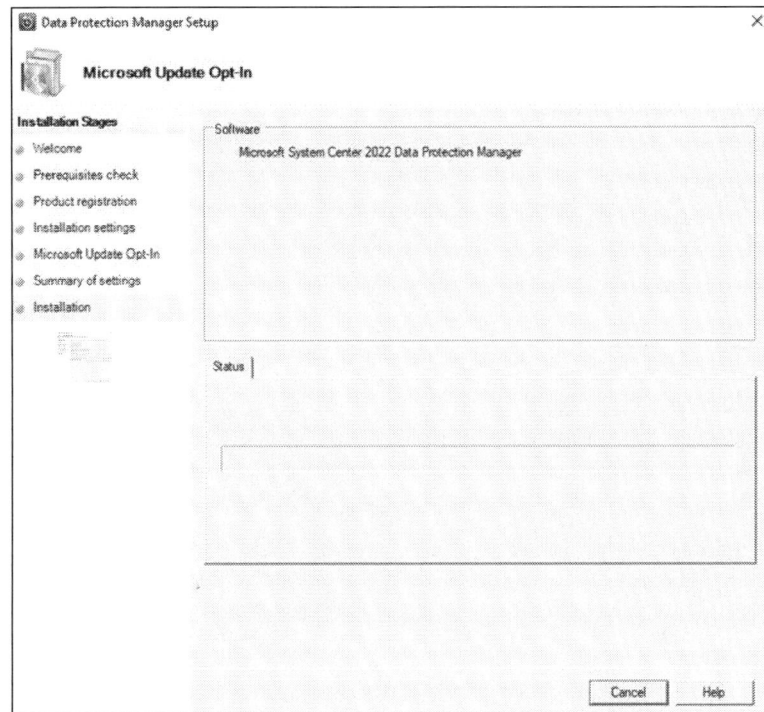

Figure 14.2: SCDPM 2022 installation status

Technology backup configuration

With the exception of supporting the backup of Microsoft native products, this can also be extended into the VMware stack also.

In order to do this, we need to perform some configurations to get this enabled which is where we will go into the procedure of how to set this up.

Manage VMware credentials

VMware vCenter servers are used to pull in the information from your VMware environment in order to add them into protection groups, and this is done by simply using managed credentials which is used to discover the vCenter servers, similar to how run as accounts are used within SCOM.

To do this, perform the following:

1. Open the **Microsoft System Center 2022 DPM** console.
2. Go to the **Management** tab.
3. Click on **Production Servers** and then click on the **Manage VMware Credentials**.

4. Click the **Add** button and then enter the details for your credentials then click Add.

You should now see something similar to *Figure 14.3*:

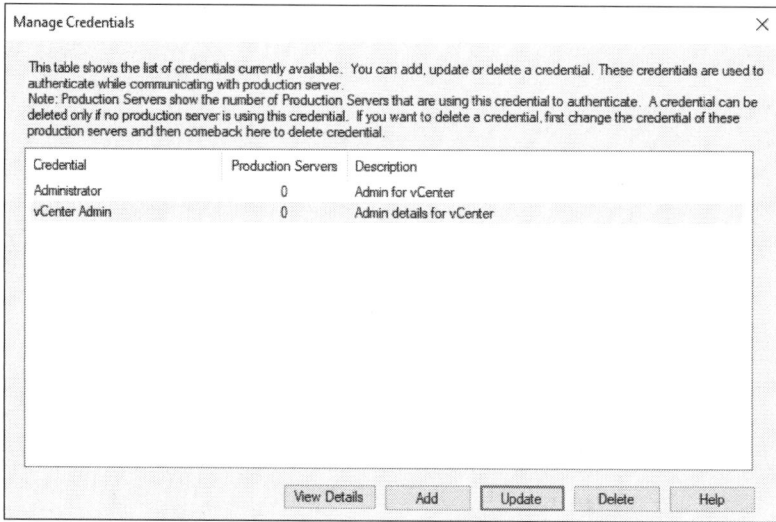

Figure 14.3: Manage VMware credentials window

Alternatively, there is also the default credentials of Administrator, which also by default does not contain a password, so if you do want to update this, you can simply highlight the credentials and select the **Update** button. This will then give you an option to enter the password for the default credentials as seen in *Figure 14.4*:

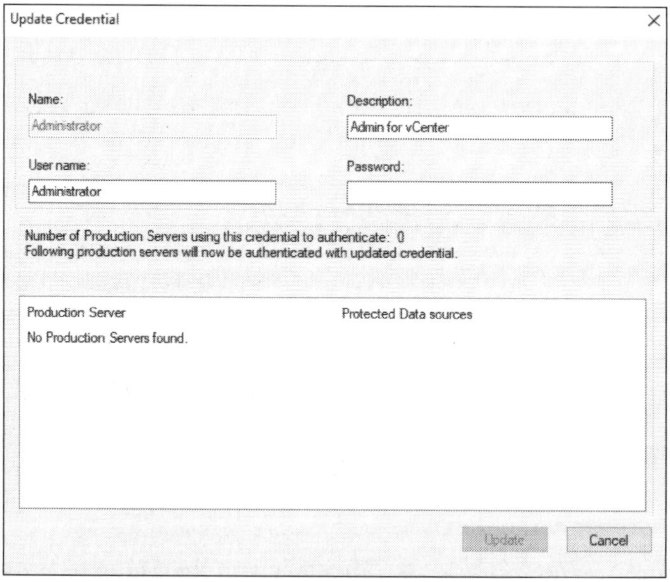

Figure 14.4: Manage VMware update credentials window

Administration of Data Protection Manager

At this point, we have everything we need to start adding to our DPM 2022 environment. Now, we can start to look into the administration tasks that can be used to configure our environment.

Add storage

Before we start scheduling backups, we first need to prepare DPM 2022 with storage which can be used to store the backups, as well as the initial temporary replica which is created beforehand.

To add disk storage, perform the following:

1. Open the **Microsoft System Center 2022 DPM** console.
2. Go to the **Management** tab.
3. Click on **Disk Storage**.
4. On the top left-hand corner, select **Add**.
5. **Add disk storage:** Once you see the disks you require, highlight it and select the add button where you will see it in the **Selected volumes** pane as shown in *Figure 14.8*. Once done then click **OK** where you will be presented with a notification for the desk requiring formatting to be used within DPM 2022 as seen in *Figure 14.6*. You can also provide a friendly name for the disk so once you see this listed as available storage you will be able to identify the required disks if you have planned for storage to be segregated.

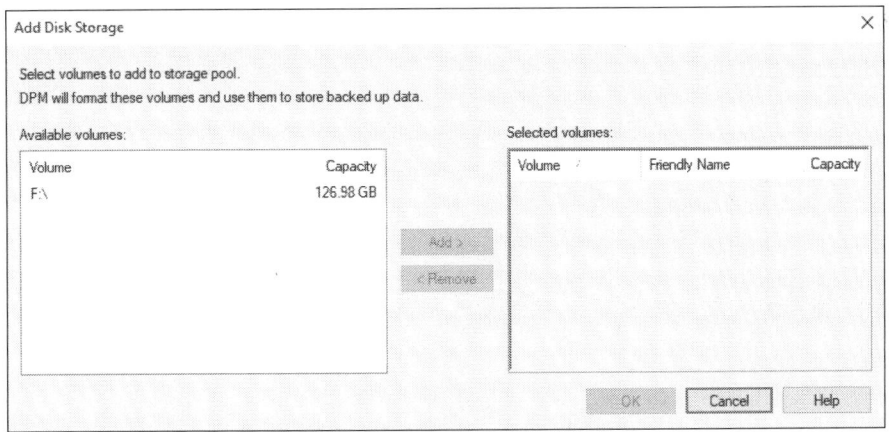

Figure 14.5: Add disk storage wizard

The following figure shows the notification message referenced in *step 5* of adding storage to DPM:

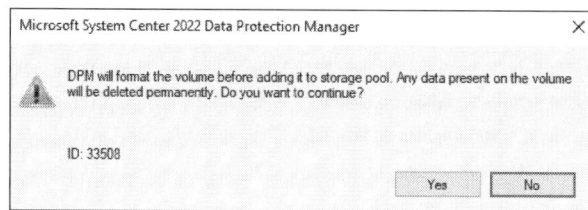

Figure 14.6: Add disk storage format notification

Once completed, you should see your added storage as well as disk details on its status and usage, as shown in *Figure 14.7*:

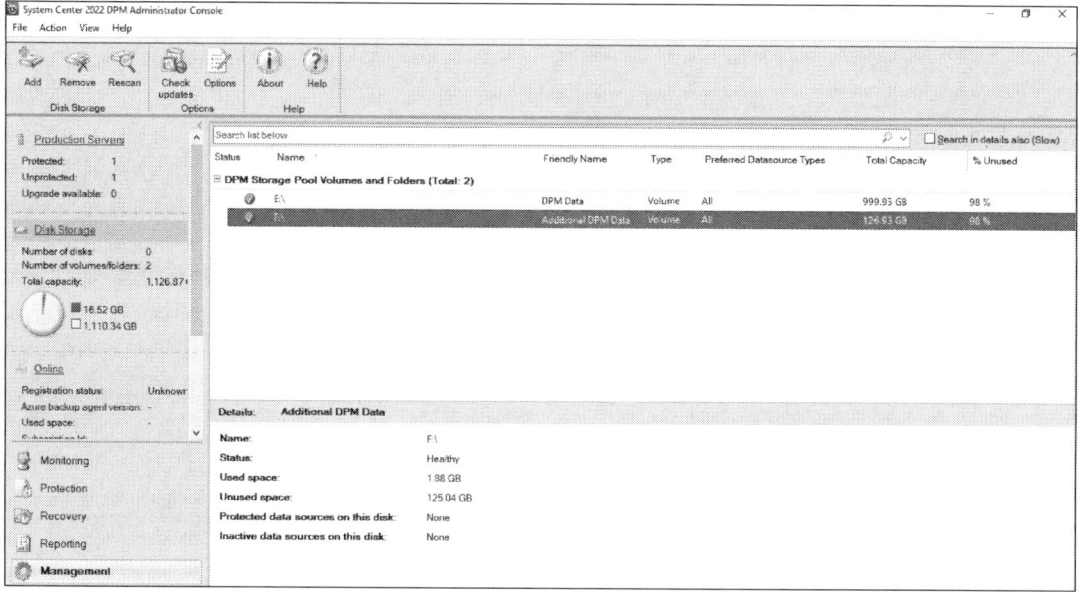

Figure 14.7: SCDPM 2022 disk storage view

> **Note:** This can also be applicable if you are using network storage such as iScsci or fibre channel which is being advertised to the target server which holds the DPM role. Selecting the Rescan button in the view shown in *Figure 14.7* may have to be used to either rediscover or refresh additional disks once they are added.

Add servers

Now, that we have storage ready for our backups, we can look at adding to our fabric by getting some servers managed through the DPM 2022 agent.

Windows servers | Not behind firewall

To add the Windows servers to your environment, perform the following:

1. Open the **Microsoft System Center 2022 DPM** console.
2. Go to the **Management** tab.
3. Click on **Production Servers.**
4. On the top left-hand corner select **Add**.
5. **Select Production Server type:** Windows Servers, then click **Next**.
6. **Select Production Server type: Select agent deployment method** | Select install agents, then click **Next**.
7. **Select computers**: Enter the name of the computer on you have manually installed the agent on, then click **Add** so that it shows on the **Selected computers** section. Then, click **Next**.
8. **Enter credentials**: Enter the credentials having administrative rights to the server to perform the attaching of the agent-managed server to the DPM server, then click **Next**.
9. **Select computers: Choose restart method** | Select if you want to have the server rebooted right after the DPM agent has been installed or if you wish to manually reboot after, then click **Next**.
10. **Enter credentials: Summary** | Review the configuration, then click **Install**.

Note: This can also be applicable if you are using network storage such as iScsci or fibre channel which is being advertised to the target server which holds the DPM role. Selecting the Rescan button in the view shown in *Figure 14.7* may have to be used to either rediscover or refresh additional disks once they are added.

Windows Servers –Behind firewall | Trusted domain

The process here slightly differs from the previous one as this requires you to have the agent installed beforehand, so you are performing an *attached* method of getting the server managed by DPM.

The first part we need to perform is installing the agent manually. To do this, perform the following:

1. Open the installation media.
2. Double-click the `setup.exe` file.
3. On the splash screen, select **DPM Protection Agent**.
4. **Microsoft Software license terms**: Click the **Accept** button once you have read through the license terms.
5. Wait until the process completes, then press *Enter* and close the window:

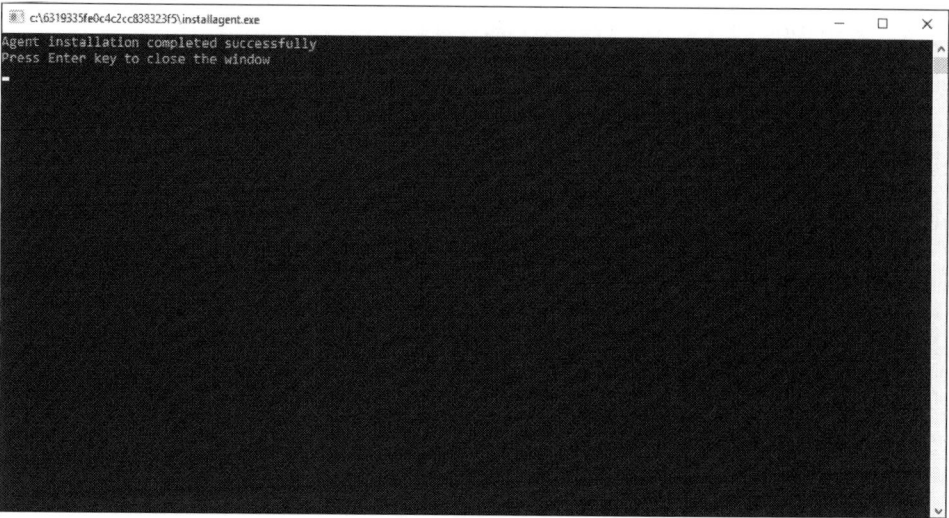

Figure 14.8: *SCDPM 2022 agent installation*

Once the agent has been installed, we can return to the DPM 2022 console and perform the following instructions:

1. Open the **Microsoft System Center 2022 DPM** console.
2. Go to the **Management** tab.
3. Click on **Production Servers.**
4. On the top left -hand corner select **Add**.
5. **Select Production Server type:** Windows Servers, then click **Next**.
6. **Select Production Server type: Select agent deployment method** | Select "**Attach agents**", then select "**Computer on trusted domain**", then click **Next**.
7. **Select computers**: Enter the name of the computer that you have manually installed the agent on, then click **Add** so that it shows in the **Selected computers** section. Then, click **Next**.
8. **Enter credentials**: Enter the credentials that has administrative rights to the server to perform attaching of the agent-managed server to the DPM server, then click **Next**.
9. **Enter credentials: Summary** | Review the configuration, then click **Attach**.

Windows Servers | Behind firewall | Non-trusted domain

To add windows servers which are in non-trusted domains, perform the following steps:

1. Open the **Microsoft System Center 2022 DPM** console.
2. Go to the **Management** tab.

3. Click on **Production Servers.**
4. On the top left-hand corner, select **Add**.
5. **Select Production Server type:** Windows Servers, then click **Next**.
6. **Select Production Server type: Select agent deployment method** | Select "**Attach agents**" then select "**Computer in a workgroup or untrusted domain**", then click **Next**.
7. **Select computers**: Enter the **Fully Qualified Domain Name (FQDN)** in the computer name field and provide the credentials that have administrative rights to perform the attach, then click add until you see the server listed in the **Selected computers** section. Click **Next**, as shown in the following figure:

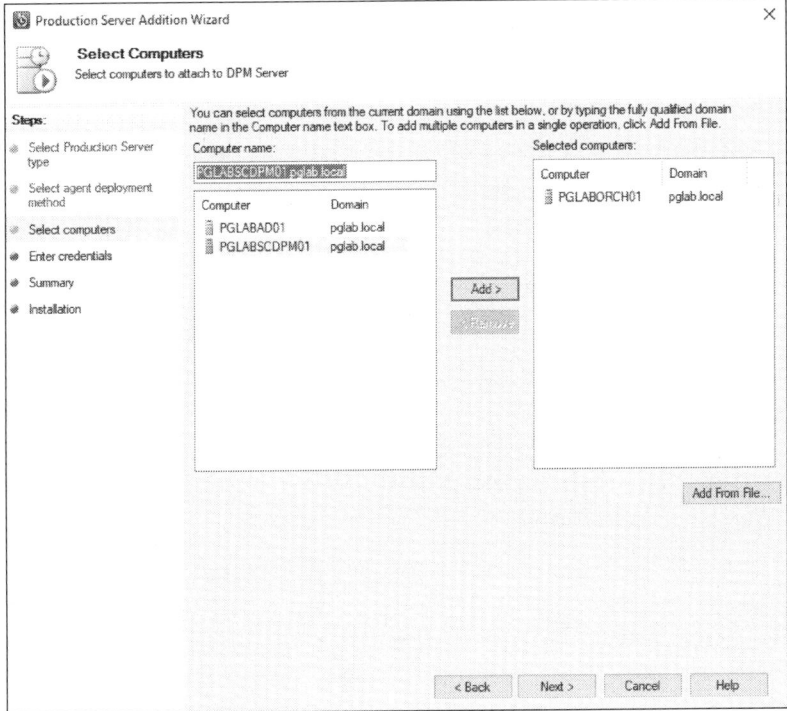

Figure 14.9: Production server addition wizard

8. **Enter credentials: Summary** | Review the configuration, then when ready, click **Attach**.

VMware servers

To add VMware servers to DPM, please perform the following:
1. Open the **Microsoft System Center 2022 DPM** console.
2. Go to the **Management** tab.

3. Click on **Production Servers.**
4. On the top left-hand corner, select **Add**.
5. **Select Production Server type:** Select VMware Servers, then click **Next**.
6. **Select computers: Select VMware Servers** | Enter the name or IP address of the vCenter server or ESXi host to add, then select the specified credential you wish to use. Click the **Add** button until you see the VMware server in the **Added VMware Servers** window. Then, click **Next**.
7. **Enter credentials: Summary** | Review the configuration, then click **Attach**.

Create protection group

At this point, we have storage and servers managed within our DPM 2022 environment. With our fabric updated, we can now proceed into creating a protection group which will allow us to put our backup designs into motion. To do so, perform the following steps:

1. Open the **Microsoft System Center 2022 DPM** console.
2. Go to the **Protection** tab.
3. On the top left-hand corner, select **New**.
4. **Welcome to the New Protection Group Wizard: Welcome** | Click **Next**.
5. **Select group members:** Select **Servers**, then click **Next**.
6. **Select group members:** Select the server components and then select the objects that you want to add to the protection group until you see them listed in the **Selected members** section on the right. When done, click **Next**.
7. **Select Data Protection Method**: Provide a name for the protection group and select the Disk protection method, then click **Next**.
8. **Specify short-term goals:** Select the retention range you want to use and the synchronization schedule. Then modify the file recovery points for what your backup will be using, then click **Next**.
9. **Specify short-term goals: Review disk storage allocation** | Wait for the data size calculation to complete and when ready select the appropriate disk below which you will store the backups on, then click **Next**.
10. **Choose a replica creation method**: Select if you want the replica to be created automatically over the network alongside a scheduled time, or if you want to perform the transfer manually. Then, click **Next**.
11. **Choose replica creation method**: Choose consistency check options | Select if you want to perform a consistency check on your backups depending on the next inconsistency status or if you want to perform one daily, then click **Next**.
12. **Summary: Summary** | Review your configuration, then click **Create Group**.

Manage protection group

Once you have created the protection group, you will see your protection group listed as seen in *Figure 14.10*:

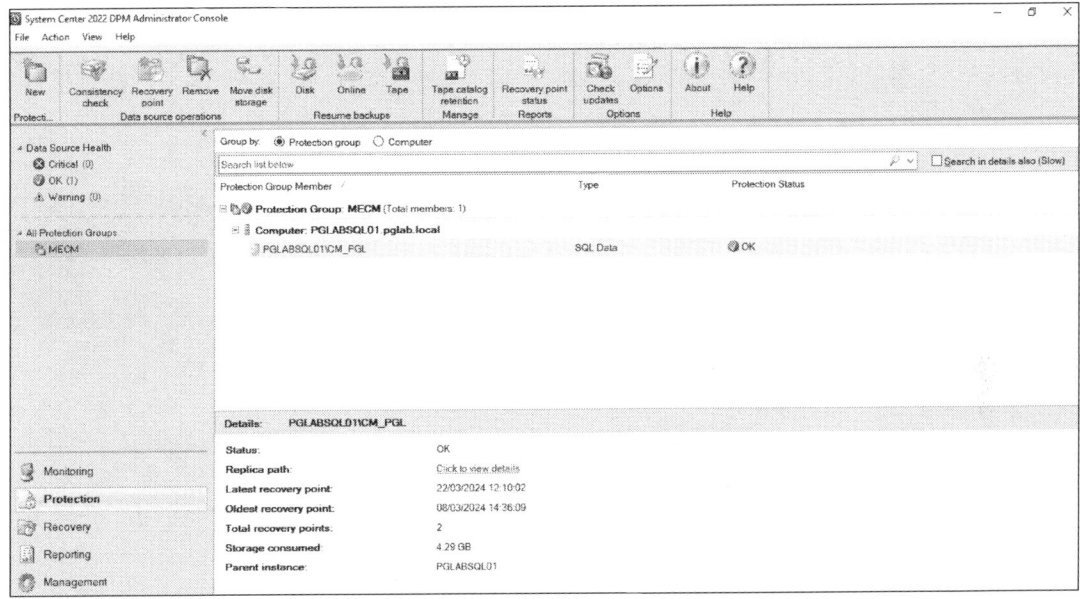

Figure 14.10: System Center DPM 2022 protection tab

With this, you now have some administration options available for your protection group.

Adding new group members

This process allows you to add additional objects to be backed up as part of your protection group.

To do this, perform the following:

1. Open the **Microsoft System Center 2022 DPM** console.
2. Go to the **Protection** tab.
3. Right-click your protection group in the main treeview, as shown in *Figure 14.10*, and select **modify protection group**.

Here, you will be presented with the Modify Group wizard, as seen in *Figure 14.11*, this process goes through similar steps of creating a new protection group:

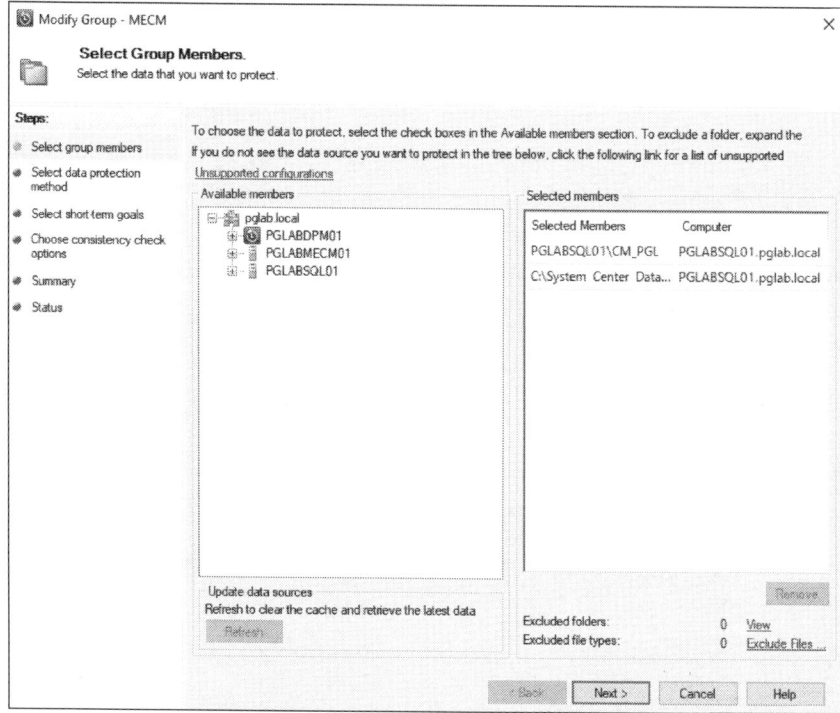

Figure 14.11: Modify group wizard

Perform consistency check

A consistency check goes through the integrity of the backup against the replica to ensure its status is healthy and with view to recover when required.

By default, with protection groups, you would have defined a schedule for when to perform a consistency check for when it would be in a status of inconsistency. However, you can perform an independent check when needed.

To perform this, do the following:

1. Open the **Microsoft System Center 2022 DPM** console.
2. Go to the **Protection** tab.
3. Right-click your protection group in the main treeview, as shown in *Figure 14.20*, and select **Perform Consistency Check**.

Recover from protection group backup

When the time comes for a disaster recovery scenario or to perform a test run to ensure you can perform a disaster recovery **User Acceptance Test (UAT)**, you will have the option to select not only what you want to recover but further options, such as:

- Date and time of the backup you wish to recover.
- Scheduling of when the recovery will take place.
- The backup be recovered on the original server or a different server.

To action a recovery, perform the following:

1. Open the **Microsoft System Center 2022 DPM** console.
2. Go to the **Recovery** tab.
3. In the browse pane, select the objects you have included within your protection group, and you will then see the recovery point times for your protected objects, as shown in *Figure 14.12*. Right-click the object from the **Path** window-pane, then **select recover**:

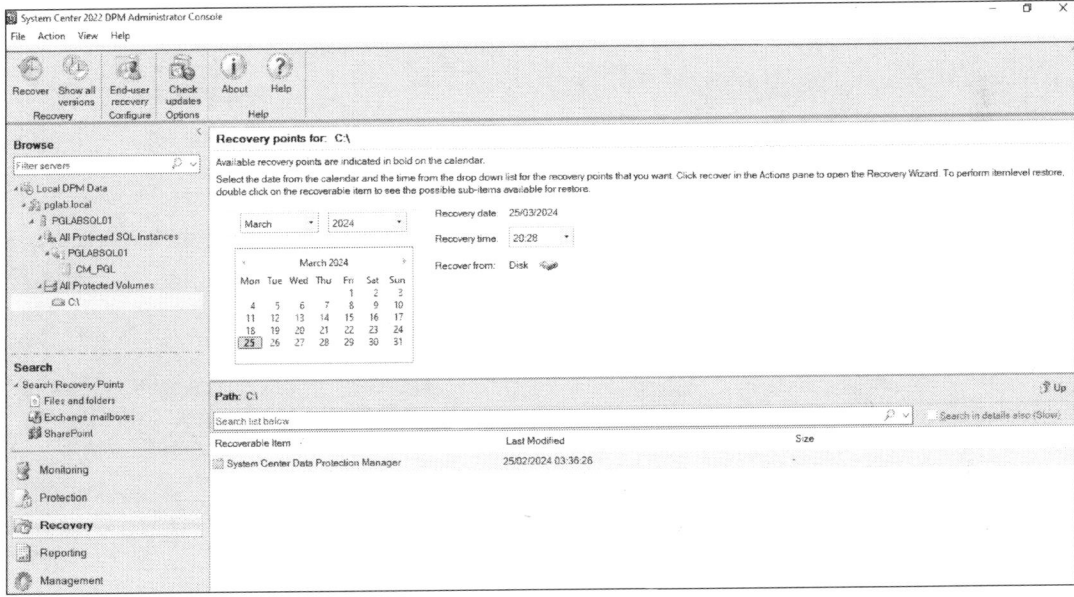

Figure 14.12: System Center DPM 2022 recovery tab

4. **Review recovery selection:** Click **Next**.
5. **Review recovery selection: Select recovery type** | Select the recovery type, then click **Next**.
6. **Review recovery selection: Specify recovery options** | Select what the appropriate action will be on the existing version and its restoring of security settings, then click **Next**.
7. **Review recovery selection: Summary** | Review the configuration and once happy click **Recover** to begin the process.

> **Note:** The instructions listed are based on the recovering of files/folders. If you were to perform this process using a SQL database, then with the product recognition features of DPM 2022 you will see SQL specific options on whether to recover to the original instance or a different instance.

Alert monitoring

For any tasks or jobs you perform within DPM 2022, you will be able to see their status in the Monitoring tab categorized by status, like In progress, completion and failed.

This can be seen in *Figure 14.13*:

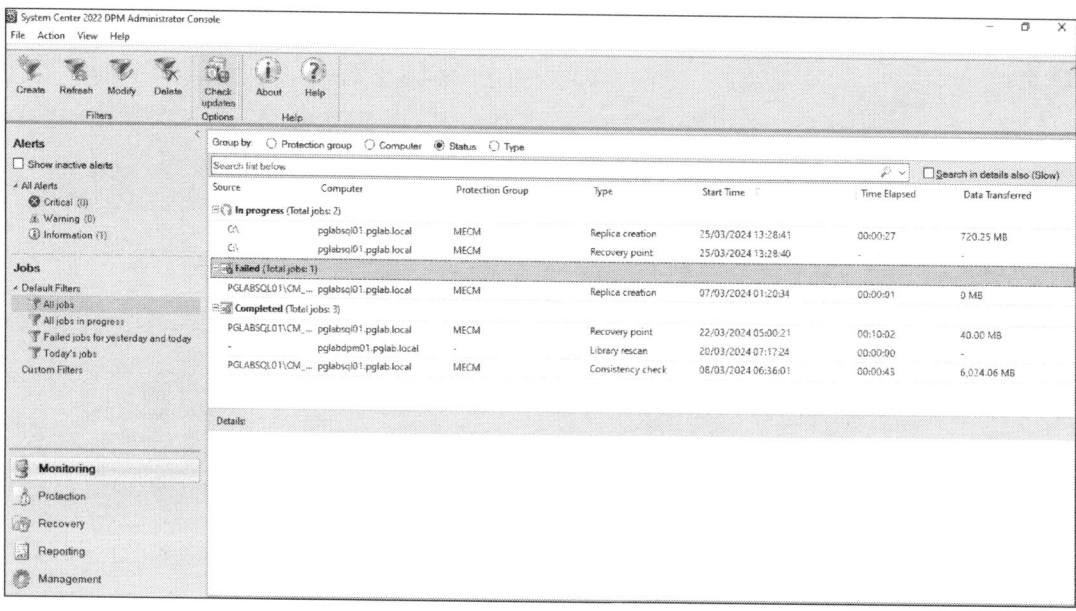

Figure 14.13: System Center DPM 2022 Monitoring tab

Report administration

Default native reports come with DPM 2022 upon the initial installation performed, as well as being the main reason SSRS is required to be installed on the SQL Server.

These can be found in the **Reporting** tab of the DPM 2022 console where you see the following reports' Disk Utilization:

- Recovery
- Recovery Point Status
- Status
- Tape Management
- Tape Utilization

Figure 14.14 shows an example of a status report:

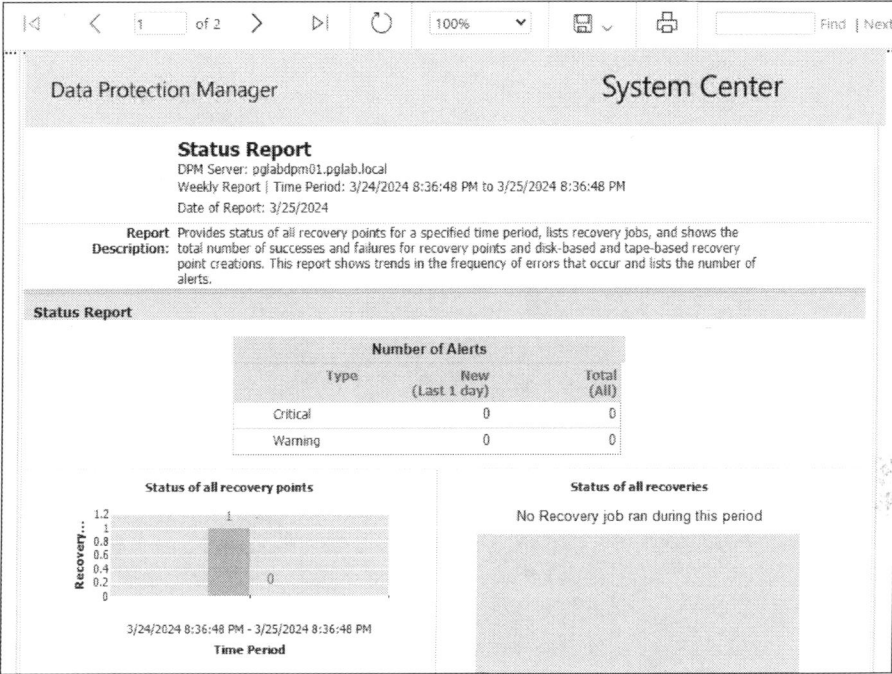

Figure 14.14: System Center DPM 2022 Status Report

Upgrade Data Protection Manager

To ensure that you keep your DPM environment updated, you will need to install the latest Update Rollups that become available for the System Center, which may include a new **update rollup (UR)** for DPM.

At the time of writing this book, the latest version for DPM 2022 is Update Rollup 2 Refresh KB5033755, which can be downloaded from here **https://www.catalog.update.microsoft.com/Search.aspx?q=5033755**

> Note: The UR2 you are seeing is known as refresh. At the time of writing this book, the UR2 released had some issues that needed to be resolved resulted in a refresh UR to be released. To see notes of the original release, you can find this here: https://support.microsoft.com/en-gb/topic/update-rollup-2-for-system-center-2022-data-protection-manager-254d23f2-2adf-46b8-9ec8-27b868073ede

To see all of the fixes and updates of the UR2 refresh, you can go to the following link: https://support.microsoft.com/en-gb/topic/update-rollup-2-refresh-for-system-center-2022-data-protection-manager-cc6dbea6-b0ed-4390-8a7f-e59af8dd1ec0

Before performing the update install, you need to ensure the following things beforehand:
1. Make a backup of the DPM 2022 SQL database.
2. Update the DPM 2022 server first.
3. Update the DPM 2022 protected server agents.

To perform the installation, do the following:
1. Download the UR updates from **https://www.catalog.update.microsoft.com/Search.aspx?q=5033755**
2. You should have three files downloaded: one for the DPM server, central console server, and the management shell.
3. Double-click the **DPM-kb5033755 file:**

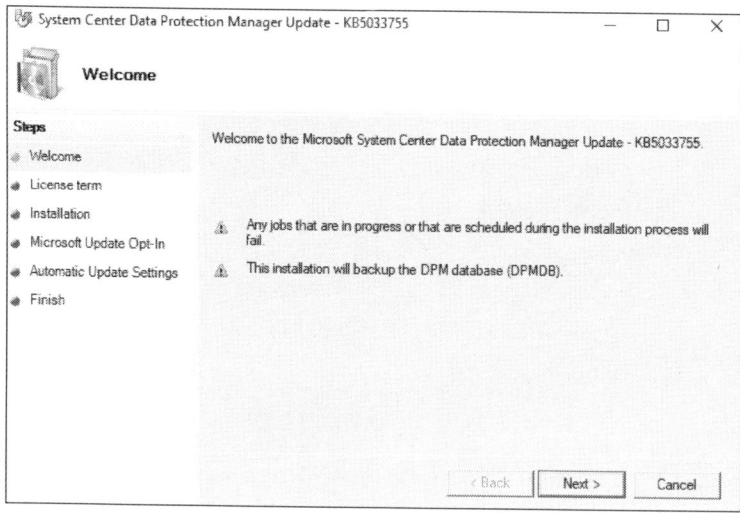

Figure 14.15: System Center DPM Update Wizard

4. **Welcome: Click Next.**
5. **Microsoft Software License Terms: Read through the license terms, then click I agree, then click Install.**
6. **Installation: Wait for this part to be completed and it will automatically proceed to the next step.**
7. **Microsoft update opt-In: | Select if you want to use Microsoft Update to automatically check for updates for DPM, then click Next.**
8. **Microsoft update opt-In: Automatic Update Settings | (Seen only if you ticked yes on the preceding step) Define the schedule for when you want the updates to be checked, then click Next.**
9. **Installation completed: Finish | Click close.**
10. **Double-click the dpmcentralconsoleserver-kb5033755 update.**

11. **Wait for this to complete, then close the command prompt window.**
12. **Double-click the dpmmanagementshell-kb5033755 update.**
13. **Wait for this to complete, then close the command prompt window.**
14. **Reboot the DPM 2022 server.**

Once this has been completed, you can then start to upgrade the protected server agents in the console.

To do this, perform the following:
1. Open the **Microsoft System Center 2022 DPM** console.
2. Go to the **Management** tab.
3. **Select the Production Servers on the left-hand side. You should also see a statistical breakdown of upgrades available.**
4. **Right-click the servers which are protected by an agent and select Update.**
5. **Once upgraded the servers, will need to be rebooted in order for the changes to take effect.**

Best practices

Here we will go through all of the best practices which are applicable for DPM. These help to ensure that you administer the product in the best way possible.

Disk pool structure

When utilizing disk storage for DPM, ensure that the disks only have sufficient amount, but also are part of a bigger infrastructure where your disks information is being backed up, so you do not have any downtime when it comes down to a disaster recovery situation.

Real-world scenarios

Real-world scenarios help us understand what is currently being done in most environments and are reflective of scenarios which apply when best practices might not necessarily the right thing for that environment.

Tape backup

Though there remains a heavy emphasis of utilizing tape backup technologies to store your backups as well as using them as protected storage, the reality of this is that tape backup technology is rarely used and, in most cases, considered obsolete. Especially taking in consideration the introduction of Azure backups (will be covered in the next chapter) as well as the continued usage of file and storage services.

Product placement against other third-party products

DPM is unfortunately not commonly used when it comes to other products heavily used for backup, such as Veritas. It is unfortunate that, as a product, this integrates well with all its System Center counterparts, and having this framework can really enhance how you perform your backups.

Conclusion

With DPM 2022 concluded, we can see that although the product does not contain a vast or complicated list of functions and tasks other than to construct precise and granular backup scheduling, its simplicity is what gives it the power to showcase what it can do for your environment, though may also be the reason of the product being overshadowed.

Overall DPM 2022 is a solid tool to use and with its product recognition capabilities, you really can start to design DR solutions all within a System Center recognized workflow.

In the next chapter, we will look at how we will analyze how we can use the System Center Suite (and Configuration Manager) to help us construct and manage an environment within a hybrid setting where both on-premise and cloud environments are integrated.

Points to remember

- DPM requires storage to be added to utilize the backing up of data from protection groups.
- VMware credential manager allow adding ESXi hosts to be protected by protection groups.
- Consistency checks are used to check the integrity of the backup being taken against the replica backup.
- DPM contains default reports for disk utilization, status of jobs and recovery point information.

Multiple choice questions

1. Name the methods used to backup storage from a protection group.
    a. Online Storage
    b. Tape Storage
    c. Disk Storage
    d. SD Card Storage

2. When protecting servers that are behind the firewall, it is not required to install the agent on the server beforehand.

   a. True

   b. False

3. DPM does not require the use of domain credentials as service accounts.

   a. True

   b. False

4. What do you need to run to allow DPM 2022 to install to a remote SQL Server?

   a. DPM Central Console

   b. DPM Remote Administration

   c. DPM Protection Agent\

   d. DPM Remote SQL Prep

5. If you want to add additional objects from different servers into your protection group, how is this achieved?

   a. Recreate protection group.

   b. Modify the protection group.

   c. Turn off protection on the servers.

   d. Rename protection group.

6. What is one of the reasons why you may not want to have a frequence consistency check on backups?

   a. Increased CPU resource usage.

   b. Failing backups.

   c. Unable to recover.

   d. Upgrade of DPM agent by mistake.

Answers

1. a, b, c
2. b
3. a
4. d
5. b
6. a

Key terms

- **DPM**: Data Protection Manager
- **DR:** Disaster Recovery
- **ESXi**: Elastic Sky X Integrated
- **UR:** Update Rollup
- **SQL**: Structured Query Language
- **VM**: Virtual Machine
- **FQDN**: Fully Qualified Domain Name

Join our book's Discord space

Join the book's Discord Workspace for Latest updates, Offers, Tech happenings around the world, New Release and Sessions with the Authors:

https://discord.bpbonline.com

CHAPTER 15
Standardizing Management and Governance for Hybrid Settings

Introduction

Another wave or addition to the overall System Center suite is the hybrid environments which we come across. Now this area is heavily debated due to the number of complexities around the overall designing of this type of environment as well as understanding the actual benefits which come from a hybrid environment as well.

In this chapter we will be discussing the previously mentioned and the policies that will have an overall effect between a hybrid setup and how System Center can work within this.

This chapter will look to cover the Cloud aspects that will play quite an integral part within this chapter, which adds another interesting layer to the centralized management covering both on-prem and Cloud-based solutions.

Structure

This chapter will cover the following topics:
- Managing hybrid environments using Microsoft System Center

- Governance policies and compliance across hybrid infrastructure
- Integrating Cloud platforms for centralized management

Objectives

Now that we have covered all the System Center products, which have taken a look into the on-premises side, the next objective is to look closer at these products to show the reader how they can help for the management and integration of the Cloud environments that you have.

In this chapter, you will identify various ways of technology helping bridge the gap between the centralization and management of both your on-premises and Cloud environment.

Managing hybrid environments using Microsoft System Center

For organizations that have not made a full transition to modern management, they will be utilizing a hybrid environment which will allow them to be active within both on-premises and the Azure environment.

This type of structure helps those who might be unable to switch over to Azure completely, since it can be quite a complicated structure to manage as well as maintain.

The Microsoft System Center suite (as well as Configuration Manager) are able to provide features and functionality which can help the administration of a hybrid environment. We will look into specific products within the suite and detail exactly what they provide in terms managing a hybrid environment effectively.

Microsoft Configuration Manager

Though no longer in the System Center suite, Configuration Manger is perhaps one of the core technologies that can be used to help manage the hybrid environment, with its integration with endpoint manager (also known as Intune, which we will cover more in the *Governance policies and compliance across hybrid infrastructure* section.).

So, let us cover and recap the following areas of interest:

- **Co-management**: Co-management is the structure where devices can be controlled by both the Configuration Manager and Endpoint Manager (Intune) or can be changed to be solely managed by one product. There are workloads in which both technologies shared, and in order to be able to toggle to which workload a technology can be responsible for is defined by the affinity controls.

The configuration for Co-management can be viewed within *Chapter 4, Microsoft Configuration Manager: Deployment and Administration* to understand the step-by-step process on how this is essentially set up from using the Cloud Attach feature in the Configuration Manager.

- **Cloud Management Gateway (CMG)**: CMG allows for devices that are not within an office network on a regular basis and where devices can connect to an internet-based management point server which will route them back into the on-premises Configuration Manager.

  Technically speaking, a CMG is not necessarily a feature that has much bearing on the management of a hybrid environment. The definition of a hybrid environment is more to do with devices registered in both Entra ID and Configuration Manager; however, in cases where CMG is used, it is perceived as getting close to the point of being ready to get into modern management. CMGs are registered within Azure as a virtual machine set (from version 2203) which is used to balance the availability of the CMG that connects into an internal Configuration Manager server role named a CMG connection point.

  Where Endpoint Manager would take over this side is where the management of remote devices would be concerned as they do not require an agent installation like how Configuration Manager does. Although, a CMG can still be used even with Endpoint Manager looking after those devices at a certain point the bigger picture would be to utilize Endpoint Manager primarily until some analysis has been done to transition into modern management, excluding Configuration Manager from the picture.

- **Autopilot reporting**: In the Configuration Manager, you have native reporting which contains some interesting information which can aid in the assistance of managing hybrid environments, with one example being the native report which contains a list of all the devices hardware hashes.

  Now, hardware hashes are used to upload devices into Autopilot in Endpoint Manager. This is a process in which, the most common cases are performed by a manual import of a CSV file, which may contain just one hardware hash after running a script; in this case with the report in Configuration Manager, you can export these in bulk for all Configuration Manager managed devices which can then be imported into Autopilot all at once.

> **Note:** This is useful if devices have not been imported into Autopilot already or if they are managed in Endpoint Manager but have not had an Autopilot Profile assigned to a group that contains these devices.

Figure 15.1 contains an example of how this report looks:

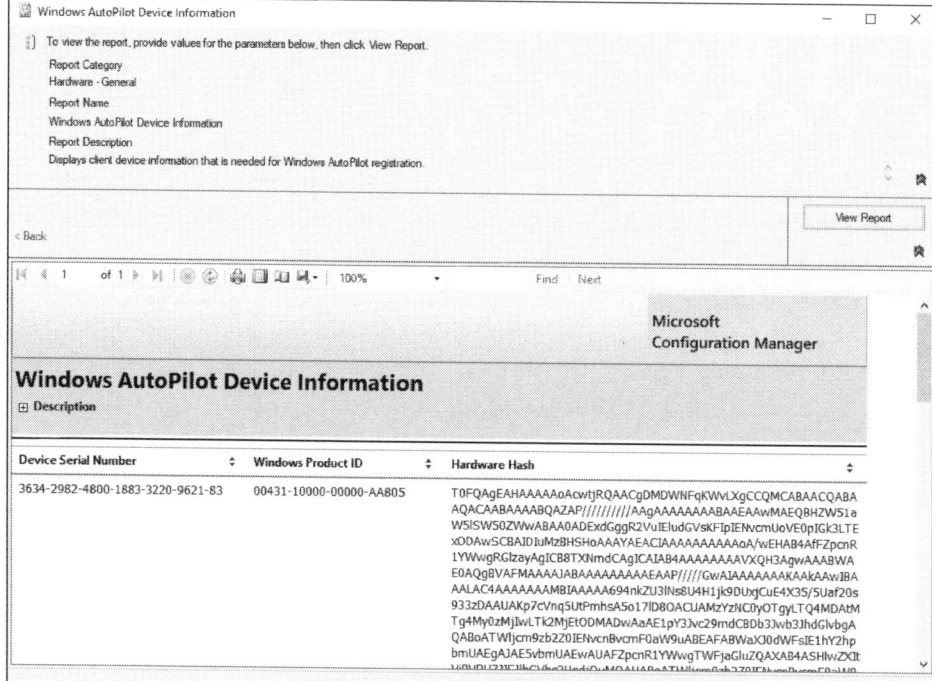

Figure 15.1: *Windows Autopilot device information report*

This report can be found in the **Hardware | General** section and is known as the Windows Autopilot Device Information.

Once this report has been run, you can then export this into a CSV format, which you can then import into the Autopilot portal at **https://intune.microsoft.com**

- **Task sequence onboarding**: Task sequences are done within the Configuration Manager in order to build bare metal machines and have them managed within Configuration Manager.

With the plan being to transition into hybrid and then eventually full modern management, there is an option in which you can develop a task sequence which will allow you to onboard your devices from Configuration Manager into Intune with Autopilot. This works well for hybrid environments and when building devices at a company standard level for where you still require Configuration Manager. This can be leveraged to allow devices to be onboarded in this manner whether you are using co-management or not.

Before you can go ahead to create the task sequence you first need to download the Autopilot profiles from Intune and formulate these into a JSON file which would then be packaged within Configuration Manager.

A detailed step-by-step guide can be seen on how to do this from the link here: **https://learn.microsoft.com/en-us/autopilot/tutorial/existing-devices/setup-autopilot-profile**

To develop a task sequence to perform a function such as this can be done by performing the following steps:

1. Open the **Microsoft Configuration Manager** console.
2. Go to **Software Library** | **Operating Systems** | **Task Sequence**.
3. Right-click and select **Create Task Sequence**.
4. **Create New Task Sequence:** Select the **Deploy Windows Autopilot for existing devices**, then click **Next**.
5. **Task Sequence Information: Specify task sequence information** | Enter the task sequence name and select a boot image to use for your task sequence, then click **Next**.
6. **Install the Windows Operating System:** Select the image package you will use and then enter a valid product key to use if not using another form of activation. Select if you will use a randomly generated password for your local administrator account or if you will define one, then click **Next**.
7. **Install Configuration Manager:** Install **the Configuration Manager Client** | Confirm the Configuration Manager client package being selected and add any additional installation properties which might be required, then click **Next**.
8. **Include updates: Include software updates** | Select if you want to have software updates applied during the build then click **Next**.
9. **Install applications:** Select any applications that you want to add to the task sequence build, then click **Next**.
10. **System preparation: Prepare System for Windows Autopilot**: Select the package that contains the JSON file package of your Autopilot profile, then click **Next**.
11. **Summary**: Confirm the settings | Review the information of your task sequence, then click **Next** to complete the creation.

If we open up the task sequence, we can have a better view of the structure of the specific step that does the applying of the Autopilot profile, as seen in *Figure 15.2:*

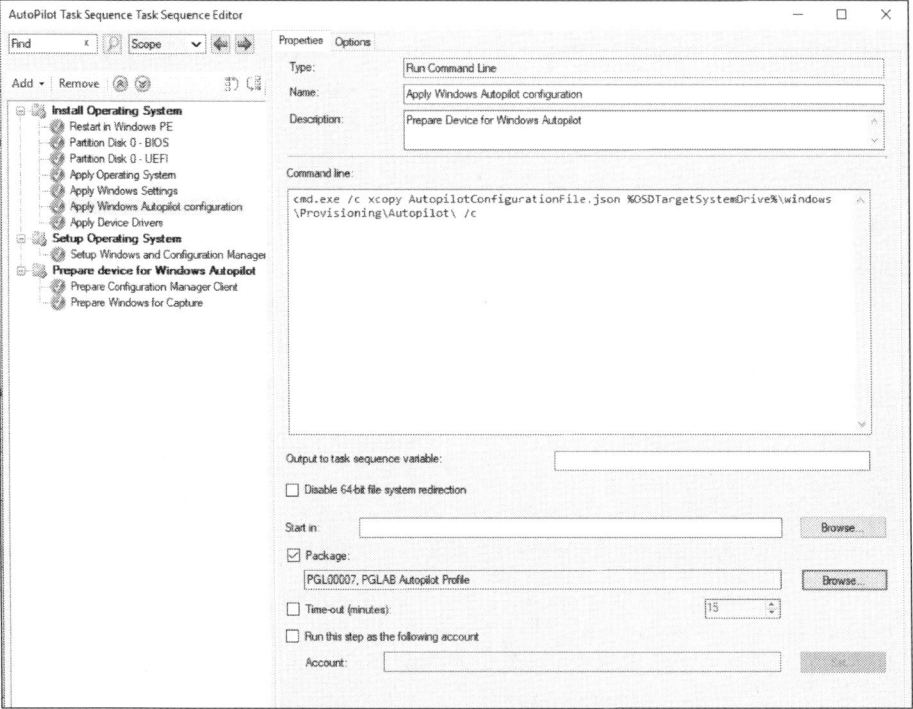

Figure 15.2: *Autopilot task sequence*

You can also view the package that has been selected which is the same as what we had picked within the wizard before the creation of the task sequence.

Once this has been done, you can then deploy this task sequence to a collection that contains these devices.

> **Note: Technically, you could have this available to All Unknown Computers if you wanted, but this would really be assuming that every device would want to be assigned to that Autopilot profile. If you do have a generic Autopilot profile you wanted to use which all devices from Configuration Manager would be part of then by all means you can perform it this way.**

To deploy the task sequence, let us perform the following steps:

1. Open the **Microsoft Configuration Manager** console.
2. Go to **Software Library** | **Operating Systems** | **Task Sequence**.
3. Right-click and select **Deploy**.
4. **General: Specify general information for this deployment** | Select the collection you want to deploy to. Note a specific collection will apply to only those devices whilst "**All Unknown Devices**" will make it available for all devices. Click **Next**.

5. **Deployment Settings:** Specify settings to control this deployment | Select from the **Make available to the following** and select the appropriate option for how you want the Task Sequence to be made available, then click **Next**.

> Note: If this has not been mentioned in the book already, then I would advise not to change the Purpose to Required. Required means ASAP without any prompt or user interaction and for task sequences depending on the need this can cause major issues. Tread very carefully around this option.

6. **Scheduling: Specify the schedule for this** deployment | Click **Next**.
7. **User experience: Specify the user experience for the installation of this software** | Make any changes necessary to the user experience, then click **Next**.
8. **Alerts: Specify Configuration Manager and Operations Manager alert options**: Configure any alert options which you require, then click **Next**.
9. **Distribution points: Specify how to run the content for this program** | Select the run options for your task sequence, then click **Next**.
10. **Summary**: **Confirm the settings for this new deployment** | Review the deployment configuration for your Autopilot task sequence deployment, then click **Next** to create the deployment.

Governance policies and compliance across hybrid infrastructure

Going forward, once you have established your environment within the hybrid state, the next part will be to start formulating policies that will be used to configure, customize and validate compliance within your environment. This is achieved by using Intune.

In the past, Configuration Manager was also able to have similar functions of control for policies natively, but these features have since been retired where governance policies are primarily used within Intune, and the focus is around a hybrid infrastructure group policy is also a factor.

Intune

When we look into Intune, we have different types of policies we can look into, such as the following:

- Compliance policies
- Hybrid Autopilot profiles
- Configuration files
- Conditional access
- Group policy analysis

Compliance policies

These types of policies ensure that any managed devices are compliant with a specific-criteria before they can access company resources within the network.

By default, the first condition when devices are managed or onboarded into Intune is to check if they have a compliance policy assigned to them and if they have met the criteria to be a compliant device.

Where a hybrid environment is concerned, it is important for devices in general to be compliant, but if you are managing devices that are either co-managed with Configuration Manager or if they are in a hybrid environment between on-premises and Intune, then you may want to set up some compliance policies which may reflect this.

Let us take a look at the forming of a compliance policy to fit this type of scenario. Here, we want to have devices that need at least a default policy to be compliant against, so we form a policy based on the platform of devices that we have and, in this case, it is Windows devices.

So, we would start to create a compliance policy with the following compliance rule configuration, as seen in *Figure 15.3*:

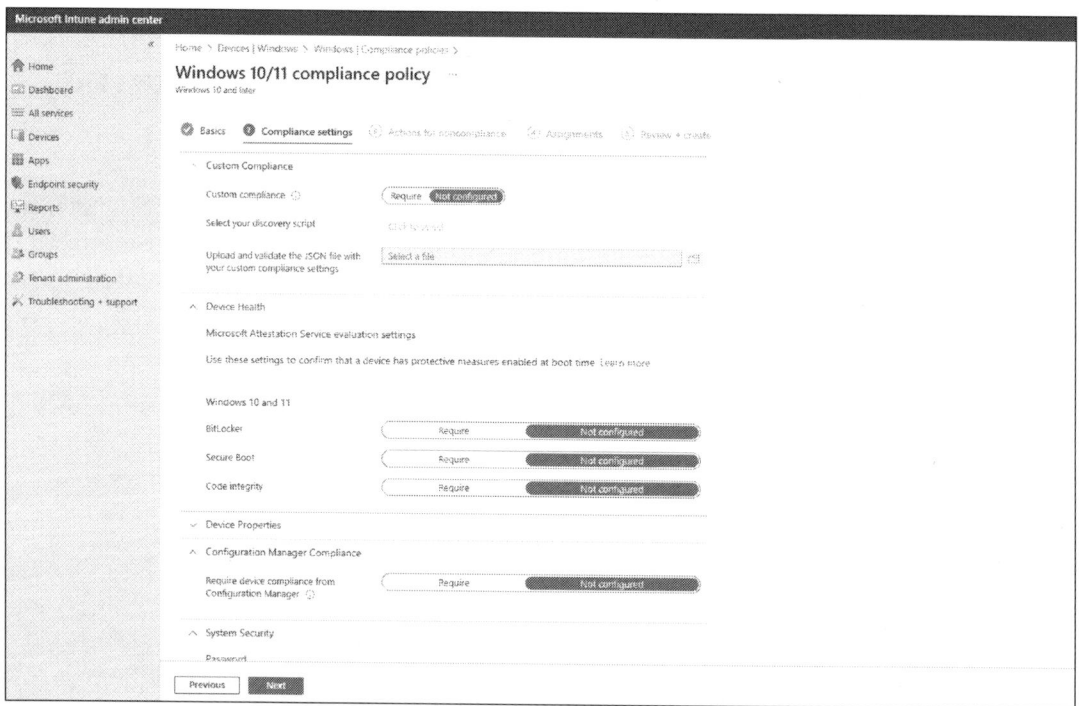

Figure 15.3: *Windows 10/11 compliance policy*

If you notice the lower part of *Figure 15.3*, there is an option that can be used for Configuration Manager compliance that allows for co-management compliance between both Configuration Manger and Intune. Now, this option works for environments that are co-managed between both technologies.

> **Note: Do not get confused between co-management and hybrid. Co-management means that a device is managed by both technologies whilst hybrid generally means that a device is managed by an on-premises domain and Entra ID. Though co-management is mostly common in hybrid environments the terms should not be confused.**

Once we have defined how we want our compliance policy structure set, we want to structure how we will handle devices that do not meet the compliance requirements next, this can be seen in *Figure 15.4*:

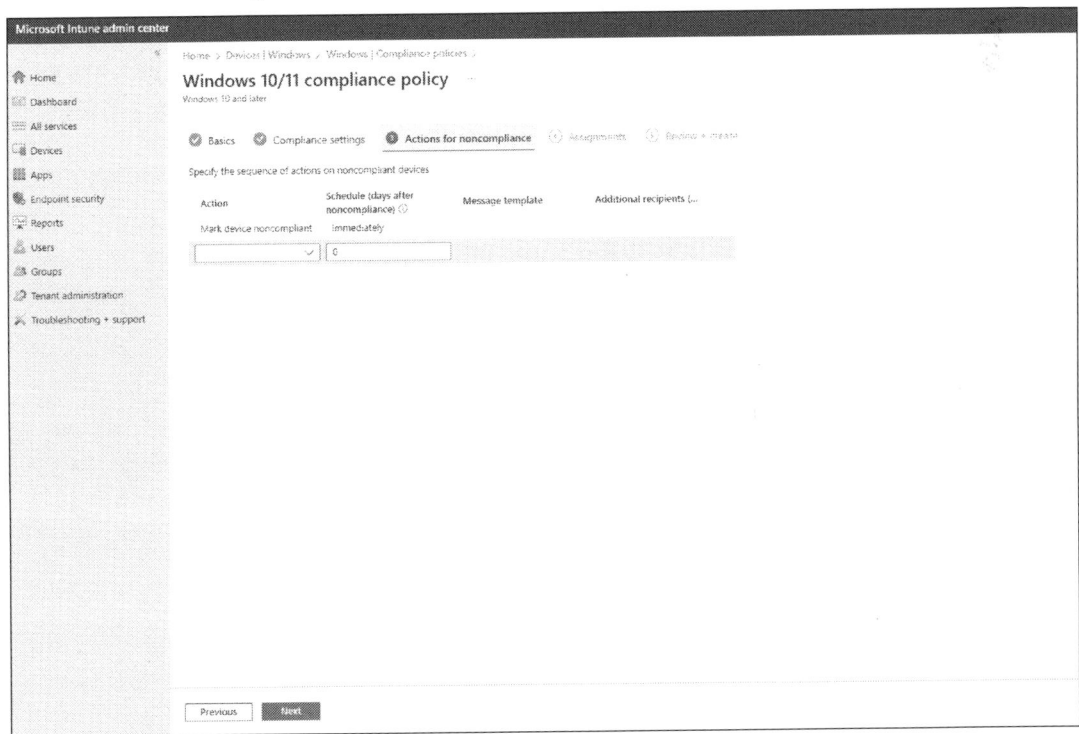

Figure 15.4: Actions for noncompliance window

By default, the immediate action is to mark the device as compliant, but you also can configure additional options, such as:

- **Add device to retire list**: This will retire the device from Intune, but can perform this after a certain number of days that have passed once the device has been marked as non-compliant.

- **Send email to end user**: After being found non-compliant, an email can be sent to the user and additional recipients are required to inform them of the non-compliance. This part does require further configuration in the "**Notifications**" section of Intune.

The last part to complete is the assignment of the group to which this compliance would apply. This will carry into the next section, in which we will discuss the significant role Hybrid Autopilot profiles play.

Here, we need to understand how our Intune estate is looking and if it is any of the following:

- All devices hybrid joined
- Mixture of hybrid and Entra ID joined
- All devices Entra ID joined

Now, it is not uncommon to have multiple compliance policies depending on the reasons and how far the segregation will go for devices, but if you happen to have all devices in one specific joined state then it maybe best to utilize one compliance policy fitting for the company standard to which devices should adhere to.

Hybrid Autopilot profiles

However, if you want to separate the devices from hybrid-joined devices, what you could do is create groups within Intune which will be just for hybrid devices from either a dynamic or assigned rule which can be assigned to your Autopilot profile.

In this case, devices being onboarded in this manner will automatically go into the group we defined for this. It would have a compliance policy assigned to the same onboarded devices, which would allow you to maintain the separation between both, as we can see in *Figure 15.5*:

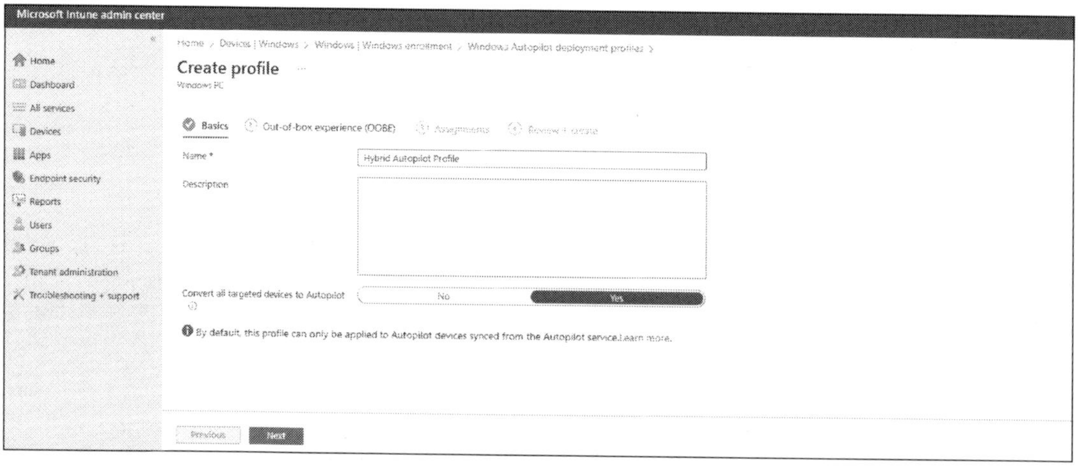

Figure 15.5: Autopilot profile creation

When we look at the configuration of an Autopilot profile, let us see how this can play a part in how we manage our hybrid estate. With the first initial option of **converting all targeted devices to Autopilot**.

Now, how this plays a part is if you want to separate devices that were hybrid joined or any type of criteria you defined, the assignment group for this Autopilot profile would convert any devices that are already managed in Intune which are *not* registered in Autopilot as Autopilot devices. So, any devices that have been onboarded by a different avenue, which are hybrid, would then be registered to be an Autopilot device where it can go through the process at any time, whether this is from an Autopilot reset, wipe, or a reset my pc option.

Proceeding into the next step of a hybrid Autopilot profile within *Figure 15.6*, we select the hybrid Autopilot option that will allow the devices to be onboarded and joined not just to the Entra ID, but also to your on-premises domain. More can be seen in this process in *Chapter 3, Streamlining OS and Optimizing Application Deployment with Microsoft Configuration Manager*, and *Chapter 4, Microsoft Configuration Manager: Deployment and Administration* of this book.

The hybrid autopilot configuration can be seen in the following figure:

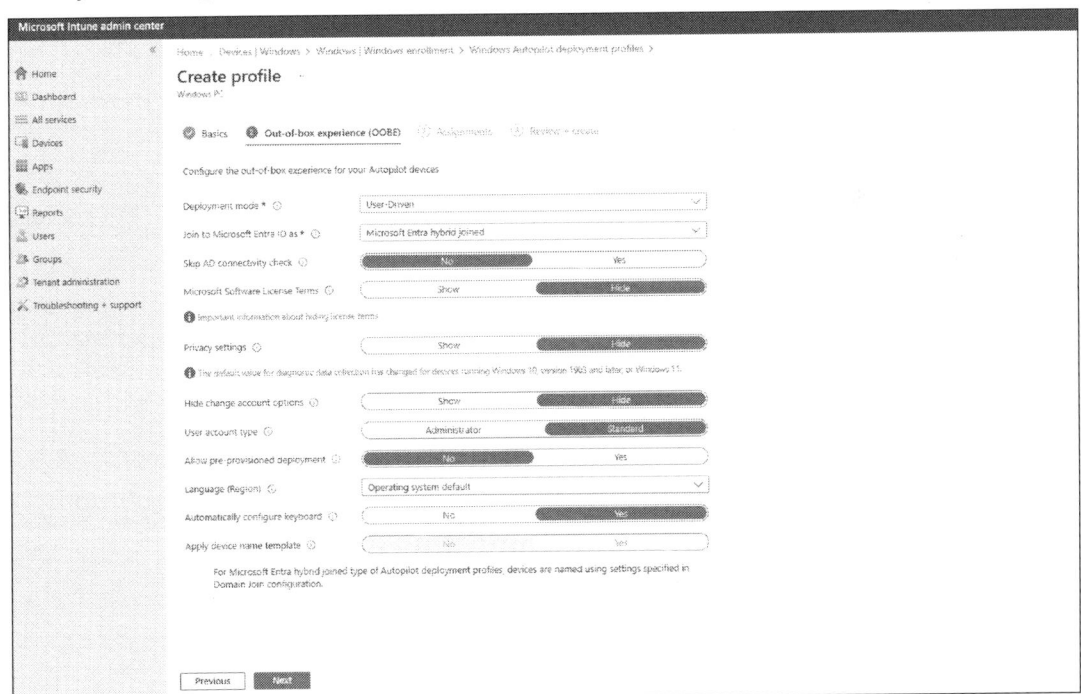

Figure 15.6: *Hybrid Autopilot configuration*

Group policy to Intune migration

With this structure, you will have the option to create configuration profiles which can replicate the same function as group policies within your on-premises domain.

Migrating group policies can support whether you are actively working on the transition to go into full modern management or if you want to retire specific policies within your on-premises domain to be utilized primarily within Intune in general.

One feature that can allow you to not only analyze these options and provide you within an option to migrate is the **Group Policy Analytics (GPO)** feature within Intune.

This is where you can export your GPO policies in an XML format and upload them into the group policy analytics, where it will output a result to showcase which policies are supported within Intune and which are not, as seen in *Figure 15.7*:

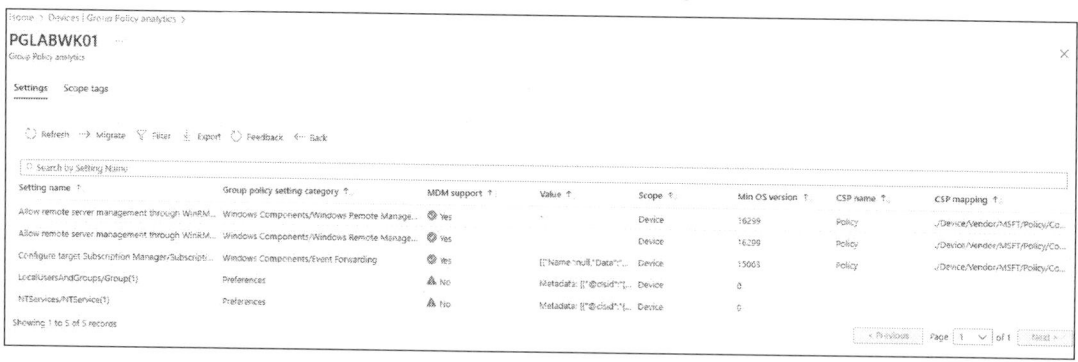

Figure 15.7: *Group Policy migration results*

Here, you have an option to migrate them directly into a configuration profile and with option to review the GPOs which cannot be carried over, but can be structured differently to be able to provide the same company standard settings.

> **Note:** If any GPOs do flag as unknown or unsupported, this means there may not be a configuration profile or compliance policy which will fit it. This could still be achieved by means of scripting methods of PowerShell, or perhaps other configuration items may have alternative settings which maybe able to provide a similar or more enhanced version of the GPO which you were looking to migrate over.

Integrating Cloud platforms for centralized management

Various products within the System Center stack also provide great integration points for Cloud services, such as Azure and Office 365.

In this topic, we will look into the rest of the products to understand how they can integrate with Cloud computing platforms.

System Center Operations Manager

Azure and Office 365 Monitoring

Operations Manager 2022 has native management packs and connectors that allow you to connect directly to your Azure environment and to your Office 365 environment allowing you to integrate the monitoring into your hybrid environment.

Management packs

This may perhaps be more on the advanced side. Typically, management packs on just the perspective of the XML code would be more applicable for an on-premises environment. Some third-party management packs (including Microsoft) may have some other forms of connecting to another technology or Cloud plugin from the use of agent-based or forms of **Simple Network Messaging Protocol** (**SNMP**) polling.

However, it is possible to have a management pack that can use a method such as oAuth authentication, which can help to plug into an enterprise application registered with your Azure environment allowing you to pull information from your hybrid environment. It will also allow you to start structuring monitors for the information you are able to poll from your custom application within your Cloud environment.

In summary, further integration can be achieved from the writing of a management pack to include authentication protocols to have communication with areas of your hybrid environment.

To learn more about oAuth authentication, you can read more about this here **https://oauth.net/articles/authentication/**

System Center Virtual Machine Manager

Azure profiles

In the *Chapter 11, Virtualization with System Center Virtual Machine Manager,* and *Chapter 12, Deployment and Administration of System Center VMM,* we covered mostly the on-premises profiles but one which we did not cover was the Azure profiles.

These are used to help add virtual machines to your server hosting fabric. They can then be managed by your Azure environment from assigning them to either the Azure Update Management for the Cloud patching process, or to be managed with basic actions as an Azure Virtual Machine using the Azure VM Management profile.

To find out more about the Azure VM Management feature for VMM 2022 this can be found here **https://learn.microsoft.com/en-us/system-center/vmm/manage-**

azure-vms?view=sc-vmm-2022 and for the Azure Update Management this can be found here **https://learn.microsoft.com/en-us/system-center/vmm/vm-update-management?view=sc-vmm-2022**

To configure this please perform the following:
1. Open the **Virtual Machine Manager** console
2. Go to **Library** | **Profiles** | **Azure Profiles**
3. Right-click and select **Create Azure Profile**.
4. **General:** Enter a name for your profile and select the correct Cloud provider for your Azure environment. Next enter a valid Subscription ID for your Azure environment then select to which profile type you will use.
5. **Update Management/Azure VM Management** | Configure the authentication then click **Next**.
6. **Summary** | Review the configuration, then click **Create**.

System Center Data Protection Manager

Online Backups: Data Protection Manager has also the ability to allow for backups to be done through online storage via your Azure environment using Azure Backup.

Azure Backup allows for backups to be done into the Cloud however it does require an active subscription to this service firstly, which more can be found about this here: **https://azure.microsoft.com/en-in/products/backup/**

Once you have this then the next action to be done would be to install the Azure Backup Agent on the DPM server which will then allow to start the development of online storage to use for your on-premises backups within DPM managed machines.

Conclusion

More and more environments are transcending into the hybrid way of working, whether this is down to being at a safe point to assess their readiness to go fully into the Cloud or to simply having the best of both worlds. However, on either scenario, we can see how the various products within the System Center suite and Configuration Manager can help manage and maintain the integration between both worlds.

The goal is to display and enable the reader to utilize everything that has been learned about each product which can integrate with the Cloud, but also how the Cloud can integrate with the same on-premises products, starting with the foundation of the Entra ID synchronization with your on-premises Active Directory domain.

The next chapter will conclude the whole book to understand what we have learned as well as analyzing the future trends which System Center and Configuration Manager will take.

Points to remember

- Configuration Manager stands is a core component for integration with Microsoft Endpoint Manager (Intune).
- Microsoft Endpoint Manager has the ability to co-manage your Configuration Manager environment with affinity controls for policy control.
- Group policies can be migrated to Microsoft Endpoint Manager to ease the transition for the future of being managed by Entra ID.
- Operations Manager can integrate with Azure and Office 365 to perform extended monitoring capabilities.
- DPM can integrate with Azure to perform extended backup capabilities for online storage backup solutions.

Multiple choice questions

1. What is the name of the process that is used to manage devices by deploying a profile for Azure AD or Hybrid Azure AD devices?
   a. AD Connect
   b. Autopilot
   c. Co-Management
   d. Enrollment Status Page

2. What is the name of the process which allows for migration of Group Policies to be turned into policies within Microsoft Endpoint Manager?
   a. Group Policy Analytics
   b. GPEdit.msc
   c. Configuration Profiles
   d. Compliance Policies

3. Which product is used to integrate with Azure and Office 365?
   a. Virtual Machine Manager
   b. DPM
   c. Configuration Manager
   d. Operations Manager

4. What is the name of the template used to help create SQL Server virtual machines?
   a. SQL Server profile
   b. Application profile

c. Capability profile

d. Hardware profile

5. Select other ways in which devices can be onboarded into a Hybrid Environment?

   a. Co-Management

   b. Operations Manager management packs

   c. Online backups

   d. Task sequence deployment via Configuration Manager

6. Operations Manager has the ability to have management packs imported which can monitor other areas of the Cloud.

   a. True

   b. False

Answers

1. b
2. a
3. d
4. a,b
5. c
6. a

Key terms

- **CMG**: Cloud Management Gateway
- **SNMP**: Simple Network Managing Protocol
- **MP**: Management Pack
- **DPM**: Data Protection Manager
- **SCOM**: System Center Operations Manager
- **GPO**: Group Policy Object
- **AD**: Active Directory
- **ID**: Identity

CHAPTER 16
Conclusion and Future Trends

Introduction

As we now reach the end of this book, we want to have an in-depth summarization of everything we have gone through per each technology within the System Center suite, as well as the entire family in general. This involves all the key concepts and our overall understanding of the book.

We will also look into the future of the System Center to see what is in store for us in areas such as roadmaps, futuristic trends, and the overall advancements made within the System Center, which will accommodate all of those changes.

This will be our conclusion chapter and will ensure that the reader has a thorough understanding of the System Center, and it's the latest version.

Structure

This chapter will cover the following topics:
- Recap of key concepts and learnings
- Future trends in data center management using System Center

Objectives

Now that we have covered all the System Center products and taken a look into the on-premises side, the next objective is to look closer at these products to show the reader how they can help with the management and integration of the Cloud environments that you have.

From this chapter, you will identify various ways of how each technology has its own way of bridging the gap between centralization and management of both your on-premises and Cloud environment.

Recap of key concepts and learnings

Now that we have reached the final chapter of the book, we will recap the key elements of each technology and the overall importance they play within your environment as well as analyzing the suitability and unsuitability of the product depending on the scenarios faced.

Microsoft Configuration Manager

The Configuration Manager is an important and integral piece to the System Center suite even if, now officially it is no longer part of the suite.

We must also understand that this product now firmly sits as a milestone for organizations to remain at the midway point of being within a hybrid environment with the goal of transitioning into modern management using Intune/endpoint manager.

Those who want to remain in an on-premises environment will find the Configuration Manager to be a powerful technology suite within itself. It will prove a strong user case to be utilized for appropriate centralization management of their environment with various options to extend into the Cloud for management of devices that may sit in hybrid or remote working scenarios.

However, administrators or stakeholders are encouraged to diligently assess the scalability and, more importantly, the longevity of using the Configuration Manager as there is debate over its long-term existence. So, it is advisable to plan ahead in this particular scenario.

System Center Operations Manager

Best summarized as a powerful monitoring solution, which within reason, can monitor anything and everything. Operations Manager boundaries can most certainly be pushed depending on the methodologies used to provide bespoke monitoring solutions, which can be done natively but can be elevated through means of management packs.

Management packs ultimately play a huge role in your monitoring, especially where there may be applications that are bespoke or perhaps may not have an official product management pack already in place where you would possibly have to seek a third-party provider for a management pack-based solution to have ultimate support for that product.

An administrator will find that being proficient in knowing how to develop and write XML within Visual Studios and additional third-party tools, such as **Visual Studios Authoring Extensions (VSAE)** will provide tremendous benefits.

With everything being said about the monitoring of other systems, it is also important to note how crucial the maintenance of **System Center Operations Manager (SCOM)** systems are, which is to ensure that your monitoring solution is pushing out correct data, as incorrect monitoring information can be just as damaging, if not even more, than having no monitoring solution at all.

System Center Service Manager

To keep a solution which can fill all of your **Information Technology Service Management (ITSM)** needs, then Service Manager is a great way to do this.

Overall, the Service Manage compliments all the integrations within your System Center family suite as well as the backbone Microsoft products required to keep your environment managed.

Having said this, the Service Manager can, at times, be overshadowed by other products within the same space, specifically technologies, such as ServiceNow being a very popular ITSM tool. However, the Service Manager has the capability of not only maintaining core Microsoft products of centralized management, but also its ability to integrate into ServiceNow also, if you want to go down this route.

Bear in mind that the same type of boundaries can be stretched for the Service Manager, in the same reminiscence way how the Operations Manager can do this by its usage of management packs.

Management packs evidently play an interesting part in the Service Manager, but not just on how you can develop custom ones to build your own ITSM frameworks. You also have the option to integrate with the Operations Manager to allow the expansion of the **Configuration Management Database (CMDB)** population of the Service Manager, so you have a full-scale inventory of your environment also.

Its overall place in the future can be tricky with the transition again being focused around Cloud management, and as the Service Manager does not boast any Cloud type capabilities, is where the demand and requirement for a technology such as this may decline in value. Those who want to stay within a hybrid environment will find this technology vastly useful.

System Center Orchestrator

A glue that can hold everything together is a great way of describing the overall function which the Orchestrator plays.

With the previous chapters, we dived into how powerful this technology is, though it is not a significantly big tool. Its integration components bring the System Center, Microsoft, as well as third-party products together, making it a great choice.

The best way to summarize its overall pros is its adaptability to building automated workflows, which can consist of normal **Buisness As Usual (BAU)** tasks together to formulate a granular workflow.

In terms of its cons, it works out similarly to its pros. Meaning that in order for you to understand how to fully utilize this technology, you need to have an in-depth understanding of what tasks your IT team is carrying out on a regular and non-regular basis. Knowing this information is key to fully equip the Orchestrator the role of formulating these automated tasks.

Task automation, while has great benefits, can also pose huge risks overall if they are not structured correctly as well as having a meaningful purpose. This applies to automation in general let alone bringing into the fold other System Center technologies, which can cause catastrophic results if automated incorrectly (famously Configuration Manager) and then as well adding a technology such as Active Directory into the fold.

System Center Virtual Machine Manager

To recap the Virtual Machine Manager, this is a technology overall will help you to centralize all of your Microsoft Hypervisor estate. The reader should understand how the tool is possessed to handle the virtual environment with just as much granularity and centralization as other competing technologies, such as VMware ESX servers managed by a vCenter.

Also taking into account its scalability in the future with it being able to integrate well within your Azure environment to allow for further interaction of VDI machines and making use of setting up your own private Cloud infrastructures from this technology.

A part of the recap is to note the versatility of the product where we have full control on building bare metal servers, as well as looking after the lifecycle of patching vulnerabilities from various in-house roles which the Virtual Machine Manager has such, as the update server and PXE servers.

It is also key to know how you will choose to design the Virtual Machine Manager around your environment with its added complexities of being able to automate, or dynamically deploy virtual **Configuration Items (CI's)** across your estate, and being able to take full advantage of the profiles, templates as well as carefully maintained estate is key. The

Virtual Machine Manager, being applicable to all technologies in general, will work in the environment you maintain.

It means that if you have hypervisor servers which are not maintained in security, capacity and availability, it can be quite harmful to the Virtual Machine Manager, hence preventing you from adding the scalability you require to move forward.

System Center Data Protection Manager

Data Protection Manager is best summarized as the technology that you may have but did not think you needed. Its simplicity is perhaps what makes it appealing along with completing a very important area within your environment lifecycle, that is, providing the ability to prepare for disastrous scenarios.

Data Protection Manager, overall, has quite an uncomplicated infrastructure, meaning that there are not really many roles other than just the main management server and the agents that report to it.

Storage can be sourced locally from disk-attached storage, file server services and with further integration into the Cloud with Azure backup storage.

To view and see how Data Protection Manager can be utilized in the future is to view where the future roadmap is within your environment, as the backing up and integration features of Data Protection Manager can aid quite well with the versatility of being within the hybrid environment, and eventually making the transition into modern management.

Future trends in data center management using System Center

With the System Center holding up strong, there are various things to watch out for, such as the latest releases and planning for its overall future and purpose within the IT sector.

System Center 2025

Recently, the arrival of System Center 2025 has been announced, due to be available in the latter part of 2024.

The confirmed products of System Center 2025, will be the following:
- Virtual Machine Manager
- Data Protection Manager
- Operations Manager
- Service Manager
- Orchestrator

To see more information on the System Center 2025 release, viewed the following link: https://techcommunity.microsoft.com/t5/system-center-blog/announcement-system-center-2025-is-here/ba-p/4138510

Configuration Manager updates

Keeping on top of the latest Configuration Manager updates is another part of the overall due diligence which takes place when being a System Center administrator. The latest version to be released at the time of writing this book is 2403.

To see the new features available for this version, visit the following link: **https://learn.microsoft.com/en-us/mem/configmgr/core/plan-design/changes/whats-new-in-version-2403.**

To ensure that you can start pulling in new updates to be available for you to start upgrading or be in preparation for upgrading, Figure 16.1 shows the section where you will view these updates:

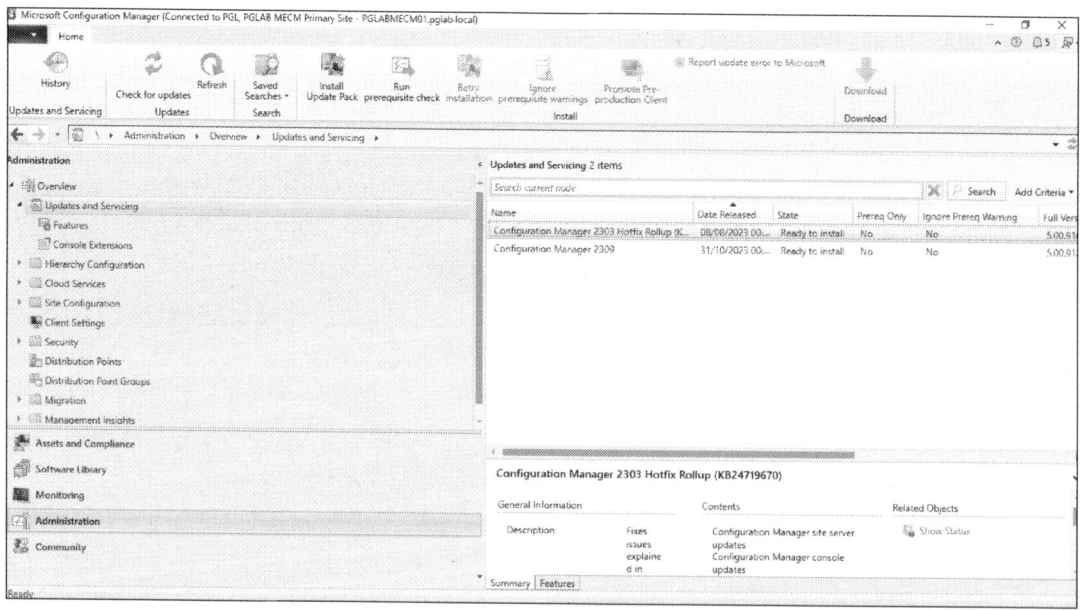

Figure 16.1: *Configuration Manager Updates and Servicing console view*

Not only that, but new features grow with each version, including a pop-up window that will help the administrator be notified of any of the latest bulletins regarding the Configuration Manager in general or specific areas within Configuration Manager. This can be seen in *Figure 16.2*, which is normally seen from the initial launch of the console:

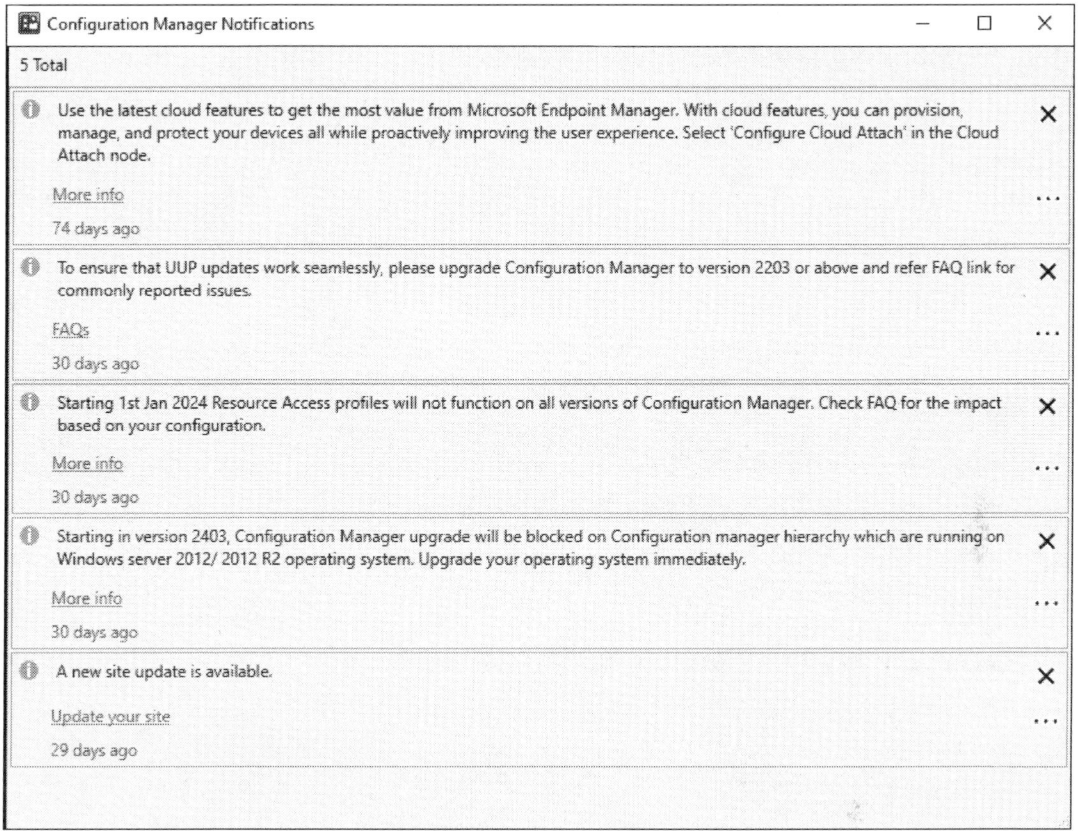

Figure 16.2: Configuration Manager Notification window pop-up

Entra ID and modern management

Modern management, as the next logical step, is becoming an increasing demand across all organizations that are able to go this route, assuming that they do not have any legacy-dependent components that will hold them back from moving forward.

Modern management is known for the present as well as future trends as more and more organizations start to transition into this area.

Entra ID is a new name that is getting more popular, which, by definition, is the new name for an Azure Active Directory and is, of course, playing a crucial part in identity and access management. It is a checkpoint to which a lot of organizations are moving or at the very least, synchronizing within their hybrid environment linked between both the on-premises active directory and the Entra ID information.

Figure 16.3 shows the dashboard page of Intune which shows vital statistics of your Modern Management:

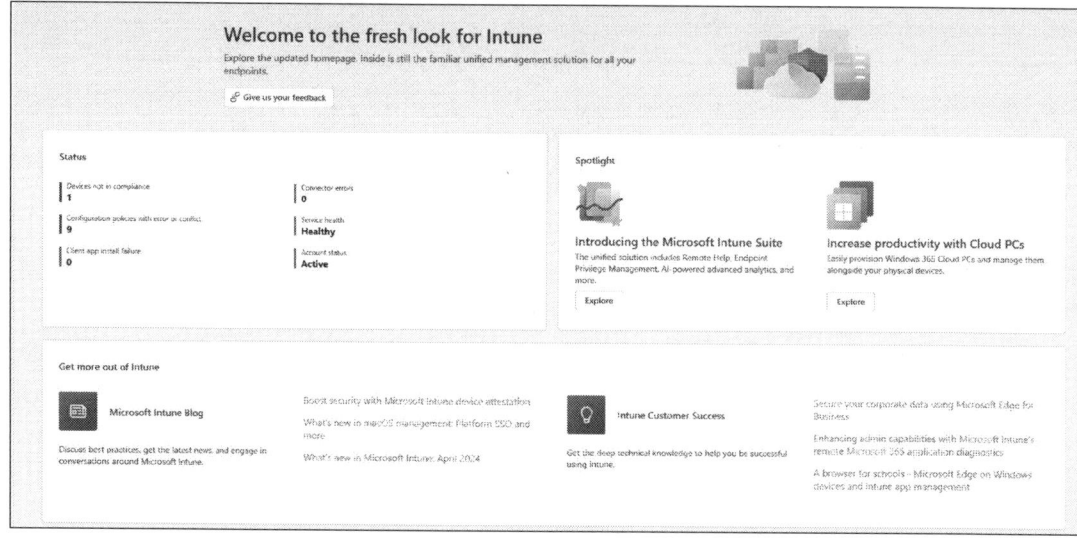

Figure 16.3: Intune dashboard page

Future of the System Center

With the System Center 2025 on the horizon and the current Configuration Manager updates still being produced, all the preceding sections mentioned, come together to illustrate a bigger summary of keeping your ears to the ground for the latest updates.

Notable links to follow

Activity within the community is always thriving with knowledge and information when it comes to areas such as:

- System Center
- Entra ID
- Modern management
- Configuration Manager

To have your ears to the ground and to see the latest trends, here is a list of notable groups, websites, and newsletters which is great to look out for as a starting point:

- **Modern endpoint management group**: It is a great group on LinkedIn and has regular and rapid content around Intune, modern management, Entra ID, Configuration Manager, and much more.
- **SCOMathon:** It is a huge hub for all things Operations Manager, with several Microsoft MVPs and SCOM experts regularly sharing content and performing live webinars and presentations for the latest advancements in SCOM. Each year a big

event is conducted called the SCOMathon, and the next event is the upcoming SCOMathon 2024.
- **Intune newsletter by Andrew Taylor:** A talented author, blogger, and Microsoft MVP, *Andrew Taylor*, has a newsletter that consists of the latest contributions within the community for areas such as Intune and modern management. These are super beneficial to get the scoop on the latest that the technical community has to offer.

Conclusion

Now, we have reached the end of the book.

To summarize – the main goal of this book was to cover the entire System Center suite, Configuration Manager, and Intune to give a more in-depth generalized breakdown of how every product works, how they can be integrated, and, more importantly, its core usage.

A lot of IT Professionals might be proficient in one or perhaps two more, but what we want to do here is shed light on the products that the reader may not be fully familiar with so that we are able to address and close the skills gap between them.

Even though products, such as Data Protection Manager might be singled out as the lesser used product, that may not necessarily apply to everyone as you can easily find an IT administrator who is just as unfamiliar or in the dark with a product such as Configuration Manager or Operations Manager.

In this chapter, we want to provide in-depth aspects of each and outline their powers individually, and integrated.

Where future trends are concerned, the IT industry already moves at a rapid pace, so the System Center stack and Endpoint Manager are no different. Hence, it is always important to stay ahead of the game to understand the latest and greatest things that affects them all.

References

- *Modern Endpoint Management Group* - **https://www.linkedin.com/groups/8761296/**
- *SCOMathon* - **https://scomathon.com/**
- *Intune Newsletter by Andrew Taylor* - **https://andrewstaylor.com/**

Join our book's Discord space

Join the book's Discord Workspace for Latest updates, Offers, Tech happenings around the world, New Release and Sessions with the Authors:

https://discord.bpbonline.com

Index

A

Active Directory Service
	Interfaces (ADSI) 64
ADSI, steps 64
Autopilot 51
Autopilot, methods
  driven autopilot 51
  pre-provisioning 51
Azure Monitor 112
Azure Monitor, aspects
  log analytics 114
  Operation Manager,
	integrating 114
  SCOM 113

C

CAS, aspects
  Directory Schema,
	extensions 63
  Firewall, optimizing 66, 67
  pre-installation,
	prerequisites 67, 68
  primary site, installing 68-71
  SQL Server 66
  Windows ADK 64
CAS Hardware, requirement
  clients 42
  disk, space 41
  manager roles, configuring 40, 41
  site system 40

CAS, prerequisites
  OS Server, installing 61
  server, features 61
  server roles 60
  WSUS, database 61
CAS, sites
  primary 38, 39
  secondary 39
Central Administration Site (CAS) 38
CMDB, key areas
  item classes, configuring 172
  up-to-date, information 171
Co-management 13
Co-management, workloads
  click-to-run, apps 48
  client apps 48
  compliance, policies 47
  device, configuring 47
  endpoint, protecting 48
  resource access, policies 48
  window update, policies 48
Configuration Manager 11-13
Configuration Manager, administration
  active, directory 81
  client account, installing 82
  cloud attach, managing 85
  device, deploying 84
  device, discovering 81
  group boundary, setup 83
  roles, adding 79
Configuration Manager, components 77-79
Configuration Manager, concepts
  central, administration 71-73
  primary site, optimizing 74, 75
  site server, configuring 73, 74

Configuration Manager, future trends 368
Configuration Manager, key point
  Cloud Management Gateway (CMG) 36
  management point 35
Configuration Manager, key steps
  consolidate 54
  multi-server, environment 54
Configuration Manager, role
  asset, intelligence 53
  legacy device, managing 52
  vulnerability, patching 52
Configuration Manager, topology
  consolidate 36, 37
  multi-server role 37
  site server 37

D

Data Protection Manager (DPM) 312
Data Retention 110
DPM, ability
  operations, managing 316
  product, recognition 314, 315
  System Center Orchestrator 316
  VMware, managing 315
DPM, architecture
  environment, upgrading 341, 342
  group, managing 337-339
  protection group, creating 336
  server, optimizing 332
  storage, adding 331
  VMware, server 335
  window, server 333

DPM, aspects
  data retention,
      planning 317, 318
  protection group,
      structuring 317
DPM Backup,
      configuring 329, 330
DPM, best practices 343
DPM, infrastructure 319, 320
DPM, key concepts 367
DPM, key points
  firewall, requirements 327, 328
  server, managing 324
  SQL, server 325
DPM, role
  central, console 312
  server, managing 312
DPM, scenarios
  tape backup 343
  third party, placement 344
DPM, structure
  hardware, requirement 313
  OS, requirements 313
  single management server 312
  SQL, requirements 313

E

Enrollment Status Page
      (ESP) 51
Entra ID 369
Entra ID, future trends 369

H

Hybrid Entra ID 48
Hybrid Entra ID, components
  Domain Join, profile 52
  Intune AD Connector 52

Hybrid Entra ID, prerequisites
  device setting, configuring 49
  Entra ID, connecting 48
  MDM Policy, configuring 48

M

Management Packs, types
  community-based management 105
  management pack, authoring 106
  microsoft management 103, 104
  third-party management 104
  Visual Studio VSAE 106, 107
MECM, best practices
  administration 88
  assets, compliance 90
  monitoring 89
  software library 89
MECM Real-World, scenario
  administration 91
  assets, compliance 92
  Monitoring 91
  software library 92
Microsoft Intune 46, 47
Microsoft Intune, key points
  application, migration 49
  prerequisites, managing 49
  update process, migration 50
Microsoft System Center
  about 2
  architecture 3
  products 2
Microsoft System Center, areas
  autopilot, reporting 349
  Cloud Management Gateway
      (CMG) 349
  Co-management 348
  task sequence, onboarding 350

Microsoft System Center, aspects
   SCO 7, 8
   SCOM 3-5
   SCPDM 10, 11
   SCSM 8-10
   SCVMM 6
Microsoft System Center,
      key concepts 364
Microsoft System Center, policies
   compliance 354-356
   GPO 358
   hybrid autopilot, profiles 356, 357
Multihoming 111
Multihoming Disaster, recovery 112
Multihoming, environments 112
Multihoming, purposes 111
Multihoming, scenarios 111
multi-runbook server,
      installing 239-241

O

Operating System Deployment
      (OSD) 12
Operations Manager, administration
   Azure Log Analytics,
      setup 148, 149
   construction, console 139, 140
   installation media, adding 145, 146
   management packs, installing 138
   new agents, adding 143
   Operational Manager, console 144
   resource pools, creating 141
   Run-As Account, creating 141
   Run-As, profiles 142
   UNIX/Linux, creating 142
   UNIX, operations 147, 148
   Window Agent, adding 144

Operations Manager, best practices
   administrate, optimizing 153
   alerts view, creating 152
   environment, testing 154
   management packs, tuning 153
Operations Manager, lab
   demilitarize zone server 116
   multihoming server 117
   multi-management server 116
   single management server 115
Operations Manager,
      world scenario 154
Orchestrator 212
Orchestrator, aspects
   data protection, integration 223
   integration packs 215, 216
   Microsoft-based integration,
      packs 217
   native integration, packs 216, 217
   SCVMM, integrating 221, 222
   service manager, integrating 221
Orchestrator, best practices
   consoles, integrating 258
   effective error, handling 256, 257
   integration pack,
      connections 256
   PowerShell, handling 258
Orchestrator, causes
   data store, configuring 228
   DPM, integrating 228
   runbook, servers 227
Orchestrator, key points
   integration packs, configuring 244
   manager task, deploying 241, 242
   rollups, updating 255
   runbooks, creating 247
   runbook servers, deploy 243

Orchestrator, roles
  runbook, designer 212
  runbook, server 212
  server, managing 212
  Web API, service 213
  web, console 212
Orchestrator, scenarios
  authorization, clearing 259
  DCOM 259
  integration pack,
       upgrading 258
  runbook, limits 259
Orchestrator, structures
  hardware, requirement 214
  multi-runbook server,
       topology 213
  OS, requirement 214
  single runbook server,
       topology 213
  SQL, server 214
Orchestrator, topology
  consolidated 228
  scalable 229
OS, key terms
  role, limitations 45
  server, supporting 43, 44
  windows 10, supporting 44
  windows 11, supporting 44

P

Performance and Resource
    Optimization (PRO) 307
PXE Servers 270

S

SCO, key concepts 366
SCOM, features
  account, dependency 23
  alert closure, enrichment 22
  azure migrate, integrating 23
  enhancement, tracking 23
  experience, enhancing 23
  FQDN, alerts 23
  NTLM 22
  RBAC 22
  REST API 22
  SHA2, supporting 22
  sort, overrides 23
SCOM, key concepts 364
SCOM, key points
  data retention 110
  hardware, requirements 101
  management, packs 103
  Microsoft 365 110
  operation manager,
       limitations 102
  OS, requirements 101
  override strategy 109
  run-as, account 108
  SQL Server 102
SCOM MI 113
SCOM, topologies
  demilitarize zone 100
  multi management 100
  operation manager, roles 98, 99
  single management 100
SCSM Environment, terms
  active directory,
       setting up 195

alert connector,
    setting up 196
configuration manager,
    setting up 196
data warehouse,
    setting up 193, 194
Operation Manager CI,
    setting up 198
Orchestrator Connector,
    setting up 198
Virtual Machine Manager,
    setting up 199
SCSM, key concepts 365
SCVMM, key concepts 366
SDK, levels 76
Self-Service Portal 199
Service Management
    Automation (SMA) 224
Service Manager 158
Service Manager,
    best practices 207
Service Manager, concepts 185
  data warehouse server 180
  data warehouse, server 191
  firewall, requirements 185
  key backup, encrypting 188
  management server 180
  prerequisites 183
  self-service, portal 181
  server, instructions 186
  server role, console 182
  SSRS, prerequisites 189, 190
  Window Server OS,
      installing 182
Service Manager, connector
  active directory 164
  alerts, synchronizing 165
  center orchestrator 165

configuration manager 164
data warehouse 163
exchange 166
pack, integrating 166
SCOM 164
SCVMM 165
Service Manager, key points
  database views, configuring 205
  management pack 200
  manager object,
      configuring 201
  self-service portal,
      publishing 202
  service, upgrading 206
  templates, optimizing 201
  workflows, creating 202
Service Manager, methods
  server, managing 173
  storage backup, securing 173
Service Manager, process
  activity, managing 169
  change, managing 169
  incident, managing 169
  problem, managing 169
  release, managing 169
  service, request 170
  template, developing 170
  workflow, developing 171
Service Manager, roles
  data warehouse, server 158
  self-service, portal 159
  server, managing 158
Service Manager, scenarios 207, 208
Service Manager, structure
  hardware, requirements 160
  multi-management server 160
  OS, requirements 161

single management server 159
SQL, server 162
Service Manager, terms
  data warehouse 174
  multi management server 175
  single management server 174
single management server,
      key points
  management server,
      installing 127
  operation console, installing 128
  report server, installing 130
  services collector,
      installing 130, 131
  web console, installing 129
single runbook server,
      installing 234
single runbook server, setup
  firewall, configuring 237
  .NET Framework, installing 235
  Orchestrator, account 236
  prerequisites, installing 237, 238
  splash screen, installing 234
SMA, connectors
  custom, connectors 227
  Orchestrator Runbooks,
      syncing 227
SMA, setup
  Orchestrator, optimizing 226
  PowerShell, module 225
  runbook, worker 225
  web, service 225
SMSD 122
SMSD, aspects
  firewall, requirements 125
  service account,
      requirements 125

single managment server,
      installing 126
Window Server, installing 123
Window Server,
      prerequisites 124
SMSD, environment 131, 132
SMSD Resource,
      deploying 134-137
Software Development Kit
      (SDK) 75
SQL, configuring 42, 43
System Center,
      components 18-21
System Center, features
  configuration, managing 25
  SCDPM 25
  SCO 24
  SCOM 22
  SCSM 25
  SCVMM 23
System Center,
      future trend 367
System Center, scenario
  Disaster, recovery 27
  order, upgrading 26
  pre-production, testing 27
  requirement level,
      supporting 28
  side-by-side, upgrading 28

V

Virtual Machine Manager (VMM) 264
VMM, aspects
  Hardware 266
  Hypervisor Platform,
      managing 268
  infrastructure role,
      planning 268-270

limitation, indicating 267
network, planning 272
OS 266
SQL 267
storage, planning 271
VMM, concepts
  Bare Metal, deploying 304
  host, adding 294-297
  host, managing 305
  infrastructure server,
    adding 290, 291
  machine template,
    creating 302, 303
  networking 293
  Pre-boot Execution,
    server 292
  profile, creating 299
  rollup, updating 306
  storage, adding 292
  VHDs, importing 303
  VM, optimizing 301
VMM, key steps
  physical host profile,
    designing 274, 275
  profile, designing 275, 276
  templates, designing 277
VMM, prerequisites
  firewall, requirements 286
  service accounts,
    optimizing 286
  splash screen,
    visualizing 287, 288
  SQL Command Line 285
  Window Assessment
    Deployment 284, 285
VMM, roles
  GUI, console 264
  server, managing 264
VMM, scenarios 307, 308
VMM, server
  Library 264
  PXE 265
  Update 265
VMM Server, deploying 289, 290
VMM, terms
  hypervisor environment,
    configuring 279, 280
  single management, server 279

W

Windows ADK 64
Windows ADK, parts
  ADK Kit 65
  WinPE 65
Windows ADK, steps 65, 66
Windows Autopilot 51

Made in United States
Orlando, FL
22 May 2025

61502283R00225